Lincoln and the Triumph of the Nation

THE LITTLEFIELD HISTORY OF THE CIVIL WAR ERA

GARY W. GALLAGHER & T. MICHAEL PARRISH, EDITORS

Supported by the Littlefield Fund for Southern History,

University of Texas Libraries

Lincoln

and the Triumph

of the Nation

Constitutional Conflict in the American Civil War

MARK E. NEELY JR.

The University of North Carolina Press   Chapel Hill

Designed by Kimberly Bryant and set in Miller with American Scribe display
by Rebecca Evans. Manufactured in the United States of America. The paper
in this book meets the guidelines for permanence and durability of the Committee on Production Guidelines for Book Longevity of the Council on Library
Resources. The University of North Carolina Press has been a member of the
Green Press Initiative since 2003.

Library of Congress Cataloging-in-Publication Data
Neely, Mark E.
Lincoln and the triumph of the nation : constitutional conflict
in the American Civil War / Mark E. Neely.
p. cm.—(Littlefield history of the Civil War era)
Includes bibliographical references and index.
ISBN 978-0-8078-3518-0 (hardback)
1. Constitutional history—Confederate States of America.
2. Constitutional history—United States. 3. United States—History—
Civil War, 1861–1865—Law and legislation. 4. Habeas corpus—United
States—History. 5. Civil rights—Confederate States of America—History.
6. Lincoln, Abraham, 1809–1865—Views on the Constitution. I. Title.
KFZ9001.5.N44 2011   342.7302'9—dc23   2011022144

15 14 13 12 11   5 4 3 2 1

Contents

Lincoln and the Triumph of the Nation

Prologue

CAPTURING THE FLAG, CAPTURING THE CONSTITUTION

Much has been written since 9/11 about the various attempts in American history to "capture the flag" for one political cause or another.[1] Historians commonly accuse the Republican Party of attempting to capture the flag during the Civil War. The Democrats by no means conceded the flag to their opponents, but their parallel effort was to capture the Constitution.

The Democracy Attempts to Capture the Constitution

An ingenious Democrat from Pennsylvania named Francis W. Hughes came up with the strategy in the second year of the war. He conceived of designating September 17 — the date that the constitutional convention in Philadelphia approved the final draft of the U.S. Constitution and sent it to the states for ratification — for annual celebration (and partisan exploitation). Beginning with a campaign to mark the September 17 date in the off-year elections of 1862, the movement might have reached a crescendo in two years' time for the all-important presidential canvass. After that, had Hughes and the Democrats played their cards right, September 17 would be as important a feature of the modern calendar as the Fourth of July and Thanksgiving.[2]

At a meeting of the Democratic State Central Committee held on July 29, 1862, Hughes and other party organizers passed a resolution "that the Chairman call upon the loyal men of Pennsylvania, through the Democratic Standing Committees of the several counties, to meet in the several cities and counties of the State . . . on the 17th of September next, to celebrate that day as the anniversary of the day of the adoption of the Constitution."[3] The proposal ran into bad luck almost immediately, for a little over a month after Hughes's call, the Confederates invaded Maryland. That alarmed Pennsylvanians next door, especially in the state capital, Harrisburg, a potential target of the Confederate attack. The chairman of the local Democratic County Committee postponed the celebration in order to focus the state's energies on repelling the invaders.[4]

The Democrats launched their campaign for the Constitution in July, and the designated date fell five days before the president announced the preliminary Emancipation Proclamation. The Democrats' alarm for the Constitution thus was not driven mainly by the Emancipation Proclamation. Still, the Lincoln administration had already provided many constitutional issues on which the Democrats might pin their hopes for revival.

In parts of Pennsylvania less threatened by invasion in 1862 the day was duly observed. Democrats in Pittsburgh, located in the western part of the state and therefore perhaps feeling a little safer, did recognize the anniversary.[5] Throughout Pennsylvania, Democrats made impressive gains in the October elections, and it was assumed that the anniversary of the Constitution would be a marked date for 1863, when the state would hold a gubernatorial election.

The Confederates invaded Pennsylvania in 1863, but thanks to the Union victory at Gettysburg, they were driven from the state well before the time came to arrange for mass meetings to celebrate the adoption of the Constitution in September. Hughes was no longer chairman of the Democratic State Central Committee, but his successor and other party workers adhered to what still seemed a good plan. The Democratic leaders improved on the idea by designating six places in the state where "monster mass meetings" would be held to mark the anniversary: Philadelphia, Lancaster, Williamsport, Scranton, Meadville, and Uniontown.[6] That way the party could ration its most effective speakers.

These rallies for the Constitution, in fact, kicked off the autumn political canvass. Railroads offered special excursion fares for the date, and political groups prepared parade floats, banners, and marching bands. The party sent in special speakers to the designated locations. The Democratic candidate for governor, George Washington Woodward, was a justice of the state supreme court and therefore pledged not to campaign, but he put in an appearance at the Lancaster meeting. Jeremiah Black, recently the attorney general under President James Buchanan, gave a biting speech. Democrats claimed that ten thousand people were present.[7] Hughes spoke at the Scranton meeting, and the Meadville rally began with a six-mile-long procession.[8] The Constitution may not have been the subject of such spectacle and celebrations since its eighteenth-century ratification. For weeks after the meetings in 1863, newspapers throughout Pennsylvania reprinted notable addresses delivered at the rallies that celebrated the adoption of the Constitution — and promoted the wartime ideals of the Democratic Party.

The Pennsylvania Democrats lost the gubernatorial election in 1863, but the idea of commemorating the Constitution had apparently proved its merit, and in 1864 the Democratic national nominating convention called on the party's adherents throughout the country to mark the September 17 anniversary. The convention met so late that year, at the very end of August, that it proved difficult to comply with the party's request to commemorate the seventeenth of September. The presidential canvass had to be very compressed, especially in Pennsylvania, where voting for all offices other than the presidency occurred in early October. It was widely believed that the October election was a bellwether for the November election, and the canvass of necessity aimed at the October election date, making the campaign season in Pennsylvania extremely short in 1864. But did the Democrats want to put a premium on constitutional issues? There was not much time to think about it.

Other issues were vying for the party's attention in September 1864, and, more problematic, naming one date as a major rallying point for a national political campaign was impractical because good speakers could not be everywhere at once (hence the Pennsylvania Democrats' six-city designation the year before). Moreover, the undisciplined American election calendar could undermine September 17 as a campaign kick-off date because different states voted at different times — even in different seasons of the year. Only the presidential election was held on the same day everywhere. In 1864 the results of the annual elections in Maine were already known by September, and the seventeenth was simply too late to start campaigning in a crucial state like Pennsylvania.

Coincidence also served to crowd the anniversary date in 1864. Hughes had begun his crusade to mark the date in July 1862, weeks before the Battle of Antietam, which happened to be fought on September 17, 1862. The hero of that battle, General George B. McClellan, became the Democratic presidential nominee two years later. In 1864, because of the particular presidential nominee, the Constitution had to share the limelight with the anniversary of the battle as a date for Democrats to commemorate. Thus the *New York Herald* described the big September 17, 1864, meeting in New York City this way: "Saturday being the anniversary of the battle of Antietam, as well as the anniversary of the adoption of the federal constitution, that memorable occasion and the services rendered to the country by

General George McClellan at Antietam were held prominently forth in the mottoes borne by the processions."[9]

McClellan was not the ideal man to feature in constitutional celebration. The real problem for the Democrats and September 17 in 1864 was not the coincidence of anniversaries but the candidate's record: General McClellan had played a role in bringing about the arrest of members of the Maryland legislature in 1861 to prevent secession of the state and had "no apology to make" for this "act necessary for the safety of the military position."[10] His record on constitutional issues was less clean than many Democrats desired. Against that stubborn fact, the movement to commandeer the anniversary of the Constitution for the Democratic Party began to falter as soon as McClellan was nominated. After the war, the anniversary movement fared no better, even though McClellan was out of the way as a Democratic candidate, and constitutional issues still loomed large for Democrats during Reconstruction. But constitutional issues were not the only ones then, nor, at times in the North, the most compelling ones. It limited political flexibility to lock onto a particular issue year in and year out when different issues arose that offered partisan opportunities.

Pittsburgh offers an example of the problems arising from the imposition of a fixed political anniversary in the presidential campaigning season. As early as 1868 labor issues began to clamor for Democratic attention, and in Pittsburgh a major mass meeting on labor "reform" took place on September 18, 1868.[11] That, of course, was the day after the anniversary of the Constitution, and the city's Democratic clubs could not make themselves available every night of the week for marching and cheering and "displaying mottoes." Naturally, the constitutional anniversary movement lost momentum. In the presidential election of 1868, Pittsburgh Democrats hung their partisan hopes on a mass meeting to be addressed by George Pendleton of Ohio (who had been McClellan's vice presidential running mate four years earlier). Apparently for logistical reasons, the meeting could not be held until October 5. That reduced the status of the September 17 meeting. Only five wards participated on the seventeenth.[12]

In the presidential election summer of 1872, the Democrats in the city failed to have a meeting to commemorate the Constitution at all. The Republicans that year managed to schedule a major convention of war veterans, the "Boys in Blue," in Pittsburgh (as part of their own continuing attempt to capture the flag), and the "Boys" endorsed the Republican national ticket on the seventeenth. The presidential candidate endorsed by the Democratic Party in 1872, Horace Greeley, who was also the nominee of the Liberal Republicans, came to the city on the nineteenth.[13]

The panic of 1873 then caused a major shift in public issues, from Reconstruction and retrospective Civil War questions to the economy. In Pittsburgh, as elsewhere, the anniversary of the Constitution passed quietly out of the political calendar as an important date. In the end, nothing came of the Democratic attempt to commemorate (and capture) the Constitution. Yet it is still instructive for constitutional history to examine the meetings that were held while the movement was alive during the war.

Democrats had no more fondness for the Constitution, no more awareness or knowledge of it, than did their Whig rivals in earlier times or the Republicans at midcentury. All parties had to respect the Constitution, all parties needed to put forth programs that had at least constitutional plausibility and legitimacy, and all parties attempted to exploit the provisions of the Constitution to their advantage. Beyond these firm parameters, however, no party enjoyed a monopoly of veneration for the Constitution or reserved a more special place for it than the competing parties. Likewise, the voters in the parties, as opposed to the policy-making leaders, had more reverence for the document than knowledge of its specific content.[14] Therefore, the attempts to commemorate the Constitution in Democratic mass meetings proved downright comical in some instances.

Again, Pittsburgh provides vivid examples of the problem. Democrats there held a rally at Eckert's Hotel for the first anniversary attempt, September 17, 1862. Newspaper coverage of the event, though apparently a little garbled, makes it obvious that the Democrats in western Pennsylvania were unclear on the year the Constitution was written and sent to the people for ratification. The document had long since been heavily overlaid by political myths within the party, especially the ideas of compact theory and state rights devised in the Kentucky and Virginia Resolutions of 1798 and 1799. Everyone seems to have been clear on the importance of the anniversary of the Declaration of Independence, but beyond knowledge of that vivid date their historical footing was not as firm. Henry Phillips, the president of the Pittsburgh meeting, began by saying that the men who had led "the war of 76" were "the identical patriots of '98, that made this vast country what it is." At this point in the history of the Democratic Party, the dates that stuck in memory were 1776 and 1798 (not 1787).

The Kentucky Resolutions and Constitutional Myth

In the 1850s the old Jacksonian era fixations of constitutionalism within the party — what Joel Silbey has identified as "traditional themes" of "limited and narrow constitutionalism, originating in Jackson's day"— had given way under the pressures of sectional conflict to emphasis on the Kentucky and Virginia Resolutions of 1798 and 1799, in other words, to the compact theory of the Constitution and a doctrine of state rights. So the "ingrained traditional Democratic beliefs about limited government, the Constitution, and conservative social policy," as Silbey describes them, were not as ingrained as he thought and were changing on the eve of the Civil War to a version more adaptable to the needs of the slaveholding South.[15] That left the people at the time confused.

The legacy of the Kentucky Resolutions will figure in the book later, and this is a good time to introduce them. Drafted by Thomas Jefferson and James Madison as protests against the Alien and Sedition Acts of 1798, acts that were passed by Congress under the John Adams administration, the resolutions struck an ambiguous blow for freedom of speech, freedom of the press, and the legitimacy of an opposition party. The Virginians sought refuge in the Tenth Amendment to the Constitution, which affirmed that the "powers not delegated to the United States by the Constitution, nor prohibited by it to the States, are reserved to the States respectively, or to the people." In protesting the Sedition Act, Jefferson did not first emphasize the First Amendment's insistence that "Congress shall make no law . . . abridging the freedom of speech, or of the press." Rather Jefferson now introduced the compact theory of the Constitution, the ultimate basis for secession doctrine.[16]

Thus when protesting the Sedition Act, Jefferson did not first reach for the *text* from the Constitution that supported his position, the First Amendment, but instead offered a *theory* of the Constitution:

> The several States composing the United States of America, are not united on the principle of unlimited submission to their General Government; but . . . by a compact under the style and title of a Constitution . . . and of amendments thereto, they constituted a General Government for special purposes, — delegated to that government certain definite powers, reserving, each State to itself, the residuary mass of right to their own self-government; and . . . whensoever the General Government assumes undelegated powers, its acts are unauthoritative, void, and of no force; . . . this compact each State acceded as a State, and is an integral party, its co-States forming, as to itself, the other party: . . . the government created by this compact was not made the exclusive or final judge of the extent of the powers delegated to itself; since that would have made its discretion, and not the Constitution, the measure of its powers; but . . . as in all other cases of

compact among powers having no common judge, each party has an equal right to judge for itself, as well of infractions as of the mode and measure of redress.[17]

An advocate of a stronger Union could easily find objectionable interpretations in Jefferson's theory. The Tenth Amendment, which Jefferson had in mind, does not leave the residuary powers to each state, but "to the States, or the people." Some, including Alexander Hamilton, writing in *The Federalist*, no. 78, did believe from the start that the U.S. Supreme Court was made a "final judge" in such conflicts. Of course, the famous preamble to the Constitution did not say that "the several States" formed the Constitution but that "we, the people" did. It was not clear that "each State acceded" to the Constitution "as a State, and . . . integral party," but instead the people acceded as represented in popular ratifying conventions organized by state. Jefferson's was only one theory of the Constitution, but it proved to be a powerfully persuasive one. Abraham Lincoln would devise an equally powerful theory in opposition to this one in his First Inaugural Address, the subject of the first chapter of this book.

Though not always used to the ends of nullification or secession, the compact theory was the heart and soul of state rights theory and thus crept into the Southern-dominated platforms of the Democratic Party in the 1850s. In 1852, for example, the Democratic national platform contained the following resolution: "That the democratic party will faithfully abide by and uphold the principles laid down in the Kentucky and Virginia resolutions of 1798, and in the report of Mr. Madison to the Virginia legislature in 1799; that it adopts those principles as constituting one of the main foundations of its political creed, and is resolved to carry them out in their obvious meaning and import."[18] As late as 1864, the Ohio Democratic Party platform contained this familiar resolution: "That the Democratic party is . . . devoted to the Constitution as transmitted to us by the framers of that instrument, and expounded by Jefferson, Madison, and Jackson, and as construed in the Virginia and Kentucky resolutions of 1798 and 1799, and as construed in the report thereon in the Virginia Legislature."[19]

The Pennsylvania Democrats and Constitutional Myth

Precise historical knowledge and meaning failed the Democrats in Pittsburgh on the constitutional anniversary in 1862. Some said that the landmark date was September 17, 1777. The resolution adopted by the Pittsburgh meeting began this way: "Whereas, the men of '77, who formed the Federal compact only recognized 'white inhabitants' to be enrolled into the service of the country, and the men of that day were the men of '98, who formed the American Constitution," and then went on to declare its political point. For Democrats, recent political history had made 1798 a more important landmark date than 1787. The final verdict pronounced on the Pittsburgh meeting by the local Democratic newspaper spoke volumes through error: "The meeting was a great success, and will have a telling effect with the people who love the men of '98."[20] The men of 1798, though their protest began in the name of liberty, were all Southerners, advocates of state rights and nullification. The men of 1787 were not. And it was a fact, apparently poorly recalled, that Thomas Jefferson, the author of the resolutions of 1798, was not even in the country in 1787 to have a hand in drafting the Constitution or aiding to ratify it.

The principal reason the Democrats failed to convert the anniversary of the Constitution into a lasting national holiday was the nakedly partisan purpose of the movement, turning the day into a nationwide opportunity for Democratic ratification meetings and not some sort of meeting called without regard to party. It was difficult to push party politics beyond its accustomed boundaries, and national anniversaries tended to lie beyond those boundaries. Unlike the brilliant Sarah Josepha Hale, who would lead the way during the Civil War in establishing a new national holiday, Thanksgiving Day, the Democrats had no talent for creating such a civic festival.[21] For one thing, the Democrats made no effort to conceal the partisan purpose behind the celebration of the Constitution. Unlike earlier war rallies for the Union advertised as "irrespective of party," their September 17 observances were overtly billed as "ratification" meetings to endorse recently nominated party candidates, or as the initiation of the season's political canvass, or simply as meetings for Democrats.

From the start, Francis W. Hughes had made that partisan mistake, filling the letter in 1862 containing the original call for observance of September 17 with the usual vitriolic Democratic boilerplate. The Constitution was under assault by secessionists and abolitionists alike, he said, and the latter, "from under the cloak of recently declared friendship and patriotism, are seeking to thrust their traitorous stilettos into the heart's blood of the nation."[22] When he spoke at the September 17 rally in Scranton the next year, even a Democratic newspaper characterized Hughes's oration as "highly argumentative."[23] No one thought that the proper tone for a Fourth of July oration, by contrast, should be "argumentative." In 1864 the September 17 meetings were candidly referred to as "ratification" meetings — that is, traditional public rallies held to endorse the nominations of the summer's national party nominating convention and to launch the intense period of can-vassing and campaigning. When Maryland's Reverdy Johnson responded to an invitation to address such a meeting, his public letter, declining the invitation but meant to be read aloud there, thanked the people who had invited him "to the meeting to-morrow of the Democratic and Conserva-tive organizations in your city . . . to ratify the recent Chicago nominations." Although Johnson was one of the most important constitutional thinkers in the Democratic Party and argued cases before the U.S. Supreme Court, he did not mention the anniversary in his letter, only the overtly political oc-casion of endorsing George B. McClellan's nomination for president.[24] The political purpose swamped the memorial one, and the memorial purpose was lost.

Capturing the Flag (and the Fourth of July) in the Civil War

From the Democratic experience in the Civil War era, we can draw a conclu-sion about the Constitution and the American nation: they were not synon-ymous. The nation could not be entirely merged with constitutionalism. No one could make the nation one with the Constitution. But no one could say that the Constitution was not a vital part of the nation. That was a Repub-lican problem during the war. The party struggled to steer clear of saying that the Constitution was not made for war and that it should be put aside temporarily as a national inconvenience.[25] From the very first Union rallies in New York City staged after the fall of Fort Sumter, it is true, the motto *"inter arma silent leges"* (law is silent in the midst of arms) occasionally rang out, and the phrase perhaps too often found its way into legal opinions written by Republican judges.[26] But such statements were unusual, and the Republicans continued to embrace the Constitution and appeal to it. They simply had to interpret it. But the Democrats did that, too: they did not so much appeal to the Constitution, in their minds, as to the theory of the Constitution devised in the Kentucky and Virginia Resolutions of 1798 and 1799. American nationalism cannot be identified completely as a "civic nationalism," or at least not one in which the civic part was defined entirely by the Constitution. Likewise, it can be said that attempts to convert Ameri-can nationalism into a form of "ethnic nationalism"— always a danger in the Civil War era with its urgent appeals to racism — was never successful either.[27]

The Constitution sits at the boundary between patriotism and nation-alism, between the sentiment and the theory that justify and define our "imagined community."[28] As the Democrats discovered, in a way, the Constitution carries limited emotional punch as a symbol and needs always to be explained and interpreted. The flag is all emotion and often defies precise explanation.

The nation's great symbolic holidays proved stubbornly resistant to partisan exploitation and were, generally, beyond the boundaries of political culture. In the Civil War the Republican attempt to capture the flag was not a mere matter of ceremony and symbol. On the hustings and even from the bench on occasion, the Republicans made outright accusations of treason and disloyalty. But to the degree they attempted to capture the symbols as well, the Republicans met with a fate analogous to that of the Democrats in their attempt to capture the Constitution. The Republicans failed also.

Thus Glenn C. Altschuler and Stuart M. Blumin were correct to point out that there were areas of society and culture in the United States where politics did not enter, but the authors went astray when they argued that the Civil War broke the barriers down and increased political intrusion on the nonpartisan sphere. "The war," they said, "breached the carefully constructed boundary between politics and other communal institutions — the church, the school, the lyceum, the nonpartisan citizens' meeting."[29] What is striking is the reverse: how seldom that breakthrough occurred, even in the Civil War. For the most part, the invisible barriers held firm. Republicans seldom attempted to shatter them, and Democrats proved generally willing to remain within their confines. A brief examination of the Fourth of July in the Civil War will serve to make the point. For this, our example will be Cleveland rather than Pittsburgh.

The nonpartisan patriotism of the typical Fourth of July celebration in the North during the Civil War was at odds with the customary modern picture of the Republican Party. The Republicans, we have been told over and over again, often attempted to commandeer national feeling as their exclusive property and to cast the Democrats as traitors. As Melinda Lawson expressed the idea, while exempting President Abraham Lincoln from that party strategy, "Lincoln did not suggest, as did many Republicans, that there could be no patriotism outside" the Republican Party.[30] It is true that many Republicans cast Democrats as traitors often and indiscriminately, but it is important to understand that they did so, for the most part, only in political settings — on the stump and on the editorial page. In nonpolitical settings, they literally joined Democrats in praising the nation and its history. Thus there were limits to their partisan allegations.

Awareness of the self-consciousness and overt manipulation of loyalty was not high in the middle of the nineteenth century. It was almost instinctive to merge partisan and national identities. Americans of the mid-nineteenth century had not experienced the loyalty scares typical of the Cold War and McCarthyism in the mid-twentieth century. The loyalty crusade of most recent vintage at the time of the Civil War, the Know-Nothing movement, was seen more as a matter of religious prejudice than of national loyalty, though there was a substantial theme of fear of foreigners in Know-Nothingism. Besides, the problem was seen to be different: for immigrants, it was a matter of forgetting old national loyalties and forming new attachments to the United States, not of having withdrawn or perverted one's attachments to America from their original base. Treason was a fundamentally different matter.

Fourth of July ceremonies generally lay beyond the boundaries of partisanship. The local Democrat with whom a Republican shared the Fourth of July platform was deemed sound enough in his patriotism. It must have been difficult for Republicans to comprehend how such ordinary citizens could associate with the traitors they imagined in the rest of the opposition party elsewhere. Such convenient and conventional compartmentalizing tricks of the mind were commonplace in American politics because of a general belief in democracy. Party leaders regularly exempted from their charges of perfidy against the other party the masses of that party. The mass of the people on the other side were only misguided and misled; they were not at bottom unsound. The democratic mass was almost always deemed sound.

In sum, the ceremonies of patriotism were for the most part just that: patriotic exercises largely exempt from conscious political manipulation. In fact, they were from all appearances consciously manipulated to contain *no* partisan content.

The height of loyalty scares in the North came in 1863, and the nonpartisan patriotism of the Fourth of July in that year was endangered. It was likely the most partisan July 4 on record. That year orators of the day included the disaffected Democrat and ex-president Franklin Pierce, on the one hand, and on the other, the divisive and confrontational Wendell Phillips and Dr. Oliver Wendell Holmes Sr. Pierce recommended in his defeatist speech in front of the state house in Concord, New Hampshire, on July 4, 1863, the exertion of "moral force, and not . . . military power" in the Civil War. In an oration in Boston, Dr. Holmes, the seemingly detached and scientific poet, denounced the North's internal enemies this way:

> At a time when every power a nation can summon is needed to ward
> off the blows aimed at its life, and turn their force upon its foes; when
> a false traitor at home may lose us a battle by a word, and a lying

newspaper may demoralize an army by its daily or weekly *sillicidum* of poison, they insist with loud acclaim upon the liberty of speech and of the press; liberty, nay license, to deal with government, with leaders, with every measure, however urgent, in any terms they choose, to traduce the officer before his own soldiers, and assail the only men who have any claim at all to rule over the country, as the very ones who are least worthy to be obeyed.[31]

Dr. Holmes's characteristic language drawn from his world of medicine, nature, and biological structure was present, but the tone of alarm is surprising. As for the Confederates, the "Southern people," he said, were "the Saracens of the nineteenth century," and the North was in the position of Europe when it was "threatened by the Saracens before Charles the Hammer defeated them."[32]

After 1863 and reassuring election results in Connecticut, Pennsylvania, and Ohio, where gubernatorial candidates identified with the peace wing of the Democratic Party went down to defeat, Fourth of July celebrations returned to ice cream and patriotic platitudes.[33] The ceremonies in Cleveland, Ohio, in the summer of 1864 offer a good example of the lengths gone to in order to keep the important day patriotic and nonpartisan. The best way to escape partisan exploitation was to focus on the veterans of the war. Late in June, the city's leaders announced that the Fourth of July celebration in Cleveland would feature the reception of the returning Seventh and Eighth Regiments of Ohio Volunteers. The program was in accordance with "the universal wish of our citizens to celebrate the anniversary of our National independence in a becoming manner, and to appropriately honor the return of the war-worn veterans," remarked the Democratic *Cleveland Plain Dealer*.[34] Words like "universal" and "appropriately" came from the vocabulary of nonpartisanship.

The railroad companies offered half fares for the day, and the crowds from the city and the surrounding area who flocked to the ceremonies were treated to an oration by a lawyer named George Wiley, who tiptoed carefully around the issue of slavery. He set as his goal in the speech answering the question, How did the country get from its wonderful values of 1776 and institutions of 1787 to the terrible Civil War that engulfed it now? He did not then launch into the customary partisan description of the war's origins. Instead, he said: "It is not for me, on this occasion to trace the gradual but steadily advancing causes which culminated in the rebellion. It is enough for me to know, at least it is enough for us to be thankful for forever, that when the first overt act of treason was committed, when the first direct assaults [were] made upon the Government, the whole Northern people sprang forward to the rescue."[35] Democrat and Republican alike recalled with wonder their relief at seeing the nonpartisan throngs who rallied around the flag at the news of Sumter's fall. Those post-Sumter rallies were for nearly everyone in the North the hallmark of nonpartisan patriotism. In the mid-nineteenth century what the phrase "the whole Northern people" really meant was "the people of both political parties."

Wiley felt compelled to offer an answer to the question he raised in the speech, and there was no ignoring the issue of slavery altogether after the Emancipation Proclamation. He argued that free labor dictated the growth of the North in one direction, and other institutions dictated the South's fatal path in another — away from free government and free public schools. "Free labor and free institutions are vital to a free government," he insisted, "and anything less than those must, in the long run be fatal to it." The war was "in fact a war between a higher and a lower grade of civilization." Wiley ended by addressing directly the assembled veterans of the Ohio regiments. He had obviously talked about slavery as a cause of the war, but he never actually uttered the word "slavery" itself. The speech was thus studiously patriotic. The Democrats in Cleveland seemed relieved. "For several years past," observed the *Plain Dealer* afterward, "the Fourth of July has been but indifferently celebrated by our citizens. Yesterday was a return to time-honored usages."[36] It is difficult to read an account of the celebration without concluding that Cleveland's city fathers were working to increase national passion and to prevent partisan intrusion.

This brief discussion of the place of nationalism in Northern ceremony and ritual brings to mind an important point. This book does not take the view that nationalism is necessarily dangerous to the Constitution and the liberties it protects. It does not take the view that nationalism and humanitarianism were opposites in the middle of the nineteenth century, so the historian's proper question might be to ask whether Lincoln was more a nationalist than a humanitarian or whether he was more willing to stretch the Constitution to save the Union than to free the slaves.[37] To make such assumptions is to fail to understand the modern idea of nationalism devised by Benedict Anderson in *Imagined Communities: Reflections on the Origin and Spread of Nationalism.* Among the most important insights of that influential book is this one: "In an age when it is so common for progressive, cosmopolitan intellectuals . . . to insist on the near-pathological character of nationalism, its roots in fear and hatred of the Other, and its affinities with racism, it is useful to remind ourselves that nations inspire love. The cultural products of nationalism — poetry, prose fiction, music, plastic arts — show this love very clearly in thousands of different forms and styles."[38]

The essential idea that nationalism was not then a "near-pathology" is perhaps most important for understanding the enthusiastic support given the national cause by religion during the Civil War, but the history of the Emancipation Proclamation, the subject of the third chapter, cannot be understood under other assumptions about nationalism. We cannot be haunted by the specter of pathological nationalism if we are to understand the role of nationalism in the constitutional history of the Civil War.

Introduction

The American Constitution was twice tested during the Civil War and then radically reshaped by the amending process, a movement well under way when the war ended. I say the Constitution was "twice" tested because the Constitution of the Confederate States of America was a deliberately imitative cousin of the U.S. Constitution, and, as far as war powers were concerned, an exact copy. Yet, despite the obvious importance of this subject, no one has ever written a constitutional history of the American Civil War. By that I mean that historical consideration of both the U.S. Constitution and the Confederate Constitution essential to a constitutional history of the Civil War has never been attempted in one volume.[1]

Of course, there are constitutional histories and textbooks of the whole sweep of American constitutional history from 1787 all the way to modern times, but these of necessity consider the Civil War as only a chapter in a much greater work.[2] Over the last hundred years, there have been two extremely valuable constitutional histories written about the North in the Civil War, but neither of them showed any interest in covering the Confederacy. The modern work, Harold M. Hyman's *A More Perfect Union: The Impact of the Civil War and Reconstruction on the Constitution*, contains only two sentences on the Confederate Constitution.[3] James G. Randall's *Constitutional Problems under Lincoln*, written almost fifty years before Hyman's book, refers often to the Confederacy, but only as an object of Union policy, as a belligerent, or as a place to confiscate property. It contains no reference to the Confederate Constitution.[4]

Randall's *Constitutional Problems under Lincoln* is encyclopedic in its coverage, but it is now eighty-five years old. Hyman's *A More Perfect Union* helped introduce legal history as a modern field of study, but its coverage of the constitutional history of the war itself was briefer and more thesis-ridden than Randall's. Both Randall's and Hyman's books remain indispensable, but neither was impressed with the Constitution as an asset to the war effort. Randall saw it, as his title suggests, fundamentally as a "problem," and Hyman argued vigorously that the Lincoln administration and Republicans in general eventually found the Constitution "adequate." On the contrary, this book concludes that the Democrats were the ones who insisted on the entire adequacy of the Constitution to the times. I take the view that the U.S. Constitution was an underestimated asset to the Union cause, and that its Confederate cousin could by no means be pointed to as a cause of Confederate defeat, even in a culture that encouraged its interpretation by state rights principles.

The North, oddly enough, has been better served than the South. For the Confederacy, there exists no book that is the equal of Randall's. That may seem astonishing given the Confederates' claim to a heritage of especially strict attention to constitutional matters. The long-winded apologia written 140 years ago by the former vice president of the Confederacy, Alexander H. Stephens, *A Constitutional View of the Late War between the States*, is what it professed to be, a participant's "view." It is not an impartial history.[5] Modern study began with Frank Lawrence Owsley's *State Rights in the Confederacy*, now over eighty-five years old. Though an inspired work, it deals with neither the Constitution nor the courts.[6] Marshall L. DeRosa's useful but brief book on *The Confederate Constitution of 1861: An Inquiry into American Constitutionalism* obviously deals directly with the Confederate Constitution and contains an insightful discussion of important court cases in a seven-page section on "state judicial supremacy."[7] However, as a political scientist, DeRosa was mainly interested in political philosophy and the relationship between the Anti-Federalists, John C. Calhoun, and the constitutional ideas that animated Confederate leaders.

To highlight the utility of the Constitution in *two* great national efforts at once may sound triumphalist, but this book is not. Few people — least of all Abraham Lincoln — could deny that the U.S. Constitution was a serious obstacle to emancipation, and Lincoln came to believe that emancipation was essential for winning the war. Constitutional historians of the "adequate Constitution" school of thought would often simply rather not talk about emancipation, which makes the Constitution look quite inadequate. The chapter on emancipation in this book, by contrast, is one of the two longest.

The neglect of the constitutional history of the Civil War in general is but part of a much larger problem, one that transcends the study of that conflict. To find the equivalent of Randall's book for other American wars is not easy. There is none for the War of 1812 or for the Mexican-American War.[8] Most modern work touching the constitutional history of American wars narrows the focus to civil liberties and the First Amendment or to the general question of presidential power. In light of that overall neglect, the Civil War seems well served indeed, but the fact remains that there is no book that chronicles, let alone analyzes, the constitutional history of both the United States and the Confederate States in the Civil War.

Much has been lost by this failure to consider both of the American constitutions in the Civil War. Since the constitutions were markedly similar in content, the historian has the opportunity to see the document tested in two different societies at the same time. The opportunity for comparisons is unequaled in history. And ultimately our judgments on the role of the Constitution in war should appear doubly sound.

This book aims to remedy some of the problem of neglect, not by supplying a comprehensive history of the Constitution in the Civil War but by stimulating interest in the constitutional history of that war and, by implication, others as well. The aim is not to kill the subject with claims of "definitive" treatment but to prove that there was genuine drama in the constitutional history of the Civil War, the equal at times of its much-studied military history. The book argues that the drama went beyond the single question of civil liberties in times of war — the role of freedom of speech and the press — which has received extended treatment in modern times. The constitutional conflict in the Civil War reached the largest questions of national existence. Therefore this is a book about the Constitution and about nationalism as well — hence the title "Lincoln and the Triumph of the Nation: Constitutional Conflict in the American Civil War."

Methods and Sources

This book does not contain a relentlessly focused argument. It does contain several arguments, but the point of this book is not consumed, as it would be in a monograph, by setting the historiography straight on one particular point. Instead, part of its objective is to familiarize readers with the content of sources that have been substantially neglected or short-changed in the writing of Civil War history. Therefore, readers will find stretches of text aimed at describing the variety and types of arguments and opinions about Civil War issues that can be found in judicial opinions and pamphlet literature. The original texts themselves are sometimes allowed to spread over the page so readers can encounter constitutional arguments and materials whole, as they were laid out at the time.

In earlier books I approached constitutional history from the bottom up, examining the history of civil liberties based on statistical study of civilians arrested by military authority in both the Union and the Confederacy. This book is more a study of the constitutional history of the North and a study of the constitutional history of the Confederacy, based on the actions of the presidents and the justices and judges. It is true, however, that this work avoids exclusive focus on the highest realms of constitutional discourse — at the level of the U.S. Supreme Court, for example — and looks at judicial history from the bottom up, from the level of state courts. The Confederacy had no supreme court, and the Supreme Court of the United States rarely enjoyed an opportunity to say anything about the war before it ended. At all levels the judges were concerned, as constitutional struggle had long been, more with power than with right. The judges did not discuss questions of conscription as problems of individual liberty, equity, and hardship as much as they approached them as problems of power struggles between the national army and state militias.[9]

This book places special emphasis on the parts of those judicial opinions dealing with the nation. The Civil War offers a rare opportunity to hear the judges' extrajudicial opinions on national subjects because of the temporary revival of the broadly "political" charge to the grand jury. Moreover, the judges and justices found it difficult to ignore the dire national crisis even in their customarily tightly focused opinions on legal matters brought before them in individual cases. Finally, the book provides constitutional history, as opposed to constitutional law, by placing the opinions of the judges in their proper contexts, and for the quotidian events and attitudes in which their jurisprudence was rooted, I have relied heavily on the political newspapers of the day.

No constitutional history of this period could possibly make sense by looking at courts and cases only. Up to the end of Reconstruction, constitutional history was not the preserve of the Supreme Court of the United States or the state supreme courts. Constitutional issues were matters for presidents and members of Congress and other politicians on the stump. We find ourselves back at the hustings in this discussion. Constitutional history was made there too, and we can never get away entirely from the men on the platforms who spoke to the people.

This book also relies on comparisons. Observations and conclusions about the history of the Civil War are arrived at here by considering similarities and differences across time. Comparing across nations has generally proved difficult, in part because of the unusual constitutional history of the United States: the country had a written constitution and only one from the late eighteenth century until 1861. It also had more than thirty state constitutions. But a cross-national comparison can be built into the history of the Civil War. Two national constitutions in two different societies were in conflict in the Civil War, and comparisons of the U.S. Constitution with the workings of its cousin, the Confederate Constitution, are important. Unlike the U.S. Constitution, the Confederate Constitution left no legacy, of course, but examining its history — surprisingly neglected to this day — can help us determine the way the war powers really worked.

Comparisons across time are important to the investigations and conclusions of this book. We have many books suggesting that the Mexican-American War was somehow a significant "rehearsal" for the Civil War, but this book argues that the aptest comparisons come from the War of 1812. Unlike the war with Mexico, the war against Great Britain of 1812–15 was a desperate struggle that produced in its very midst sharp constitutional conflicts and urgent demands for numerous constitutional amendments. Losing the War of 1812 was more than a remote possibility, and, similarly, losing was a possibility for the North and a reality for the Confederacy.

A constitutional history of the Civil War necessarily privileges elite sources likely to embody coherent constitutional arguments. Constitutional history made on the stump and in newspapers lacked the rigorous content of judicial opinions and presidential proclamations. A manageable compromise between the esoteric opinions of the jurists and the more sensationalist doctrines shaped for popular consumption on the political platform I have found in the political pamphlet, a major form of political communication in the era, so characteristic of the times that collectors then and afterward sought to gather them in great numbers and to bind them in volumes for preservation. The pamphlet represents a happy medium between political popularity and systematic, lengthy constitutional precision and technical rules of interpretation.

Pamphlets were characteristic of the vigorous political culture of the nineteenth century's party politics. One could hardly help noticing them. Thus in Daniel Webster's famous Second Reply to Hayne, given in 1830, perhaps the most famous American speech of the nineteenth century except for the Gettysburg Address, Webster referred to them in such a way as to denigrate partisan debate. They were "forgotten and moth-eaten two-penny pamphlets." South Carolina's Senator Robert Y. Hayne had "stretched a drag-net over the whole surface of perished pamphlets, indiscreet sermons, frothy paragraphs, and fuming popular addresses; over whatever the pulpit in its moments of alarm, the press in its heats, and parties in their extravagance, have severally thrown off in times of general excitement and violence."[10] Their use persisted, and in the time of the very greatest excitement, the Civil War, pamphlets became peculiarly characteristic of the politics and social debates.

As historian Frank Freidel pointed out, in February 1863 three great engines of pamphlet production were founded in the North "within five days of each other," in a moment of profound reconsideration of the meaning of national existence.[11] These organized societies piled their pamphlets on top of the already prodigious production of pamphlets by familiar political organizations and customary methods, especially the printing and distribution of speeches in Congress. The result was just short of a marvel: together, all of these sources produced more than one copy of a pamphlet for every single person who voted in 1864.[12] Their content was somewhat elevated in significance. The political parties of nineteenth-century America had long since mastered public opinion. They were so efficient in their methods that they compiled a record never matched before or since: in elections for president from 1840 to 1892, some 78 percent of qualified voters, on average, went to the polls.[13] Speeches and newspapers were their tools of choice with which we are most familiar. But the parties also relied on pamphlets — to get the best speeches to an audience larger than the crowd at the open-air meeting; to put into print materials that were too long to be reproduced in a newspaper, which had also to print advertisements, editorials, and the local shipping news; and to provide, in more lasting, more targeted, and less cumbersome form than a sprawling news sheet, the key and telling arguments for their cause. Pamphlets played a role in bringing about the parties' mastery of nineteenth-century public opinion, and the concerned leaders of the Civil War felt they must redouble the effort in a struggle for more than the next presidential term, in a struggle for existence. The patriots took a page from the partisans' book: in the midst of the crisis, they decided to look to pamphlets to save the Constitution and the Union from ruin. Happily for the constitutional historian, lawyers eagerly used their pens to write about constitutional issues for a public larger than the one found in a single courtroom.

The pamphlets were not only spread broadcast by the newly energized organizations and alarmed patriots of the Civil War, they had their influence even in high places. Columbia University's Francis Lieber was thrilled to discover he had influential readers of his work on the laws of war. On February 20, 1863, he boasted to General in Chief Henry W. Halleck, "I observe from some orders of General [William S.] Rosecrans that he has used my pamphlet on 'Guerrilla Warfare.'"[14] Supreme Court Justice Robert C. Grier received a copy of the famed lawyer Horace Binney's pamphlet, *The*

Privilege of the Writ of Habeas Corpus under the Constitution, early in 1862. No one else among his intimates had a copy yet, and his "was much sought after — and borrowed by one from another till it was *lost to me*."[15] Though we tend to think of newspaper articles that are reprinted to make pamphlets, the influence often went in the other direction, especially in the case of pamphlets on complicated constitutional questions. The editors of the *New York Evening Post*, when they covered the trials of the Legal Tender Act in New York courts in early 1863, admitted they had believed that only gold and silver could be legal tender in the United States until they read a 42-page pamphlet containing the argument of lawyer Bernard Roelker in *The Legal Tender Clause*. Afterward, they could see the legitimacy of using paper money as legal tender.[16]

Political pamphlets represent a medium particularly identifiable with the Civil War era. Joel H. Silbey noticed them years ago, walking the stacks of the Cornell University Library. In his book on the Democratic Party in the Civil War era, published in 1977, Silbey reserved a special place in his bibliographical note for pamphlets:

> The nineteenth century was an age of political pamphleteering. In every election, and in between as well, short and long and highly partisan pamphlets were issued in floods by local, state, and national party organizations and such groups as the Society for the Diffusion of Political Knowledge (for the Democrats) and the Loyal Publication Society (for the Republicans). The pamphlets include reprints of individual speeches by prominent men, formal addresses to the people by state and local party conventions, and details of the records of themselves and their opponents. It is a vast literature buried in rare book rooms and archives. Frank Freidel, *Union Pamphlets of the Civil War* . . . provides a good sample of some of them. Andrew D. White, then a New York state senator, collected many of them and his collections are bound in more than one hundred volumes in the Cornell University Library.[17]

Those Cornell pamphlets are now in the rare book room, disbound, and separately cared for.

Eventually, Silbey found an opportunity to publish a selection of the political pamphlets in the John Harvard Library series that also saw the publication of Frank Freidel's selection from the Civil War North. *The American Party Battle: Election Campaign Pamphlets, 1828–1876*, a two-volume collection, was confined to pamphlets published by political parties and "in . . . campaign season."[18] That focus forced Silbey to defend the somewhat ephemeral content of pamphlets so closely tied to partisan campaigning. "They were not written by Jeffersonian political intellectuals," he said, "and did not reflect the subtleties of the earlier group of writers, well-educated elites conversing with one another about the nature of power and proper governance."[19] On the other hand, it must be said that not all pamphlets were the products of party hacks. The Civil War in particular and constitutional conflict in general called forth the efforts of lawyers and judges who did, some of them, contrary to the pamphlets featured in *The American Party Battle*, "deal extensively, directly," and "in a sophisticated way with large and abstract themes of the nature of political sovereignty and systems of government."[20]

Historians, in fact, owe a debt to the sensitivity of nineteenth-century collectors like Andrew Dickson White (who later became the president of Cornell) who somehow recognized right away the importance and characteristic significance of these pamphlets to the history of the era.[21] Such collections lie at the heart of Civil War research in other libraries as well. At the Pennsylvania State University, the pamphlet collection of Justice John M. Read, of the Pennsylvania Supreme Court, offers a similar monument to a contemporary political and constitutional observer who recognized the importance of pamphlets to the history of his times. As a prominent lawyer and judge, Read was especially interested in sophisticated pamphlets that dealt with government (to borrow Silbey's language). His sixty-one volumes of bound pamphlets, containing some 1,250 different publications, require five library shelves to hold them (and now are kept in the rare book room).[22]

There would have been parallel collections of Confederate pamphlets as well, but collecting in that field could not be confined to pamphlets as the peculiar medium for political-constitutional debate and conflict. There were too few pamphlets. But the great historian Francis Parkman recognized immediately after Appomattox that the historical society in Boston should send emissaries to collect all the printed paper literature surviving from the attempt to form a Confederate States of America. These now make up the notable collection of Confederate Imprints in the Boston Athenaeum and have, in turn, served as the basis for the fundamental Confederate bibliographies.[23]

Parkman, Read, White, and others even at the time of the war had a sense of the power of these pamphlets to open up the meaning of the era. The pamphlets are long enough to offer intellectual substance but short enough to fit the political attention span of a presidential campaign or of a season of war. Neither books nor platforms and handbills from the era can quite equal the explanatory power of the pamphlets. Their significance has been sensed in recent times as well. In 1967 Frank Freidel edited *Union Pamphlets of the Civil War, 1861–1865,* reprinting fifty-two of the hundreds that have survived. He introduced them this way:

> When the ideological struggle between the South and the North disintegrated into a resort to arms, the generation-long war of words continued in intensified, often virulent, fashion. . . . It was essential in such a long and uncertain struggle that soldiers know why they were fighting. Northerners especially went to considerable pains to supply troops with verbal ammunition. Moreover the people of the North among themselves engaged in endless self-examination and sharp internal disputes. In effect they kept asking themselves why they should be fighting. What was the meaning of the war; how should it be conducted; what should its objectives be? What was the essence of the Federal Union they were sacrificing their young men to preserve? Politicians, lawyers, journalists, publicists, and intellectuals all contributed to the great symposium which ranged from crude propaganda to finely wrought treatises on constitutional theory.[24]

Freidel noticed that the competition for the attention of the reading public had grown since the early days of pamphleteering in the seventeenth and eighteenth centuries, with abundant newspapers and magazines available at low prices in later times, but that pamphlets "continued vital in the American Civil War." He guessed that "the pamphlets may well have found proportionately more readers than those appearing in either earlier or later crises." Even so, some, he pointed out, "in the complexity and sophistication of argument" equaled "the revolutionary tracts and the *Federalist.*"[25]

When Freidel thought about the pamphlets of the Civil War, he recalled "the revolutionary tracts" of the eighteenth century, and his volumes were successors to the landmark edition of those pamphlets edited in 1965 by Bernard Bailyn. *Pamphlets of the American Revolution* included a selection of 72 of some 400 that survived, and Bailyn's introductory essay established a new paradigm for interpreting the Revolution and much of American history afterward.[26]

For some reason, the publication of the Union pamphlets by Freidel did not do for Civil War scholarship what its predecessor volume of Revolutionary pamphlets had done for an earlier period of American history. In political history the energies of historians were principally absorbed at the time of the publication of Freidel's work in voting analysis and what was called the New Political History, which was little concerned with ideology and constitutional history. Other historians were spurning sources that might have appealed to a reading elite; these social historians pursued the history of common people. In the study of the Civil War itself, military history received an urgent push in the late 1970s in the direction of reading, not pamphlets about constitutional questions but the letters of common soldiers, in search of the view of the war from the trenches rather than from the headquarters. Military history took on a new prestige because of that focus, which caused much of the energy of study of the Civil War period to flow back into military history, now construed in new ways. Constitutional and legal historian Harold Hyman read the pamphlet literature diligently for *A More Perfect Union: The Impact of the Civil War and Reconstruction on the Constitution*, published in 1973, but after that, the constitutional history of the era and the pamphlets essential to understanding it mostly went begging.

This book seeks to resurrect Hyman's example and to remind historians of the wonderful variety of arguments that exist within the white, cream, tan, blue, yellow, and light green paper covers of Civil War–era pamphlets. The variety of ideas reminds us of an important quality of pamphlets identified by an admirer of them as a medium of expression, George Orwell:

> The pamphlet is a one-man show. One has complete freedom of expression, including, if one chooses, the freedom to be scurrilous, abusive, and seditious; or, on the other hand, to be more detailed, serious and "high-brow" than is ever possible in a newspaper or in most kinds of periodicals. At the same time, since the pamphlet is always short and unbound, it can be produced much more quickly than a book, and in principle, at any rate, can reach a bigger public. Above all, the pamphlet does not have to follow any prescribed pattern. . . . All that is required of it is that it shall be topical, polemical, and short.[27]

The individualism of the pamphlet is also one of its striking features. That quality will be readily apparent in Chapter 2. It is a quality that is missing from other everyday political literature. The resolutions of mass meetings in an election year were often similar, and party platforms were national. But the individual voices of the pamphleteers, holding forth on political and constitutional questions, can be heard at sufficient length to appreciate the individuality of outlooks and arguments.

The disparity in the number of sources available for the Confederacy, as compared to the Union, is nowhere more evident than in the case of political pamphlets. The Confederacy produced few pamphlets on constitutional and political questions — part of the problem addressed in Chapter 7. The secession crisis preceding the Confederacy, however, was different; during that period the Southern presses printed an avalanche of political and constitutional literature, much of it in pamphlet form. Jon L. Wakelyn, like Freidel almost thirty years earlier, recognized their importance and published an edition of selected titles in 1996. These offer some of the critical evidence for Chapter 6. But once the war began, paper and ink grew scarce, and so did the opportunity to write about politics and the Constitution in the midst of a doomed struggle for existence. Dramatic changes in political culture (the absence of political parties and the absence of the crucial presidential contest) eliminated the usual motives for pamphlet production. The Confederates managed the loyalty of their people without a lot of pamphlets. As a result, it has always been a little more difficult to describe the salient constitutional issues in the history of the Confederacy. Chapters 7 and 8, on state rights and civil liberties in the Confederacy, were all the tougher to write for want of such sources.

The Purpose

I have attempted in this book to explore how lawyers, judges, justices, and government officials thought about the Constitution. In some places, historical argument is subordinated to description and analysis of the kinds of arguments employed during the Civil War to explain (occasionally) and to capture (most often) the U.S. Constitution for one's political purposes. These old constitutional arguments will likely be unfamiliar, as constitutional and political historians have most often described the policy outcome of the arguments and not the sort of reasoning that got the thinkers to their conclusions. I have attempted to render the arguments lovingly, in their ingenuity, intricacy, and inconsistency (often). But I have attempted to keep in mind that the protagonists of this book are not best described as "thinkers." Rather, they were men who were concerned with political policies and constructed arguments about them. Almost all of their arguments served a political purpose. Some were devised artificially, for legal clients, and did not necessarily reflect sincerely even the mind of the person who conceived the argument. Almost all the people studied in this book were lawyers or politicians. Therefore, because of the limitations of nineteenth-century social ideas, they were all men. The constitutional ideas and influence of women in this period will await another book. What is new in this book, in other words, does not come from the cast of characters. Many of them were prominent in the period, some were famous, and a few came to have periods of history named after them. What is new does not come, for the most part, from archival discovery, either. Instead, it comes from looking at what has been too often overlooked even in plain sight: judicial opinions, political pamphlets on constitutional questions, and public proclamations.

This book will begin the modern study of the Constitution's role in America's wars by looking at the Civil War. With the Constitution under a strain without parallel, the presidency, the Congress, the political parties, and the courts during the Civil War laid bare its strengths and weaknesses. Much of the text that follows is meant only to convince readers how much of interest lies in the opinions of the judges, newspaper editors, politicians, and political pamphleteers of the Civil War era. Once historians are convinced of that, then surely the more complete constitutional history of the Civil War will follow.

Part 1

The President and the Nation

It is of the nature of war to increase the executive
at the expense of the legislative authority.
— *The Federalist*, no. 8 (Alexander Hamilton)

Secession and Anarchy

LINCOLN'S VIEW OF THE CONSTITUTION AND THE NATION

When Confederates fired on Fort Sumter on April 12, 1861, they put the nation and its Constitution to the first life-threatening test since the War of 1812. The results of the previous test by arms had not proved particularly encouraging. The United States all but lost the War of 1812. Diplomatic negotiation salvaged much for the country in the peace treaty, and the United States learned its lesson: ambitious economic development was essential to create a country based on something other than mere sentiment. As Thomas Jefferson, renouncing his earlier agrarianism, told Benjamin Austin about a year after the War of 1812 ended, "Experience has taught me that manufactures are now as necessary to our independence as to our comfort."[1]

Although no one could point to the Constitution as a cause of American military defeat in the War of 1812, in fact, the Constitution had proved to be problematic. Federalists, especially in New England, were unhappy with the Republican war against England. They showed it by fruitless votes against appropriations for the war in Congress (they were too few in number to block legislation), and, more effectively, they showed it at the state level by attempting at every opportunity to interfere with the nationalization of the militias for the war. By 1814, some Federalists were so frustrated that they were beginning to resort to what now became the constitutional gambit of beleaguered American minorities: compact theory, nullification, and threats of secession.

The problems were resolved decisively, first, by Andrew Jackson's military victory at New Orleans early in 1815 and by the artful peace negotiations in Europe that preceded it. Second, they were resolved by the American people themselves, who fled the Federalist Party in droves, tarnished as it now was with a reputation for treason. The party collapsed, and American politicians learned a critical lesson that became a part of the country's unwritten constitution: members of Congress could not vote against supplies for soldiers in the field (as the determined Federalists had consistently done). Other issues were left unsolved: nationalizing the militias, mobilization and conscription, nullification, even secession.

Instead, unhampered by the tarnished Federalist Party or by old-fashioned doubts among small-government and pastoral Republicans like the early Jefferson, the country embarked on a period of determined nationalization. In that atmosphere of nationalism that followed the near defeat in the War of 1812, Abraham Lincoln grew up. He was six years old when the war ended. The old-fashioned works on Lincoln written in the shadow of Frederick Jackson Turner's frontier thesis of a century ago paid little attention to the relevance of national economic development to Lincoln's earliest life on the frontier. Historians tended to freeze his image in a coonskin cap with a log cabin in the background.

Sources of Lincoln's Constitutional Ideas

Nationalism was the first source of Lincoln's ideas on the Constitution. He likely imbibed that sentiment as a boy growing up in Indiana, reading about the battles of the American Revolution. We know this not from any documents surviving from that early period of Lincoln's life but from what he recalled much later when American nationalism was challenged by secession. Faced with the departure of seven states as a fait accompli after he was elected president in 1860, Lincoln thought harder about the nation and its Constitution than ever before in his life. On his way to Washington, D.C., for his inauguration, he spoke before the New Jersey legislature in Trenton, where he reflected on his youth:

> May I be pardoned if, upon this occasion, I mention that away back in my childhood, the earliest days of my being able to read, I got hold of a small book, such a one as few of the younger members have ever seen, "Weem's Life of Washington." I remember all the accounts there given of the battle fields and struggles for the liberties of the country, and none fixed themselves upon my imagination so deeply as the struggle here at Trenton, New-Jersey. The crossing of the river; the contest with the Hessians; the great hardships endured at that time, all fixed themselves on my memory more than any single revolutionary event;

and you all know, for you have all been boys, how these early impressions last longer than any others.[2]

The sentiment of nationalism was surely the earliest force shaping Lincoln's ideas of the Constitution, but he was not called upon to express his views by any national crisis of his youth or early manhood. The nullification crisis erupted in 1832, the year when Lincoln ran for the first time for the Illinois legislature, but he spent most of that year as a volunteer in the Black Hawk War, had little time to campaign for office, and faced mostly issues of local economic development. He lost the election and spent 1833 scrambling to make a living and find a trade.

Nationalism expressed itself in Lincoln's ideas earliest as a program of economic development for the West and the nation. Lincoln knew and understood very well the economic structure needed for American national development, but at first he saw it mainly from the standpoint of individual opportunity for economic advancement in life for a poor boy who toiled on hardscrabble farms for his illiterate father. Thus the second source of constitutional ideas for Lincoln was the Whig Party and Henry Clay's vision of economic development, the American System. It was difficult, if not impossible, to be an economic development–minded Whig and believe in strict construction of the Constitution. Put simply, canals are not mentioned in the document. One had to derive constitutional plausibility for programs of government-supported economic development from some sort of broader construction of the Constitution. Apparently Lincoln found it easy to accept such principles. In a speech on a program of internal improvements given during his term in the U.S. Congress, he said characteristically: "No one, who is satisfied of the expedience of making improvements, needs to be much uneasy in his conscience about it's [*sic*] constitutionality."[3]

The third source of constitutional ideas for Lincoln has, surprisingly, often been slighted in the literature: the antislavery movement. By the 1850s Lincoln had fully appropriated the antislavery view of the Constitution. He articulated this position most eloquently in his famous speech against the Kansas-Nebraska Act at Peoria in 1854. Succinctly expressed, the antislavery myth of the Constitution was, as Lincoln said in a speech in Springfield, Illinois, in 1854, that the "theory of our government is Universal Freedom. 'All men are created free and equal,' says the Declaration of Independence. The word 'Slavery' is not found in the Constitution." Thus the Constitution did not affirm slavery; it looked forward to its "ultimate extinction."[4] He explained the antislavery view of the Constitution with the most precise historical references in his Cooper Institute speech of February 1860; the first half of the speech resembled a lecture in constitutional history.

Nationalism, the Whig Party, and the antislavery movement overlapped in their effects, but the strand of influence most obvious in Lincoln's early political career was the one of economic development derived from the Whig Party. Although Henry Clay's American System was nationalistic, offering a vision of the country united by regional economic specialization, the initial appeal of this economic program was as much existential as nationalistic to a poor frontiersman like Lincoln seeking economic opportunity. We do not know exactly when he comprehended the value of economic development to national unity and strength.[5] Among other things vital to the Union, the course of economic development pursued for more than a generation after the War of 1812 had forged the bonds of union between the Old Northwest and the East. Eventually, east-west railroads made trade along the north-south route on the Mississippi River old-fashioned: the river trade did not represent the wave of the future. The most important development for nationalism, as Michael F. Holt has argued in pointing out its dramatic effects on America's political parties, was "the completion of the trunkline railroads between the Atlantic coast and Western waters — the Erie in 1851, the Pennsylvania in 1852, the Baltimore and Ohio in 1853, and the New York Central in 1854."[6]

The overlap of nationalist ideas could be reinforcing and consistent, but they could also get in each other's way in the course of a long career in politics, and Lincoln had a very long career; some thirty-three of the fifty-six years of his life were spent in politics. Here is an example of the problems. In 1848, after years of resting content with the constitutionality of internal improvements, Lincoln developed a new argument. In answer to President James K. Polk's mild suggestion that there might be internal improvements important enough to justify amendment of the Constitution to make them legal, Lincoln decided at last to weigh in on that question in a speech in the House of Representatives:

> I wish now to submit a few remarks on the general proposition of amending the constitution. As a general rule, I think, we would [do] much better [to] let it alone. No slight occasion should tempt us to touch it. Better not take the first step, which may lead to a habit of altering it. Better, rather, habituate ourselves to think of it, as unalterable. It can scarcely be made better than it is. New provisions, would introduce new difficulties, and thus create, and increase appetite for still further change. No sir, let it stand as it is. New hands have never

touched it. The men who made it, have done their work, and have passed away. Who shall improve, on what *they* did?[7]

There were no amendments to the Constitution passed in Lincoln's lifetime, but he would become less conservative on the question later. It was hardly possible to foresee in 1848 a time when the slave states would remove themselves from the position in the Union to block constitutional amendments touching slavery (indeed, fifteen slave states voting solidly could have blocked such an amendment to this day). But then that was the problem with a long career in politics: the politician had to encounter unexpected developments — such as war.

The Mixed Legacy of the Whig Party

The history of Abraham Lincoln's ideas about the Constitution would fit a fairly simple linear narrative were it not for the complicated nature of the legacy of the Whig Party. The Whigs were resounding nationalists until 1846, when the Mexican-American War caused them to change course. The sudden change is most jarring in the career of the great Whig leader Henry Clay. As a Republican at the time of the War of 1812, Clay was a leader of the "War Hawks," who pushed for war against Great Britain. But the outbreak of the war with Mexico, under the administration of Democratic president James K. Polk, caused Clay to change course dramatically from War Hawk to extreme dove. Clay, unlike Lincoln, was not in Congress during the war and enjoyed the luxury of taking a stance of extreme opposition. In a speech in Lexington, Kentucky, given late in 1847, Clay expressed his agreement with the "Immortal Fourteen" Whig members of Congress who had voted against the declaration of war with Mexico.[8]

Lincoln entered Congress after the declaration of war but before the peace was negotiated. Like most Whigs, he voted for supplies but otherwise opposed the war policies of the administration. Although such a stance did not directly challenge any views on the Constitution that Lincoln had already formed, it did cause him for the first time to articulate his ideas about the Constitution and war. Now the constitutional questions did prick his conscience and provoked a stricter construction of the document than he had heretofore been accustomed to.

The problem was complaints from his home district, embodied in sharp disagreement on the war voiced by his law partner, William Henry Herndon. Lincoln always prided himself on the consistency of his opposition to the Mexican-American War. He maintained that "it was a war of conquest brought into existence to catch votes."[9] In other words, he conceded the likelihood of the popularity of expansionist policies and maintained that that was the chief allure of the aggressive war against Mexico for Polk. Or, as he stated in an autobiographical statement written for a campaign biographer in 1860, Polk started the war "to divert public attention from the surrender of 'Fifty-four forty or fight' to Great Brittain [*sic*], on the Oregon boundary question."[10] On January 3, 1848, Congressman Lincoln voted for the Ashmun Amendment (attached to a resolution of thanks to General Zachary Taylor) declaring the war "unnecessarily and unconstitutionally begun by the President of the United States."[11] Lincoln later explained that the war was unnecessary "inasmuch as Mexico was in no way molesting, or menacing the U.S." More important for the discussion here, he contended that the war was unconstitutional "because the power of levying war is vested in Congress, and not in the President."[12]

Herndon's objections to Lincoln's vote on the Ashmun Amendment, expressed in a letter to the Illinois congressman, elicited an uncharacteristic, lecturelike response. To his junior partner, Lincoln wrote:

> The provision of the Constitution giving the war-making power to Congress, was dictated, as I understand it, by the following reasons. Kings had always been involving and impoverishing their people in wars, pretending generally, if not always, that the good of the people was the object. This, our Convention understood to be the most oppressive of all Kingly oppressions; and they resolved to so frame the Constitution that *no one man* should hold the power of bringing the oppression upon us. But your view destroys the whole matter, and places our President where kings have always stood.[13]

Herndon's letter to Lincoln has disappeared, and we do not know exactly what Herndon's constitutional argument was. What we do know is that by the time of the Civil War, there would be many who would claim that Lincoln himself stood "where kings have always stood."

Effie Afton

All three of these strands of influence — the economic growth program of the Whig Party, nationalism, and the antislavery movement — likely had greater influence than another putative source of Lincoln's ideas about the Constitution: his profession as a lawyer. In fact, he could have held these ideas on the Constitution without ever stepping inside a court of law. A sentiment of nationalism and devotion to programs of economic development preceded Lincoln's decision to become a lawyer. Antislavery feeling preceded it as well. He said that he could not remember when he did not think slavery was wrong, and he could certainly remember much that preceded his admission to the bar in 1836. Still, issues arising from his legal practice occasionally overlapped the views of law and Constitution he derived mainly from politics. He was a politician and a lawyer, not a theoretician or a political economist, so he was most likely to articulate his ideas on economic development and the Union only in the course of achieving a practical end. Usually these occasions were political, but sometimes they involved his law practice. Lincoln was reminded of the importance of economic development to the nation in a case he tried only four years before the Civil War. His client was a railroad bridge company, and the case has come to be called the *Effie Afton* case. It was officially recorded as *Hurd et al. v. Rock Island Bridge*.

In 1856 fire destroyed a new paddle-wheel steamer, the *Effie Afton*, after it ran into a pier of the bridge that had been built to span the Mississippi River from Rock Island, Illinois, to Iowa. The bridge, constructed by the Rock Island Bridge Company, a subsidiary of the Chicago, Rock Island, and Pacific Railroad, carried the company's trains over the new road. Jacob S. Hurd, the owner of the ship, sued the bridge company for posing a hazard to water traffic, and the case found its way into the federal court in Chicago in 1857. Abraham Lincoln was part of the team of lawyers who defended the bridge company, and he made a famous summation to the jury in the case on September 22–23, 1857.

The bridge was the first one to reach over the Mississippi River and thus dramatized the possibilities of east-west trade across the American continent. The Mississippi had long stood as a symbol of steamboat traffic carrying goods north and south from St. Louis. The railroad ran east and west. The bridge had only opened in April 1856, and in less than a month the great steamboat had come to grief on its pier. The ensuing legal case would test the law's relationship to the future of the American nation.[14]

In his summation, Lincoln assured the court that he "had no prejudice against steamboats or steamboatmen nor any against St. Louis." But he went on to say that "there is a travel from East to West, whose demands are not less important than that of the river." He then pointed out "the astonishing growth of Illinois, having grown within his memory to a population of a million and a half," and added to his argument the importance of the railroad traffic to "Iowa and the other young and rising communities of the Northwest." Lincoln insisted that "this current of travel has its rights, as well as that north and south. If the river had not the advantage in priority and legislation, we could enter into free competition with it and we could surpass it." He had thus introduced into the case not only the vision of the growing West but also the economic principle of free competition. Both, he thought, ought not to be impeded by the law.

As lawyers might in a modern brief, counsel for the bridge company had introduced into evidence statistics showing the volume of traffic on the railroad that had passed over the bridge while the Mississippi River was frozen into commerce-stultifying ice. Lawyers for the steamboat objected, but Justice John McLean, who was sitting on the federal circuit court bench in the case, ruled in favor of the defense.[15] Lincoln recognized the impressive quality of the statistical documentation presented earlier and carefully included it in his summation to the jury: "It is in evidence that from September 8, 1856, to August 8, 1857, 12,586 freight cars and 74,179 passengers passed over this bridge. Navigation was closed four days short of four months last year, and during this time, while the river was of no use, this road and bridge were equally valuable."[16]

The case showed Lincoln at his most forward-looking and innovative as a legal practitioner. Justice McLean, who delivered the charge to the jury, was a Whig-turned-Republican like Lincoln, and he obviously shared the same vision of development of the western empire. McLean told the jurors:

> Although there may be something in this case to enlist the conflicting interests of different communities, it is a common occurrence, which results from the increase of population and the consequent increase of trade. It is felt more or less by all nations and all communities. To any one who will take a general view this is high evidence of a rising and prosperous country. Bountiful as Providence has been in supplying our country with great lakes and mighty rivers, they are found inadequate to the wants of society. They are the great arteries of commerce, but like the human system, the body cannot be preserved in its healthful vigor unless the veins shall connect with the arteries and impart health and action to every part.
>
> New fields of industry and enterprise necessarily open up new avenues of intercourse. This is the law of progress, and it cannot fail so long as civilization shall be progressive. And it will be found in the future as it has been in time past, that this progress will greatly add to instead of diminishing from the general wealth of the country. And however sectional jealousies may arise out of this progress it will be seen and acknowledged that the prosperity of the whole country is consistent with the prosperity of its different parts.[17]

Aided by the judge's obviously loaded charge to the jury, Lincoln thus played his part in shaping American law to the dynamic of capitalism. The argument also testified to his accustomed forward-looking economic views.[18] One other aspect of the nation's future was at work in the case: the Union itself. In his summation Lincoln noted briefly in passing that counsel for the *Effie Afton*'s owners had "alluded to the strife of the contending interests, and even a dissolution of the Union."[19] In 1857 sectional questions were everywhere, even in Chicago courtrooms. Lincoln understood from this point on, if he had not before, that the solidarity of a North welded by railroad iron east and west could be relied upon in season and out. During the Civil War he would waste less time than most on worry about the fidelity of the states of the Old Northwest to the Northern cause. He hailed from one of them, Illinois, and he had every confidence they would cling to the Union.

The Inaugural Address, March 4, 1861

Four years after the *Effie Afton* case, Abraham Lincoln delivered his First Inaugural Address as president of the United States and at last focused his attention on the relationship between the Constitution and the nation's survival. *Effie Afton* and east-west commerce were only a bedrock prelude to the nationalistic document he produced for that occasion. Though capitalism was another vital source of ideas for Lincoln, he did not mention any economic arguments in the inaugural address. He came up with other ideas to make his case for union. Lincoln did not invent American nationalism at that moment. The union of Northeast and Northwest already rested solidly on iron rails. But could one be sure of the sentiment for union in America's hearts? Southerners were apparently in danger of losing the sentiment, and Lincoln found that he must articulate a systematic vision of the nation for the first time in his long political career, spanning a generation from the Age of Jackson to secession.

On March 4, 1861, when he took the oath prescribed for the president by the Constitution and delivered the much-anticipated address, the situation seemed to require — in addition to indications whether he was going to accede to Southern demands or go to war — an explanation of the errors of secession and the necessity of perpetual union. The task was not easy for Lincoln because he had spent most of the previous decade defending liberty from the perceived assaults of a slaveholding aristocracy. Now he was put in the position of defending authority over liberty. The antislavery sources had been foremost in that decade for him. Only a year before the inaugural, in the Cooper Institute speech, he had, more or less, worked up a lecture embodying the antislavery interpretation of the Constitution. He had not then been articulating a systematic theory of the importance of national power, and now he had to work up another kind of lecture.

Moreover, overconfident about the security of the Union, Lincoln had apparently not thought much about secession. He did not develop any serious theoretical interest in the problem of secession in his earlier career in politics. He had little interest in political theory of any sort. Only days before his murder in April 1865, Lincoln was still trying to dismiss the issue:

> I have been shown a letter . . . in which the writer expresses regret that my mind has not seemed to be definitely fixed on the question whether the seceded States, so called, are in the union or out of it. . . . I have *purposely* forborne any public expression upon it. As [it] appears to me that question has not been, nor yet is, a practically material one, and that any discussion of it, while it thus remains practically immaterial, could have no effect other than the mischievous one of dividing our friends. As yet, whatever it may hereafter become, that question is bad, as the basis of a controversy, and good for nothing at all — a merely pernicious abstraction.[20]

But when Lincoln was elected president in 1860, others thought it was important to understand his record on the question of secession. The president-elect had to admit that he really had none. On the very day that the South Carolina secession convention first met — after a generation of debate and controversy had brought the issue to a head — Lincoln, then still the president-elect, received a letter inquiring about his views on secession. It came from Thurlow Weed, the right-hand man of William H. Seward (soon to be appointed President Lincoln's secretary of state) and someone whom Lincoln simply had to answer. Lincoln replied that there was "but little, if any thing, in my speeches, about secession; but my opinion is that no state can, in any way lawfully get out of the union, without the consent of the others; and that it is the duty of the President, and other government functionaries to run the machine as it is."[21] About a week after South Carolina's secession, Lincoln responded to a letter asking him about secession this way: "Yours kindly seeking my view as to the proper mode of dealing with secession, was received . . . but . . . I could not answer it till now. I think we should hold the forts, or retake them, as the case may be, and collect the revenue. *We* shall have to forego the use of the federal courts, and *they* that of the mails, for a while. We can not fight them in to holding courts, or receiving the mails."[22] There was nothing theoretical in what Lincoln said and nothing with a tone of exasperation or intellectual outrage at the doctrine. Lincoln kept his focus on the practical.

The problem for Lincoln was that seven Southern states had seceded from the Union, and nothing in the Constitution explicitly declared secession illegal. Nothing in the Constitution explicitly declared the Union perpetual.[23] As Don E. Fehrenbacher wrote, the "law inheres most essentially in the text of the document," and Lincoln had to do the best he could without much actual text to back him up.[24]

Lincoln began to consider the problem around February 1861, about a month before his inauguration. He might not even have begun that early, but he was going to take a circuitous route to Washington for his inauguration — a whistle-stop tour — and he wanted to have his inaugural address finished in draft before he left on that arduous journey meant to cultivate public opinion.

Lincoln sat down in Springfield in a borrowed office to draft his inaugural address. He obtained a copy of the Constitution from his law partner.[25] When he examined it, he discovered, perhaps to his surprise and certainly to his dismay, that it offered no straightforward solution. Even the feeble Articles of Confederation had said at least that the Union was perpetual — had said it more than once, in fact. The very title of the document was "Articles of Confederation and Perpetual Union." But the Articles had been tossed onto the rubbish heap of American history long ago, and nothing in the Constitution declared the Union perpetual.

In his inaugural address, Lincoln laid out four different arguments for union — constitutional, legal, historical, and practical. His constitutional argument was weak, and, of necessity, skirted textual analysis. "I hold," Lincoln said, "that in contemplation of universal law, and of the Constitution, the Union of these States is perpetual." In that formulation of doctrine, universal law came first, not the fundamental American legal document, the Constitution, and it was only "in contemplation" that the Constitution was perpetual. "Perpetuity," Lincoln argued, "is implied if not expressed, in the fundamental law of all national governments." The United States — he did not say so directly, of course — was among those national governments in which perpetuity was "not expressed."[26] Strict construction, constitutional literalism, may not have led inexorably to a doctrine of secession, but it could not save the Union either.

Lincoln followed with a legal argument that attempted to answer the favorite theory of the secessionists, the "compact" theory of the Constitution, on their own terms. "If the United States be not a government proper," Lincoln asked, "but an association of States in the nature of contract merely, can it, as a contract, be peaceably unmade, by less than all the parties who made it? One party to a contract may violate it — break it, so to speak; but does it not require all to lawfully rescind it?"[27] That point he left as a question rather than an affirmation, even though it may have represented his firmest belief, the argument against secession he already had at hand back in December, when Thurlow Weed asked about his views.

Perhaps the most memorable effort followed: a historical argument. "Descending from these general principles," he said, "we find the proposition that, in legal contemplation, the Union is perpetual, confirmed by the history of the Union itself." He proceeded to invent a mythical national past for Americans, one that did not look mythical at all. It fact, it looked the opposite, drily and analytically precise, referring to old legal documents rather than to heroic events from the past, and confined to a tight, almost scholastic, chronology:

> The Union is much older than the Constitution. It was formed in fact, by the Articles of Association in 1774. It was matured and continued by the Declaration of Independence in 1776. It was further matured and the faith of all the then thirteen States expressly plighted and engaged that it should be perpetual, by the Articles of Confederation in 1778. And, finally, in 1787, one of the declared objects for ordaining and establishing the Constitution, was *"to form a more perfect union."*[28]

Lincoln had more to accomplish in devising this mythological chronology than denying state rights and secession. As an antislavery Republican he also desired to secure a fundamental place in the constitutional history of the United States for the Declaration of Independence, with its affirmation that all men are created equal. That was the problem he had worked on mainly in the 1850s.

By the time of his famous debates with Stephen A. Douglas in 1858, Lincoln had already formulated his view that "the declara[tion] that 'all men are created equal' is the great fundamental principle upon which our free institutions rest; that negro slavery is violative of that principle; but that, by our frame of government, that principle has not been made one of legal obligation."[29] When the original declaration was made, the authors "meant simply to declare the *right*, so that the *enforcement* of it might follow as fast as circumstances should permit. They meant to set up a standard maxim for [a] free society, which should be familiar to all, and revered by all; constantly looked to, constantly labored for, and even though never perfectly attained, constantly approximated, and thereby constantly spreading and deepening its influence, and augmenting the happiness and value of life to all people of all colors everywhere."[30] In the inaugural address, Lincoln remained faithful to the antislavery sources of his constitutional ideas and carefully included the Declaration of Independence as one of the documents of the historical series that confirmed that "in legal contemplation, the Union is perpetual."

He had spoken the truth about American history perhaps, but not the whole truth.[31] The weakest part of the historical argument lay in the section that dealt with the weak Articles of Confederation. True, their very title was "Articles of Confederation and Perpetual Union," and Article XIII affirmed that "the union shall be perpetual." Yet Article II affirmed with equal forthrightness that "each state retains its sovereignty," whereas Article III styled the nature of the Union as no more than "a firm league of friendship."[32] Lincoln did not mention Articles II and III.

More important, the true history of the Articles of Confederation interrupted the linear flow of the history of the American nation Lincoln was attempting to construct. What Lincoln claimed — namely, that "the faith of all the . . . thirteen States" had been "expressly plighted and engaged" that the Union "should be perpetual," with the *drafting of the Articles* — was not entirely accurate. Ratification by the states after the Articles were drawn up was a protracted and tortured process, finally brought to a conclusion only by the application of outside force. Maryland held out from ratification for years, until 1781. When the British threatened to invade the South, however, the state became alarmed and requested the protection of the French navy. France's envoy, the Chevalier de la Luzerne, extracted ratification of the Articles as the price of naval protection for Maryland (France, aiding the American colonies at the time in their war for independence, naturally wanted the colonies united in their fight against England).[33] Finally, the Constitution of 1787 was actually a wholesale repudiation of the weak government under the Articles. To place the Articles of Confederation with the Constitution on a progressive continuum was to iron out the very considerable political struggle to achieve unity in the American past.

Sources Transformed

In composing the inaugural address, Lincoln did not take his arguments straight from the sources he consulted. He had borrowed from his law partner William H. Herndon copies of Andrew Jackson's famous antinullification message of December 10, 1832, and Henry Clay's speech on the Compromise of 1850 as well as a copy of the Constitution.[34] Later he also obtained a copy of Daniel Webster's famous reply to Robert Y. Hayne, a speech, Herndon informs us, that Lincoln had read back in New Salem.[35] A look at these sources will give us renewed appreciation for Lincoln's innovation and discrimination in argument.

President Jackson had viewed the Articles of Confederation as enemies of nationalism and noted their "defects": "Under its operation we could scarcely be called a nation. We had neither prosperity at home nor consideration abroad. This state of things could not be endured, and our present happy Constitution was formed, but formed in vain, if this fatal doctrine [of nullification] prevails."[36] Later in the message Jackson, in a passage followed closely by Lincoln in his inaugural address, said: "The unity of our political character . . . commenced with its very existence. Under the Royal Government we had no separate character; but opposition to its oppressions began as UNITED COLONIES. We were the UNITED STATES under the confederation; and the name was perpetuated, and the Union rendered more perfect, by the Federal Constitution."[37] More important, Jackson, a Democrat and Tennessee slaveholder with no antislavery convictions or goals in facing down nullification, did not mention the Declaration of Independence specifically in his own mythical history of the Union. Lincoln significantly transformed Jackson's nationalist doctrine.

Despite those differences, Lincoln had taken part of his argument from Jackson.[38] Kenneth Stampp has noted that

> Jackson's conclusion appears to be the model from which Lincoln drew inspiration for some critical statements in the first inaugural address. Jackson warned the people of South Carolina that he would fulfill the obligation imposed on him by the Constitution "to take care that the laws be faithfully executed." In this he had no discretionary power, for "my duty is emphatically pronounced in the Constitution." Therefore, if an attempt at disunion should lead to "the shedding of brother's blood," that result could not be attributed to "any offensive act on the part of the United States." Having urged South Carolinians to consider the dangers they risked, Jackson closed on a softer note with an appeal to their love for the Union.[39]

That does sound like a summary of Lincoln's inaugural:

> I shall take care, as the Constitution itself expressly enjoins upon me, that the laws of the Union be faithfully executed in all the States. Doing this I deem to be only a simple duty on my part. . . . I trust this will not be regarded as a menace, but only as the declared pur-

pose of the Union that it *will* constitutionally defend, and maintain itself.

In doing this there needs to be no bloodshed or violence; and there shall be none, unless it be forced upon the national authority.[40]

Lincoln also consulted Henry Clay's speech on the Compromise of 1850, of February 5–6, 1850, apparently borrowing ideas from the following passage of Clay's:

> I think that the Constitution of the thirteen States was made, not merely for the generation which then existed, but for posterity, undefined, unlimited, permanent and perpetual. . . . It is to remain for that posterity now and forever. Like another of the great relations of private life, it was a marriage that no human authority can dissolve or divorce the parties from and, if I may be allowed to refer to this same example in private life, let us say what man and wife say to each other: We have mutual faults; nothing in the form of human beings can be perfect; let us, then, be kind to each other, forbearing, conceding; let us live in happiness and peace.[41]

Lincoln transformed Clay's comparison, employing it to describe geographic determinants of the nation:

> Physically speaking, we cannot separate. We cannot remove our respective sections from each other, nor build an impassable wall between them. A husband and wife may be divorced, and go out of the presence, and beyond the reach of each other; but the different parts of our country cannot do this. They cannot but remain face to face; and intercourse, either amicable or hostile, must continue between them.[42]

Lincoln's transformation of Clay's comparison again reminds us that what Lincoln modified and ignored in his predecessors was important for understanding his view of the nation and the Constitution. Clay, for example, may have been a Southern man with Northern principles, but he *was* a Southern man. In other remarks on the compromise made on July 22, 1850, Clay insisted that "my rules of interpreting the Constitution of the United States are the good old rules of '98 and '99."[43] The "rules" to which Clay referred were the ideas embodied in the Kentucky and Virginia Resolutions of 1798 and 1799, documents that formed the original source of nullification and the threat of secession that lay in the compact theory of the Constitution. Lincoln left those principles where they lay in Clay's speeches.

What Lincoln ignored in Andrew Jackson is significant enough to merit extended comment as well. The defense of the U.S. Constitution embodied in the antinullification message of 1832 contained, among other things, a familiar Jacksonian affirmation of the importance of the presidential office:

> The people of the United States formed the Constitution, acting through the State Legislatures in making the compact, to meet and discuss its provisions, and acting in separate conventions when they ratified those provisions; but the terms used in the construction, show it to be a government in which the people of all the States collectively are represented. We are ONE PEOPLE in the choice of the president and the Vice-president. Here the States have no other agency than to direct the mode in which the votes shall be given. The candidates having the majority of all the votes are chosen. The electors of a majority of the States may have given their votes for one candidate, and yet another may be chosen. The people, then, and not the States are represented in the Executive branch.[44]

The omission of Jackson's ideas about the executive provides proof that Lincoln had no premeditated expansion of presidential power in mind when he took office before war broke out.[45] Lincoln's nationalism conspicuously contained none of the pathological seeds of one-man rule or the cult of personality of dictatorship to be found in deeply troubled nationalisms of the twentieth century.

Lincoln's inaugural address also offered a fourth argument for the nation, a practical one. If secession be seen as legitimate, Lincoln insisted, "why may not any portion of a new confederacy, a year or two hence, arbitrarily secede again[?] . . . Plainly, the central idea of secession, is the essence of anarchy." He continued with words that Southerners were likely to notice: "A majority, held in restraint by constitutional checks, and limitations, and always changing easily, with deliberate changes of popular opinions and sentiments, is the only true sovereign of a free people. Whoever rejects it, does, of necessity, fly to anarchy or to despotism."[46] Southerners, of course, feared rule by national majorities and doubted the continuing viability of the "constitutional checks" Lincoln mentioned in passing.

The events of the next four years would test this proposition about anarchy—and prove it wrong repeatedly. Chapter 6 examines the process of secession closely, but for now the following considerations should suffice to show the error of Lincoln's prediction. Secession in the Southern states, which Lincoln had been witnessing, was itself an orderly and legalistic parliamentary process that followed constitutional state boundaries.[47] The subsequent history of the Confederacy has more often been described as authoritarian than anarchic, though both descriptions are wrong. We may note now the following three salient facts of Confederate history that make any assertion of anarchic tendencies implausible. First, only West Virginia seceded from the Confederacy, and that occurred, in essence, early, while the configuration of the Confederate States was in formation. Second, even after the trans-Mississippi Confederacy was severed by the fall of Vicksburg from the Richmond government's practical control in mid-1863, the West did not secede from the East. The fall of Vicksburg came two years out in the history of the Confederacy, exactly the time Lincoln mentioned, but no further secessions occurred then. Third, the "anarchic" areas of the Confederacy, such as East Tennessee, only mirrored the turbulent areas of society in similar Border States of Lincoln's own Union. "Anarchy," or contested authority over the control of the state government, in these discontented and poorly controlled mountainous areas was endemic and not a later development that mimicked the precedent of secession.

Anarchic impulses were not unleashed in the North, either. All the talk later in the war of a great Northwest Conspiracy to secede and join the Confederacy proved to be just talk. And distant places like California, only remotely controlled by Washington, D.C., remained fast and true to the Union throughout the war. The lure of secession was not particularly great. The lure of strong nationhood recovered its superiority quickly.

Lincoln was wrong about anarchy, but his contribution in his inaugural address to the myth of a common American past, on the other hand, has been underestimated.[48] That becomes clear if we compare the inaugural address to a third source of Lincoln's ideas, Daniel Webster's Second Reply to Hayne, of January 26–27, 1830, perhaps the most famous single source of American nationalist ideas of the antebellum period. Webster's withering response to South Carolina's nullification doctrines in that speech offered an early defense of the power of the national government. But Lincoln did not find Webster's formulation completely usable, either.

Webster emphasized the essential role of the judiciary in American nationalism. First, Webster quoted the supremacy clause of the Constitution from Article VI: "The Constitution, and the laws of the United States made in pursuance thereof, shall be the supreme law of the land, any thing in the constitution or laws of any State to the contrary notwithstanding." Then he added: "To whom lies the last appeal? This, Sir, the Constitution itself decides also by declaring, *'that the judicial power shall extend to all cases arising under the Constitution and laws of the United States.'* These two provisions cover the whole ground. They are, in truth, the keystone of the arch! With these it is a government; without them it is a confederation."[49] Lincoln did not rest his case in 1861 by asserting the supremacy clause and pointing to the U.S. Supreme Court because the Court lay in the hands of Chief Justice Roger B. Taney and the other architects of the infamous *Dred Scott* decision of 1857.

Lincoln realized from the aggressive stance Taney took in defending slavery and racism in the *Dred Scott* decision that the chief justice could not be relied upon as the keystone of the arch of Union, that anyone who might go as far as Taney had in defense of slavery might not stop at threatening the means to save the Union. Still, Webster and the U.S. Constitution indicated that the Supreme Court was supposed to settle such conflicts of power, and Lincoln had, reluctantly, to address the role of the Court in the secession crisis:

> I do not forget the position assumed by some, that constitutional questions are to be decided by the Supreme Court. . . . The candid citizen must confess that if the policy of the government, upon vital questions, affecting the whole people, is to be irrevocably fixed by decisions of the Supreme Court, the instant they are made, in ordinary litigation between parties, in personal actions, the people will have ceased, to be their own rulers, having, to that extent, practically resigned their government, into the hands of that eminent tribunal.[50]

Lincoln did not retreat to the judiciary for help and opted for a more democratic ethos.[51]

Lincoln had had plenty of time to think about judicial review (as opposed to secession), and he now shifted the weight of his ideas more toward democracy than in the past. Taney had been chief justice for most of Lincoln's political career (from 1836 on), but Lincoln had had little to complain about even so until the *Dred Scott* decision.[52] That opinion, which declared that Congress had no power to prevent the spread of slavery to the territories, undermined the central plank of the Republican platform. Under pressure from Stephen A. Douglas, who chided the Republicans for "offering violent resistance" to an opinion of the Court, Lincoln absolutely had to devise an answer.[53] His political instinct was to remind Douglas of embarrassing inconsistencies from the Democratic Party's past. And who, to date, had been the greatest challenger of the authority of the U.S. Supreme Court in American history except the very founder of the Democratic Party himself, Andrew Jackson?

Lincoln did not raise the question of the Court's decisions protecting Indian nations from hostile state legislation that Jackson largely defied;

instead, he brought up the more famous veto of the bill to recharter the Second Bank of the United States and the message Jackson wrote in defense of his veto. In part, this put Lincoln in the position of a departmental understanding of constitutionalism — that is, that each branch of government was to interpret the Constitution as it saw fit (a problematic doctrine that left unanswered the question of resolution of the ultimate conflicts between the branches).

Seeking to embarrass Douglas in 1857, Lincoln quoted Jackson's justification, with its democratic skepticism about the final authority of the Supreme Court. Lincoln featured these words, among others, from the veto message:

> It is maintained by the advocates of the bank, that its constitutionality, in all its features, ought to be considered as settled by precedent, and by the decision of the Supreme Court. To this conclusion I cannot assent. Mere precedent is a dangerous source of authority, and should not be regarded as deciding questions of constitutional power, except where the acquiescence of the people and the States can be considered as well settled.[54]

In his 1857 critique, Lincoln himself did not put as great an emphasis on people, confining his criticism of the *Dred Scott* decision to jurisprudence rather than democracy:

> If this important decision had been made by the unanimous concurrence of the judges, and without any apparent partisan bias, and in accordance with legal public expectation, and with the steady practice of the departments throughout our history, and had been in no part, based on assumed historical facts which are not really true; or, if wanting in some of these, it had been before the court more than once, and had there been affirmed and re-affirmed through a course of years, it then might be, perhaps would be, factious, nay, even revolutionary, to not acquiesce in it as a precedent.[55]

Lincoln did not embrace a doctrine of popular constitutionalism, incorporating the opinions of the people into constitutional consideration. He referred to "legal public expectation" and not simple public opinion in 1857.[56]

But in the inaugural address, he was bolder and revealed, for the first time, a tendency to be seduced by the democratic doctrines of Andrew Jackson. In 1861 he contrasted a people who were determined to be "their own rulers" and not surrender to the authority of "that eminent tribunal," the Supreme Court. He had no further criticism of the court as an institution. Still, when Lincoln adopted a political position out of opposition to another party's measures, as he had to in the aftermath of the *Dred Scott* decision, it caused him to think about the question, and if he thought about it long, he was likely to reach for democratic justifications for his newly articulated position. After four years to think about the problem of a perverse decision of the Supreme Court, he was inching toward democracy.

Certainly Daniel Webster in his important nationalist answers to South Carolina nullification never approached the views of Jackson on judicial review. On the contrary, Webster's answer to nullification *was* a flat constitutional insistence on the finality of judicial review. Lincoln was not going to embrace that, nor was he to adopt Webster's version of American constitutional history. Webster held an extremely negative view of the government of the United States under the Articles of Confederation. Power was what that government had famously lacked. Webster asked what was to be done if South Carolina thought a tariff ought not to be paid and Pennsylvania thought it should. "If there be no power to settle such questions, independent of either of the States, is not the whole Union a rope of sand? Are we not thrown back again, precisely, upon the old Confederation?"[57] In 1861 Lincoln chose to rest his argument on the inviolability of the Union rather than the brute fact of its constitutional or legal power. He saw a continuity in the progress of American history from the Declaration of Independence, through the Confederation period, and to the formation of the more perfect Union under the Constitution of 1787. The resulting doctrine was less confrontational and perhaps more appealing. And Lincoln's scheme left a prominent niche for the role of the Declaration of Independence. *That was crucial for an antislavery politician.* To be sure, that somewhat demoted the prestige of the Constitution in Lincoln's thought, for the Constitution was a problem for antislavery men and the Declaration of Independence was an inspiration. Neither Webster nor Jackson, of course, drew significantly on the antislavery tradition, and therefore neither Jackson nor Webster had as important and clear a role for the Declaration of Independence in American history.

Even so, Lincoln was the heir of the work of the fathers of American nationalism: Andrew Jackson, Daniel Webster, and Henry Clay. He picked, chose, and refined arguments. He did not invent them. And he was not partisan in choosing as sources Jackson, Webster, and Clay. One source was Democratic and the others Whig. Lincoln knew that he could not offer a national vision that appealed to the ears only of partisans of one creed. He accepted the greatest gift to the nation of the second party system: the embrace of nationalism by both political parties.

Conservative Nationalisms of the Future Not Prefigured nor Conservative Nationalisms of the Past Recalled

Civil War historians have sometimes seen Lincoln's inaugural address as a starting point for a drama of development of doctrines of conservative nationalism. Constitutional historian Michael Les Benedict, for example, initiates his discussion of the Civil War this way:

> The war for the Union deepened northerners' sense of nationalism, leading to the widespread acceptance of an idea growing in Europe: that a nation is defined not by a social contract among its citizens but by the common feelings, customs, language, and culture of its people. Many northerners now argued that Americans had become a national people through common experience and culture even before they had adopted the Constitution. Lincoln articulated this understanding in his inaugural address. The Union was older than the Constitution, he said. Americans were united not only by a Constitution but by "mystic chords of memory, stretching from every battlefield and patriot grave to every living heart and hearthstone all over this broad land."[58]

Benedict exemplifies those historians who have seen Lincoln articulating in the Civil War a distinctly European idea of nationhood based on tradition rather than on contract. When Lincoln put forward his ideas on the nation, then, would it be accurate to say he was somehow "inventing" a new nation?[59] Was he invoking conservative ideas once discarded in America? Was he embracing authoritarian ideas of some mystical sort?

Benedict's drama of ideas about the nation does not capture the nature of Lincoln's enterprise, though he is correct to realize that Lincoln's view deserves a place in even a brief textbook on the Constitution. At this point Civil War history can be rescued by the ideas of Benedict Anderson. In his influential book *Imagined Communities: Reflections on the Origin and Spread of Nationalism*, Anderson makes a point crucial for interpreting the political ideas of this period: "In an age when it is so common for progressive, cosmopolitan intellectuals . . . to insist on the near-pathological character of nationalism, its roots in fear and hatred of the Other, and its affinities with racism, it is useful to remind ourselves that nations inspire love, and often profoundly self-sacrificing love."[60] When we recognize nationalism in the political ideas of Abraham Lincoln, we need not recoil in horror or even get nervous. We should not assume the worst: that they hearken back to reactionary ideas or that they prefigure totalitarianism and fascism. In the middle of the nineteenth century, nationalism was not pathological.

Though Lincoln may have struggled with interpretation, his argument for nationhood focused mainly on interpreting the Constitution. Had the Constitution offered him the clear textual basis he needed, his argument might have stopped there. His original historical argument, which offered a more seamlessly linear history for the nation than it had actually experienced at the end of the eighteenth century, nevertheless proceeded from document to document, from the Articles of Association, to the Declaration of Independence, to the Articles of Confederation, to the final Constitution of 1787. It was as though Lincoln had looked into the lockbox of American history at the nation's bank and pulled out a bunch of old foolscap agreements that proved the nation existed prior to the states.

Later in the address, Lincoln added: "Physically speaking, we cannot separate. We cannot remove our respective sections from each other, nor build an impassable wall between them." He did not, as others would during the war to come, wax rhapsodic about the hills and valleys of that landscape, nor did he point to the freedom of flow of the Mississippi River, long a staple of nationalist arguments in the United States and another point to be made often in the war years to come (and in 1863, by Lincoln himself). Lincoln had as a young man floated products down the Mississippi from the Old Northwest to New Orleans. In 1861 he might have woven into the speech fetching anecdotes of the union of North and South he saw then. But he did not. He did point out the difference between a union bound by contract and one bound by geography. "A husband and wife may be divorced, and go out of the presence, and beyond the reach of each other; but the different parts of our country cannot do this." A listener might see North and South as an unhappy married couple deciding glumly to stick to their union—hardly an inspiring image of nationhood. Lincoln did not vividly enlist Nature itself on the side of America.

As for "feelings, customs, language, and culture," Lincoln said nothing about them nor did he try to appeal to them with imagery—that is, until the end of the address, when he said: "The mystic chords of memory, stre[t]ching from every battle-field, and patriot grave, to every living heart and hearthstone, all over this broad land, will yet swell the chorus of the Union, when again touched, as surely they will be, by the better angels of our nature."[61] But these were not really Lincoln's words and, more to the point, not exactly Lincoln's way of thinking about the subject. It never occurred to him to appeal to sentiment and national feeling. He did not yet really know how to do it except in the service of liberation. He was good at making stirring appeals to liberty and republicanism, of course, and had been doing so in service to the antislavery cause for most of the previous decade, but when it came to nationhood, he simply was not up to it.[62] Such things were more in William Seward's line, and so, when Seward read a draft of Lincoln's proposed address, he suggested:

> The argument is strong and conclusive, and ought not to be in any way abridged or modified.
>
> But something besides or in addition to argument is needful — to meet and remove prejudice and passion in the South, and despondency and fear in the East.
>
> Some words of affection — some of calm and cheerful confidence.[63]

Lincoln heeded Seward's advice to include "something besides . . . argument." Seward suggested the language that Lincoln subsequently revised into the memorable "mystic chords of memory" that concluded the address. What is significant here is the fact that Lincoln could not come up with such an appeal on his own, even with his fervent patriotism and his gift for language. Without outside assistance, Lincoln could not summon traditionalist and sentimental ideas of nationhood, even when they were needed.[64]

Interpreting the Address at the Time

Many Americans read the inaugural address closely, but they were looking for policy, not philosophy. If we may judge from newspaper commentary on the speech, few in the North cared about the theory of national unity Lincoln had offered. The *New York Herald*, distinguished among major newspapers by its relative political independence and its dismissive and withering tone, was among the few to comment substantively on the content of the nationalist argument, and it did so with ridicule: "The Union, Mr. Lincoln reminds us, has not provided, in the national constitution, for its own destruction; but, 'in contemplation of universal law,' it must be 'perpetual' — indeed, this should greatly console the Bourbons and the Rajah of Scinde, 'perpetuity is the fundamental law of all national governments.'. . . Later, however, he pays a tribute to the 'right of revolution,' with which his first declarations are hardly consistent." The *Herald* editors were close readers, it must be said. They noted that the address contained "the finger-marks of Mr. Seward, from the exordium to the poetical peroration."[65]

The earnest and Republican *New York Tribune* complimented Lincoln on "the admirable treatment of the Secession question," but it did not go into particulars.[66] The *Philadelphia Press* did not quarrel with the substance but with the originality of the antisecession argument. "In his remarks in reference to the character of our institutions and the impossibility of legal secession without the consent of all the States," the editors wrote, "he only reiterates, in forceful terms, the views . . . repeatedly expressed by all the great statesmen of our country."[67] James G. Randall, himself a constitutional historian, surveyed newspaper reactions to the inaugural address and followed their lead by commenting mainly on questions of conciliation versus coercion as practical matters in the crisis over federal property in the seceding states.[68]

The lack of commentary on the nationalist philosophy in the address suggests that Northerners' minds were already made up on the value of the Union. The people simply wanted to know whether Lincoln was going to war to save it or not. They looked for indications that the new president might compromise on questions of federal property in the seceded states, or that he might invade the South, or that he might surrender U.S. forts there. They wondered whether he would irritate the South by interfering with the apprehension of fugitive slaves, the first substantive issue he dealt with in the address. But, for whatever reason, most Americans in the North were already sold on the nation. They were not waiting to pick a side. They already knew whose side they would be on if the verdict was war. They did not really respond to the philosophical arguments or the mythical history.

Modern Interpretation

There have been those who would attempt to rescue even the First Inaugural Address from characterization as nationalistic. The great constitutional lawyer Akhil Reed Amar, for example, interprets the address in the opposite way from Michael Les Benedict. Amar admires Lincoln's invocation of the preamble to the Constitution. He believes the U.S. Constitution is fundamentally a radically democratic document and that the beginning words, "We the people," should be taken seriously. He has said that in "Lincoln's First Inaugural Address, the reference to the Preamble's 'more perfect Union' was explicit; at Gettysburg, Lincoln's allusion was more subtle, playing on the grand 'We the People' phraseology."[69] Amar refers to the phrase in the Gettysburg Address of 1863, "government by the people, of the people, and for the people."

Although it is true that Lincoln did refer to the preamble of the Constitution in the inaugural address, he did not do so for the purpose Amar ascribed to him. At the end of his historical argument, Lincoln said: "And finally, in 1787, one of the declared objects for ordaining and establishing the

Constitution, was 'to form a more perfect union.'" But Lincoln was attracted only to the dry logic of the preamble, not to its populist poetry. Rather than quote the "we the people" phrase, Lincoln said, "If destruction of the Union, by one, or by a part only, of the States, be lawfully possible, the Union is *less* perfect than before the Constitution, having lost the vital element of perpetuity."[70] Lincoln was still straining to smuggle perpetuity into the text of the Constitution of 1787. This was not a search for democratic inspiration. In fact, he did not actually quote the "we the people" part of the preamble in either the First Inaugural Address or the Gettysburg Address two years later.

Lincoln could at times be witheringly logical in matters of political philosophy. There is a notable example of that in a brief speech he gave in Indianapolis on his way to Washington on February 11, 1861:

> What is the particular sacredness of a State? . . . If a State, in one instance, and a county in another, should be equal in extent of territory, and equal in the number of people, wherein is that State any better than the county? Can a change of name change the right? By what principle of original right is it that one-fiftieth or one-ninetieth of a great nation, by calling themselves a State, have the right to break up and ruin that nation as a matter of original principle? . . . Where is the mysterious, original right, from principle, for a certain district of country with inhabitants, by merely being called a State, to play tyrant over all its own citizens, and deny the authority of everything greater than itself.[71]

In the end, Lincoln was a serious statesman interested in saving the nation; he was not as interested in scoring debating points with secessionists. The statement above was less devastatingly logical than it was playful in context. It provoked laughter from the crowd in Indianapolis at least twice. And immediately before the definition of a state, Lincoln had set the tone by saying this of the perspective of the secessionists: "In their view, the Union, as a family relation, would not be anything like a regular marriage at all, but only as a sort of free-love arrangement, — [laughter] — to be maintained on what that sect calls passionate attraction. [Continued laughter] But, my friends, enough of this."[72]

Frederick Douglass and the First Inaugural Address

Amar would have been on firmer ground had he located the more democratic interpretation of the Constitution not in Lincoln but in one of his sharpest critics, Frederick Douglass. In one way, the reaction of Douglass to Lincoln's inaugural address was typical for Americans in its indifference to philosophy. Douglass readily admitted that the president gave "a very lucid exposition of the nature of the Federal Union." "His argument is excellent," Douglass said, "but the difficulty is that the argument comes too late. When men . . . openly insult [the government's] flag . . . it would seem of little use to argue with them. If the argument was merely for the loyal citizen, it was unnecessary. If it was for those already in rebellion, it was casting pearls before swine."[73] Like most Americans in the North, Douglass was moved by the "insult" of Southern secession, not by explanations of its untenable legality.

Douglass's extended analysis of the speech appeared in *Douglass's Monthly* in April 1861, before the firing on Fort Sumter. It is a surprisingly neglected source.[74] For the bulk of his essay about Lincoln's address, Douglass dwelt on its truckling tone rather than on its intellectual and historical content. Douglass brilliantly began his essay by comparing Lincoln to a fugitive slave, noting that the president-elect had been forced by threats of assassination to sneak into Washington for the event. "We have no censure for the President at this point," Douglass observed. "He only did what braver men have done. It was, doubtless, galling to his very soul to be compelled to avail himself of the methods of a fugitive slave, with a nation howling on his track."[75] But the damage to Lincoln's reputation was done, and no one knew it better than Douglass, who used the ironic comparison to set the stage for a denunciation of the inaugural address for failing to stand up bravely to the threat of Southern secession. Throughout, Douglass's editorial is laced with the language and imagery of cowardice.

Douglass employed the occasion mainly to offer a forward-looking radical analysis of the U.S. Constitution. Consideration of the Constitution was crucial for Douglass. He had long ago broken with William Lloyd Garrison over the nature of the Constitution and forged his own path toward political antislavery. Garrison considered the Constitution a proslavery document and hence, in a moment notorious to many Americans, burned a copy of it in the public square in Framingham, Massachusetts, on July 4, 1854. To Garrison, the Constitution was a "covenant with death." Long before Garrison's infamous act, Douglass had been influenced by another radical antislavery advocate, Gerrit Smith, to regard the Constitution as an antislavery and basically liberal document. Smith argued that the Constitution, read literally, did not mention the word "slavery" but did promise to "secure the blessings of liberty." Slavery was incompatible with that ideal, plainly stated in the preamble, and therefore inconsistent with the Constitution. Literal interpretation was crucial to Smith, and he insisted that the framers' *intentions* be ignored. Considering their intentions could lead to proslavery interpretations of the document's language.[76]

Douglass could not make sense of such an approach to constitutional interpretation. To him the intentions of the framers obviously mattered. He had to convince himself that those intentions were fundamentally liberal before he could come around to full fealty to the Constitution of the United States. By 1861 Douglass had done that. The president, in discussing what he regarded as the constitutional obligation to return fugitive slaves, had stated that "the intention of the law-giver is the law." Douglass believed that statement true only if the intention was itself lawful — that is, right and just. Even supposing that one granted to Lincoln the principle that the intention of the lawgiver was the law, Douglass argued, "two very important questions arise — first, as to who were the makers, and, secondly, by what means are we required to learn their intentions?"[77]

"Who made the Constitution?" Douglass asked. He was not satisfied with the conventional answer that the fifty-five members of the Philadelphia constitutional convention of 1787 made the document. He would never be content to consult only the intentions of those fifty-five men. Instead, Douglass insisted that "the preamble to the Constitution answers that question. 'We the people, do ordain and establish this Constitution.' The people, then, made the law." In other words, original intent would properly have to take into account the intentions of the various ratifying conventions and of the voters who selected the delegates to those conventions. "The fact is," Douglass suggested, "there is no evidence whatever that any considerable part of the people who made and adopted the American Constitution intended to make that instrument a slave-hunting or a slaveholding instrument, while there is much evidence to prove the very reverse." Douglass did not actually have much evidence himself, but he had developed a profound principle of constitutional interpretation for others to pursue. Lincoln was perhaps heading in that direction a little, with his newly developed fondness for Andrew Jackson's insistence that judicial review must somehow include the acquiescence of the people and the states, but he would never get as far as Douglass did.[78]

Douglass differed from the men who shaped Lincoln's speech — especially Senators Orville Hickman Browning and William H. Seward, the two compromising politicians who brought about the most important revisions in the original draft of the inaugural address. Browning and Seward had somewhat tamed and toned down a draft characterized by Lincoln's ablest modern biographer as "a no-nonsense document" that declared the Union "indestructible," denounced secession as "illegal," and vowed "to enforce the laws."[79] Douglass, unlike Browning and Seward, was looking for a policy of defiance, not concessions or a political philosophy of nationalism. "When men deliberately arm themselves with the avowed intention of breaking up the Government," Douglass insisted, "when they openly insult its flag, capture its forts, seize its munitions of war, and organize a hostile Government, and boastfully declare that they will fight before they will submit, it would seem of little use to argue with them. . . . To parley with traitors is but to increase their insolence and audacity."[80]

"Traitors," Douglass roared. Lincoln mentioned the word in the first draft but not the final version of the address.[81] What we see in the inaugural address is Republican policy shaped by several voices in crisis. What we do not see is the intensity of Lincoln's nationalism. We see only the type of nationalist he was. Like most Northerners Abraham Lincoln was already a nationalist, and he therefore believed, as he said in the first draft, "that no State, upon its own mere motion, can lawfully get out of the Union, — that *resolves* and *ordinances* to that effect are legally nothing; and that acts of violence, within any State or States, are insurrectionary or treasonable, according to circumstances." In the final version, he said "insurrectionary or revolutionary."[82] The Republican platform adopted at the Chicago convention that nominated Lincoln for president asserted that "the threats of disunion so often made by Democratic members" of Congress constituted "an avowal of contemplated treason."[83] In the final version of the inaugural address, Lincoln deleted his original profession of "duty . . . as well as . . . inclination" to follow "the Chicago Platform."[84] Douglass was right: Republican advisers had persuaded Lincoln to truckle a good deal more than he was personally inclined.

The seeds of Frederick Douglass's own profound American nationalism were already present, too — in his reference to the insult to the flag, for example, an obvious indicator of emotional identification with symbols of American nationalism. But his experience, and that of African Americans in the North generally, had been too searingly unhappy and frightening since the *Dred Scott* decision of 1857 for Douglass to feel a complete commitment to the American nation, even with a Republican assuming its presidency. Douglass was still planning a visit to Haiti, wondering whether white descriptions of the deplorable state of government and society there were accurate or whether it might offer a haven for refugees from an increasingly racist United States.[85]

The Commander in Chief's Address

On July 4, 1861, about eleven weeks after the fall of Fort Sumter, Lincoln sent a Message to the Special Session of Congress called to ratify the war measures he had been forced to take so far and to make essential appropriations for the war. It was a sort of Second Inaugural Address, necessitated because the situation had changed so critically — from peace to war — and thus introducing another new president, the commander in chief.

Lincoln shared the people's confidence in the Union, though he developed a more philosophical understanding of the nation's appeal than most. After the fall of Fort Sumter he was confident that if Democrats and Republicans remained united behind the war, and not all of the Border States seceded, American nationalism was equal to the task of quelling the rebellion. He did not deem it necessary later in his presidency, after initial efforts in 1861 at arguing with secession, to justify or arouse nationalism in the North through his own efforts as speaker or writer, despite much of what is said about his words being his "sword." Even when he announced the preliminary Emancipation Proclamation on September 22, 1862, the wartime document he wrote that was most likely to be read and analyzed by the most Americans, Lincoln phrased it not in inspiring language but in cold and "pettifogging" legalese.[86]

"The people will save their government, if the government itself will allow them," Lincoln wrote in a preliminary version of part of the special message to Congress of July 4, 1861.[87] Thus Lincoln seemed to have come to a realization of the true situation. In this follow-up to the First Inaugural, now after the fall of Sumter and mobilization for war and first blood, we find more antisecessionist arguments along with a labored explanation of extraordinary presidential powers already embraced to quell the rebellion (these will be discussed in the next chapter).

The best explanation for the antisecessionist arguments is that secession was not over — or rather, no one knew it was. Lincoln was already committed to attempting to hold Maryland and Missouri by military force, and Kentucky's fate appeared equally doubtful. It was worth thinking up more arguments against secession, therefore. The attempt at times seems a little desperate, but it does suggest Lincoln's resourcefulness in constitutional argument. For example, here we see his first attempt to put to use the long-neglected powers in Article IV, section 4: "The United States shall guarantee to every State in this Union a Republican Form of Government, and shall protect each of them against Invasion; and on Application of the Legislature, or of the Executive (when the Legislature cannot be convened) against domestic Violence." This was the part of the Constitution most obviously shaped in reaction to Shays's Rebellion, but it had since been found useful only in the Dorr War in Rhode Island in the 1840s. Lincoln tried to make it useful now:

> The Constitution provides, and all the States have accepted the provision, that "The United States shall guarantee to every State in this Union a republican form of government." But, if a State may lawfully go out of the Union, having done so, it may also discard the republican form of government; so that to prevent its going out, is an indispensable *means*, to the *end*, of maintaining the guaranty mentioned; and when an end is lawful and obligatory, the indispensable means to it, are also lawful, and obligatory.[88]

I have never seen this constitutional argument used anywhere else in the secession debate, and surely the reason is its strained quality. Yet we can see that Lincoln was good at scouring the Constitution to find in it previously hidden powers. He would return to Article IV, section 4, in more fruitful and forward-looking ways when he began to think about Reconstruction toward the end of 1863. For now, however, this argument seems to have led to no particular advantage, and it was conspicuous that the president did not want to call attention to the parts of Article IV, section 4, that he scrupulously avoided quoting. Had the legislatures or governors of the Southern states asked to be invaded to protect their republican forms of government? Was it a protection from invasion to be invaded? It is little wonder that he dropped this argument from his antisecession arsenal of ideas.

Other arguments devised were nearly too clever to follow. He noted that the Constitution of the Confederate States of America did not embrace or reject secession. Therefore to be consistent in interpretation, Lincoln said, they must now secede from each other "whenever they shall find it the easiest way of settling their debts, or effecting any other selfish, or unjust object."[89] Since reducing the number of states by secession reduced the resources available to pay the nation's creditors, was that fair to the creditors?[90] Surely that was not an argument that gained much traction. He devised others, but all were more or less like the one based on the guarantee of a republican form of government — they raised as many questions as they answered. The president was intent on proving that secession was revolutionary and treasonable and not legal. As an answer to the practical situation in the Border States, those states had seen the consequences of secession for other states — bloody war and invasion — and surely the question did not much matter.[91] Of course, it justified the coercive measures of the government if secession were illegal, but surely the patriotic uprising of the people of the North so far was the best all-around answer. He knew the people would save the government if the government would let them; they needed no more convincing of the righteousness of their cause. There were strong parts of the message, especially where Lincoln stated the political problem of the war succinctly as the necessity to prove that republics were not inherently weak and unable to prevent dissolution.

The clearest part of his argument was that the states were not sovereign, that the word "sovereign" did not even appear in the Constitution, and that he did not think it appeared in any state constitutions, either. "This relative matter of National power, and State rights, as a principle," Lincoln said, "is no other than the principle of *generality*, and *locality*. Whatever concerns the whole, should be confided to the whole — to the general government; while, whatever concerns *only* the State, should be left exclusively, to the State. This is all there is of original principle about it."[92] The antisecession parts of the message were received with intellectual indifference by an already fervidly nationalistic populace.[93] The tepid reaction of the Republican *New York Times* to the Fourth of July message was telltale: "The argument of the Message against the right and justice of a State seceding sounds something too much like the President's Indianapolis speech. . . . The subject does not admit of argument."[94] The *New York Tribune* proved even more dismissive. "The President's argument against the pretended Right of Secession," said the *Tribune*'s editors, "is clear and forcible; but it is very much like arguing that a man's leg has no right to secede from his body. The traitors never supposed they had any other right in the premises than that founded in the strength of their battalions. Whenever they find themselves whipped, the Right of Secession will be no more."[95] Frederick Douglass had made the same point forcefully in his early reaction to the inaugural address.

The unpredictable *New York Herald* proved surprisingly sympathetic, saying that the address offered "a learned argument, pointed and pungent withal, against the heresy of secession." Perhaps more to the point, the *Herald* readily endorsed the aggrandizement of presidential power exemplified in the period between the fall of Fort Sumter and the special session of Congress. Here, if the press had any memory, the editors might have recalled the Bourbons and the Rajah of Scinde. Instead, the *Herald* commented mildly and patriotically: "In all these proceedings, the President, in anticipating the authority of Congress, had no doubt of its approval, nor do we suppose that any one else has had the slightest doubt on the subject."[96]

The *Philadelphia Inquirer* had a reporter in Washington, D.C., who gained some knowledge of the Fourth of July message before it was issued; he told his paper that he had "ascertained one fact in regard to it, which will set at rest many idle rumors. It is emphatically a war message. The Inaugural Address breathed peace."[97] People were evidently relieved, then, to see that the tone had changed. The *Inquirer*, after publishing the message, expressed appreciation for the "terse yet thorough exposition of the unsoundness, and, indeed, utter absurdity of the theory of Secession."[98] It otherwise dealt with the welcome news of putting the nation on a war footing.

Sidney George Fisher, also of Philadelphia, was impressed with the message of July 4:

> Read it with great satisfaction. . . . It shows . . . remarkable power of thought & argument. The . . . right of secession is treated in a manner at once clear, comprehensive and original. It contains the following happy definition of a sovereign state, "a political community without a political superior," which is so terse & complete, that it deserves a place in the science of politics. . . . In this hour of its trial, the country seems to have found in Mr. Lincoln a great man. . . . Should he prove equal to the promise given by his speech, his message and his conduct thus far, he will be an unspeakable blessing to the nation. He was got, however, by accident, by the chance of a caucus nomination. His selection was a surprise to himself and to the people.[99]

This rare observation allows us to see better what others saw in Lincoln's speech. Fisher, himself soon to be the author of a theoretical work on the Constitution, appreciated the degree to which Lincoln's speech approached "political science." What Fisher liked most was the proof that Lincoln was more than an "available"— that is, attractive vote-getting — party politician. Fisher's were essentially elitist concerns that fell outside appreciation for the nationalist appeal in the message to Congress.

The *Chicago Tribune* characterized the message as "certainly the most important public document that has been given to the country since the adoption of the Constitution," apparently because it showed a will to save the Constitution. The editors also complimented the "argument against the secession dogma" as "masterly and exhaustive," but they said nothing more about that part of the speech.[100]

What Frederick Douglass noticed about the message to Congress was different from what any of the white commentators singled out: "In the late Message of our honest President, which purports to give an honest history of our present difficulties, no mention is, at all, made of slavery. Any one reading that document, with no previous knowledge of the United States, would ever dream from anything there written that we have a slaveholding war waged upon the Government."[101]

As in the case of the First Inaugural Address, Frederick Douglass offered the most searching criticism of the president's Message to the Special Session of Congress of July 4, 1861.

Two

Habeas Corpus, the Nation, and the Presidency

President Lincoln's first regular message to Congress, of December 3, 1861, laid to rest his arguments about secession. "The inaugural address at the beginning of the Administration, and the message to Congress at the late special session," he wrote, "were both mainly devoted to the domestic controversy out of which the insurrection and consequent war have sprung. Nothing now occurs to add or subtract, to or from, the principles or general purposes stated and expressed in those documents."[1] He never again showed any interest in the question.[2]

Although he had not done so in his First Inaugural Address, in the Message to the Special Session of Congress of July 4, 1861, Lincoln quoted the preamble to the Constitution to populist purposes. He criticized the secessionists for being "not partial to that power which made the Constitution, and speaks from the preamble, calling itself 'We, the People.'"[3] He continued in his December 3 message an attractive argument identifying the "insurrection" as "a war upon the first principle of popular government—the rights of the people." And then he attempted to argue (anticipating some modern academic arguments) that societies with a master-slave relationship in their labor system tended naturally to despotism. At that point originality failed him or he ran out of time to prepare, and he fell back on old arguments he had made in a speech before the Wisconsin State Agricultural Society on September 30, 1859, describing the advantages of free labor over slave labor in eliminating a permanent class of wage laborers unable to better themselves and rise in the economic order. He continued to insist that there was "not, of necessity" a class of people who were fixed in the condition of laborer for life.[4] The new subjects were slavery and colonization. The next chapter deals directly with those subjects.

Old subjects would continue to trouble the administration, however. The July 4 message had introduced the persona of the commander in chief, who had seen that there was "no choice . . . left but to call out the war power of the Government."[5] About the role of the commander in chief there would continue to be much constitutional debate. The person who initiated the debate — and whom Lincoln had to answer in the July 4 message itself — was the chief justice of the U.S. Supreme Court, Roger B. Taney.

Ex parte Merryman

Ex parte Merryman was intended to be a landmark in the constitutional history of the Civil War. The chief justice of the U.S. Supreme Court wrote the decision in May 1861, confronting the president of the United States less than two months after the firing on Fort Sumter. The route to the nation's capital passed through Maryland, a slave state, and Union troops rushing south were met by violent mobs in Baltimore. Afterward the railroad bridges to the city were burned. The provision in the Constitution for suspending the writ of habeas corpus seemed written to meet just such domestic violence and sabotage. Lincoln suspended the writ, and on May 25, 1861, Union officers arrested a civilian named John Merryman outside Baltimore. For once, the chief justice could make something happen. He did not have to wait for a case to come to him on appeal, because he could issue a writ of habeas corpus for a Federal prisoner directly. Merryman's lawyer came to Taney, who issued the writ. The officer who held Merryman refused to bring him into the court, and Taney wrote an opinion stating that the president was not empowered to suspend the writ of habeas corpus without the authority of Congress.

In the president's mind and in the minds of historians ever after, the suspension ranks second only to the decision to go to war with the Confederacy as the supreme expression of nationalism by the executive. Were "all the laws, *but one*, to go unexecuted, and the government itself go to pieces, lest that one be violated?" Lincoln asked rhetorically in July as he defended the actions taken by his administration in the aftermath of the firing on Fort Sumter. Two years later the president was more extreme in his claims for the importance of the suspending power. Suspension of the writ, he explained, facilitated the arrest, without charge, of people in the North who were "damaging the army, upon the existence, and vigor of which, the life of the nation depends."[6] Abraham Lincoln, in short, was not about to let the writ of habeas corpus stand in the way of the life of the nation. Years later James G. Randall, Lincoln's biographer, concluded: "Perhaps no other feature of Union policy was more widely criticized nor more strenuously defended."[7]

In the mind of Chief Justice Taney, suspending the writ of habeas corpus was not a presidential power. As constitutional historian Daniel Farber lucidly summarized it, this was Taney's case:

> He made three major points. First, the suspension clause is found in Article I, devoted mostly to the legislative power, not in Article II, devoted to the executive power. This placement seemed unlikely for a constraint on the president. Second, after long struggles on behalf of liberty, the English monarch had been completely deprived of the power to suspend the writ. Would the Framers have given the president more draconian powers than those possessed by George III? Third, eminent judicial authorities and commentators such as Chief Justice Marshall and Justice Story had described the suspension power as congressional. Thus, Lincoln's actions contradicted the accepted reading of the clause.[8]

Taney was not a nationalist, or not much of one. There were limits to the sacrifices he would make to save the Union. He would settle for two nations rather than exceed those limits. That was the case for others as well, but the limit was not for them so near and clear. In a private letter written on June 12, 1861, after the *Merryman* decision had been reported widely in the press, Taney expressed to former president Franklin Pierce, who had a surprisingly weak identification with the nation for a war veteran and an ex-president, his hope "that the North, as well as the South, will see that a peaceful separation, with free institutions in each section, is far better than the union of all the present states under a military government, and a reign of terror preceded too by a civil war with all its horrors, and which end as it may will prove ruinous to the victors as well as the vanquished."[9]

Despite the wide gulf of belief that lay below the narrow confrontation of Lincoln and Taney over habeas corpus, the crisis between president and chief justice passed. The reason was not forbearance on the part of either strong-willed man.[10] The Supreme Court lacked the original jurisdiction to force other issues and had to wait thereafter, impatiently, for appeals to come its way. For his part, the president had his hands full without further challenging the authority of the only branch of government the Republicans did not control. It is testament to the power of national sentiment that Taney's lead in the *Merryman* case enjoyed little following.[11]

Taney's opinion might have died a quiet death from want of eager fol-lowers, but it riled up the opposition. Some Northern intellectuals brooded over the opinion and, in the end, could not sit silent and let Taney's views pass.

The President's Defenders: Joel Parker

The first unsolicited defense of Lincoln's policy came from a surprising source, a professor at the Harvard Law School. Joel Parker first tried out his ideas on his students on June 11, 1861, soon after news of the *Merry-man* decision reached Cambridge. Then he broadcast them in the *North American Review*.

Article I, section 9, of the Constitution stated: "The privilege of the Writ of Habeas Corpus shall not be suspended, unless when in Cases of Rebel-lion or Invasion the public Safety may require it." No one had ever carefully explained what those words meant. Parker himself did not much dwell on the *words*. His argument was, at bottom, based mainly on practical con-siderations. He argued for a circumstantial martial law, a condition that obtained when there was war. It need not be imposed by anyone, and it was not derived from the Constitution itself. There was no agency and no text involved. Habeas corpus was not the same in war and peace, he insisted. Although civilian control of the military was fundamental to the American Constitution, it simply could not apply to the army camp, the field of battle, and the march on campaign. Civil process could not be used in those places; martial law ruled in war, whether declared in official proclamation or not. At its simplest, Parker's argument boiled down to locality: martial law held sway naturally in camp, on the march, and in the field in times of war.

Parker recognized that "it is not sufficient that we reach the conclusion by intuition."[12] He needed some text and precedent. He went on to assert, first, that Taney misread the provision in the Constitution as a grant of power and not a restriction. It was clearly the latter, Parker maintained, and therefore restricted an existing power to suspend that was somehow independent of Congress. Second, he said that *Luther v. Borden* "covers the whole ground," because Taney's decision in that case in 1849 upheld martial law, which had been imposed in Rhode Island during the Dorr War. Finally, Parker reached this definition of the power that governed Merry-man: "Martial law, then, is that military rule and authority which exists in time of war, and is conferred by the laws of war, in relation to persons and things under and within the scope of active military operations in carrying on the war, and which extinguishes or suspends civil rights, and the remedies founded upon them, for the time being, so far as it may appear to be necessary in order to the full accomplishment of the purposes of the war."[13] In truth, as that crucial definition reveals, the professor had not really got much beyond "intuition." For him, martial law simply existed in war by virtue of the laws of war customarily embraced by civilized nations.

Still seeking learned authority for his position, Parker then invoked John Quincy Adams, not as president or secretary of state but as a member of the House of Representatives after he left the presidency. In debates over the Texas question, Adams in April 1842 had asserted that the laws that came into place in time of war included the power to free the slaves of the enemy. Smart Southerners were alarmed by the release of this argument from the bag of political thought, and Louisville's S. S. Nicholas, for one, attacked Adams's argument relentlessly, from its first issuance through the time of the Civil War. Before reading Adams's argument, Nicholas snorted, he had "supposed that, in the estimation of all intelligent men in the country, martial law stood upon the precise same footing, and none other, as Lynch law, Regulators' law, or mob law." In "a legal or moral sense they all have the precise same basis."[14] Parker did not mention the slavery context of the Adams-Nicholas debate.[15]

In the end Parker relied heavily on the practical: on practical results and on practical reasoning. Like many lawyers, he sought immediately factually provable conditions. All one had to do, he maintained, was to contemplate "the practical result" of allowing the halt of military operations by the civil process of some "silly" judge.[16] An appendix to the second edition of Parker's pamphlet answered criticism aimed at the original magazine article: in particular, that a declaration or recognition of war was required for martial law and Congress had not declared it. Parker answered with opinions from cases involving ships captured by the blockade (that would soon form part of the *Prize Cases* of 1863), identifying the present situation in the United States as a war *in fact.*

Parker's argument, considered as a Harvard Law School lecture, which was its first formulation, gained surprising circulation. Besides the *North American Review* version, which appeared in the October 1861 issue, Harvard's printer, Welch and Bigelow, also published a pamphlet edition in 1861. J. Campbell in Philadelphia brought out a second edition in 1862, sometime after April.

Phillip S. Paludan has said of the professor's argument:

Parker held up the conditions . . . for Taney and others to view. He was surprised that the jurist [Taney] had been able to ignore them.

Insurrectionary mobs threatened the capital, setting fire to bridges in an attempt to isolate the city. The President had declared martial law. Yet Taney had ignored these things and decided that Merryman must be freed. But were army officers to await the pleasure of civil courts before arresting mobs and arsonists? Parker admitted that the military should always be subject to the civil power in time of peace — but this was not a time of peace, nor was the place of arrest a place of peace.[17]

Such arguments draw attention to close context. Parker himself realized that specificity was problematic. "How far does the principle apply upon which this exemption from civil responsibility rests? The cases which have occurred, and which are likely to occur hereafter, are not cases of an attempt to serve the writ of *habeas corpus* on the actual battlefield, or on the immediate march to it."[18] Still, Parker did not think the principle reached very far, literally, in miles or even feet.

Taney had laid his ground on that point carefully in *Ex parte Merryman*. He did not mention conditions of war or insurrection, of invasion or rebellion — the conditions stipulated in the Constitution. Instead, he spoke only of the availability of courtrooms and judges:

[The military authority] in this case has gone far beyond the mere suspension of the privilege of the writ of habeas corpus. It has, by force of arms, thrust aside the judicial authorities and officers to whom the constitution has confided the power and duty of interpreting and administering the laws, and substituted a military government in its place, to be administered and executed by military officers. For, at the time these proceedings were had against John Merryman, the district judge of Maryland, the commissioner appointed under the act of congress, the district attorney and the marshal, all resided in the city of Baltimore, a few miles only from the home of the prisoner. Up to that time, there had never been the slightest resistance or obstruction to the process of any court or judicial officer of the United States, in Maryland, except by the military authority. . . . There was no danger of any obstruction or resistance to the action of the civil authorities, and therefore no reason whatever for the interposition of the military.[19]

Parker, as Paludan pointed out, had attempted to create a rather different impression of the circumstances on the first page of his pamphlet. This was Parker's depiction of the scene:

Merryman was arrested by a military force, without any warrant from a magistrate, on charges of treason and rebellion founded upon certain acts done by him at, or immediately after, the attack by a mob upon the Sixth Regiment of Massachusetts Volunteers, in its passage through Baltimore; the mob being incited to violence through the agency of secessionists inhabiting that city, and the regiment being on its way to Washington to sustain the government of the United States, — the capital itself being threatened by the leaders of the insurrection. Troops from Pennsylvania proceeding to Washington for the same purpose were attacked and turned back by the same mob. It was alleged, especially, that Merryman had participated in the destruction of the railroad and bridges, with the design of preventing other troops from reaching the capital by the route through Baltimore. Fort McHenry, in the immediate vicinity of Baltimore, was at the time of the arrest held and occupied for the purposes of the war, which had then just commenced, and was regarded as a very important military post, serving among other purposes as a check — and perhaps for the time as the only effectual check — upon the disaffected population of Baltimore.[20]

The question of access to Washington through Baltimore was the key to Merryman's arrest, to the suspension of the writ of habeas corpus, and, at bottom, to Parker's argument.

In fact, the close context supported Taney rather than Parker, Paludan, and Lincoln, if one accepts access to courts of law as proof that no serious social disorder exists. John Merryman was arrested on May 25. By that time, the bridges had been repaired, railroad contact with the North had been reestablished for over a week, and Baltimoreans were reading the New York newspapers once again.[21] On May 1 a local judge charged the grand jury in the City Criminal Court to make presentments against the rioters who had caused Baltimore's disaster of April 18–19:

> The excitement and alarm which has prevailed in our city since that time has been appalling.
>
> The peaceful pursuits of trade are almost abandoned. The laborer no longer has his hire, and our citizens await in anxiety the reestablishment of law in our midst to assure them of safety to their wives and children.
>
> . . . The very existence of society depends on your faithful discharge [of duty] . . .

Besides the loss of life, the violence done to property, the breaking into stores, the assuming unlawful authority, the irregular and *illegal* army of troops without compliance with the militia laws of the State, and the attempt by organizations, unknown to the law, to usurp lawful government, also deserve your attention.[22]

The situation had once been dire as this charge to the grand jury makes clear, and Taney never acknowledged that, but was it dire when Merryman was arrested—long after the City Court was indicting rioters? On May 5, for example, an alleged rioter named Augustus Johnson was indicted.[23] In addition to the City Criminal Court, the Court of Common Pleas, the City Circuit Court, the Superior Court, the Circuit Court for Baltimore County, and the Court of Appeals of Maryland in Annapolis all met before the arrest of Merryman.[24]

Geography seemed to matter, though the Constitution mentioned only "public safety" and not "local safety" among its conditions for suspending the writ. For a time, President Lincoln confined his suspensions of the writ of habeas corpus to limited geographic areas, but he soon moved to national suspension in certain categories of cases. In the summer of 1863, he argued vigorously against the view that the Constitution limited military arrests of civilians in wartime to "localities where rebellion actually exists":

> Inasmuch . . . as the constitution itself makes no such distinction, I am unable to believe that there is any such constitutional distinction. I concede that the class of arrests complained of, can be constitutional only when, in cases of Rebellion or Invasion, the public Safety may require them; and I insist that in such cases, they are constitutional *wherever* the public safety does require them—as well in places to which they may prevent the rebellion extending, as in those where it may be already prevailing—as well where they may restrain mischievous interference with the raising and supplying of armies, to suppress the rebellion, as where the rebellion may actually be—as well where they may restrain the enticing men out of the army, as where they would prevent mutiny in the army—equally constitutional at all places where they will conduce to the public Safety, as against the dangers of Rebellion or Invasion.[25]

The simple fact was that Parker's introduction of the subject of martial law served only to confuse, not to clarify. Martial law was, in many people's minds, completely and clearly a matter of local and immediate temporary conditions. We can imagine its invocation, say, to permit the summary punishment of looters until flood waters recede. The suspension of the writ of habeas corpus contemplated by the men who drafted the U.S. Constitution was meant to deal with emergencies that threatened the public safety too, but somehow its conception was different from the very limited and circumstantial conception of martial law. Surely the writ of habeas corpus could be suspended out of sight of pennants on army tents and glistening bayonets.

The President's Most Important Defender: Horace Binney

The president defended himself, of course, in his Message to the Special Session of Congress of July 4, 1861. What Lincoln wrote then has been scrutinized repeatedly, and James G. Randall, for one, has noted that it was written in the passive voice and showed Lincoln's "deep concern" over the policy and his "reluctance" to embrace it. All of that seems to point only to the ineffectiveness of the wordy and labored defense. The main problem was that Lincoln as much as admitted constitutional violation. In the most frequently quoted passage, he said: "Are all the laws, *but one*, to go unexecuted, and the government itself go to pieces, lest that one be violated?" After the attempt in the message to defend his action, Lincoln apparently decided not to talk about it anymore. When he took up the subject again almost two years later, he did not admit any violation of the Constitution.[26] Surely legal publicists and constitutional polemicists would not have felt the necessity to go to the president's defense in 1861 and 1862 had he offered in the message a satisfactory defense himself. Evidently Attorney General Edward Bates's defense of the policy was not highly regarded either, probably because of the obligatory nature of an argument by an administration legal officer.

The defense of the suspension of the writ of habeas corpus regarded at the time as most effective came from Horace Binney, a retired octogenarian lawyer of considerable reputation in legal circles who was now writing a book on the origins of George Washington's Farewell Address.[27] His pamphlet, *The Privilege of the Writ of Habeas Corpus under the Constitution*, more than fifty pages in length, appears to be the most widely circulated tract on the subject. The Online Computer Library Center (OCLC) reports sixty-eight libraries holding copies of the first edition published by C. Sherman in Philadelphia in 1862. There seems to have been a second edition, and a Philadelphia publisher, T. B. Pugh, also released a version that contained the original and a "Second Part" (that is, another pamphlet on the subject that Binney wrote to answer his critics). By comparison, the highly influential pamphlet by Charles Janeway Stillé, entitled *How a Free People Conduct a Long War*, the first edition of which was also issued in Philadelphia in 1862, finds only fifty-three libraries reporting copies in OCLC. There is no comparison in readability. The Binney pamphlet can only be described as technical; the Stillé pamphlet was inspiring. George M. Fredrickson, the historian who made both Stillé and Binney famous, said of Stillé's work: "This pamphlet, reprinted several times in 1863 to counter the growing 'disloyalty' problem, eventually sold over 500,000 copies, making it probably the most widely distributed single piece of Northern patriotic literature."[28]

Binney was egged on to discuss the habeas corpus problem by Columbia University's Francis Lieber, a self-professed political scientist and an eager nationalist. Binney was a nationalist, too. Immediately after the firing on Fort Sumter, he was one of the signers of a broadside containing the following text:

> The unparalleled event of the past week has revealed to the citizens of the United States, beyond question or possibility of doubt, that a peaceful reconciliation under the form of our Constitution is repelled and scorned, and that secession means, in the hearts of its supporters, both treason and war against our country and nation. We, therefore, the undersigned, loyal citizens of the United States, and inhabitants of the city of Philadelphia, responding to the proclamation of the President of the United States, hereby declare our unalterable determination to sustain the government in its efforts to maintain the honour, the integrity, and the existence of our National Union, and the perpetuity of the popular government, and to redress the wrongs already long enough endured. No differences of political opinion, no name or badge of diversity upon points of party distinction, shall restrain or withhold us in the devotion of all we have or can command, to the vindication of the Constitution, the maintenance of the laws, and the defence of the flag of our country.[29]

Before Taney issued his opinion in the *Merryman* case, Binney had confined his efforts in aid of the Union cause to service on a commission "to provide for the poor families of the mechanics who have become volunteers."[30] But an able article on the habeas corpus question in the conservative *National Intelligencer* caught his attention on June 22, and he was captivated by the problem:

> It is a paper of that class which gets the mind out of a rut. On some subjects the ruts of the mind are so deep that it is the hardest thing

in the world to get out of them. It requires a pull beyond ordinary strength. This of Habeas Corpus as a universal, ever-continuing right, is one of them; though one cannot see any good reason why, if enemies or rebels suspend the operation of all other laws, a military commander should not suspend or resist the Habeas Corpus writ to bring about their restoration. I may make a remark on the clause in the Constitution, which the writer of the article does not make, — viz., that it is not in time of war that the suspension becomes allowable, but only in time of invasion or rebellion, — violent outbroken opposition to law, — facts which locally displace the operation of the laws. If the enemy and rebel do this, why should he be protected by Habeas Corpus in his liberty, to repeat it to the end? In fine, the whole question, as I think I told you, is whether the commander in chief, in times of invasion and rebellion, may not make military prisoners, and keep them prisoners. As a war right, it seems to be very clear, when one gets out of the rut.[31]

In some ways the "rut" was obvious: the familiar mantra that the writ of habeas corpus was a bulwark of liberty like Magna Charta really did not go into detail on how the writ worked in war and peace. Without being jolted out of the rut, one simply repeated the mantra. But Binney, too, had noted "facts which *locally* displace the operation of the laws," and such facts were on Taney's side in this case. In Binney's mind must have been the consideration that suspension by the president made sense while he fought an enemy invader or rebels on American soil, but it should not happen in a foreign war. But he would carry that idea to the point of believing that only the president could suspend the writ and only under those conditions.

Horace Binney needed to be pulled out of his very deep rut of suspicion of presidential power as well. That, too, the article in the *National Intelligencer* did. Binney had a brief political career in the 1830s, when he had been elected to the House of Representatives to defend the Second Bank of the United States. He had therefore been a sharp critic of Andrew Jackson's expansive view of presidential power. The anonymous author in the *National Intelligencer* not only read the part of the Constitution dealing with the writ of habeas corpus (and Chief Justice Taney's exposition of it) carefully, he also took a bold view of the powers of the presidency. Naturally, he repeatedly referred favorably to Andrew Jackson. Binney could never bring himself to do that.

The *National Intelligencer* article made four fundamental points, all of them marked by originality and bold thinking. First, the author stated that it was obvious that in wartime, when the public safety was threatened, certain parts of the Constitution were meant to be ignored and had to be ignored. The Second and Fourth amendments, for example, if rigidly adhered to, were simply incompatible with quelling rebellion. How could a war be waged on American soil and the right to bear arms not be somehow interfered with, and likewise without the searching and seizing of private property? The same was true of the writ of habeas corpus, especially given the situation in Maryland, which teemed with people eager to join and to help the Confederacy. Second, he demonstrated that some of Taney's statements in *Ex parte Merryman* about the text of the Constitution were false. Was it true that nothing in Article I, section 9, had to do with the powers of the executive? No, for there was a provision dealing with payments from the Treasury, and that was part of the executive branch. Was it true that Article I dealt only with the powers of Congress and that placement of a clause therein meant it was a congressional matter? Certainly not, for Article I, section 10, dealt with powers denied to the states and dealt alone with the states. The writer also noticed what might have been in Taney's opinion but was not: for example, reference to General Andrew Jackson's suspension of the writ of habeas corpus in New Orleans at the end of the War of 1812.

Too much of what the author had said so far rested "alone on general reasoning," and any jurist worth his salt would not be comfortable without some precedent on his side. He thought he had one, and it came from Taney's own pen. This was the third impressive argument in the *National Intelligencer* article. In *Luther v. Borden*, a decision of 1849 stemming from the Dorr War in Rhode Island seven years earlier, the chief justice himself had sustained the declaration of martial law by the government of Rhode Island and the violation of individuals' property rights thereunder. The ability to do such things, Taney had said, was fundamental to the government of any state. As for the role of the courts in such situations, Taney said there were political questions as well as legal ones and the court was not the arbiter of the former.

Fourth and finally, the writer stated that the powers of the president, as described in the Constitution, were unlike those of the legislature and the judiciary. The powers of the two last named were enumerated, but the president's were not. Article II said only that "the executive power shall be vested in a president of the United States of America." The document did not identify what those "executive" powers were. To have described all of them exhaustively would have made the fundamental document read like a legal code, not a constitution. The author argued simply that the Constitution meant that all powers that can be depicted as executive in nature were the president's unless specifically forbidden to him or specifically limited. The president's powers, then, worked on a principle of constitutional interpretation opposite to the one used in examining congressional and judicial powers.

But he was the president of the United States and not the Rajah of Scinde, to borrow the caustic language of the editors of the *New York Herald*, and were the president's powers equal to those of such an unlimited head of state? For all its almost scary expansiveness about the powers of the president, the *National Intelligencer* article actually took a narrower view of the president's power to suspend habeas corpus than the Lincoln administration did. The writer insisted that the suspension was limited to specific cases depending on peculiar contingencies in each instance and was therefore a military power. The administration came to believe that the power granted to Congress in the Constitution to suspend the writ in an invasion or rebellion would result in a general suspension denying the writ to everyone in various specified classes of cases.[32]

The recipient of Binney's letter about the *National Intelligencer* was Francis Lieber, who thought the president deserved a better defense than the one provided by his attorney general, Edward Bates. Lieber encouraged Binney to work on the question, and in the end Binney prefaced his pamphlet with a letter to Lieber, revealing that the pamphlet that followed was a response to Lieber's encouragement.[33]

Lieber was himself the likeliest man in America to provide the president's defense, but he could not because he was on record in his famous textbook *On Civil Liberty and Self-Government* saying that "we have seen already under what circumstances our constitution permits the suspension of the habeas corpus, and that this cannot be done by the president alone, but by congress only, need hardly be mentioned."[34] Lieber was beyond the period of his greatest productivity as a scholar, having spent a great effort of scholarly production to get out of South Carolina, where he taught unhappily for years, to the Northeast. Instead, America's putative first political scientist then became America's first public intellectual. He defended the Republican cause in pamphlets. He lent his skills to the Republican administration directly and drafted codes of laws for guerrilla warfare and then for all warfare. He oversaw the vast publication effort of the Loyal Publication Society. And he prompted Horace Binney's defense of the president.

The defense would be a stretch for Binney also, but his record on presidential power was buried in an obscure past, some thirty years distant and confined to speeches reported in the press and in Congress.[35] By now Binney was thinking along the same lines as the president. The question why, "if enemies or rebels suspend the operation of all other laws, a military commander should not suspend or resist the Habeas Corpus writ to bring about their restoration," as Binney said in his letter to Lieber about the *National Intelligencer* article, anticipated Lincoln's defense of his suspension put forth in his Message to the Special Session of Congress on July 4, only eight days later: "Are all the laws, *but one*, to go unexecuted, and the government itself go to pieces, lest that one be violated?"[36] Once pulled out of his intellectual rut, Binney then proceeded in his own direction and provided an argument of great originality that was, in fact, not much modeled on the specific arguments of the anonymous newspaper jurist.

Part of the peculiar power of Binney's pamphlet, *The Privilege of the Writ of Habeas Corpus under the Constitution*, which he finished writing at the end of 1861 and published early in 1862, lay in its sterile isolation from previous or current political conflict. He showed a single-minded and deliberate focus on the legal and constitutional question in the immediate foreground, as though he were arguing a case before a judge and not a political one before a mass reading public. Surprisingly, Binney managed to avoid circumstantial arguments based on the desperate times in which he was writing. He avoided political or moral appeals. The pamphlet contained no invocations of basic patriotism, though that was its ultimate inspiration. The document was as dry as dust and therein, ironically, lay its power.

In the course of an ordinary legal career, or of an extraordinarily distinguished one like Binney's for that matter, a lawyer in antebellum America might never examine the clause in the Constitution governing the writ of habeas corpus. In fact, Binney was willing to conclude, cautiously, after several months of study, that "this question . . . has never been argued with any care, or perhaps argued at all, by a Court, or by Counsel in Court."[37] As soon as the article in the *National Intelligencer* caused this Philadelphia lawyer to look closely, he had his case. Article I, section 9, clause 2, of the Constitution stated, "The privilege of the Writ of Habeas Corpus shall not be suspended, unless when in Cases of Rebellion or Invasion the public Safety may require it." The key lay in the triggering conditions, invasion or rebellion. Those events were not synonymous with "war," which Congress alone had the power to declare. Rather, invasion and rebellion were factual conditions to be identified and combated immediately, whether Congress was in session or not. "The *gist* of the question seems then to be this," Binney wrote, "whether it requires an Act of the Legislature to declare that Rebellion or Invasion exists in the Country . . . if it does not, then the power of enforcing the execution falls necessarily to the Executive."[38] Thus Binney had clearly set as his task answering Taney, for the argument that suspension was an exclusive power of Congress was the point of *Ex parte Merryman*.[39]

Binney also offered a close historical analysis of the placement of the habeas corpus clause in Article I, the portion of the Constitution dealing with the powers of Congress. He said it was originally proposed at the constitutional convention in Philadelphia in 1787 to be placed in the section dealing with the judiciary. Obviously, placement did not signify.

Like Taney, Binney dealt with analogies to and precedents from England. Binney argued that the Constitution did not imitate the British government, because the United States rejected parliamentary supremacy and was more democratic. Thus the president, who was elected by the people, need not be feared as the king was feared. In Great Britain the habeas corpus guaranteed against the king in particular. The U.S. Constitution guaranteed the writ against anyone, not only the executive, except during rebellion or invasion. Binney dismissed *Ex parte Merryman* out of hand as having no judicial authority, noting that the argument in the opinion depended in part on "an elaborate depreciation of the President's office, even to the extent of making him, as Commander-in-Chief . . . no more than *an assistant to the Marshal's posse*: the deepest plunge of judicial rhetoric." At that point, significantly while discussing the power of the president and Taney's assault on it, Binney took the nearest thing to a swipe at Taney's loyalties. "The opinion, moreover," Binney said, "has a tone, not to say a ring, of disaffection to the President, and to the Northern and Western side of his house, which it is not comfortable to suppose in the person who fills the central seat of impersonal justice."[40] Besides, Binney pointed out, with the sharp eye of a longtime practitioner in an adversarial legal system, Taney's proofs of the president's want of power under the Constitution proved only how correct and safe it was to entrust such a president with the authority to suspend the writ of habeas corpus.

Nationalism and Horace Binney's Defense

The historian who called Horace Binney to modern attention was George M. Fredrickson. He saw in Binney's defense of Lincoln the work of "one of the last of the Federalists," the sort of person who would find cause for "rejoicing" in the revival of the spirit of the Alien and Sedition Acts.[41] There is little truth in such a view of Binney; Fredrickson's interpretation was based on an assumption that nineteenth-century nationalism was a "near pathology," to borrow the language of Benedict Anderson. It is true that Binney was old when he came to the president's defense and could remember the days of the Federalists. But he was only eighteen at the time of the passage of the Alien and Sedition Acts in 1798, and though he identified with the Federalist Party early in life, his views on the internal security measures of the administration of John Adams are unknown. Besides, his defense of the president stopped well short of endorsing any unconstitutional limitation on the First Amendment, which the Sedition Act was.

More important, Binney's disagreement with the opinions of Roger B. Taney preceded the *Merryman* decision and the question of dissent in the Civil War and had, at first, nothing to do with buttressing the authority of the national state. Binney thought that the *Dred Scott* decision of 1857 ought not to "have the least authority whatever." "It is a political or party result," he argued. If it stood, it would "divide this country into irreconcilable sections, while it dishonours the men of the Revolution, the men of the Constitution, and the Constitution itself."[42] Later, in 1863, Binney said he had always believed that Taney's *Dred Scott* ruling was the cause of the war, for it was the aged chief justice who "first told all the rest of the States that common sense and long-sanctioned interpretation of plain language were as nothing against the interests of slavery."[43] Before the outbreak of the Civil War, Binney regarded the secession of the Southern states as "the natural product of their state of society divided between masters and slaves." And before the administration publicly embraced a policy of emancipation he explained to Francis Lieber, "God knows I disapprove of the institution of slavery every way, — for its effect upon the slaves, still more for its effect upon the masters, most of all for its incompatibility, growing and incurable incompatibility, with such a government, black slavery pre-eminently."[44]

On race, obviously, Binney was no Wendell Phillips, but he was liberal. In January 1865 he called his judgment on "the universal suffrage of free blacks . . . suspended." He boasted: "Fifty years ago, as a judge of election, I ruled that a free black native of Pennsylvania, who had paid his tax, was entitled to vote; and there was no dissent." The restriction of suffrage to whites only by Pennsylvania in the 1838 state constitution he blamed on Democrats bent on accommodating the South. In early Reconstruction he remained cautious, inclining "to leave the question of suffrage to the States until after the next census, perhaps longer; but after, say, ten years to give the right of suffrage to every freeman."[45] In short, Binney's disagreements with Taney stemmed from a combination of antislavery sentiment *and* nationalism — that is, Lincoln's tradition and the force that won the Civil War. Though it may have been partisan, it was not reactionary and authoritarian, as Fredrickson would have us believe. Horace Binney was not bent on reviving high Federalism.

On the other hand, Binney was not entirely consistent. In the past he had little good to say about presidential power. After the fall of the Federalist Party, he was elected to a single term in the U.S. House of Representatives in 1832. Binney then detested Andrew Jackson's expansive views of the power of the presidency (as evidenced, in part, by Jackson's exercising his veto power over the bill to recharter the Second Bank of the United States). To Binney, Jackson was attempting to elevate the executive branch above all other departments of the government.[46]

When Binney ran for Congress on an anti-Jackson ticket in 1832, he gave a speech that echoed the fears of executive tyranny commonplace among the political opposition in that era. He began his address to a mass meeting in Philadelphia by urging the people to go to the polls. Voicing their will through "the medium of free election," he said, "may, thank heaven, be still exercised with safety. How long it will continue so, or how long the enjoyment of it will be of any value to you, are questions upon which the short remainder of the present year will probably furnish materials for a decisive judgment." Binney accused President Jackson of aiming at the "*prostration of all the departments of government except that which he fills.*" He warned that "invasions of the Constitution are like invasions in war; they must go on or back." One newspaper at the time summarized the message of the speech this way: "Our Federal Government has, in fact, been converted into a Dictatorship."[47] In other words, Binney's fondness for presidential power in the Civil War was new and a repudiation of his old anti-Jackson views, though he never said so. Taney had made a similarly dramatic ideological migration from his earlier views. Taney was also a former Federalist and an octogenarian, but he had been one of Andrew Jackson's cabinet members. *Ex parte Merryman* expressed a newfound fondness for a weak presidential office.

Horace Binney reversed his position not only on the power of the chief executive, but also on the power of the U.S. Supreme Court. Back in 1832, when he had been intent on describing Jackson's view of the powers of the presidency as a threat to democracy and the Constitution, he had focused less on Jackson's veto of the bill to recharter the Second Bank than on the president's defiance of the Supreme Court in cases involving Indian tribes in Georgia. In *Cherokee Nation v. Georgia* and *Worcester v. Georgia* the Supreme Court had denied the power of the state of Georgia over Indian tribes. At that time, Binney had praised the Court as "the great moral substitute for *force* in controversies between the people, the States, and the Union" and accused President Jackson, who largely ignored the Court's rulings, of attempting "to impair the influence of that sacred voice." In Jackson's bank veto message, Binney pointed out, the president "denies, and *goes out of his way* to deny, that the judgment of that Court upon the meaning and effect of the constitution, can lawfully control *him, or any other person whatever*, sworn to support the constitution."[48] Years later, it did not bother Binney when Lincoln refused to be controlled by the chief justice in the matter of suspending the writ of habeas corpus.[49]

When the presidency was in Democratic hands Binney was critical of the president's power, and when it was in Republican hands he buttressed the president's power. Still, Binney's unconscious impulse was partisan; it was not authoritarian. Seeing the nation through partisan eyes, as nearly everyone did in the nineteenth century, could put any politician on the brink of ignoring the country in its hour of need in certain circumstances. Binney himself, back in 1832, had been speaking to the rally in Philadelphia not only in the midst of a presidential election canvass but also in the midst of the crisis over South Carolina nullification. Binney was arguing, in effect, that the serious constitutional issue of the day was Jackson's threat to the authority of the Supreme Court and not South Carolina's threat to the nation. In other words, a reader of Binney's 1832 speech might have surmised that Jackson threatened the Union more than South Carolina did.

And yet, like most partisans, Binney was blind to his own partisanship. When Lincoln was elected president in 1860, Binney wrote a letter of recommendation for a man seeking the post of federal district attorney in Philadelphia. Influencing patronage appointments was the very essence of partisanship, of course, but Binney insulated himself from any realization of his hypocrisy by saying to the president-elect that he recommended the person only if the office were already vacant. At the end of the letter, Binney said: "Let me add, that I ask no attention to this note, on the score of political affinities to party. I heartily desire the success of your administration of the Government, upon your own principles, as you have stated them. In this respect I perceive no departure from those which I imbibed as a youth during the administration of Washington, and to which probably I shall adhere for my remainder of life."[50]

William Whiting Defends the "War Powers"

If Lincoln was grateful for Binney's defense, he never said so. The only defender of the constitutionality of the habeas corpus suspensions about whom Lincoln expressed an opinion was William Whiting, a lawyer from Boston who became the solicitor for the War Department. By 1865, Whiting was in poor health and seldom on the job; when the War Department was considering his resignation, Lincoln commented that he liked him "very much."[51]

Whiting's historical reputation has been enhanced by Harold Hyman, who found in his arguments an important example of the idea of the "adequate Constitution." It is true that Whiting deserves attention, for he had a special claim on lasting fame as a commentator on the role of the Constitution in the Civil War. His long pamphlet on *The War Powers of the President and the Legislative Powers of Congress in Relation to Rebellion, Treason and Slavery*, first published, apparently, in the spring of 1862, was repeatedly expanded and reached a tenth edition by 1864 and a forty-third by 1871.[52] I know of no other constitutional commentary born of the war that showed such staying power.

But Whiting did not really find the Constitution adequate, and that was because his first interest came in the area in which the Constitution was clearly inadequate: emancipation. In fact, Boston's Emancipation League was largely responsible for keeping his pamphlet in print up to the tenth edition of 1864.

Before Whiting received his appointment in the War Department in November 1862, he wrote *The War Powers of the President*. The central problem, from the preface to the final chapter, entitled "Slavery," was the constitutional power to emancipate slaves. Apparently the office of "solicitor" was created for him later — early in 1863 — and died when he resigned from the position in April 1865.[53] From the start, Whiting put emphasis on a careful "distinction between emancipating or confiscating slaves, and abolishing the laws which sustain slavery in the Slave States. The former merely takes away slaves from the possession and control of their masters; the latter deprives the inhabitants of those States of the lawful right of obtaining, by purchase or otherwise, or of holding slaves."[54]

Whiting laid claim, all right, to finding the Constitution adequate for his purposes. "The learned reader," he said, "will . . . notice, that the positions taken in this pamphlet do not depend upon the adoption of the most liberal construction of the constitution."[55] But Whiting protested too much; in truth, his ideas did hinge on very liberal construction of the Constitution — and ultimately not on the Constitution at all but on international law.[56] Whiting's argument depended on the usual slippery advocacy. "If the ground-plan of our government was intended to be more than a temporary expedient, — if it was designed, according to the declaration of its authors, for a *perpetual* Union, — then it will doubtless be found, upon fair examination, to contain whatever is essential to carry that design into effect."[57] It can be said, perhaps, that men of the same generation wrote the Constitution and declared the Union "perpetual," but the men who declared the Union "perpetual" were, specifically, the ones who wrote the Articles of Confederation. The men who wrote the Constitution in 1787 did not say the Union was perpetual in that document, and it replaced the Articles.

It was equally deceptive to say that Whiting did not rely on "the most liberal construction," for even the most cursory reading of his pamphlet shows reliance on the extraconstitutional. On that point, constitutional historian Phillip Shaw Paludan made valuable corrections to the pioneering work of Hyman:

> Faced with the need to justify executive efforts to defeat the Confederacy, Whiting provided the War Department and the President with practically a blank check. . . . Whiting argued that the government was not chained by any restrictive interpretation of the Constitution. It had complete power to preserve itself in any manner that it saw fit. Since Southerners had ignored the Constitution, they might not be protected by it. He advanced the general welfare provision of the preamble and asserted that it allowed almost unlimited government action. The only check was the power of the people to elect new officials. Whiting went on to claim broad powers for the government on the basis of many other constitutional provisions. The goal in most of these claims was emancipation. Congress, he said, might emancipate using its treaty powers. It could use the power of eminent domain for the same purpose; it could emancipate to secure domestic tranquility, to suppress insurrection, or to maintain a republican form of government. Whiting's catalogue of powers left the federal government virtually unrestrained.[58]

Once exposed for their constitutional brashness, even desperation, Whiting's arguments betray other weaknesses, including political ineptitude. His assertion that the government had the constitutional right to confiscate property in peace or war was proclaimed under an all-caps heading "THE RIGHT IS FOUNDED IN REASON."[59] When he described the extravagant powers the U.S. government enjoyed as a belligerent, the all-caps heading came right out of a Democrat's nightmare: "THE LAW OF NATIONS IS ABOVE THE CONSTITUTION."[60] In reality, Whiting was the epitome of the Democratic caricature of "higher law" Republican constitutionalism or even abolitionist fanaticism. He actually described in so many words "the sovereign and almost dictatorial powers" that the government could claim in wartime.[61]

It is obvious from the Frémont imbroglio, to be discussed in Chapter 3, that President Lincoln wanted nothing to do with a frank embrace of "dictatorial" powers, and the use of such outré language — and perhaps outré constitutional interpretations as well — should cause us to question whether this blustering defense of the president actually reflected the president's own views on the subject. From the start, Whiting, though he defended the president, conspicuously parted ways from the president's manner of defending himself. Whiting was bent not only on defending emancipation but also on finding in Congress the power to make holding slaves illegal ever after. "The right of the Executive to strike this blow against his enemy," wrote Whiting, "does not deprive Congress of the concurrent right or duty to emancipate enemy's slaves, if in *their judgment* a civil act for that purpose is required by public welfare and common defence, for the purpose of aiding and giving effect to such war measures as the commander-in-chief may adopt." "Congress," he concluded, "may destroy slavery by abolishing the laws which sustain it."[62]

Lincoln's views on the constitutionality of emancipation never coincided with Whiting's. When Lincoln was first forced to think about the question systematically, under pressure for an explanation of his revocation of General Frémont's emancipation proclamation for Missouri, he believed that the president could not free the slaves, that to do so would amount to dictatorship, and that Congress might free the slaves by law. By the time Lincoln had decided that the president had power as commander in chief to free the slaves, he no longer thought Congress could free them by law. Lincoln was on the verge of showing a draft of the Emancipation Proclamation to his cabinet in July 1862, when, in a message explaining his objections to the Confiscation Act of July 17, he said: "It is startling to say that congress can free a slave within a state." But then he went on to say that one must assume that treason causes an owner to forfeit ownership to the government, and then Congress decides that the government's slaves shall be free.[63] His doubts only grew, and in his message accompanying the pocket veto of the Wade-Davis Bill of July 1864, Lincoln said that he was "unprepared to declare . . . a constitutional competency in Congress to abolish slavery in States."[64] Lincoln did not invoke the law of nations first as authority for emancipation, and he always invoked Article II of the U.S. Constitution making him commander in chief. Lincoln was a politician, grateful always for political support and not particularly interested in the reasoning process the supporter used to arrive at the same position. Yet he cared that his own positions be constitutionally plausible.

Historians have made too much of William Whiting, and they have misunderstood the roots of his radical constitutional views: he had to stretch his constitutionalism, but he was clearly determined to find authority for the abolition of slavery. Paludan has offered a valuable interpretation — exposing the absurd desperation of a scheme to emancipate millions of souls from a web of constitutional and legal institutions lasting centuries by the power of eminent domain! The only improvement we can make on Paludan is to note carefully that Whiting did not go to the constitutional lengths that he did for the sake of the president. Despite his willingness to use the term "dictatorial power," no nationalist infatuation with one-man rule, looking forward to twentieth-century totalitarianism, lurked in the enthusiasms of the clever patent attorney from Boston. Whiting's was a radical constitutional view concocted in the service of abolitionism, for he was at least as keen on the powers of Congress as of the president — as long as those powers were used to free the slaves.

One thing that may have fooled us into taking Whiting too seriously is the peculiar publishing history of his works on the Constitution in wartime. Hyman, for example, seems to have been impressed with Whiting's publishing record: a tenth edition by 1864 for *War Powers under the Constitution* (the title given the original 1862 pamphlet after other matters concerning government of hostile territory were added) and a forty-third in 1871. A check of OCLC, however, reveals that *no library holds an edition between the tenth in 1864 and the forty-third in 1871*. It could well be that the Boston lawyer practiced the same gentle deception that many a publisher did: claiming on the title page an exaggerated and unverifiable number of copies sold or of editions printed.

An interesting and apt comparison is the publishing history of a parallel Copperhead work, John A. Marshall's *American Bastile*, the Book of Martyrs of the peace wing of the Democratic Party. First published in 1869, it claimed to have reached its "twenty-seventh thousand" copy in 1885. Did it ever really sell that many copies? We will likely never know, but the publication history of Marshall's book can at least be traced much more fully and incrementally than Whiting's. Two prospectuses existed before its publication. My university library alone holds a fifth, sixth, eighteenth, twenty-second, and twenty-fourth edition of the book. A check of OCLC shows a detailed publishing history with editions, after the first in 1869, in 1870, 1871, 1872, 1874, 1875, 1876, 1877, 1878, and 1880 before the 1885 edition.

Historians have somehow been overly impressed with Whiting's credentials. Stephen C. Neff, for example, misidentifies Whiting as "a former Harvard Law School professor."[65] Neff, in turn, seems to have been too much influenced by Hyman's exaggerated claim for the quality of the War Department's gaggle of lawyer appointees under Secretary of War Edwin M. Stanton. "Stanton and Whiting," Hyman wrote, "were joined in the War Department's legal secretariat by patent attorney Peter Watson, former cabinet officer Joseph Holt, constitutional scholar Francis Lieber, and lawyers-become-generals Ethan Allen Hitchcock and Henry W. Halleck. From 1861–65, no university law faculty or private firm in the nation equaled this association of lawyers."[66] In truth, Lieber, who was a Columbia Law School professor, was never an appointed official in the War Department. Instead, he worked for one month on a special board established by the department at the behest of General in Chief Henry W. Halleck to draft a code of the laws of war to govern the armies in the field.[67] A more likely explanation for the nature of the group of lawyers in the department is that Stanton was a patent lawyer and knew other patent lawyers. Before he turned to pamphleteering in the Civil War, Whiting was also a patent attorney.[68]

Hyman perpetuated Whiting's personal myth. The eulogistic memoir of Whiting printed in Boston after his death in 1873 stated, "As our armies vindicated the unity of the country against its foes in the field, Mr. Whiting vindicated the sufficiency of the constitution as a legal bulwark against the narrow and false constructionists who would have left it powerless at the feet of rebellion."[69] Whiting claimed that he found the Constitution adequate, but in fact he did not, in his specific arguments, which were generally based on international law and came perilously close to the infamous "higher law" doctrines that so frightened the Democrats. Besides, even were we to adopt as a definitive interpretive scheme for the constitutional history of the Civil War, the rise of the "'adequacy of the Constitution school of thought,'" surely it matters that its practitioners differed in where the adequacy lay.[70] Lincoln and Whiting did not agree. Finally, the whole scheme seems inadequate, when we reflect on the fact, overlooked by Hyman and Neff, that the heartiest champions of the Constitution's adequacy were the Democrats. But the Democratic point of view was all but ignored by Hyman. For example, John A. Marshall's *American Bastile* is never referred to in *A More Perfect Union: The Impact of the Civil War and Reconstruction on the Constitution*, though Hyman's book is otherwise a goldmine of citations for pamphlets on the Constitution.

Lincoln Defends Himself

Horace Binney completed his pamphlet on the suspension of the writ of habeas corpus on December 23, 1861. A year and a half later the president found himself in need of explanations for the policy once again, and he did not look to Binney or Parker or the attorney general or William Whiting for help. This time, the president helped himself. He had been keeping notes and memoranda, apparently awaiting the occasion or necessity to use them. When the arrest of Ohio politician Clement L. Vallandigham aroused widespread Democratic mass meetings across the North, Lincoln knew that the time had come.[71]

In June 1863 Lincoln chose to respond to a letter sent from a mass meeting held in Albany, New York. The first signer was Erastus Corning, and Lincoln's letter has ever since been known as the "Corning letter." It was a very different thing from the labored and technical defenses offered by Horace Binney. Lincoln's was a blistering and uncompromising justification of the internal security measures of his administration, replete with the tough language presidents use in war when the enemy gets near the gates. In fact, the Corning letter of Abraham Lincoln is the strongest statement ever made by any American president asserting the power of the government to restrict civil liberty.

The Corning letter is remarkable for four assertions by the president. Unlike Binney's pamphlet or the president's own previous defense of the policies in his Message to the Special Session of Congress in the summer of 1861, the Corning letter of the late spring of 1863 included a quotable passage conjuring up a vivid image:

> Must I shoot a simple-minded soldier boy who deserts, while I must not touch a hair of a wiley agitator who induces him to desert? This is none the less injurious when effected by getting a father, or brother, or friend, into a public meeting, and there working upon his feelings, till he is persuaded to write the soldier boy, that he is fighting in a bad cause, for a wicked administration of a contemptable [*sic*] government, too weak to arrest and punish him if he shall desert. I think that in such a case, to silence the agitator, and save the boy, is not only constitutional, but, withal, a great mercy.[72]

It is impossible to ignore that vivid passage, but other important things in the letter have sometimes escaped notice.

Thus a second assertion — the one with which Lincoln began his case, in fact — was that the war was the result of a conspiracy a generation in the making. "The insurgents had been preparing . . . more than thirty years," he insisted, "while the government had taken no steps to resist them." That imagined circumstance of planning had given the rebels a little-noticed advantage over the Northern giant. The third and most important of Lincoln's assertions followed: that part of the long-digested plan was to leave embedded in Northern society "a most efficient corps of spies, informers, suppliers, and aiders and abettors of their cause in a thousand ways." They would be protected "under cover of 'Liberty of speech[,]' 'Liberty of the press' and '*Habeas corpus*.'" This "machinery" would be used to raise a "clamor" against the energetic measures of the administration and thus aid the enemy. In short, libertarian dissent in the North was simply "part of the enemies' programme." Lincoln virtually criminalized silence and demanded a noisy patriotism as proof of loyalty. "The man who stands by and says nothing, when the peril of his government is discussed," he said, "can not be misunderstood. If not hindered, he is sure to help the enemy."[73]

The president's fourth point did not go unnoticed at the time but has been generally overlooked in modern times. He followed his statement that the citizen's silence was tantamount to aiding the enemy with this assertion: "Much more, if he talks ambiguously—talks for his country with 'buts' and 'ifs' and 'ands.'"[74] It is, of course, members of the loyal opposition who speak for their country with buts and ifs. The Democrats said they supported the war *but* not if the Republicans changed its original goal. The Democrats said they supported the war *if* the Constitution were not sacrificed in the course of waging it. In other words, Lincoln thus moved rhetorically to threaten the loyal opposition.

The Corning letter is an example of nationalism unleashed. Its language existed just above the level of ridicule and fury. The president attempted to keep the tone presidential. When he suggested the inevitability of criticism of administration policies on internal security—a fact on which the enemy relied—Lincoln said that "they . . . knew they had friends who would make a question" of who had the right to suspend the writ of habeas corpus. An early draft of the letter had the phrase "raise a squabble" for "make a question." He also said that the "clamor" raised over the arbitrary arrest of innocent persons by mistake "might be . . . of some service to the insurgent cause." An early draft used the word "howl" for "clamor."[75]

The letter remained presidential in tone, but it came from a stern president indeed. It threatened the loyal opposition and challenged constitutional protections essential to the environment of an open and competitive party system. It is vital to understand the immediate context of this vigorous assault on freedom of speech and the press. Robert E. Lee's army was poised to invade the North in the military campaign that would lead, in a little over three weeks' time, to the Battle of Gettysburg. Besides that nerve-wracking military context, there was a political context that cannot go without mention: Lincoln released his letter to the Northern press the day after the Democratic state convention of Ohio nominated Clement L. Vallandigham for governor. Governors of the states played a much larger role in military mobilization than they do now, and Vallandigham as a congressman had abstained from voting on bills to supply the troops in the field. For a nervous president it may no longer have been clear that the opposition was loyal.

No one was more on Lincoln's mind than Robert E. Lee, of course, but Clement Vallandigham may have run Lee a close second in the summer of 1863. We can gain some appreciation of the weight of that concern for the president from Secretary of the Navy Gideon Welles's description of his meeting with Lincoln after Ohio's election day and Vallandigham's defeat in October 1863:

> I stopped in to see and congratulate the President, who is in good spirits and greatly relieved from the depression of yesterday. He told me he had more anxiety in regard to the election results of yesterday than he had in 1860 when he was chosen. He could not, he said, have believed four years ago, that one genuine American would, or could be induced to, vote for such a man as Vallandigham, yet he has been made the candidate of a large party, their representative man, and has received a vote that is a discredit to the country. The President showed a good deal of emotion as he dwelt on this subject, and his regrets were sincere.[76]

Lincoln never said exactly what prompted him to release the Corning letter when he did. Historians would like to know whether the military or the political context was the paramount influence. But we cannot say for certain. However, we can say that the president followed up his wide-ranging and pugnacious defense of the arrest of Vallandigham with yet another public letter aimed directly at the gubernatorial contest in Ohio. Here the Ohio Democrats certainly played into the president's hands. A delegation from the party convention that had nominated Vallandigham on June 11, 1863, went to the White House to hand the president a copy of the resolutions passed at the convention. Lincoln met with them on June 25, then published another long letter on the same subject as the Corning letter on the twenty-ninth. This letter, perhaps because of its more obvious political context, has not received as much attention from historians as the Corning letter.

Though the letter to Matthew Birchard and the other Ohio Democrats, dated June 29 by Lincoln, covered much of the same ground as the letter published earlier in the month, it did contain at least one interesting new result of Lincoln's thinking on the subject. The Ohio letter centered its argument more on the importance of the presidential office:

> You ask, in substance, whether I really claim that I may override all the guarrantied [*sic*] rights of individuals, on the plea of conserving the public safety — when I may choose to say the public safety requires it. This question, divested of the phraseology calculated to represent me as struggling for an arbitrary personal prerogative, is either simply a question *who* shall decide, or an affirmation that *nobody* shall decide, what the public safety does require, in cases of Rebellion or Invasion. The constitution contemplates the question as likely to occur for decision, but it does not expressly declare who is to decide it. By necessary implication, when Rebellion or Invasion comes, the decision is to be made, from time to time; and I think the man whom, for the time, the people have, under the constitution, made the commander-in-chief, of their Army and Navy, is the man who holds the power, and bears the responsibility of making it. If he uses the power justly, the same people will probably justify him; if he abuses it, he is in their hands, to be dealt with by all the modes they have reserved to themselves in the constitution.[77]

This development was significant. It was a change from Lincoln's rather innocent First Inaugural Address, which, back in those days of peace, did not contemplate, despite its use of the nationalist arguments first put forward by Andrew Jackson, any expansion of executive power. The president now boldly took the responsibility.[78]

The resolutions of the Ohio Democratic nominating convention obviously raised this question in Lincoln's mind and provoked the response: "Does your Excellency wish to have it understood that you hold, that the rights of every man throughout this vast country are subject to be annulled whenever you may say that you consider the public safety requires it, in time of insurrection or invasion?"[79] But he had by the spring of 1863 found powers in the presidency that to him exceeded those of the U.S. Congress. In his view, the president (as commander in chief) could free slaves in war and Congress could not, for example. If we step back from these developments in Lincoln's ideas, do we perceive an inevitable tendency in nationalism, vigorously asserted, to enhance one-man rule? Did nationalism seriously threaten the Constitution?

The Question of Presidential Power

Abraham Lincoln, though previously a Whig in politics, had never been an earnest critic of Andrew Jackson's exercise of presidential power. In truth, he half admired it. In 1849 Lincoln was seeking appointment to a patronage office as reward for his work to elect Zachary Taylor president. Taylor's idea that the president should not imitate the vigorous ideas of Jackson and should defer to his cabinet in making appointments worked to Lincoln's disadvantage, as the cabinet members were not disposed to favor Lincoln. Lincoln told John M. Clayton, President Taylor's secretary of state, in a letter Lincoln presumptuously wished the whole cabinet and the president himself would see, that the president must not allow himself to be perceived by "the People" as "a mere man of straw." "It is said," Lincoln recalled from recent press coverage of the Mexican-American War, "Gen. Taylor and his officers held a council of war, at Palo Alto (I believe); and that he then fought the battle against unanimous opinion of those officers. This fact (no matter whether rightfully or wrongfully) gives him more popularity than ten thousand submissions, however really wise and magnanimous those submissions may be." The president "must occasionally say, or seem to say, 'by the Eternal,' 'I take the responsibility.' Those phrases were the 'Samson's locks' of Gen. Jackson, and we dare not disregard the lessons of experience."[80]

In 1861 there was much to remind Lincoln of the pertinence of General Jackson's example. When a delegation from the Baltimore YMCA visited him to protest the movement of troops across their city in April 1861, in the wake of the violence of the recent Baltimore massacre, the president exploded with nationalist wrath. "The rebels attack Fort Sumter, and your citizens attack troops sent to the defense of the Government, and the lives and property in Washington, and yet you would have me break my oath and surrender the Government without a blow. There is no Washington in that — no Jackson in that — no manhood nor honor in that."[81] One wonders what the young Christians of Maryland thought of that outburst.

Horace Binney had no such weakness for the memory of Andrew Jackson and could not go where Lincoln seemed headed. When he came to write two more pamphlets on habeas corpus, he clung to his position in the first. His original pamphlet received so many replies, some of them written "to work the question up for party use," in Binney's view, that by April 1862 he was ready to reply to them and did so with the "Second Part" of his argument. The only criticism he deemed worthy of comment was that the clause on habeas corpus in the Constitution was not a granting of a power but a restriction on the already existing power of Congress to suspend.[82] Binney dismissed that in part because the Constitution empowered Congress only to regulate the appellate jurisdiction of the Supreme Court and not otherwise to *regulate* the courts (that issued the writ). The Constitution gave Congress only the power to "constitute tribunals inferior to the Supreme Court."[83]

For some of Lincoln's critics, the U.S. Congress made the unanswerable argument for the president by authorizing the suspension of the writ. Now Chief Justice Taney's objection — that it could be done only by Congress — had been met. Congressional authorization came finally on March 3, 1863, and thereafter presidential proclamations suspending the writ of habeas corpus cited congressional authorization in their preambles. Thus the suspension of September 24, 1862, announced *before* Congress acted, began:

> Whereas, it has become necessary to call into service not only volunteers but also portions of the militia of the States by draft in order to suppress the insurrection existing in the United States, and disloyal persons are not adequately restrained by the ordinary processes of law from hindering this measure and from giving aid and comfort in various ways to the insurrection;
>
> Now, therefore, be it ordered. . . .[84]

The next year, after Congress acted, when the president suspended the writ of habeas corpus in certain kinds of cases, he began this way:

> Whereas, the Constitution of the United States has ordained that the privilege of the Writ of Habeas Corpus shall not be suspended unless when in cases of rebellion or invasion the public safety may require it, . . . and whereas by a statute . . . it was enacted by the Senate and House of Representatives of the United States in Congress assembled, that, during the present insurrection, the President of the United States, whenever, in his judgment, the Public Safety may require, is authorized to suspend the privilege of the Writ of Habeas Corpus in any case throughout the United States. . . . Now, therefore, I Abraham Lincoln, President of the United States, do hereby proclaim. . . .[85]

What might be a solution for Lincoln, who needed, practically, to suspend the writ, turned out to be a problem for Binney, who had bet his intellectual reputation on an argument for the location of the power in the executive rather than in Congress.

Lincoln and the actions taken by the administration under the suspension of the writ of habeas corpus quickly outstripped the president's early defenders. The first to pull back from his initial defense was Harvard's Joel Parker. By the time of the autumn elections in 1862, Parker was engaged in a bitter dispute with the dominant faction of the Republican Party in Massachusetts led by Governor John M. Andrew and Senator Charles Sumner. He went so far as to issue a twelve-page pamphlet addressed "To the People of Massachusetts," dated October 30, 1862, denouncing the corruptions of party power. He despised the Republicans' ideas of conquering the Southern states, treating them as territories, and thereby gaining the power to emancipate the slaves. He denounced a recent convention of Republican governors who met in Altoona, Pennsylvania, as a violation of the Constitution's provisions against states entering into treaties or alliances or confederations. He did not think the governors should coerce the president into dismissing General George B. McClellan or emancipating the slaves. He resented the pressures exerted by the Republicans in Massachusetts to make support for emancipation accomplished by such extraordinary means a condition of loyalty in fighting for the Union. If he were not already, Parker was now to become famous for his independent thinking (and sharp tongue).

Denouncing the Reverend H. M. Dexter's assertion that it was necessary to support the president and his belief in the constitutionality of emancipation, Parker said: "When a clergyman assumes to know more of Constitutional law than those who have spent their lives in the investigation of its principles, he is apt to exhibit himself an unmitigated ass; and when he makes a political prostitute of himself, pandering to the lusts of a political party, he is entitled to no greater respect than — other persons who disregard their duties."[86] Such was not the customary style for a Republican to address the clergy in the state with the strongest Puritan heritage.

Thereafter Parker never lifted a pen in support of Abraham Lincoln's presidential powers. He had never thought them as extensive as Lincoln thought them, and by the time the president could defend his powers with the likes of the Corning letter, Parker had been left far behind as a presidential apologist. Still, like Horace Binney's, Parker's roots could be found in antislavery feeling and in constitutional criticism of the *Dred Scott* decision. "God forbid that I should be supposed to entertain any sympathy with slavery," he declared early in 1865, but he always insisted that a presidential proclamation did not constitute a proper constitutional remedy. Constitu-

tional amendment on the one hand and the friction of war on the other —
that is, the destruction of the master-slave relationship in individual cases
by martial law in the field — were the only legal remedies.[87] The president's
position on the military necessity of the Emancipation Proclamation and
his position on the suspension of the writ of habeas corpus taken in the
Corning letter seem to have left Parker with no recourse other than denunciation of such "despotic" doctrines. "The allegation, substantially, that the
President may do anything which the military necessity requires, and that
he is the sole judge when the public necessity arises, and what it requires"
he depicted as despotism.[88]

Parker even offered a little art criticism by way of illustrating his dismay
with Republican doctrines on the Constitution and emancipation. After
seeing Francis B. Carpenter's famous painting depicting the *First Reading
of the Emancipation Proclamation to the Cabinet,* he noted ruefully, "Prostrate upon the floor is the Constitution of the United States!" By contrast,
the artist had painted the image of a thick calf-covered book, William Whiting's *War Powers of the President,* as though that were superior to the Constitution itself.[89] Parker, as Phillip Shaw Paludan has fully demonstrated,
had no use for Whiting.[90]

Of a piece with his denunciation of the Massachusetts clergyman as an
"unmitigated ass" was Parker's characterization of the Emancipation Proclamation, even after the Great Emancipator's martyred death, as a "great
humbug."[91] He coolly characterized Lincoln as a "despotic ruler" in terms of
constitutional powers, but he was as disenchanted with the exercise of similarly despotic powers by Congress. Behind both, Parker could see the corrupt workings of a mindless, overheated, and power-hungry political party.
He regarded political parties as the root of the constitutional troubles, and
he denounced fealty to them as a form of slavery no different from that
practiced in the South.[92]

Horace Binney was also reconsidering the question of presidential power
in the summer of 1864. In his view, members of Congress had only "be-
deviled" the issue by asserting the president's right to suspend the writ of
habeas corpus and then proceeding "to regulate partially his proceedings,
as if the power were their own." What he was referring to was the provision in the Habeas Corpus Act of March 3, 1863, requiring the president to
submit to the federal courts a list of the persons imprisoned when the writ
was suspended. If grand juries found no charges against them, judges could
release them. If the president failed to supply lists of prisoners, then the
judges had the right to dismiss the prisoners on habeas corpus. James G.
Randall characterized the law as "a sort of compromise between camp and

bench."[93] Binney was aggravated by the legislation rather than mollified. He had hung his reputation on the assertion that suspension was a presidential power. More important, what transpired under the suspensions during the war increasingly gave him pause. After the president was safely reelected in 1864, Binney now thought it possible to offer a somewhat more restrained interpretation of the law on this subject.

Publication of the resulting *Suspension of the Privilege of the Writ of Habeas Corpus: Third Part* was delayed by the "engrossing events of April" 1865 (apparently the pamphlet was completed by March 4). It was finally published in June 1865. Binney had enjoyed more time for research in British history, and he had been sobered by some of the uses to which the suspension had been put by the administration. Besides, he thought it now safe, with the president's reelection, "to show what I then wrote [in 1862] did not proceed from opinions that were hostile to the personal liberty of freemen, whatever might be their opinions, within any range that does not include treasonable designs against the United States; and that it as little proceeded from a disposition to curtail the judicial power."[94] It had dawned on Binney that he had ignored the question of the sorts of offenses for which the writ's suspension was intended, for it could not possibly have been meant to extend to all crimes and all persons. The history of the suspension in Great Britain made clear that it had always been intended to apply to cases of treason or suspicion of treason. Suspension was aimed at conspiracies against the state. That was the steady practice of the past and would have been what the members of the Philadelphia convention had in mind when they drafted the provision for the Constitution of the United States, though they said frustratingly little about this important measure. The contrast with British practice, then, was not only in lodging the power with the executive but also in confining its use to the emergencies of invasion or rebellion. Otherwise, the Americans must have meant what the British meant by it at the time, he concluded.

In terms of the American Civil War, such a tight definition of its scope had important implications for the routine policies of the Lincoln administration and Congress's endorsement of the power to suspend. Binney had never intended to see—as any careful reader of the press of the day with an eye to legal and judicial affairs must have—minors and their parents unable to appeal for a writ of habeas corpus to question the retention in the ranks of an underage soldier or of a soldier made too drunk to know what he was doing when he enlisted. Binney thought that conscription was constitutional, but he never meant that the writ of habeas corpus would be unavailable to draftees who had been conscripted in error.[95] It is likely that he had read the president's defense of the Vallandigham arrest and of the administration's internal security policies in general. Binney said pointedly, "There may be partisans and judges who countenance and promote opposition to the draft," but they were a negligible force and lacked treasonable intent in many cases.[96] Suspension was a civil and not a military power; it was not to be confused with martial law or to be instrumented by the military power. It was not even a war power to be used, say, "to assist a military draft or enlistment."[97] That exception alone would have ruled out the principal use of the suspension in the North in the later stages of the war. Though a great defender and admirer of the president, whom he was reluctant to criticize at a time when it might impede the prosecution of the war, Binney in the end had great differences from Lincoln in interpreting the power to suspend the writ of habeas corpus. Lincoln used it to accomplish more restrictions on individual freedom than Binney ever dreamed — and at that, the president stopped well short of *political* abuse of the power (to arrest members of the opposition party).

The Opposition: Benjamin R. Curtis

The critics of the suspension of the writ of habeas corpus and of the expansion of presidential power included, famously, a gaggle of lawyers in Philadelphia, stirred to action by Horace Binney's pamphlet, and a few others, besides the predictable mass of Democratic newspaper editors and politicians. If any reminder is needed that American constitutional history cannot be described as a battle between strict and broad construction, this polemical literature produced by Lincoln's critics provides it. As usual in great conflicts over the U.S. Constitution, the debate was as much a matter of differing *theories* of the Constitution as of strict or broad construction of the document itself. In the instance of the critics of Lincoln's expanding powers in the Civil War, if anything, the literal textual ground was held by Lincoln's defenders. His critics often spurned it. Like Roger B. Taney, they certainly spurned historical precedent.

A case in point was an anonymous pamphlet entitled *Presidential Power over Personal Liberty: A Review of Horace Binney's Essay on the Writ of Habeas Corpus*, which characterized Binney's work as "very subtle, and . . . the best written upon the subject." The critical author was content, if not eager, to dismiss precedent. "There have been no decisions directly in point," he admitted. "We will, therefore, not be controlled, in this discussion, 'by the crooked cord of the discretion' and opinion of Judges found in books of Reports, but 'by the golden metwand' of reason, the words of the statute, and cotemporaneous [*sic*] understanding." (As the use of the term "metwand" instead of the ordinary word "measure" makes apparent, the writer in this instance was not particularly intent, despite rushing to get his pamphlet in print, on making the reader's path to his meaning easy.) In sum, he said, "He who sticks to the letter, sticks in the bark."[98]

The reason for dismissing precedents was simple: what few there were, were all on the side of executive power. These included John Marshall's decision in *Ex parte Bollman and Swartwout*, the actions of General Andrew Jackson before he became president, and Roger B. Taney's decision in *Luther v. Borden*.

The opinion in *Ex parte Bollman and Swartwout*, a case involving alleged coconspirators of Aaron Burr, was written by Chief Justice John Marshall in 1807. Marshall ruled that the U.S. Supreme Court could issue a writ of habeas corpus only in its appellate role, but that the commitment of Erick Bollman and Samuel Swartwout to jail by a federal court in the District of Columbia circuit, constituted a decision of another court. "The criterion which distinguishes appellate from original jurisdiction, is that it revises and corrects the decisions of another tribunal," he said. Otherwise, the issuance of the writ of habeas corpus by the Supreme Court of the United States would be in conflict with the historic decision on original jurisdiction in *Marbury v. Madison* from 1803.[99] Marshall's opinion did not exactly cover the *Merryman* situation, because Chief Justice Taney had issued his writ as an individual justice, not as an act of the whole Court. Still, Marshall's opinion would have opened to investigation the question of Taney's jurisdiction in the *Merryman* case and might ultimately have called into question his ability to overrule the president in such an instance.[100] In the end, Taney might have fallen victim to his own attempt to describe the decision as one from the Supreme Court (in chambers). No one at the time questioned Congress's ability to expand original jurisdiction for individual Supreme Court justices by giving them the power to issue writs of habeas corpus.[101] The Marshall precedent, still, ran against Taney.

Andrew Jackson's precedent represented a previous use of such a power that had gone unquestioned by the Supreme Court. It was more a Democratic embarrassment than a serious challenge to constitutional opposition to Lincoln's suspension of the privilege of the writ of habeas corpus. In 1815, after the Battle of New Orleans but before official notice of the signing of the peace treaty reached him, Jackson had imposed martial law on New Orleans. Under it, he arrested a newspaperman who had criticized him for the act and, when a judge issued a writ of habeas corpus on application from the newspaperman, Jackson arrested the judge too. The judge later imposed a one-thousand-dollar fine on Jackson for being in contempt of court in refusing to answer the writ of habeas corpus.[102] Neither the president nor Congress was directly involved, and, beyond the contempt citation by the federal judge, there was no court opinion in the affray. Years later, a Democratic Congress refunded Jackson's fine with interest and praised the suspension of the writ of habeas corpus in times of war. Such actions by the founder of the Democratic Party itself were suggestive and perhaps merited some comment in any fair-minded discussion of the constitutional question.

President Lincoln, of course, brought the matter up in his Corning letter and offered a detailed, factual history of the New Orleans episode. From that incident, Lincoln concluded: "It may be remarked: First, that we had the same constitution then, as now. Secondly, that we then had a case of Invasion, and that now we have a case of Rebellion, and: Thirdly, that the permanent right of the people to public discussion, the liberty of speech and the press, the trial by jury, the law of evidence, and the Habeas Corpus, suffered no detriment whatever by that conduct of Gen. Jackson."[103] The story of Andrew Jackson's actions had been a part of Lincoln's political education, not his legal apprenticeship. The precedent of practice by the very man who appointed Taney to the Court ran against Taney.

Luther v. Borden, the Rhode Island case already mentioned in this chapter because the defenders of Lincoln so often referred to it, could hardly have been ignored by any diligent jurist and not simply because the decision was written by Roger B. Taney himself. It was a thoroughgoing attempt to sustain the fundamental military powers of government and was based on reasoning about sovereignty as much as on the Constitution, statutes, or previous judicial decisions. In short, it was the kind of conclusion reached by the same path of reasoning used by Lincoln's eager defenders. Even Taney's sympathetic chronicler, Carl Brent Swisher, has noted the inconsistencies between *Merryman* and the Rhode Island case:

> Taney's critics called attention to alleged inconsistencies between his challenge to the President and to the military in the *Merryman* case and his opinion in *Luther v. Borden* where no North-South issue was directly involved. In the earlier case the Chief Justice had asked rhetorically whether a federal court could inquire into the correctness of the decision of the President to call out the militia. If it could, and if it differed with the President, it would be the duty of the court "to discharge those who were arrested or detained by the troops in the service of the United States or the government, which the president

was endeavoring to maintain. If the judicial power extends so far, the guarantee contained in the Constitution of the United States is a guarantee of anarchy and not of order." By contrast with his disparaging comments in the *Merryman* case on the scope of Presidential power, and stress on the safeguards erected against Presidential tyranny, Taney had said in the *Luther* case, "It is said that this power in the President is dangerous to liberty, and may be abused. All power may be abused if placed in unworthy hands. But it would be difficult, we think, to point out any other hands in which this power would be more safe and at the same time equally effectual."[104]

The principal text Taney had to rely on in the opinion was the guarantee of a republican form of government in Article IV. He regarded as political questions beyond the purview of the courts the power of the state government to impose martial law and to authorize the entry of citizens' homes to make arrests and seize evidence. In this instance, Taney himself ran against Taney.

Among the critics of Lincoln there emerged one who had once been a sharp critic of Taney. Benjamin R. Curtis was famous as a shrewd dissenter in the *Dred Scott* case. Not long after, Curtis resigned from the U.S. Supreme Court and practiced law in Massachusetts. In a way, like Attorney General Edward Bates, Curtis never lost his emotional identification with the Whig Party. "I am a member of no political party," he said in 1862. "Duties inconsistent, in my opinion, with the preservation of any attachments to a political party, caused me to withdraw from all such connections, many years ago, and they have never been resumed. I have no occasion to listen to the exhortations, now so frequent, to divest myself of party ties, and disregard party objects, and act for my country. I have nothing but my country for which to act, in any public affair."[105] He criticized Lincoln in a pamphlet published in 1862 under the title *Executive Power*.

Curtis argued that the suspension of the writ of habeas corpus (particularly as embodied in the president's proclamation of September 24, 1862) and the preliminary Emancipation Proclamation of September 22, 1862, were both underlain by a vast claim to executive power. They derived from the view of the presidency voiced in Lincoln's reply, in the late summer of 1862, to a delegation of Chicago clergymen urging him to issue an emancipation proclamation. At that time Lincoln was still maintaining a posture of discouraging the hopes of such people. The press, relying on a document describing the delegation's meeting prepared later by the clergy, reported Lincoln as saying, "Understand, I raise no objections against it on legal or constitutional grounds; for, *as commander-in-chief of the army and navy,*

in time of war, I suppose I have a right to take any measure which may best
subdue the enemy."[106]

Curtis maintained that no one could derive the powers Lincoln claimed
under the suspension of the writ of habeas corpus from the clause in the
Constitution allowing for its suspension. Curtis might have been correct
about the practical results of a suspension of the writ, but he was wrong
about Lincoln's own view of the Constitution, as the Corning letter would
show in less than a year's time. Lincoln derived only the power to emancipate the slaves of the enemy from the powers of the commander in chief in
war; he did derive the extensive system of military arrests of civilians without charge from Article I, section 9, of the Constitution, where the habeas
corpus privilege was mentioned.

Curtis argued that even "the meanest capacity" could grasp the implica-
tions of a claim to be able to override any of the guarantees of rights in the
Constitution under a plea of what would "best subdue the enemy."[107] Yet
Curtis himself recognized the practical realities of war on American soil:

> The general who moves his army over private property in the course
> of his operations in the field, or who impresses into the public service
> means of transportation, or subsistence, to enable him to act against
> the enemy, or who seizes persons within his lines as spies, or destroys
> supplies in immediate danger of falling into the hands of the enemy,
> uses authority unknown to the Constitution and laws of the United
> States in time of *peace*; but not unknown to that Constitution and
> those laws in time of *war*. The power to declare war, includes the
> power to use the customary and necessary means effectually to carry
> it on. . . . And, in time of war without any special legislation, not the
> commander-in-chief only, but every commander of an expedition, or
> of a military post, is lawfully empowered by the Constitution and laws
> of the United States to do whatever is necessary, and is sanctioned
> by the laws of war, to accomplish the lawful objects of his command.
> But it is obvious that this implied authority must find early limits
> somewhere.[108]

Those limits were the sphere of "actual operations in the field," in the first
place, and in the second, they "did not prescribe rules for *future* action."[109]
Curtis noted the worry that "it is the intention of the Executive to use the
powers asserted in the last proclamation and in the orders of the Secretary
of War, to suppress free discussion of political subjects." Curtis said that he,
personally, had no such fears of the president, but of the subordinates in
the field to whom these powers would be delegated, no one could be sure.[110]

It seems rarely to have occurred to the president's critics of habeas corpus how simple a remedy there was for questions about Lincoln's power to suspend, given the dominance of the Republicans in Congress. If there really was some constitutional problem with the suspension of the writ by the president, then he could hasten to ask the permission of Congress to do it — and get it forthwith. Edward Ingersoll, of Philadelphia, a bitter critic of the administration, did realize it. "Had the executive applied to Congress," Ingersoll observed, "as he should have done, under his oath to preserve, protect and defend the Constitution, for power to suspend the privilege of the writ of Habeas Corpus, the power no doubt would have been granted him in a moment."[111] Therefore, Ingersoll, thinking of the future, when such permission would likely come from Congress, focused on narrowing the consequences of a *legal* suspension of the privilege of the writ of habeas corpus.

That Congress could and would rescue the president reminds us of an important point. None of the critics, despite their protestations that they desired Union victory, bothered to suggest in their pamphlets that the president simply get the constitutional permission he needed. They might have said, not much harm has been done up to now. Not many people have been wrongfully arrested so far. The courts can rectify those errors, and in the future the king's cure would be for the president simply to obtain the necessary permission under the Constitution. In regard to emancipation, Lincoln himself made an analogous suggestion. If there were legal problems with the Proclamation, then the "King's cure" was a constitutional amendment that he recommended and worked for.[112] There was no such genuine expression of goodwill on the part of the partisan opponents of the administration. They were grudging and opportunistic critics, for the most part, whose style was brinkmanship in challenging the party in power and not seeking consensus.

Alas, the opposite is also true. The president's defenders seem to have made no such constructive suggestion, either. The adversarial style of politics (and legal proceedings) was indelibly ingrained, and no one really thought of consensus as something that could be reached. They thought mostly of advantages to be seized.

Sidney George Fisher: The Eccentric Constitutionalist

No treatment of the habeas corpus controversy and presidential power would be complete without consideration of Sidney George Fisher, whose place as a constitutional thinker has been magnified by the fact that he wrote the only full-length book on the Constitution in the Civil War that was published during the war itself. Fisher occupied an intellectually prominent place in Harold Hyman's *A More Perfect Union: The Impact of the Civil War and Reconstruction on the Constitution*, and Hyman's student Phillip Shaw Paludan devoted two chapters to him in *A Covenant with Death: The Constitution, Law, and Equality in the Civil War Era*.[113]

Fisher was not exactly a defender of the president. He did come, to his own surprise, to admire Lincoln as soon as he read his First Inaugural Address. Moreover, Fisher hated the administration's critics, of whom he got an eyeful at very close range. He had married into one of the most pro-Southern families in the Philadelphia area, the Ingersolls. One of them became a victim of arbitrary arrest and subsequently himself a pamphleteer against the president's internal security measures. Since Fisher was financially independent, he had leisure to think about and write on constitutional questions. In that respect he was like Binney, who was essentially retired and could turn his intellectual curiosity to wartime constitutional questions.[114] He was like Binney as well in that he proved to be a nationalist stirred by the war to restless action and intellectual effort.[115]

Otherwise, Fisher was like no one else. He was the only constitutional commentator during the war to derive as a lesson from the Constitution's struggle for existence that the legislative branch should be supreme! Such a conclusion defied the logic that has always located in the executive the decision, will, and force needed for war. It also defied the wording of the U.S. Constitution. We can only conclude — what no one else heretofore has really noticed — that the constitutional thought of Sidney George Fisher was eccentric enough to be simply marginal to debate. He does not merit the place he has gained in the historical literature. He represents no powerful intellectual or political tradition in American history. Yet there are enough forerunners of American political development in his book — scientific racism, congressional government, and the intellectuals' revolt against party politics and nominating conventions, for example — that, when combined with the attention lavished on Fisher in the past, they demand one more last, long look at him.

The best explanation for his ideas is intellectual isolation — that, combined with the fact that the glimpse of American politics he caught sight of was extreme: the antics of the Ingersolls. He set out to write a pamphlet on habeas corpus but instead wrote a book on the Constitution. His racism was systematic and based, he thought, on ineluctable scientific laws. It is easy to think that in slightly different circumstances, he might have turned out to be like John H. Van Evrie, the early white supremacist and single-minded editor of *The Caucasian*.[116] But that would have entailed embracing the pro-Southern outlook of the Ingersolls, which he resisted instinctively. Fisher tacked onto his book on the Constitution as an appendix a feverishly written little piece of journalism advocating the Emancipation Proclamation. His nominal occupation was lawyer, but he denigrated the Supreme Court and in his constitutional theories diminished its role. Indeed, the Court was the biggest loser in his theories; in the end, he equated judicial review with nullification. Historians have consistently identified him as an elitist who feared democracy, but he championed the most popular branch of government as the nation's proper savior.

Harold Hyman saw Fisher as a constitutional realist who avoided the neat "geometry" and "formalism" Hyman associated with Edward Bates and Roger B. Taney; in his odd way, then, Fisher looked forward to a view of the Constitution as a living document. In reconsidering Fisher, Hyman's student Paludan concluded that "his performance revealed the enormous hypnotic power of constitutionalism in American life. After arguing that the Constitution was inadequate to the existing crisis, that it was in major degree responsible for it, Fisher insisted that the Constitution justified the remedies necessary for national survival."[117] Paludan also emphasized the limitations Fisher's fear of Jacksonian democracy ultimately placed on his otherwise very flexible view of the Constitution. For Paludan, then, Fisher was more conservative than pragmatic. The problem with using Fisher as an example of the deep fears of the tendencies of Jacksonian individualism and democracy toward anarchy is the problem of using him as evidence and example for any powerful strain in American political and constitutional thought: he was simply eccentric.

He was clever, though. The originality of his outlook on the Emancipation Proclamation will be considered in the next chapter. Fisher's analysis of the Constitution generally was simple. The first part of his book, on a "written Constitution," was actually an attack on Article V and the mechanism for amending the Constitution of the United States. The case that the article was a "fetter" rather than an "instrument" was not very persuasive. Somehow, the process described in the Constitution was too cumbersome to meet the challenges of change, but also too prone to arouse partisan passion. It was clear that if the U.S. Congress had the power that the British Parliament did to change the Constitution, the process would be less cumbersome, but the element of partisan passion — about which Fisher, a bitter and sour critic of political party behavior, cared a great deal — was not well analyzed. The best he could do to explain the difference was the following:

To put its cumbrous machinery in motion, the people must be roused, and as the most important organic changes are generally connected with the interests of sections or of classes, the people are very likely to be roused by them, to be divided into parties, to be influenced by passion. They thus become a very unfit tribunal to decide such questions, which are not likely to be tried on their merits. The contest would be for victory, not for truth, a wide field and ample opportunity would be given to the arts of demagogues, and how far the struggle would go, and what would be its result, no one, at the beginning of it, could predict.

Yet to such a tribunal does the Constitution submit organic changes, and such struggles does it invoke. First in Congress or in the State Legislatures the question must be debated, by which the alarm is sounded. Then it must be discussed before the people, then a convention be elected. Then debated again in that convention. Then again before the people or in the State Legislatures. And all these operations are to be performed by the same people and by the same leaders; for leading party men would be the managers of the process throughout. Why might not the subject be safely committed to Congress, a body as much elected by the people as a convention, and therefore, as likely to represent their wishes?[118]

All Fisher really said was that he trusted Congress and he did not trust the amendment process. He did not, for he was a man of his times, look up from his desk and lamp to examine the process of convening conventions in the Southern states for secession, though they certainly included the steps of electing a convention and debating in the convention and in at least one case having the people vote on the convention's ordinance. There was nothing empirical about his constitutional ideas and therefore nothing "realistic."

We must at all times recall that this era preceded the advent of social science, and people like Fisher were dilettantes. What professional standard required him to deal with the relevant literature in his work or to be familiar with the literature of constitutional thought? He did not, apparently, know the history of the Pennsylvania Constitution, which had offered a relevant lesson on this subject of amendment in the past. The Constitution of 1776 provided for a Council of Censors to meet every seven years to see whether any parts of the state's constitution had been violated and to call for a convention if needed. Fisher did not even compare his view of the amendment process with the views of *The Federalist*, which he had read. *The Federalist*, nos. 49 and 50, dealt at length with Thomas Jefferson's ideas about occasional appeals to the U.S. Constitution and the Pennsylvania Revolutionary Constitution's provision for periodic appeals to the Constitution. James Madison found many of the same faults in these frequent or regular appeals to amendment that Fisher did with the Constitution's own amending process, particularly the enlistment of party passion along familiar party lines. But Madison's goal was to decrease the power of the legislative branch, and Fisher's was to increase it. Madison, it must be said, rested part of his case on empirical examination of the workings of the revolutionary constitution of Pennsylvania. How closely had Fisher read *The Federalist*?[119]

What Fisher did was to reveal his unquestioning infatuation with the British constitution as the sum of the virtues of political development to date in world history. The rural Philadelphia provincial was the ultimate Anglophile.

After devoting a long section of his book to the subject of "Union," Fisher then proceeded to deal with "Executive Power." He had the benefit of reading Parker, Binney, Bates, Theophilus Parsons, and the works of his outrageous in-laws. He was not an admirer of executive power, obviously, but he was an admirer of Lincoln. That incongruity led him to undermine the whole argument of his book. For he said that, in suspending the privilege of the writ of habeas corpus while Congress was not in session, Lincoln did exactly what he should have done to save the Union. What Fisher could not understand, and he said so, was that Congress did not then step up to the plate and offer the president what the English constitution provided for: authorization after the fact for suspension in their recess. Yet this was that same Congress that was to be trusted with essentially legislative sovereignty. Through it all, Fisher remained adamant that suspension was a legislative power because "every presumption is against" the Founders' "intending to clothe" the executive "with greater power than that of the English Executive, more especially with the irresponsible power of secret and discretionary imprisonment."[120]

It was a good thing that Fisher so admired parliamentary supremacy, for otherwise a fondness for executive power would have made him an easy apologist for dictatorship and one-man rule. I do not know of a passage in Civil War literature, written as early as this one — in 1862 — that equals it in near-religious worship of the man who occupied the executive office (note also the sharp contrast with the parliamentary process that surrounded Lincoln):

The people know the necessities of the hour, and appreciate the man whose hand is on the helm. They trust him. By a few plain and simple sentences and unostentatious deeds, — by golden silence and by silvern speech, — by masterly action and by masterly inaction, this sage and hero from the backwoods has, in one short year, commanded the entire confidence of a great nation, of a people the most intellectual and forcible on earth. Before the grandeur of that sentiment the base spirit of party cowers in silence, and the venomed tongues of the demagogues are obliged to hiss in whispers. In all debates and discussions, legislative or social, it has become the custom to mention the name of Mr. Lincoln with respect. Clothed in the raiment of truth and justice, he walks unscathed through the fiery furnace of civil war, and enters without fear the murky dens of party, where the howlings and gnashing of envy, hatred and revenge are awed into silence by his presence. It is a signal instance of the magnetic power of character, which conquers, like beauty, merely by being seen. By no popular arts, by no dazzling glare of military or other renown, by no previous services to the country, by no shining or captivating graces or accomplishments, but by the quiet and unostentatious display of a national and catholic spirit, of a good heart, of perfect integrity and purity of motive, of valor to meet danger and of ability to cope with difficulty, has this man of plain manners, who in his youth worked as a farm laborer, seated himself without an effort on a throne nobler than that of King or Kaiser, — the respect and faith of his countrymen.[121]

Sidney George Fisher was the first of a long line of Lincoln worshippers in American history.

But hero worship did not turn into apologies for dictatorship, and interpreting the Constitution to meet the ends of a great war did not lead to apology for presidential power or to any new appreciation of the presidential office. Fisher thought that Congress should suspend habeas corpus for the duration of the war, indemnifying the president for past action, and making clear the principle of legislative power except when the Congress was not in session. The power of secret and discretionary arrest — he conspicuously avoided the Democratic term "arbitrary"— was otherwise an invitation to dictatorship and Caesarism.

Despite a thoroughgoing racism, Fisher managed to praise the Emancipation Proclamation and to envision for African Americans a future under white rule as persons (rather than property) destined to labor below artisan levels. It would be tempting to say, in keeping with the overall thesis of this book, that Fisher's nationalism was powerful but not pathological. Indeed, it was not as pathological as it might seem from his interest in scientific racism or his proneness, in Lincoln's case, to hero worship. The problem is that Fisher's nationalism itself was not as powerful as it might seem.

For decades, we have accepted as the standard for systematic expressions of nationalism in the North in mid-nineteenth century America the notion of "perpetual Union." That was the ideal of Union that historian Kenneth Stampp went in search of when he scoured American political thought from the Constitution of 1787 to secession in 1860. Stampp's search was certainly bolstered by Abraham Lincoln's attempt to find a sovereign standard for nationalism as he entered the presidency in 1861: the theoretical and historical parts of the First Inaugural Address aimed to explain the perpetuity of the Union. Fisher, however, was a nationalist entirely equal to the challenges posed by the Civil War and impervious to the pro-Southern ideas of his in-laws. But he did not believe in a perpetual Union. He believed the Union that existed in 1862, when he wrote his book, was more than worth fighting for, but he did not think it would be perpetual.

Fisher considered local attachment one of the wonderful attributes of the wonderful Saxon race. Ultimately, to him, sectionalism was understandable:

> This country, fully peopled or half peopled, is large enough to make five or six great nations, each with its system of central and local government. The time will come when it will be so divided, with or without such a system for each of its parts. Must there be a civil war at each division, because the Constitution has not expressly granted to Congress power to dissolve the Union? Which is better, that these inevitable changes should occur, when in the fullness of time they become necessary, amicably, by mutual consent and with a just regard to all rights and careful provision for the future, or that each separation should be attempted by rebellion, the result of which would be, if successful, a revolution, followed by years of bitterness and probable war; if unsuccessful, the forced obedience and subjection of the weaker party, in which there can be no true union. Would it not be wiser to preserve the whole Union as long as possible, by wreathing the chains of necessary authority with garlands of benefit and blessing, so that if possible none shall wish to leave it, but when a swarm is ready to have a hive of its own, to permit it to depart with good wishes and friendly adieus, so that the kindness of old fellowship and kin may be afterwards preserved?[122]

The great student of nationalism, Benedict Anderson, identified as one of nationalism's enduring qualities and powers its profound, at times religious, association with final things and with eternity.[123] Sidney George Fisher was an American nationalist—more systematic than most—whose nationalism escaped that quality. In Fisher's case we are presented with the only constitutional thinker to derive legislative supremacy from the Civil War experience *and* the only loyal commentator to derive visions of amicable secession from Union victory.

Sidney George Fisher was a constitutional thinker who must be used with great care, and that, in the end, may be all that can be said about him.

Presidential Power, the Nation, and the Constitution in War

The intellectual defenders of Lincoln's extension of presidential power by suspension of the writ of habeas corpus had Whig antecedents. The Whig theory of the presidency was not powerful at all with Lincoln, and it could be easily overridden by nationalism in the case of other former Whigs. No one wanted to go as far as the president did in the Corning letter. That had no intellectual defenders—only partisans then and historians much later. Nationalism could cause men like Binney and Parker to find excuses for modest extensions of presidential power, but these were purely patriotic and circumstantial and not deeply authoritarian in any way. The roots of their identification with Lincoln and the Republicans, in fact, stemmed more from antislavery sentiment than from authoritarianism. It stemmed mainly from nationalism, which in the nineteenth century led, not to dictatorship and the cult of the individual, but, as Benedict Anderson said, to music and poetry. In the case of the United States, it led to emancipation.

Nationalism did tend to increase executive power—a little. Joel Parker pulled back from enhancing presidential power quickly. William Whiting was as interested in increasing congressional power as presidential; he was mainly interested in finding *some* power somewhere that would authorize emancipation. Abraham Lincoln and Horace Binney were very different kinds of men, but their nationalist convictions worked for a time in the same direction, toward increased executive power. It proved to be a mild and even reasonable response to the challenge, and Binney began to pull back from the full implications of his original argument for presidential power as soon as it seemed politically safe.

Even though Binney and Lincoln were different kinds of men, in both cases the assertion of nationalism was linked to fears about the loyal opposition. Binney was almost as relieved as Lincoln had been by Clement

Vallandigham's defeat in 1863, when in Pennsylvania, Democratic gubernatorial candidate George W. Woodward also lost. On November 10, 1863,
Binney wrote a friend in England, explaining the situation in America this
way:

> Parties do not die, because the country might do better without them.
> The party opposing the government was at one time very menacing;
> and if it meant what it threatened, would have not only put us at the
> feet of the South in the great question of division, but would have
> carried over Pennsylvania and other States depending on free labour.
> That danger has disappeared for the moment, tho' it may come again.
> There is no avoiding the action of a party in time of war, whether
> civil or foreign, because it has been formed with reference to peace
> and peace policies only. The union or association of men for any great
> purpose is too useful to its leaders to be dissolved under any circum-
> stances, if they can help it. And it will be maintained, and is main-
> tained even in this civil war, on the very border of treason, and some-
> times crossing it. We cannot help this, but we may strive to disappoint
> the purpose.[124]

In the end, Binney, a relic of the Early Republic, whose political identity in
many ways was forged when political parties were considered harmful and
dangerous to republics, by 1863 was forced to acknowledge their permanence in a republic, even in time of war.

We can safely exonerate American nationalism and the Lincoln administration from allegations of tendencies to authoritarianism or one-man rule.
Both Abraham Lincoln and Horace Binney harbored fears for the loyalty
of the opposition. Both Lincoln and Binney moved a little in the direction
of enhancing presidential power, but Binney receded almost entirely from
his advance before the war was over. Lincoln himself did not have the opportunity to pull back from his cautious steps toward a Jacksonian theory
of the executive because of his murder by John Wilkes Booth.

As late as December 8, 1863, Lincoln still seemed interested in presidential power. The rousing Corning letter was behind him, but the famous
Proclamation of Amnesty and Reconstruction of that date based the power
to reconstruct the Southern states substantially on the president's pardon-
ing power. There was much resentment in the Congress and in his own
party over the creeping powers of the president. The language of the protests in the next summer against the executive veto of the Wade-Davis Bill
was strident enough to have come from Democrats. Other ambitious Republicans sniffed the vulnerability of the president, and John C. Frémont's

third-party movement drafted a platform critical of the president's record on civil liberties.[125]

Such positions, however, should not cause us to overlook Lincoln's own careful consideration of the proper power on which to base a reconstruction of the Southern states. In fact, in the proclamation of December 8, 1863, the president astutely anticipated the constitutional discovery that would come to have the greatest sway over Republicans in Reconstruction, for Lincoln also based his Proclamation of Amnesty and Reconstruction on the little-used clause in the U.S. Constitution guaranteeing a republican form of government to the states. Its great virtues were broad vagueness in content and its location of the power in no particular branch of government. The clause said only that "the United States" would guarantee a republican form of government to the states. Thus both the president and the Congress could have roles in the process. After December 1863 President Lincoln never took another step in the direction of increasing executive power, even though the war would once again go perilously against the Union side.

The tendency toward executive power in nationalism proved in the United States to be identifiable but negligible. It came nowhere near approaching the pathological. Institutionally, it simply had no lasting effect. President Andrew Johnson, after the war, could attempt a "presidential Reconstruction" only because of the congressional calendar, not because of any greatly enhanced view of the power of the president.[126] He simply was running Reconstruction after assuming the presidency until Congress returned to its session of December 1865. As soon as it did, his powers rapidly were curtailed. Moreover, the minimal enhancement of executive power in the Civil War had no lasting effect. After Johnson's impeachment, there followed an era in American political history accurately described as congressional government, when the powers of the legislative branch were as great as they had ever been.[127]

Nationalism, though a powerful force in the Civil War, did not prove to be conservative, did not find the Constitution an incumbrance to be shed, and did not lead to one-man rule or even to any long-run strengthening of the executive branch under the Constitution. An examination of constitutional history makes that clear.

A less important conclusion also seems inescapable. Frederick Douglass and Abraham Lincoln were among the greatest constitutional thinkers of their time. Proportionate to the amount of time they could devote to studying the Constitution, they were certainly very great. Neither was a college or law school professor. The president lacked the formal education to become one, and Douglass would surely have been barred on account of racial prejudice. Although Lincoln became a lawyer, the law did not offer especially good training for constitutional thinking in a political context. Lincoln was too busy with a political career and in the end coping with political crisis and war to dedicate time to cloistered study of the Constitution. Douglass lacked any legal background and was too busy leading a people to freedom to have enough time for such study.

Douglass was certainly a greater constitutional thinker than Sidney George Fisher, but it would be difficult to arrive at that conclusion by looking at the existing literature on the Constitution and the nation in the Civil War. Even a work as recent as Phillip S. Paludan's *Covenant with Death*, which was published in 1975 and which takes its title from the notorious abolitionist denunciation of the Constitution, gave to Douglass but one mention. That was to say that abolitionists "became more admiring [of the Constitution] when the war promised to destroy slavery. Frederick Douglass called the war a war 'in order to save the Constitution.'"[128] But we know that Douglass split from William Lloyd Garrison well before the Civil War occurred in order to embrace the Constitution. He thought about the Constitution long and hard enough, in war and peace, to come up with the idea of popular constitutionalism. Harold M. Hyman quoted Douglass only once in his book *A More Perfect Union*, a passage about society and not about the Constitution at all.[129] Yet Douglass was more coherent and more forward-looking as a constitutionalist than the eccentric Sidney George Fisher, who was prominently featured in Hyman's book.[130]

And Abraham Lincoln, who has, admittedly, not suffered from want of praise for his ideas about the Constitution, deserves praise not yet lavished on him. Certainly, he was a more original constitutional thinker than Kenneth Stampp gave him credit for. The sources of the First Inaugural Address — the Constitution itself excepted — do not exhaust the ideas woven together in that powerful national myth Lincoln put together when faced with the secession crisis. On the more practical side, Lincoln, though he eventually embraced more presidential power than his early systematic apologists could stomach, as nearly as we can tell from his tragically abbreviated life, ceased to embrace more when he could.[131] Moreover, he thought about the powers of the president under the Constitution in ways inspired by the ideas of political parties rather than in ways comfortable to a lawyer, and that too set him apart from the notable constitutional scholars and thinkers of his time, mired as they were in English law and history.

If we step back from the pamphleteers who defended Lincoln, we see only bizarre doctrine laboriously fashioned from reasoning unmoored in reality. Harvard law professor Joel Parker decided that martial law was not derived from the Constitution and nevertheless existed without being declared by anyone in the legislative or executive branch. He did not trust party politicians and left an important role only for judges — to say when martial law existed and precisely where.

Sidney George Fisher's looking-glass world made the judiciary the big loser and somehow managed to derive an ideal of legislative supremacy from a situation of war, the very time when almost all authorities acknowledged the necessity of a growth in executive power. A rabid nationalist, he did not actually believe in a perpetual Union.[132]

Harvard-educated patent lawyer William Whiting may have thought that slavery could be abolished by eminent domain! Most astonishing of all, Horace Binney, fabulously learned and prestigious as a lawyer, decided what no one on earth ever decided before or since, that *only* the president could suspend the writ of habeas corpus.

In the context of such strained and downright preposterous arguments, the reasoned propositions of Lincoln and Douglass stand out as islands of sane statesmanship. They arrived at their ideas because one of them was not a lawyer and because the other was able to escape the habits of thinking like a lawyer. They reasoned as statesmen do. The importance of shedding the straitjacket of a legal background will be more apparent in the next chapter, on the strains the Emancipation Proclamation placed on the Constitution.

The Emancipation Proclamation

THE TRIUMPH OF NATIONALISM OVER RACISM AND

THE CONSTITUTION

The most important constitutional development on the eve of the Civil War was the growth of constitutional racism. The U.S. Constitution of 1787 was not an expressly racist document, and the word "white" nowhere appeared in it. To take a look at the common understanding of the document seventy years after its drafting, however, is to think that maybe it did after all. Constitutional racism reached the U.S. Supreme Court in 1857, but the movement had been brewing for years.

The encroachment of racism on constitutional understanding was not entirely a matter of Southern domination of the U.S. Supreme Court. The Taney Court did not singlehandedly hijack the document in the *Dred Scott* ruling.[1] Rather, a number of decisions made by people now nameless mapped the way to a racially exclusive understanding of the constitutional order. These decisions were the work of state legislators, delegates to constitutional conventions, and masses of voters ratifying their work.

The encroachments of racism on American state constitutions from 1820 to 1860 can hardly be overlooked, but the intensifying sentiment and its new tendency toward exclusion of African Americans go well beyond any characterization of it as part of "Jacksonian democracy." Being fearful that, with an expansion of political rights and especially of voting rights, the rise of the common man might include African American men, was not the same thing as resolving to exclude African Americans altogether from residence. Here is the way that constitutional historians Melvin I. Urofsky and Paul Finkelman have dealt with the subject in the past:

In the decades between 1800 and 1860, every state in the Union revised its constitution. An analysis of the changes in these documents
shows a steady democratization of the political system and greater
awareness (at least in the North) of the need for written protections
of individual liberties especially for whites. With a few exceptions,
however, like the Rhode Island constitution adopted after the Dorr
War, these constitutions of the Jacksonian period tended to disfran-
chise blacks where they once had the right to vote, to limit the rights
of Southern masters to free slaves, and in other ways to incorporate
the racism of the era into state law.[2]

Such an approach underestimates the intensity of the trend, for white
women could not vote either, but there was no movement to exclude them
from the states altogether.

The most intense period of the movement began a little over a decade before the Civil War. It eventually found spokesmen in Chief Justice Roger B.
Taney of the U.S. Supreme Court and Senator Stephen A. Douglas of Illinois. Taney and Douglas merely articulated what others, who are largely
nameless in American history, had begun. The movement was most apparent in the state constitutions revised around the turn of the decade in 1850.
They marked the culmination of a trend begun, as Urofsky and Finkelman
argued, in the Jacksonian era. In Indiana, where Abraham Lincoln grew up
from age seven to adulthood (1816–30), the process began just after he left
the state for Illinois with his family. In 1831 the Indiana legislature passed
a law requiring any African American who wanted to settle in the state to
post a $500-bond guaranteeing good behavior while there. Such a large
sum meant, effectively, exclusion of African Americans from the state. Even
so, Hoosiers later thought the measure did not go far enough, and in the
constitution of 1851 the thirteenth article forbade free African Americans to
enter the state to settle. The article was submitted to the vote of the people
separately from the body of the constitution itself, and the racial exclusion
measure passed by what Eugene Berwanger has described as a "startling"
majority: 113,628 to 21,873.[3]

In 1851 Iowans also moved to exclude African Americans from settlement in their state. That year the legislature passed a law prohibiting black
immigration.[4]

The constitutional history of Illinois had been very like Indiana's. In 1829
its legislature required a free African American wanting to enter Illinois
to settle to post a $1,000-bond.[5] Lincoln, who moved to the state in 1830,
could not have done so had he been African American, for he was too poor

to post the requisite bond. In 1848 Illinoisans revised their constitution, authorizing the legislature to take measures to forbid African Americans to enter the state to settle. The exclusion article was submitted separately from the rest of the body of the constitution, so they had, in effect, a pure referendum on racism. It passed by a vote of 60,585 to 15,903, a greater margin than the rest of the constitution enjoyed.[6] Lincoln was in Congress at the time, and because there was no absentee voting in Illinois, he did not vote on the measure.

Late in 1857, Oregon voters passed an African American exclusion measure in their constitution by 8,640 to 1,081. Again, the provision had been submitted separately from the rest of the constitution and passed by a much greater majority.[7] The U.S. Congress admitted Oregon as a state and thus in a way condoned its African American exclusion policy in 1859, virtually on the eve of the Civil War.[8]

Two years before the admission of Oregon with its racially exclusive constitution, Chief Justice Taney's majority opinion in the *Dred Scott* case performed a strained exercise in rewriting American history to make it almost a constitutional principle that people of African descent "had no rights which the white man was bound to respect."[9] Taney documented limitations on people of African descent that proved the opinion of them was never high enough for them to be thought of as citizens under the Constitution, but he did not refer to the exclusion laws of recent history like those of Illinois and Indiana. Instead, he confined his examples to the original thirteen states. Vaguely, he was seeking original intent in these efforts, but in fact he cited legislation well past the time of the ratification of the Constitution. He must have believed that the prestige of the original thirteen states was what he needed, not the manifestations of modern Western prejudice. It is not known whether he knew of the provisions of the modern state constitutions, as no cases arising under the Illinois or Indiana laws enforcing the constitutional exclusion of African Americans ever went to the Supreme Court.[10] Emboldened in part by Taney's assertion, Stephen A. Douglas then began to formulate the only quotable phrase he had uttered in a long public career. In the first of his famous debates with Lincoln, he said:

> We are told by Lincoln that he is utterly opposed to the Dred Scott decision, and will not submit to it, for the reason that he says it deprives the negro of the rights and privileges of citizenship. . . . Do you desire to strike out of our State Constitution that clause which keeps slaves and free negroes out of the State, and allow the free negroes to flow in, and cover your prairies with black settlements? Do you desire

to turn this beautiful State into a free negro colony? . . . I believe this government was made . . . by white men, for the benefit of white men and their posterity forever, and I am in favor of confining citizenship to white men, men of European birth and descent, instead of conferring it upon negroes, Indians and other inferior races.[11]

Douglas was then championing popular sovereignty, a version of state rights, and expressed contentment with decisions of other states to allow African Americans more of the privileges of citizenship than Illinois did. Nevertheless, the clarion call for a white man's government was what others quoted later, not the "great principle of popular sovereignty."[12]

Historians of the period and Lincoln biographers have obscured the brewing revolution of constitutional racism by going down the wrong path in pursuit of making the Republicans' arguments plausible. At the time, Republicans relied on spreading alarm about a mythical Slave Power Conspiracy to frighten voters into believing that a tiny cabal of slaveholders would not stop at the *Dred Scott* decision making it unconstitutional for territories to exclude slavery, but would soon bring about a second *Dred Scott* decision making it unconstitutional for *states* to exclude slavery from their borders any longer. There was no such thing as a unified conspiracy of slaveholders, but creating aristocratic monsters to slay, like the Slave Power Conspiracy, was an effective political style of the day.[13] Historians have since attempted to exonerate the Republicans from creating this fiction by urging us to think that it might have come true. In particular, they point to the real possibility of what Republicans warned against, a second *Dred Scott* opinion. Lincoln stated the myth fully in the "House Divided" speech of June 16, 1858, the keynote address of the Republican campaign for the Senate that year:

> Put *that* and *that* together, and we have another nice little niche, which we may, ere long, see filled with another Supreme Court decision, declaring that the Constitution of the United States does not permit a *state* to exclude slavery from its limits.
>
> . . . Such a decision is all that slavery now lacks of being alike lawful in all the States.
>
> Welcome or unwelcome, such decision *is* probably coming, and will soon be upon us, unless the power of the present political dynasty shall be met and overthrown.
>
> We shall *lie down* pleasantly dreaming that the people of *Missouri* are on the verge of making their State *free*; and we shall *awake* to the *reality*, instead, that the *Supreme* Court has made *Illinois* a *slave* State.[14]

Both Don E. Fehrenbacher and Eric Foner have looked into the possibility as though it were something real and not an exaggerated bugaboo made on and for the stump.

Fehrenbacher said, "Historians, made overly wise by hindsight, have been disposed to regard the charge as more or less empty political rhetoric, ignoring the fact that even unrealistic fears may be utterly real. Actually, slavery had *already* been nationalized in various ways beyond the minimal requirements of the Constitution, and northern fear of further nationalization in the wake of the Dred Scott decision was, in the circumstances, no more unjustified than southern fear concerning the ultimate intentions of the Republican party."[15] Foner wrote, "Lincoln . . . and countless other Republicans predicted, in what Simon Cameron called 'the next step after the Dred Scott decision' . . . that the Court would deny the power of a state to exclude slavery." At that point, he moved, not to discredit the factual basis of any such allegation, but instead to say, "Many Republicans believed that slavery would be established in the North, not by a direct Supreme Court decision but by a ruling on the right of slaveholders to bring slaves into and out of free states without forfeiting their property rights." He then proceeded to describe "the Lemmon case" in New York, involving the transit of slaves from Virginia to New York.[16]

At that point historians might have done better to address the probability that the Republican charge was ridiculous, a fabrication for political effect, not to search for some possible vindication of a will-o'-the-wisp. The Democrats were flabbergasted by the absurd charge. Stephen A. Douglas, in the series of debates with Lincoln that followed the "House Divided" speech, said:

> The . . . question which Mr. Lincoln presented is, if the Supreme Court of the United States shall decide that a State of this Union cannot exclude slavery from its own limits will I submit to it? I am amazed that Lincoln should ask such a question. ("A school boy knows better.") Yes, a school boy does know better. Mr. Lincoln's object is to cast an imputation upon the Supreme Court. . . . He casts an imputation upon the Supreme Court of the United States by supposing that they would violate the Constitution of the United States. I tell him that such a thing is not possible. (Cheers.) It would be an act of moral treason that no man on the bench could ever descend to.[17]

In the early twentieth century historians had proved that there was no Slave Power Conspiracy, in part because of fundamental disagreements among Southerners themselves that kept them from cooperation.[18] The Southerners wanted to defend the slavery they had but wanted to have nothing to do with those states that disapproved of it. Theirs was largely a defensive enterprise and one aimed at proving the equality of white owners of slaves with Northern property owners.

Attempts to justify the Republicans' charge have obscured what was really happening to the constitutions of the states. What was in process of nationalization was not slavery but racism, and that was occurring in Lincoln's home state, not to mention Oregon and Indiana. Iowa seemed to be starting down the same legislative path. The outbreak of the Civil War interrupted the clear trajectory of constitutional racism, but would opening the possibility of emancipation give it new impetus?

The Revival of Colonization

Surprisingly, it seemed as though the racist trend might continue even with the advent of the first Republican chief executive. President Lincoln almost singlehandedly revived the cause of colonization. After he left behind his critique of secession and defense of the suspension of the writ of habeas corpus in his Message to the Special Session of Congress of July 4, 1861, the president moved on to a new subject in his message to the regular session of Congress on December 3, 1861. The subject was colonization, an old and largely discredited policy. Colonization had been part and parcel of the constitutionalization of racism, at least in Indiana, and its revival nationally at this time in the sectional contest was a sign that the march of constitutional racism might well continue.

Article XIII of the Indiana Constitution of 1851, which excluded African Americans from the state, stipulated that revenues paid in fines for violation of the law be applied to a fund for the colonization of African Americans who had settled in the state before its constitution was changed. There followed the creation of what might be termed a model for the Lincoln administration later. The Indiana legislature appropriated a fund for colonization and started looking for a colony. The lawmakers created a State Board of Colonization and appointed an agent, a Methodist minister named James Mitchell. Later Mitchell would serve in the Interior Department of the Lincoln administration as an emigration commissioner while the administration used a congressional appropriation to look for a colony and colonists.[19]

The constitutional exclusion of African Americans in Illinois in 1848 had come without provision for a government program to promote colonization, but Lincoln likely knew of the Indiana plan from Mitchell, who became the agent of the American Colonization Society in Springfield in 1853. During the time Mitchell was the agent, Lincoln lectured for the colonization society in Illinois.[20] Some have seen the president's expressions of interest in colonization in 1861 and 1862 as a form of political preparation for an emancipation policy to come, but that ignores the continuity of his interest in colonization and the continuity of Mitchell's work for state and national governments. Lincoln had been working for colonization, off and on, for nearly a decade before the Emancipation Proclamation. His administration constructed a government bureaucracy of sorts, on the Indiana model, to initiate the national program. Thus Lincoln's idiosyncratic interest became institutionalized.

Such developments are no proof that Lincoln ever contemplated constitutionalizing racism. But that development in other state constitutions obviously remained a threat. Lincoln's recommendation for a colonization plan in 1861 had an ominous consequence in the development of his own constitutional ideas. The acquisition of territory (to serve as colonies for freedmen) posed another constitutional problem: territorial acquisition by an ostensibly anti-imperial nation. Though as a congressman he had been a critic of the Mexican-American War, which was widely regarded as having been initiated for territorial ambitions, Lincoln had never said that the acquisition of territory was itself unconstitutional. Rather, he had said that the Mexican-American War was unconstitutional because, in Lincoln's mind, President James K. Polk provoked it, and the Constitution gave Congress the power to declare war. On the acquisition of territory, Lincoln had always been a realist. In an 1854 speech in Bloomington, Illinois, criticizing the Kansas-Nebraska Act, Lincoln, in the course of rehearsing the history of the territorial expansion of slavery, said: "Jefferson saw the necessity of our government possessing the whole valley of the Mississippi; and though he acknowledged that our Constitution made no provision for the purchasing of territory, yet he thought that the exigency of the case would justify the measure, and the purchase was made."[21] As president in 1861, now looking for real estate for a colony, Lincoln could say, "Having practiced the acquisition of territory for nearly sixty years, the question of constitutional power to do so is no longer an open one with us." He forthrightly summarized the meaning of the Louisiana Purchase of 1803, saying that "the power was questioned at first by Mr. Jefferson, who, however, in the purchase of Louisiana, yielded his scruples on the plea of great expediency."[22] On that point, Lincoln was consistently practical. He had always been content with the assertion of presidential power under circumstances of "necessity" or "great expediency."

Suddenly, in the presidential message of 1861, Lincoln injected into this discussion of territorial acquisition a hypothetical argument about race. "If it be said that the only legitimate object of acquiring territory is to furnish homes for white men," he asserted, "this measure effects that object; for the emigration of colored men leaves additional room for white men remaining or coming here." He concluded by saying that "Mr. Jefferson, however, placed the importance of procuring Louisiana more on political and commercial grounds than on providing room for population."[23] The argument was hypothetical, yet Lincoln did not dismiss it out of hand, and it had profound implications for national identity.

The argument was a disturbing outgrowth of the racist underside of the Republican Party's central free soil appeals. In the 1850s Lincoln himself stressed the importance of halting slavery's spread to the new territories as a step toward ultimate extinction of the institution, but he did on occasion express the racist case for Free Soil as well — namely, that to keep slavery out of the territories was also to keep African Americans out of the country's future settlements. At Peoria in 1854, in a famous and eloquent speech, Lincoln said of the territories: "We want them for the homes of free white people. This they cannot be, to any considerable extent, if slavery shall be planted with them. Slave States are places for white people to remove FROM; not to remove TO. New free States are the places for poor people to go to and better their condition. For this use, the nation needs these territories."[24] These perilously uncertain ideas about race and nation were soon to form the context of President Lincoln's tortuous constitutional journey to the Emancipation Proclamation.

Steps to Emancipation?

James G. Randall's *Constitutional Problems under Lincoln* has embalmed a point of view on the constitutional history of the Civil War that needs revision — that is, that the Constitution was a "problem" for the North during the Civil War. Elsewhere I have argued that we need to look at the Constitution in a different way: as an advantage to the administration in winning the war.[25] Article II of the Constitution had the practical effect of making a determined Republican the commander in chief for four long years and allowing him to ride out military defeats and remain in office to victory. The duration of Lincoln's term of office and the certainty of his persistence in attacking the rebels caused the Confederate States to abandon the advantages of defense and embark on offensive operations that proved disastrous — in Maryland in 1862 and in Pennsylvania in 1863. Dedication to offensive military campaigns complicated the mobilization problem of the Confederacy, as the Richmond government had to raise armies for such operations and not rely on nationalizing the state militias for defense — a more comfortable constitutional position in a republic dedicated to state rights. The four-year presidential term left the opposition party in the North, the Democrats, with little effective role, and the political dominance of the Republican Party made mobilization for a massive war much easier. In the instance of a war commencing with a presidential administration and with the executive in reasonably able hands, the Constitution was a great advantage. It was especially so in a country with a marked democratic ethos, for its clear delegation of military command authority and its inflexible and long term of office for the chief executive gave time and authority to ignore temporary disappointment and discouragement of the press and public opinion at the fortunes of battle.

But for emancipation the Constitution *was* a problem.[26] To the Democrats, the Constitution seemed an insuperable obstacle to emancipation. Indeed, many Republicans themselves knew it was a problem. Antislavery enthusiasts had always recognized it as such and continued to after the Civil War began — none more so than President Abraham Lincoln, who had acknowledged in the most important and widely read speech of his life, his First Inaugural Address, that the Constitution and generations of constitutional interpretation made it clear that slavery in the states where it already existed could not be touched by the federal government.

The customary approach to emancipation in history books is to walk through the events leading up to it, from salient event to salient event, most of them now famous — from General Benjamin F. Butler's declaration in May 1861 that escaped slaves were contraband of war and were not to be returned to their masters on the Confederate side, right up to Lincoln's signing of the final Emancipation Proclamation on January 1, 1863, his hand sore and tired from greeting visitors at the annual New Year's Day White House public reception. James Randall made this approach famous in *Constitutional Problems under Lincoln* with his chapter entitled "Steps toward Emancipation." Randall was bent on proving that Lincoln's plan of emancipation was moderate and not radical, so the chapter culminated in a section on "that form of emancipation which Lincoln favored in preference to any other because it came nearest to satisfying his sense of what was statesmanlike, equitable, and legally sound. This was gradual emancipation by voluntary action of the States with Federal cooperation and compensation."[27]

Oddly enough, Randall did not really dwell on the constitutional aspects of Lincoln's changing views, and he nowhere addressed the conception of the Constitution Lincoln held or where it came from or how it changed, if it did, over time. Such considerations mark the real "steps" to emancipation.

We have already seen what the three sources of Lincoln's constitutional ideas were. The antislavery movement was slighted in Randall's treatment of "Lincoln's lawyerlike caution in dealing with the slavery question as a matter of permanent law."[28] As for "lawyerlike caution," we have seen in the treatment of the habeas corpus question that legal training was not particularly helpful. Surely in the case of emancipation, it was even less so. Lincoln embraced the antislavery myth of the Constitution wholeheartedly, but at bottom he knew it could not entirely gloss over the problem that the Constitution recognized slavery.

Clinging to the Constitution and its clauses on slavery led to inequalities and unfairness to free states, and Lincoln knew it well. "In the control of the government—the management of the partnership affairs," he pointed out in a speech in 1854, Southerners

> have greatly the advantage of us. By the Constitution, each State has two Senators—each has a number of Representatives; in proportion to the number of its people—and each has a number of presidential electors, equal to the whole number of its Senators and Representatives together. But in ascertaining the number of the people, for this purpose, five slaves are counted as being equal to three whites. The slaves do not vote; they are only counted and so used, as to swell the influence of the white people's votes. . . . There is no instance of exact equality, and the disadvantage is against us the whole chapter through.

"Now all this is manifestly unfair," he said, but he would not complain. "It is in the constitution; and I do not, for that cause, or any other cause, propose to destroy, or alter, or disregard the constitution. I stand to it, fairly, fully, and firmly."[29]

Nor would he blink away the plain obligation to recover fugitive slaves laid on the American people by the Constitution. These obligations were none the less "degrading" to the free states: "We are under legal obligations to catch and return their runaway slaves to them—a sort of dirty, disagreeable job, which I believe, as a general rule the slave-holders will not perform for one another."[30] In his inaugural address seven years later, he admitted that the fugitive slave clause was "as plainly written in the Constitution as any other of its provisions."[31]

But by late 1861 Lincoln was likely already wishing he had never said what he had about the Constitution and slavery in his inaugural address, and he made sure that he said nothing about it thereafter in public. That is one of the striking things about the steps to emancipation. The other, that we may infer from this constitutionally taciturn record, is how quickly Lincoln solved the constitutional problem of emancipation. The decision to issue the Emancipation Proclamation may have come slowly, but Lincoln rather quickly figured out how to make it constitutionally acceptable if and when he deemed it expedient.

It should be said first that Lincoln's actions spoke more loudly than his words in these events, and the American people did not mistake them. He publicly disallowed most practical steps taken toward liberating slaves as a class. The most famous of these episodes was his reversal of General John C. Frémont's emancipation proclamation in Missouri on September 11, 1861. We know a great deal more about Lincoln's views on this than the public did at the time through the survival of some private correspondence. But if we look only at Lincoln's order to Frémont, the president insisted "that the said clause of said proclamation [Frémont's, in relation to the confiscation of property and the liberation of slaves] be so modified, held, and construed, as to conform to, and not to transcend, the provisions on the same subject contained in the act of Congress entitled 'An Act to confiscate property used for insurrectionary purposes.'"[32] Lincoln did not say, and he might well have, that Frémont must make his orders conform to the Constitution of the United States. The president did not use the occasion to make explicit his trustworthy adherence to the Constitution.

Lincoln did explain his view on the Constitution at great length in a confidential letter to Senator Orville Hickman Browning about Frémont. Here the constitutional obstacle seemed all but insuperable:

> Genl. Fremont's proclamation, as to confiscation of property, and the liberation of slaves, is *purely political*, and not within the range of *military* law, or necessity. If a commanding General finds a necessity to seize the farm of a private owner, for a pasture, an encampment, or a fortification, he has the right to do so, and to so hold it, as long as the necessity lasts; and this is within military law, because within military necessity. But to say the farm shall no longer belong to the owner, or his heirs forever; and this as well when the farm is not needed for military purposes as when it is, is purely political, without the savor of military law about it. And the same is true of slaves. If the General needs them, he can seize them, and use them; but when the need is past, it is not for him to fix their permanent future condition. That must be settled according to laws made by law-makers, and not by

military proclamations. The proclamation in the point in question, is simply "dictatorship."[33]

When, exactly one year later, Lincoln himself did what Frémont had done but for the states in rebellion only, he no longer thought it constituted dictatorship, of course. But how did he get to that new view of the Constitution?

We have no idea. He did not ask anyone for a digest of laws on the subject, as he had done in the case of suspending the writ of habeas corpus in April 1861. If he read anything new that was particularly persuasive to him, the record does not show it. But he did, obviously, change his mind.

His public actions remained compatible with a view of the Constitution as a document that protected slavery. In a message to Congress on March 6, 1862, Lincoln proposed a voluntary emancipation plan for the Border States. Such a plan, he insisted, "sets up no claim of a right, by federal authority, to interfere with slavery within state limits, referring, as it does, the absolute control of the subject, in each case, to the state and it's [*sic*] people, immediately interested. It is proposed as a matter of perfectly free choice with them."[34] In May he issued a public proclamation revoking an order somewhat like Frémont's given by General David Hunter at Hilton Head, South Carolina. In this instance Lincoln delivered a sort of anti-emancipation proclamation of considerable length and formality. Compared with the Frémont order, the format of this fully official presidential proclamation countersigned by the secretary of state is striking. But what was Lincoln trying to say now that he had not used the Frémont occasion to say in the same way?

The president did not say what was wrong with Hunter's order except that the general had not been authorized to give it. "I further make known," Lincoln said, giving the first indication, public or private, that he had changed his mind about the Constitution, "that whether it be competent for me, as Commander-in-Chief of the Army and Navy, to declare the Slaves of any state or states, free, and whether at any time, in any case, it shall have become a necessity indispensable to the maintenance of the government, to exercise such supposed power, are questions which, under my responsibility, I reserve to myself."[35] Hunter, a mere general, had certainly not used any such argument for "such supposed power." In other words, this revocation, sometimes only referred to as one in a series of discouragements to emancipation issued by Lincoln before the Emancipation Proclamation, should not have been so discouraging. It was a proclamation that emancipation might be constitutional, that emancipation might be only a matter of expediency hereafter to be decided by the president. Thus the constitutional problem was on its way to solution in Lincoln's mind as early as May 1862. About eight months had passed since he told Senator Browning emancipation by proclamation amounted to "dictatorship."

By July 22, 1862, Lincoln had definitely changed his mind, because on that day he showed his cabinet a secret draft of a proclamation freeing the slaves. Thereafter what he said in public clearly reflected that change in constitutional ideas, though it was never the most noticeable part of any public statement. Those statements appeared to be aimed at asserting the inexpediency of proclaiming the slaves free. The most well-known instance was Lincoln's letter of August 22, 1862, answering Horace Greeley's "Prayer of Twenty Millions" in which he asked the president to abolish slavery. Lincoln's reply was not a presidential proclamation, but it was published in the most widely read Republican newspaper in the country, and the meaning of it, like the meaning of the Hunter proclamation, seemed overtly negative but was quietly permissive on the question of constitutional power. Read in full, it did say that emancipation could come "under the Constitution." "I would save the Union," Lincoln wrote. "I would save it the shortest way under the Constitution. . . . If I could save the Union without freeing *any* slave I would do it, and if I could save it by freeing *all* the slaves I would do it; and if I could save it by freeing some and leaving others alone I would also do that."[36] The Constitution was no longer a problem in Lincoln's mind. Lincoln spoke in plain language here, and he did not supply, as he had in the proclamation of May, a formal statement of the constitutional rationale for possible emancipation (his constitutional competence as commander in chief to meet military necessity). But, of course, the president could not be contemplating emancipation as a military strategy if it were not legal to use it.

Just how great a problem for Lincoln was the Constitution? History's knowledge of documents that were private then but well known now as well as the president's own circumspect language in dealing with the subject have caused us to fail to notice that he never said after the war began that the Constitution sanctioned slavery. It was a serious problem in his own mind, but he tried to say nothing in public to remind people that it was a problem.

Loss of Political Mastery

The steps-to-emancipation approach to the Proclamation initiated by Randall has led over the years to a false impression that Lincoln's approach to emancipation was not only slow but also methodical. It was not methodical. He allowed the issuance of the Proclamation to be controlled by events, and in that regard David Herbert Donald's famous biography of Lincoln captures an important quality of the president. The first page of that book contains only these words: "I CLAIM NOT TO HAVE CONTROLLED EVENTS, BUT CONFESS PLAINLY THAT EVENTS HAVE CONTROLLED ME. Abraham Lincoln to Albert G. Hodges, *April 4, 1864.*"[37]

Historians, friendly and hostile alike to his reputation, generally agree that Lincoln was a master politician. Building on the model of Randall's steps to emancipation, some modern historians find him at his best in the period surrounding the introduction of the Emancipation Proclamation. Lincoln, we have recently been told, was a "pragmatist" and recognized that his ideals "could only be achieved in gradual, step-by-step fashion through compromise and negotiation, in pace with progressive changes in public opinion and political realities." According to this interpretation, "Lincoln the politician was a master of misdirection, of appearing to appease conservatives while manipulating them toward the acceptance of radical policies." So historians now see, in the period leading up to the issuance of the preliminary Emancipation Proclamation, not exactly the conservative course Randall perceived, but an exemplification of "political legerdemain" practiced for the sake of a radical program.[38]

It is, in fact, utterly impossible to see a rational pattern in Lincoln's record during the period between the announcement to the cabinet of his intention to issue a Proclamation on July 22, 1862, and the actual appearance of the preliminary document on September 22. At that initial cabinet meeting, Secretary of State William H. Seward argued forcefully that the Proclamation must await military victory or else be taken as a sign of weakness and desperation on the part of the administration. That advice caused Lincoln to delay public announcement pending a battlefield victory, and it obviously made any concerted effort at preparing the ground of public opinion difficult because no one knew when the Proclamation would be issued. While he waited, not knowing when the Army of the Potomac would enjoy battlefield success, Lincoln responded to critics — Horace Greeley in one instance and a group of Chicago churchmen in another — who were vexed by the delay in helping slaves and strenuously urging emancipation. The letters Lincoln wrote to them allowed historians in later years to undermine the moral authority and dignity of the Proclamation.

To these was added the meeting with African American leaders in the White House on August 14, 1862. This meeting was arranged by the administration's officer in charge of colonization, James Mitchell, the Methodist preacher and professional colonization agent who previously worked on that problem in Indiana and Illinois. In a performance that was embarrassing at the time and remains so to this day, the president made racial difference the salient point: "You and we are different races. We have between us a broader difference than exists between almost any other two races." He blamed the war on the presence of African Americans in America: "But for your race among us there could not be war." He pointed out that the "ban" placed upon African Americans by the other people in the country was "a fact with which we have to deal. I cannot alter it if I would." Lincoln concluded, "It is better for us both, therefore, to be separated." And then he launched into a sales pitch for the men present to lead their people out of the country to a Central American colony said to be rich in coal deposits![39]

Lincoln did not know how proximate the announcement of the Emancipation Proclamation was, because he had made it hostage to a Union military victory. It would be difficult to say that there was any particular timing in the scheduling of this meeting. Had there been a military victory on August 1, 1862, instead of September 17, presumably Lincoln would have issued the Proclamation as promised, and the purpose of this meeting would not have been to pave the way for emancipation. Maybe it would not have occurred at all. But it did occur, and the meeting seems like the culmination of Lincoln's long-standing interest in colonization.

Lincoln could hardly have done a poorer job of managing the news of the Emancipation Proclamation. Indeed, some newspapers could publish in their sheets the day after he issued the Proclamation Lincoln's own statement made to a group of Chicago churchmen in the White House on September 17 *before* he announced the Proclamation but only available to the press on September 23 *after* the Proclamation was issued. To these churchmen advocating emancipation Lincoln replied, "What *good* would such a proclamation of emancipation from me do, especially as we are now situated? I do not want to issue a document that the whole world will see must necessarily be inoperative, like the Pope's bull against the comet!"[40] These remarks were published by the Chicagoans after they had returned home to Illinois. Lincoln had lost control of the timing of the statement on emancipation. The result was that newspaper readers could read Lincoln on the twenty-third saying the Emancipation Proclamation, issued the day before, was "inoperative" and impractical.

Lincoln afforded his critics many opportunities by his temporary loss of political mastery.[41] Even after he issued the Proclamation, the president still failed to get a grip on the public relations of the administration. An example of Lincoln's lack of attention to timing can be seen in his issuance on September 24, 1862 (only two days after he publicly announced the preliminary Emancipation Proclamation), of a new presidential proclamation suspending the writ of habeas corpus and declaring martial law. His critics, especially Benjamin R. Curtis, would charge that both proclamations derived from the same expansive and potentially despotic theory of presidential power. By this ill-timed proclamation suspending the writ of habeas corpus, Lincoln allowed his critics to label his act of liberation a part of a pattern of despotic rule.

It does not appear that there was an emergency demanding the orders of the twenty-fourth, which responded to a situation that had been brewing for weeks. Yet it served to lend some credence to the accusations of those who found the Emancipation Proclamation rooted in a despotic view of the Constitution. We now know that Lincoln had little interest in expanding presidential power. But the president had abdicated control of the timing of emancipation. The evidence on the September 24 proclamation on habeas corpus is limited, but from all appearances, Lincoln simply lost control of timing public statements again. To the president, emancipation was one policy and military mobilization was another, and he never stopped to think what the two proclamations would look like reproduced in the nation's press at dates so near each other.

Presumably, the habeas corpus proclamation had nothing to do with cultivating public opinion and everything to do with national security. Military recruiting fell in the summer of 1862 after McClellan's disastrous Peninsula campaign, and the administration resorted to a draft of militia to fill quotas. The War Department, fearing resistance to this draft, issued a series of drastic orders on August 8, 1862, "to prevent evasion of military duty and for the suppression of disloyal practices." They included the following:

1. By direction of the President of the United States it is hereby ordered that until further order no citizen liable to be drafted into the militia shall be allowed to go to a foreign country. And all marshals, deputy marshals and military officers of the United States are directed, and all police authorities especially at the ports of the United States on the seaboards and on the frontier . . . are hereby authorized and directed to arrest and detain any person or persons about to depart from the United States in violation of this order and report to Maj. L. C. Turner, judge-advocate at Washington City, for further instructions . . .

2. Any person liable to draft who shall absent himself from his country or State before such draft is made will be arrested by any

provost-marshal or other United States or State officer . . . and conveyed to the nearest military post or depot and placed on military duty for the term of the draft, and the expenses of his own arrest and conveyance to such post or depot and also the sum of $5 as a reward to the officer who shall have made such arrest shall be deducted from his pay.

3. The writ of habeas corpus is hereby suspended in respect to all persons so arrested and detained and in respect to all persons arrested for disloyal practices.

The secretary of war stated later that Lincoln gave verbal instructions to issue these orders and read the draft of them in the secretary's presence. Another order published the same day was clearly a forerunner of Lincoln's September proclamation on habeas corpus. Lincoln directed:

1. That all U.S. marshals and superintendents or chiefs of police of any town, city, or district be, and they are hereby, authorized and directed to arrest and imprison any person or persons who may be engaged, by act, speech, or writing, in discouraging volunteer enlistments, or in any way giving aid and comfort to the enemy, or in any other disloyal practice against the United States.

2. That immediate report be made to Maj. L. C. Turner, judge-advocate, in order that such persons may be tried before a military commission.[42]

The subsequent presidential proclamation of September 24 dealt with the same militia draft problem. However, the problem had shrunk, not grown, in the meantime. On September 8, 1862, Major Turner issued an order stating that because the "quota of volunteers and enrollment of militia" had been "completed in several States, the necessity for stringent enforcement of the orders of the War Department in respect to volunteering and drafting no longer exists." He rescinded all arrests stemming from violations of the restrictions on travel and declared that "arrests for violation of these orders, and for disloyal practices, will hereafter be made only upon" his express order or that of state officials.[43] The surviving copy of the September 24 proclamation suspending the writ of habeas corpus is not written in Lincoln's hand and is only signed by him. Moreover, we know that he had already okayed the idea of the stringent August 8 orders. Presumably someone came to him from the War Department with a draft of the proclamation ready for him to sign around the twenty-fourth.

It is not clear why Lincoln issued the habeas corpus proclamation when he did. It was a mistake to do so since the problem it aimed to solve, the militia draft, was largely over with by then, and the timing left the president vulnerable to charges that he issued drastic edicts at will. If he had allowed the War Department, like the Chicago clergymen, to control the timing of the appearance of information coming from the White House, he had made a mistake — and one of a pattern with the mistakes he made before issuing the Emancipation Proclamation.

In the case of the Emancipation Proclamation, history stands witness to the longest period of loss of political mastery in Lincoln's whole life.[44] The public relations debacle recalls the original advice Lincoln received at the first cabinet meeting on the Proclamation. Postmaster General Montgomery Blair had said it would cost the Republicans the fall elections to issue the Emancipation Proclamation before November. History has applauded Lincoln's willingness to sacrifice political advantage for moral principle in spurning that advice, but, in fact, he might have done better to listen to Blair. He could have issued the Proclamation after the elections and not delayed by one second the actual freeing of any enslaved person, because the preliminary Proclamation gave the states in rebellion one hundred days to avoid the effects of the Proclamation by returning to the Union. The offer was an empty gesture, and everyone at the time knew it; Lincoln could have issued the same preliminary Proclamation in November and given the states in rebellion thirty days to reconsider their position and possibly avoid the effects of the Proclamation. In that instance, the proximity to the drastic enforcement of the militia draft, at least, would have been avoided. Moreover, the waiting period stipulated in the preliminary Emancipation Proclamation, which was of arbitrary duration, could have provided the window of time for Lincoln to implement a campaign, already devised, to cultivate public opinion.

Instead, in the actual waiting period that followed the announcement of the momentous Proclamation on September 22, Lincoln continued to stumble politically and to send mixed signals on emancipation. Almost immediately after the announcement, he expressed concern that the Proclamation might be perceived in Europe as a sign the North was losing and desperate. On September 24 he drafted a letter for American statesman Edward Everett to carry to Europe:

> Whom it may concern
>
> Hon Edward Everett goes to Europe shortly. His reputation & the present condition of our country are such, that his visit there is sure

to attract notice and may be misconstrued. I therefore think fit to say, that he bears no mission from this government, and yet no gentleman is better able to correct misunderstandings in the minds of foreigners, in regard to American affairs.[45]

Why did he not say how happy he was that an unofficial American ambassador could now be met in Europe as a messenger from a liberated land? Lincoln seemed almost naively impatient for results at the same time. When Vice President Hannibal Hamlin congratulated him on the Proclamation, Lincoln revealed that he was in a funk:

It is known to some that while I hope something from the proclamation, my expectations are not as sanguine as are those of some friends. The time for its effect southward has not come; but northward the effect should be instantaneous.

It is six days old, and while commendation in newspapers and by distinguished individuals is all that a vain man could wish, the stocks have declined, and troops come forward more slowly than ever. . . . The North responds to the proclamation sufficiently in breath; but breath alone kills no rebels.[46]

It is no wonder Lincoln marked this letter "Strictly private."

The president had not recovered his political equilibrium even by December, when he sent his annual message to Congress. Lincoln only sowed doubt by proposing three amendments to the U.S. Constitution that fell a good deal short of the Thirteenth Amendment to come in 1865. They provided that any state arranging to abolish slavery by 1900 would receive federal compensation for every slave freed. Lincoln also wished to compensate loyal masters of slaves who had already escaped to freedom "by the chances of the war." Finally, an amendment would authorize Congress to appropriate money for colonizing "free colored persons, with their own consent."[47] Was it possible that emancipation might, despite the Proclamation of September 22, be postponed until the twentieth century?

It was December 1, 1862, and emancipation was only thirty days away— or was it? No one could tell. Even now Lincoln was confusing the public, not preparing it. Then, in the same message, he backed off his earnest advocacy of colonization and argued that slavery was what made African Americans desire to leave the South; its end would cause them to stay there and not move to the North. In giving the Northern public that assurance, the president somewhat reinforced the practical utility of what I have called "constitutional racism." As his mind raced on with arguments and counter-arguments, Lincoln finally concluded that if the freedmen did emigrate to the North after all: "In any event, cannot the north decide for itself, whether to receive them?" Stephen A. Douglas could not have said it better.[48]

The point is not to dwell on what might have happened in some counterfactual scenario, but to say that Lincoln might have done better during this whole period to have sought and heeded political advice from the members of his cabinet and other politicians. Although he did accept the counsel offered by Secretary Seward, the president's other close associates seemed mystified by his decision to issue the habeas corpus proclamation on September 24. The next day, on September 25, Secretary of the Navy Gideon Welles wrote in his diary: "The President has issued a proclamation on martial law, — suspension of *habeas corpus* he terms it, meaning, of course, a suspension of the privilege of the writ of *habeas corpus*. Of this proclamation, I knew nothing until I saw it in the papers, and am not sorry that I did not." Welles did have some sense that it was a mistake to flex so much executive muscle in so brief a window of time. "I question," he wrote, "the wisdom or utility of a multiplicity of proclamations striking deep on great questions."[49]

Criticism and Defense

Though the habeas corpus proclamation of September 24 had nothing to do with the Emancipation Proclamation, it had much to do with incensing Benjamin Robbins Curtis, who quoted both documents at the beginning of his pamphlet, entitled *Executive Power*, which attacked Lincoln for his expansive view of presidential power. Here is Curtis's extensive quotation from the habeas corpus proclamation:

> Whereas, it has become necessary to call into service not only volunteers, but also portions of the militia of the States by draft, in order to suppress the insurrection existing in the United States, and disloyal persons are not adequately restrained by the ordinary processes of law from hindering this measure, and from giving aid and comfort in various ways to the insurrection:
>
> Now, therefore, be it ordered, —
>
> *First.* That during the existing insurrection, and as a necessary measure for suppressing the same, all rebels and insurgents, their aiders and abettors, within the United States, and all persons discouraging volunteer enlistments, resisting militia drafts, or guilty of any disloyal practice, affording aid and comfort to the rebels against the

authority of the United States, shall be subject to martial law, and liable to trial and punishment by courts-martial or military commission.

Second. That the writ of habeas corpus is suspended in respect to all persons arrested, or who are now, or hereafter during the rebellion shall be, imprisoned in any fort, camp, arsenal, military prison, or other place of confinement by any military authority, or by the sentence of any court-martial or military commission.[50]

Curtis then added the text of the orders issued by Secretary of War Edwin M. Stanton to implement the president's proclamation. These described an elaborate system of provost marshals whose duty it was "to arrest all deserters, whether regulars, volunteers, or militia, and send them to the nearest military commander or military post, where they can be cared for and sent to their respective regiments; to arrest, upon the warrant of the judge advocate, all disloyal persons subject to arrest under the orders of the war department; to inquire into and report treasonable practices, seize stolen or embezzled property of the government, detect spies of the enemy, and perform . . . other duties."[51]

Curtis also focused on a part of Lincoln's response to the Chicago churchmen, delivered before the Emancipation Proclamation but appearing in the press only after its issuance. From that ill-considered document Curtis highlighted the president's statement, "Understand, I raise no objection against it [an emancipation proclamation] on legal or constitutional grounds; for, *as commander-in-chief of the army and navy, in time of war, I suppose I have a right to take any measure which may best subdue the enemy.*"[52] In truth, the statement was a rough-and-ready approximation of Lincoln's views on the subject, but it did not represent the careful language Lincoln employed in the anodyne proclamation itself. Even in what amounted to a stump speech written about a year later, reiterating the grounds justifying the Emancipation Proclamation, Lincoln was more circumspect:

I think the constitution invests its commander-in-chief, with the law of war, in time of war. . . . Is there — has there ever been — any question that by the law of war, property, both of enemies and friends, may be taken when needed? And is it not needed whenever it helps us, or hurts the enemy? Armies, the world over, destroy enemies' property when they can not use it; and even destroy their own to keep it from the enemy. Civilized belligerents do all in their power to help themselves, or hurt the enemy, except a few things regarded as barbarous or cruel. Among the exceptions are the massacre of vanquished foes, and non-combatants, male and female.[53]

That statement (as opposed to the one Lincoln made to the Chicago churchmen) probably would not have mollified Curtis, but it would definitely have made Curtis's path a little rougher.

Curtis criticized Lincoln's expansive idea of the powers of the presidency mercilessly, but he did not forthrightly indicate the special problem of constitutional interpretation of the description, or lack thereof, of the president's powers in Article II. The principle of Article I had long seemed clear: the Constitution described in so many words what powers Congress had. The format was, "The Congress shall have power," and there followed a long list of powers preceded by "to," as "to regulate commerce." The principle of Article II was different, for there the Constitution said only that "the executive power shall be vested in a President of the United States of America"; it did not go on to say what "the executive power" entailed. It did stipulate that the "President shall be Commander in Chief of the Army and Navy of the United States" and that he was authorized "to make treaties" and to "fill up all vacancies that may happen during the recess of the Senate." But it was left to surmise what the executive powers were. Most thinkers presumed that the executive powers had to be used to "execute" laws passed by Congress, and certainly Lincoln was not executing any law of Congress in his two proclamations. To do so in the case of emancipation would be merely to enforce the Confiscation Acts. He wanted to go beyond those. But the powers of the commander in chief seemed more open-ended — at least to the pamphleteers who answered Curtis's argument. Curtis did not convey the meaning of the Constitution accurately when he said that "the military power of the President is derived solely from the Constitution; and it is as sufficiently defined there as his purely civil power."[54] True enough, perhaps, but Curtis should have added that the civil powers were hardly "defined" at all.

Into that great void of definition of executive power and the power of the commander in chief Lincoln's defenders leaped with ready explanations of powers to be inferred from his position in government. Curtis tried to confine the power to something roughly equivalent to the authority to give battlefield orders to enlisted men. "He is the general-in-chief," Curtis explained, "and as such, in prosecuting war, may do what generals in the field are allowed to do within the sphere of their actual operations, *in subordination to the laws of their country, from which alone they derive their authority.*"[55] That was an inference from the Constitution, a matter of sound constitutional interpretation perhaps, but not a quotation from the article on the executive. The only ideas of "subordination" actually communicated in Article II came in the provision that the president could be impeached and that his elected term lasted four years.

As practical limitations during the Civil War, neither the threat of impeachment nor the term limit proved to be much hindrance to executive power — at least until the war came to the election of 1864. The president assumed office almost exactly when the Civil War began, and therefore he was in command for a long time — long enough to have caused, fought, won, and negotiated peace in two Mexican-American wars. Impeachment was unlikely once the Southern Democrats left Congress for the Confederacy and Republicans gained firm control of Congress. Those in the North who opposed the Lincoln administration searched desperately for legal limitations on the executive.

Curtis's *Executive Power* gained considerable circulation. There were three different versions of the edition published by Little, Brown in 1862: one of 34 pages, one of 31 pages, and one of 29 pages. Another edition was printed in Cambridge in 1862, and the *New York World* put out a 15-page version. But it was not revised and reissued in 1863 or in 1864 for the presidential canvass. Today forty libraries report copies of the Little, Brown edition of 34 pages, but nearly that number have copies of the 31- and 29-page versions as well. We know that the pamphlet had an effect, for it prompted at least two exasperated responses.

When Benjamin Curtis attacked the so-called faulty view of the Constitution that underlay suspension of the writ of habeas corpus and the preliminary Emancipation Proclamation, it shocked Republicans, for Curtis had become, because of his dissent in the *Dred Scott* case, something of an antislavery hero. When the *New York Tribune* published a pamphlet edition of the notorious *Dred Scott* decision back in 1860, it included Taney's opinion and added Curtis's dissenting opinion in full (as rebuttal) along with thumbnail abstracts of other opinions and resolutions from the New York legislature denouncing the opinion.[56] Curtis provided the basic ammunition for constitutional criticism of the *Dred Scott* ruling — then and now. His attack on the president's policies could not be easily dismissed as predictable partisanship and had to be answered. Charles P. Kirkland and Grosvenor P. Lowrey, lawyers in New York, each independently decided to do it.

Kirkland rushed the first pamphlet response into print. *A Letter to the Hon. Benjamin R. Curtis, Late Judge of the Supreme Court of the United States, in Review of His Recently Published Pamphlet on the "Emancipation Proclamation" of the President* appeared before the end of 1862. Kirkland, like Curtis, maintained that he was of no party. He had voted against Lincoln in 1860 and in the most recent legislative election in New York had cast his ballot for a Democrat for state senator.[57]

Kirkland recognized the disadvantage to which the president was put by the proximity of the two proclamations, the one liberating and the other constricting liberty. He chided Curtis for not treating the two proclamations separately. Kirkland confined his arguments to what Curtis had said about the Emancipation Proclamation (at least to the degree he could separate the arguments in Curtis's work).[58]

Kirkland's principal charge was that Curtis had disguised his assault by saying it was an attack on "Executive Power." Lincoln had not justified the proclamation of emancipation as an executive power but as a power of the commander in chief, and the two were different. The latter power included the *"law of self-preservation"* (and here Kirkland reminded readers of the president's oath to "preserve, protect, and defend the Constitution"); it was not a matter of a law of Congress but of "belligerent right" and the "law of arms" and the "general principles of war."[59] His other main point was that Curtis had written as though no rebellion had occurred; he referred to the rebellious states as if they were like those in the loyal North, entitled to the protections of the U.S. Constitution.[60] Kirkland carefully pointed out that emancipation was not a punishment but a military strategy for defeating the enemy. He refused to believe that there was any important difference, as Curtis had argued, between a state as an enemy in war and the "governing majority" in a state as an enemy in war.[61]

The Proclamation liberated the property of the people in the enemy state. It was not a matter of meting out justice to individuals for the extent of their involvement in the Southern rebellion. It was a military strategy to bring victory. Kirkland asked whether anyone would deny that, if the United States were at war with a foreign nation on its border in which there were millions of slaves, there would be any problem with attempting to free those slaves as part of the war effort.[62] He denied that he was an abolitionist or a believer in the political and social equality of the white and black races, and he criticized Curtis for talking about slave insurrection.[63]

Grosvenor P. Lowrey's *The Commander-in-Chief; A Defence upon Legal Grounds of the Proclamation of Emancipation; and an Answer to Ex-Judge Curtis' Pamphlet, Entitled "Executive Power"* was the other pamphlet-length answer to Curtis. The first edition was published in New York in 1862, and a version with more extensive footnotes appeared in 1863.[64] If evidence from surviving copies in libraries can be trusted, it did not have quite the circulation of Curtis's pamphlet, but it was an able defense of the president and far more readable and less technical than the defense of the suspension of the writ of habeas corpus offered by Horace Binney earlier in the year.

Even so, Lowrey's pamphlet was well researched. He uncovered a number of events from American history that aided his case and to this day are little known. He did not reach back into a distant British past of common law precedent. He found a letter of President James K. Polk, of March 23, 1847, that endorsed military governments over enemy citizens.[65] But the most important work involved precedents for treating enemy slaves as property that could be legitimately confiscated in war. Lowrey did not rely, as most did, on John Quincy Adams's famous speeches on the Texas question for such doctrine. As a right in international law he could cite England's assertions in the American Revolution and in the War of 1812, France's in Santo Domingo in 1793–94, and Spain's "in Columbia, through General Morillo." Most interesting were the complex cases involving fugitive American slaves captured in war by American generals. He could point to the actions, in the Seminole Indian War, of General Thomas S. Jessup, who used fugitive slaves as guides and spies, then freed them and sent them west. "The administrations of Van Buren and Tyler sanctioned and approved his acts," Lowrey said. The escaped slave of a man named Pacheco who had fought in the same war against the United States was taken by the United States and, when Pacheco demanded his return, the slave was considered a prisoner of war and freed. Congress, he pointed out, rejected a bill to compensate Pacheco for his loss. Zachary Taylor, who was a slaveholder himself and had no antislavery reputation, refused to return escaped slaves to Florida owners who demanded them in the Seminole War of 1838, declared them prisoners of war, and freed them. General Edmund P. Gaines likewise refused to surrender to their owners fugitive slaves who had been fighting beside Seminoles, treated them as prisoners of war, and sent the former slaves to be relocated with the Indians in the West, effectively freeing them.[66] Unlike the slaves in the Confederacy, some of those captured in previous wars had sided with the enemy—but were freed anyway.

But these legal precedents, arising from situations of complicated loyalties, did not really make Lowrey's argument. Though he did not dwell on the difference as much as Kirkland did, Lowrey recognized the significance of the title of Curtis's pamphlet—*Executive Power*—and entitled his to mark the crucial contrast: *The Commander-in-Chief*. He said that the president derived his office of commander in chief directly from the Constitution but that the functions of the president as commander in chief "are extra-constitutional." The point was made in startling language, but the idea was a little more tame: the office of a commander in chief was not original with the Constitution, and its powers were not derived from the document but from the laws of war.[67] He depicted these as being different from the president's civil powers, which were original to the Constitution and were adequately described. He did not go into the vagueness of the "executive."

Lowrey also made an important distinction between the way a commander dealt with slave property and with the other property of the enemy. "The right, in time of war, to seize, destroy, convert, and transfer, the property of the enemy, is uncontroverted," he said, but the enemy's horse or wagon must actually fall into soldiers' hands to be seized. The case of the enemy who held slaves, on the other hand, was different. "The only possible way to deprive him of his horse and wagon, is to lay hands upon them — but we may reach his slave by proclamation, and invite him, as our ally and by our authority, to lay hands upon himself," he pointed out shrewdly.[68] And therein lay the answer to future generations of cynics who derided the Emancipation Proclamation for not really freeing anyone because it applied only to slaves in territory controlled by the enemy.

Lowrey then touched on a subject that the president would surely rather he had not:

> It is said that servile insurrection will ensue, and that non-combatants and innocents will suffer. Such is not the necessary consequence; and who has the requisite knowledge to affirm that it will take place? The object is to weaken the enemy by reducing his means of sustenance, and if insurrection by the freed laborers should transpire, it will be one of those unavoidable misfortunes which [Hugo] Grotius illustrates by the case of rapine in a captured town; and the destruction of women and children in a pirate-ship.[69]

The famous Dutch writer on international law had admitted that towns could be assaulted even though soldiers sometimes looted the places afterward and that naval vessels could fire on pirate ships even though their prisoners might suffer in the bombardment. Lowrey went on:

> Would it be considered by any one, contrary to the laws of war to encourage, in the centre of Alabama, resistance by loyal white men to the confederate government? And, if not, what is there about a black insurrection, except the bare possibility that the debased black — for whose continued debasement, in the midst of Christian civilization, the enemy alone is responsible — may be more cruel in his proceed-

ings; and which result, the enemy, but for misguided persistence in treason, might surely prevent?[70]

In this passage Lowrey had touched on the racist underpinnings of grand strategy. No one faulted Lincoln for encouraging the uprising against the Confederacy in East Tennessee. Parson Brownlow and other white East Tennesseans became heroes. Slave insurrection was another matter. The president never ventured out on such dangerous waters. Instead, he included in the revised and final version of his Emancipation Proclamation the following advice: "I hereby enjoin upon the people so declared to be free to abstain from all violence, unless in necessary self-defence; and I recommend to them that, in all cases when allowed, they labor faithfully for reasonable wages."[71]

Lowrey ended with a clear, systematic summary of his argument:

First: Abraham Lincoln, as Commander-in-chief in time of war, embodies all the executive war powers of the nation. Second: These powers are extra-constitutional, having their origin in the nature of things, and are recognized as an established code by all civilized nations. Third: Principal among them, is the right to end war and obtain security for the future, by destroying the cause of the war. Fourth: The proclamation in question is intended to have that effect, and is considered necessary to that end by the nation, speaking through its supreme military authority.[72]

Lowrey's principal direct complaint about Curtis's argument was that he refused to consider the Confederates as belligerents; rather, he viewed them as citizens with the protections and rights of the Constitution.

If Curtis chose not to explain the problems of interpretation of Article II of the Constitution and Lowrey exploited that great loophole, it must be said that Lowrey slighted some obvious problems of constitutional interpretation as well. He argued that the commander in chief had the necessary power to win the war with which he was tasked by the nation, and having that power meant that he could address each war's central purpose. In this particular conflict, the central purpose was to restore the rebellious states to their former constitutional relationship with the government. For Curtis, that was to return to a nation whose Constitution protected slavery. Lowrey wanted to prove that slavery was not part of the essential constitutional arrangement to which the states were to be returned. He contended: "Though often carelessly spoken of as a constitutional right, it [slavery] had no special constitutional warrant, over any other property right, but rested under the same general provision which reserves to the states all powers for the regulation of their local concerns not granted to the general government."[73] To win the war the president could certainly for the time destroy the enemy's right to this horse or that horse. And the same was true of slaves.

But slavery did apparently have constitutional status above that of horses. Horses were not mentioned in the Constitution and slaves were — three times, though not by name. It might be the case that the only protection of slavery was the reserved powers of the states, but Lowrey owed his readers some explanation of the three specific recognitions of slavery in the Constitution — in the three-fifths clause, in the clause about the termination of the international slave trade, and, perhaps most problematically, in the fugitive slave clause.

Some Unexplored Precedents

The pamphleteers in general missed some obvious bets. Lowrey did find a letter of Polk's endorsing military government of enemy territory, but there was more in the judicial record from the Mexican-American War. It was an international war instead of an insurrection, true, but it was waged under the administration of a Democratic president in the shadow of the expansive view of the presidency taken by the founder of the party, Andrew Jackson. All one had to do was to look at the Supreme Court reports, as former Supreme Court justice Benjamin R. Curtis and the enterprising Charles P. Kirkland did, to find at least two cases of interest. And it was well known that trials by military commission had been devised first in the Mexican-American War — under the presidency of Democrat James K. Polk. Curtis found the *Mitchell v. Harmony* case (though, according to Grosvenor Lowrey, Curtis misinterpreted it), and Kirkland found the embarrassing *Cross v. Harrison* case.

No doubt it was difficult to locate the precedents. On the surface, *Mitchell v. Harmony* and *Cross v. Harrison* had nothing about them to call attention to their being war-related cases, and they were decided years after the Mexican-American War was over — in 1851 and 1853, respectively. But one suspects that the Republicans might not have been eager to explore the possibilities for models of government action in the history of the Mexican-American War, since antislavery men did not recall it fondly and many former Whigs in the Republican Party had opposed the war and the measures of the Democratic president. Most important, that was the case with the Republican president during the Civil War: Abraham Lincoln had sharply criticized Polk and the Democrats in opposing the war in Mexico as unnecessary and unconstitutional.[74]

Lincoln had always been careful in discussing the Mexican war and the stance he took on it while serving his only term in the U.S. Congress. In 1858, when he was running against Stephen A. Douglas for the Senate, Illinois Democrats searched his record, and the *Chicago Times* attacked Lincoln for having allegedly opposed a bill appropriating money for medicines and nurses for the American soldiers in the war.[75] The Democrats were mistaken. As Lincoln confidently told the editor of the *Chicago Tribune*, "You may safely deny that I ever gave any vote for withholding any supplies whatever, from officers or soldiers of the Mexican war. I have examined the Journals a good deal; and besides I can not be mistaken; for I had my eye always upon it."[76] Once again, what mattered most in Lincoln's constitutional education was not his law practice or his knowledge of English history or the crabbed books on pleading and evidence he read, but his broad practical knowledge of American political history. He knew, well before he went to Washington, about what we can call today America's unwritten constitution. The War of 1812 and its aftermath had established, by the example of the speedy demise of the Federalist Party, which opposed the war, that no party could vote against supplies for the soldiers already in the field and hope to survive. The novice representative from Illinois knew that.

Still, it was generally embarrassing if not constitutionally telling that the president now presiding over the greatest war in American history in 1862 had in some fashion opposed America's previous war — against Mexico. The Democrats never managed to exploit that effectively, but here and there they tried. Thus some members of the Ohio Democratic convention, which had nominated the notorious Clement L. Vallandigham for governor in 1863, recalled Lincoln's term in Congress:

> During the war with Mexico many of the political opponents of the [Polk] Administration . . . thought it their duty to denounce and oppose the war . . . with equal reason it might have been said of them, that their discussions before the people were calculated to discourage enlistments, "to prevent the raising of troops" & to induce desertions. . . .
>
> When gentlemen of high standing . . . including your Excellency opposed in discussions before the people, the policy of the Mexican War, were they "warring upon the Military" & did this "give the Military constitutional jurisdiction to lay hands upon them?[77]

Once again, Lincoln could safely rebuff such critics, but this time he had to be more careful — in fact, he had to be downright sly. Before he got to the meat of his argument with them on the constitutional power to suspend the writ of habeas corpus and institute under that umbrella a broad internal security program, he explained to the Ohio Democrats: "I dislike to waste a word on a merely personal point; but I must respectfully assure you that you will find yourselves at fault should you ever seek for evidence to prove your assumption that I 'opposed, in open discussions before the people, the policy of the Mexican war.'"[78] Lincoln had not given any speeches in Illinois against the war, which broke out at about the time he was elected, but he did give a well-known address about the war while a member of Congress (copies of which he eagerly franked home to his constituents). Technically, perhaps, such a speech did not come "in open discussion before the people."

We will never know whom the legacy of the Mexican-American War would have embarrassed the most in the political battles of the 1860s or how they might have shaped constitutional interpretation, but it is worthwhile to examine the constitutional record more closely than most of the politicians in the Civil War did. Just after the issuance of the *Merryman* decision, an anonymous contributor who signed his article "C.M.E.," offered "Some Points for . . . Taney" on "Martial Law" in the *New York Times*. He noted that Roger B. Taney had "ruled in favor of military seizure of private goods" in *Cross v. Harrison* and "in favor of a war tariff" in *Mitchell v. Harmony*.[79] The notion was later lost, but the author was right that the opinions were relevant, and he was probably correct in seeing that they were problematic for the author of the *Ex parte Merryman* ruling. *Cross v. Harrison* almost certainly could have been put to use by the president's Republican defenders. Decided by the Taney Court in the December term of 1853, the complicated case involved a claim by the New York import-export firm of Cross, Hobson and Company that it was due a refund of duties paid the government on goods imported into California at the end of the Mexican-American War. The United States had imposed a war tariff while occupying California as conquered enemy territory, and then some delay ensued before California was brought under U.S. tariff laws and a proper collector of customs was in place. Much of the merchants' claim hinged on the period after the treaty of peace ending the war, but the issue of the wartime tariff also figured in their complaint. The Supreme Court, in refusing an award to the merchants and holding the customs collector not liable, ruled on the constitutionality of some actions of the commander in chief.

In rehearsing the facts of the case, the attorney general noted:

> In the war with Mexico, the port of San Francisco was conquered by the arms of the United States, in the year 1846, and shortly afterwards

the United States had military possession of all of Upper California. Early in 1847 the President . . . , as constitutional commander-in-chief of the army and navy, authorized the military and naval command- ers . . . in California to exercise the belligerent rights of a conqueror, and to form a civil and military government for the conquered ter- ritory, with power to impose duties on imports and tonnage for the support of such government, and of the army, which had the conquest in possession.

This was done, and tonnage and import duties were levied under a war tariff, which had been established by the civil government for that purpose, until official notice was received by the civil and military Governor of California, that a treaty of peace had been made with Mexico.[80]

Justice James M. Wayne wrote the opinion of the Court, in which he ruled that "no one can doubt that these orders of the President, and the action of our army and navy commander in California, in conformity with them, was according to the law of arms and the right of conquest, or that they were operative until the ratification and exchange of a treaty of peace."[81] Wayne did not elaborate much on that point, but he did say that "such would be the case upon general principles in respect to war and peace between na- tions."[82] It was a long way from this position to the one on the powers of the commander in chief taken by Lincoln's defenders later, but there was nothing in *Cross v. Harrison* to complicate matters for Lincoln. "General principles" of "war and peace" explained the commander in chief's powers, not powers specifically delegated to him by the Constitution. Once again, the precedent, such as it was, fell on the side of the administration. *Cross v. Harrison*, which the diligent Charles Kirkland discovered, would have been of use to Grosvenor Lowrey, who argued, among other things, that the laws of war invested in the power of the commander in chief meant that "we may suspend his [the enemy's] civil government, and establish military rule in it, for the management of civil affairs."[83]

The case of *Mitchell v. Harmony* was not as much help to Lincoln's oppo- nents as Curtis thought (as Lowrey, in criticizing Curtis, shrewdly pointed out). This complicated opinion, written by Roger B. Taney himself in the December 1851 term of the Court, made a U.S. colonel liable for nearly $100,000 for merchandise, wagons, and mules lost by a merchant named Manuel X. Harmony. Harmony was a Santa Fe Trail trader who became involved in General Alexander W. Doniphan's campaign in the Mexican- American War. He followed in the wake of the American army, trading goods with conquered Mexicans as part of the administration's policy to mollify the local inhabitants and prevent an uprising of the people of Mexico. But as the campaign for Sacramento heated up, Doniphan and Colonel David D. Mitchell forced a reluctant Harmony to continue with them farther into enemy territory, and he eventually lost all of his wagons, animals, and goods. In New York, a federal jury held the colonel liable for the property. The U.S. Supreme Court upheld the decision.

Benjamin R. Curtis thought he saw in the decision grist for his mill of criticism of the Emancipation Proclamation. "The case of Mitchell *vs.* Harmony," Curtis wrote, "presented for the decision of the Supreme Court of the United States the question of the extent of the right of a commanding general in the field to appropriate private property to the public service, and it was decided that such an appropriation might be made, in case it should be rendered necessary by an immediate and pressing danger or urgent necessity existing at the time, and not admitting of delay, but not otherwise."[84] He quoted at some length from Taney's crystal clear opinion in the case, then concluded: "The wagons, mules, and packages seized by General Doniphan, in that case, were of essential service in his brilliant and successful attack on the lines of Chihuahua. But this did not save him from being liable to their owner as a mere wrongdoer, under the Constitution and laws of the United States."[85] Lowrey very properly commented later: "The professional reader will be embarrassed to discover how the case of Mitchell *vs.* Harmony. . . , which Judge Curtis cites, can apply to the power of the Commander-in-chief to take the property of an armed enemy. That was an action against a lieutenant-colonel for seizing, unnecessarily, the property of a loyal citizen, and it would almost seem that the Judge had forgotten that the persons whose property it is now proposed to take, *are armed rebels, who have no standing except in the tribunal of war.*"[86]

Lowrey had a point, but so did Curtis. That Curtis did not make it clear that Harmony was an American and not a Mexican belligerent was slippery and smacked of courtroom advocacy. Still, two points could be argued. First, the question of the enemy status of Confederate slaveholders was not well established and would not be until the decisions in the *Prize Cases* were reported. Second, and more important, was the sort of tight reasoning about private property in which Curtis indulged—following in this case the lead of Taney himself, who pointed out as the lesson of the case, after citing a British precedent, that "this case shows how carefully the rights of private property are guarded by the laws in England; and they are certainly not less valued nor less securely guarded under the Constitution and laws of the United States."[87] Curtis thus argued:

In time of war, a military commander, whether he be the commander-in-chief, or one of his subordinates, must possess and exercise powers both over the persons and the property of citizens which do not exist in time of peace. But he possesses and exercises such powers, *not in spite of the Constitution and laws of the United States, or in derogation from their authority, but in virtue thereof and in strict subordination thereto.* The general who moves his army over private property in the course of his operations in the field, or who impresses into the public service means of transportation, or subsistence, to enable him to act against the enemy, or who seizes persons within his lines as spies, or destroys supplies in immediate danger of falling into the hands of the enemy, uses authority unknown to the Constitution and laws of the United States in time of *peace*; but not unknown to that Constitution and those laws in time of *war.* The power to declare war, includes the power to use the customary and necessary means effectually to carry it on. As Congress may institute a state of war, it may legislate into existence and place under executive control the means for its prosecution. And, in time of war without any special legislation, not the commander-in-chief only, but every commander of an expedition, or of a military post, is lawfully empowered by the Constitution and laws of the United States to do whatever is necessary, and is sanctioned by the laws of war, to accomplish the lawful objects of his command. But it is obvious that this implied authority must find early limits somewhere.

And where exactly were those limits? Curtis's answer was "that over all persons and property *within the sphere of his actual operations in the field,* he may lawfully exercise such restraint and control as the successful prosecution of his particular military enterprise may, in his honest judgment, absolutely require."[88] This position was close to Joel Parker's analogy between the suspension of the writ of habeas corpus and the rules governing a military encampment.

Examined closely, Curtis's argument is really not helpful for understanding the Emancipation Proclamation or the underlying authority of the commander in chief. However, that was the way lawyers thought. And Lincoln was a lawyer and sometimes thought that way, too. There is not much difference in reading Curtis, above, and reading Lincoln as he lectured his old friend Orville Hickman Browning on the difference between General Frémont's authority to seize property and the emancipation of slaves. After Lincoln's analysis, also quoted earlier, he said the farm and field (and slave) temporarily seized by the general did not have their future condition decided by the general. Lawmakers had to determine that. Similarly, Curtis concluded, "The military power over citizens and their property is a power to *act*, not a power to prescribe rules for *future* action. It springs from present pressing emergencies, and is limited by them. It cannot assume the functions of the statesman or legislator, and make provision for future or distant arrangements."[89]

Lincoln, unlike Curtis, changed his mind later. When President Lincoln explained the revocation of Frémont's proclamation he was writing to Senator Browning, a noted lawyer and an aspirant to the Supreme Court, and Lincoln might even have exaggerated the lawyerliness of his approach to the subject. But we can see, once again, that the lawyer's way of thinking was not really very helpful. Curtis admitted he was not considering "the functions of a statesman." The lawyer needs the precision of physical conditions. A military necessity to him is an action that must be taken to avoid being killed or surrounded by the enemy *now*. Then the lawyers can go about establishing the degree of danger according to witnesses — How many miles away was the enemy? Did the enemy have superior numbers and arms? How many rations were left for our army? Was there daylight for an attack? Was it getting cold so that the farmer's fence rails were essential to avoid frostbitten hands that very night? Such thinking could lead to a fair and quantifiably precise judgment of liability, but it was not exactly the same thing as geopolitical matters of foresight, statesmanship, and grand strategy. Without unsettling the security of the enemy's slave property, the war might have been lost, but Lincoln could not prove in court that the Union, with its vast armies and resources and open lines of communication, was going to lose a great battle tomorrow in Tennessee without the action of the slaves. He could not prove that freeing the slaves would help the armies keep warm in a particular camp that night. The task of the commander in chief was not to dwell on matters of tactics and proximate threats of extinction of military lives. He was to think of matters of grand strategy and a whole war and a whole nation for a long time to come. Such matters were more in the line of work of a commander in chief than what Curtis or Parker or Lincoln himself (in talking to Browning) described. It was telltale that Curtis likened the commander in chief to the general in chief.

Furthermore, the commander in chief simply could not be held to such a precise standard. He could not, as Lincoln sensibly informed Browning, explain what he would *not* do to the enemy. Likewise, the commander in chief could not determine with any precision whether the strategic measure was necessary to avert defeat the next day and at Washington or any other particular place. That would be to lend to the enemy the advantage of depressing public opinion at home. It might even cause panic and financial depression. The president had to say, artfully, that these measures were necessary for victory — not that they were necessary to avoid looming defeat. Surrender, not action, would be the result of the application of such a precise legal standard. For the commander in chief's grand strategy, the jury had to be out longer.

The length of time for judgment might not be as long in the case of suspension of the writ of habeas corpus and domestic civil liberties. If that program was ultimately intended as or was distorted into a program for destruction of the loyal opposition, the republic could not hold back judgment on that. Lincoln seemed to have known that instinctively. He seemed to see the Emancipation Proclamation and the suspension of the writ of habeas corpus both as derived from the Constitution but from different parts of the Constitution (the one from Article II making the president commander in chief and the other from Article I, section 9, permitting the suspension of the writ of habeas corpus). To question one was not necessarily to question the other. It was a shame that the two proclamations, emancipation on the twenty-second and suspension on the twenty-fourth, had to come together so closely as to permit someone like Curtis to see them both as rooted in the same uncontrollably expansive view of the executive. Lincoln did not really have such a view. He was a problem-solver, looking here in the Constitution for the authority to solve this problem and there in the Constitution for the authority to solve that problem.

Even examined closely, the legalistic arguments of Lincoln as a lawyer talking to Browning, or of Curtis or of Parker or of Taney assessing Doniphan's liability for the wagons and mules and merchandise of the merchant Harmony, brought precision but not genuine clarity. As Lowrey said, it simply made a difference whether the problem concerned civilians who were friendly and marching along with one's own army or concerned civilians whose allegiance was owed to an enemy government dedicated to destruction of one's army. And someone needed to make the tough judgment about civilians who lived within the boundaries of such a hostile government's jurisdiction but were by choice or necessity bystanders when one's armies appeared.

It did not help to see the commander in chief as a glorified colonel. Legalistic thinking could advance the debate no further. Even the law schools had failed: Parker was a professor at Harvard. Curtis and Parker had an old-fashioned view of the commander in chief — as George Washington, a president who could, if necessary, leave his desk and mount a horse and be the chief commander in the field. Time and technology had made it so that the Constitution had at the very least to be sensibly interpreted to fit modern times and new styles of command.[90]

In a book that argued that the president and the Republicans found the Constitution "adequate" to the necessary war effort, Harold Hyman had surprisingly little to say about the Emancipation Proclamation, and Lincoln deemed the Emancipation Proclamation necessary to win the war.[91] The problem for Hyman was surely this: The Constitution was not exactly "adequate" for emancipation. Lincoln's key defender on the question — Grosvenor Lowrey, the Horace Binney of emancipation — made the argument that the office of the commander in chief was derived from the Constitution but that the powers of the commander in chief were, frankly, "extra-constitutional."

The best work on the subject is Allen C. Guelzo's volume, *Lincoln's Emancipation Proclamation: The End of Slavery in America*. It is the only book, for example, that deals fully with the critical pamphlet literature. But the study, essentially definitive, has left a little room for correction. In the first place, Guelzo is too dismissive of the pamphlet defenders of the Proclamation. "No scorecard tallied up the points made by each debater," he concludes, "but taking the debate as a whole, it is hard to see the Proclamation's defense counsel as anything but marginally successful in making a direct constitutional case for it." He goes on to say: "Grosvenor Lowrey admitted that the war powers he spent so much time applauding as 'the faithful friends and servants of the Constitution . . . are not constitutional powers; and I am compelled to call them extra-constitutional for want of a better name.' Parker and Curtis believed they already knew what that name was — *illegal* — and Lowrey's admission can only have brought dry smiles to the Boston jurists' faces."[92]

But here we can see, if nowhere else, the virtues of constitutional history. That dismissal of the defense counsel underestimates the nature of constitutional interpretation and in particular the inherent differences in interpreting the powers of the executive in Article II and those of the legislature in Article I. "Extra-constitutional" may well be a slippery and often dangerous term, but in this instance at least it cannot properly be equated with "illegal." What Lowrey meant was only that the powers of the executive are not enumerated in the document in the same systematic way the powers of the legislature are, and therefore it requires knowledge of things outside of the U.S. Constitution to understand executive power and the power of the commander in chief.

Moreover, in showing proper respect for constitutional argument and, especially, in emphasizing Lincoln's own respect for constitutional argument, Guelzo cannot quite release himself from the thrall of thinking of Lincoln as a lawyer. It was not Lincoln's ability to think as a lawyer that enabled him to justify and draft and defend the Emancipation Proclamation, it was his release from that way of thinking. While he thought and reasoned and argued in a lawyerly fashion, as he did in the letter to Browning about Frémont's proclamation, Lincoln could only think of proving liability and anything grander was dictatorship. The abandonment of such reasoning freed Lincoln to emancipate the slaves. Think for a moment where close — even brilliant — legal reasoning took Horace Binney: to the position that suspending the writ of habeas corpus was actually an executive power and not a congressional one at all, a position held by no one else anywhere before or since.

Of all times, this was the one when Lincoln lost political control in at least two instances. In the first, having abdicated control of the timing of emancipation, he then allowed himself to give two disastrous interviews — "proto-news conferences" we might call them. Such a venue was not suited to Lincoln's talents. The colonization meeting was embarrassing to anti-slavery advocates, outrageous to African Americans, and unconvincing to enemies of emancipation. In the case of his inimitable statement to the Chicago clergymen about the pope's bull against the comet, he left the timing of the appearance of his remarks to the dawdling sermonizers from Chicago, and they got around to issuing their statement *after* the Proclamation appeared. Worse, the casual setting caused Lincoln to state his powers as a commander in chief in cases of military necessity too loosely. In the case of the September 24 proclamation on habeas corpus, he abdicated it to the fortunes of war and the bureaucracy of the War Department. Again, because Guelzo's book on the Emancipation Proclamation is not primarily a constitutional history, it does not much concern itself with the general question of presidential power in the Civil War and thus understates the blunder of the September 24 proclamation.

The Emancipation Proclamation, as it turned out, was going to fare all right in American public opinion, despite prevailing racism, because of its essential nationalism, but the Proclamation might have enjoyed even smoother sailing had Lincoln not stumbled politically. We can hardly blame him, as a practicing politician all his life, for remembering a little too well what beat him in his last political loss — Stephen A. Douglas's inventive and relentless race-baiting in 1858 (which will be dealt with below). But it seems wholly out of character for Lincoln to have made so many political mistakes in so short a time. The only explanation seems to be that he, like many others in that era, was unsure that in times of crisis political parties should or would continue business as usual.

The rare glimpse Lincoln gave us of his theories on political parties in 1852 has been underestimated and too little used to understand him. In a eulogy on Henry Clay, Lincoln found himself forced to explain away Clay's having spent his life — as Lincoln was spending his — in the service of political party. Inadvertently, in the course of doing that, Lincoln allowed historians a rare glimpse of one of his assumptions — a common assumption in the day — about the nature of political parties. He said: "A free people, in times of peace and quiet — when pressed by no common danger — naturally divide into parties. At such times, the man who is of neither party, is not — cannot be, of any consequence. Mr. Clay, therefore, was of a party."[93]

Ten years later, of course, Lincoln and the American nation were being pressed by common danger. Were political parties natural then, too? Lincoln and other Republicans seemed a little surprised when the Democrats organized so vigorously to contest the elections of 1862. Indeed, early in September 1862 Senator Lyman Trumbull of Illinois wrote the president to inform him: "The Democrats are organizing for a party contest this Fall. They have called a state convention and are calling congressional and county conventions of a purely party character throughout the state."[94] It is difficult to imagine any other even-numbered year in which a senator would feel that a president needed to be informed of such organizing. Perhaps thinking that those elections would not be as contested as usual had enabled Lincoln to spurn Montgomery Blair's advice to delay announcing the Emancipation Proclamation until after the autumn elections, when in fact delay would not have hurt anything and might have helped the Republicans and the emancipationists. In other words, Lincoln may have been assuming that there would be little political challenge from the opposition in the fall of 1862 because of the existence of war, and his ordinarily keen political instincts were on more than one occasion lulled into carelessly unguarded public statements issued in uncontrolled and uncontrollable circumstances.

Kentucky and Emancipation

Constitutional history, though essential to understand the Emancipation Proclamation, can carry us only so far. It may be clear enough that the Constitution was a problem for emancipation in a way that it was not for the war effort, but it was obviously not all of the problem Lincoln faced in contemplating emancipation. When we realize how quickly he solved the constitutional problem, we must ask ourselves, well, then, what was holding the president back? Otherwise, we run the risk, always present in constitutional history, of overemphasizing the role of the Constitution in practical political affairs.

The obvious answer to the question of what, besides the Constitution, at first held Lincoln back is twofold: first, the military and strategic importance of the Border States, and second, racism. Lincoln famously acknowledged the military problem of emancipation. In his initial letter to General Frémont addressing the general's own proclamation in Missouri in the summer of 1861, he pointed out as the reason to rescind the proclamation: "I think there is great danger that . . . [it] will alarm our Southern Union friends, and turn them against us — perhaps ruin our rather fair prospect for Kentucky."[95] He realized that so important a moral issue should not be given second place to a political-military calculation of expediency, and when he explained the Frémont affair to Browning — in the letter from which a lengthy passage is quoted above — he said Kentucky was important but not controlling:

> The Kentucky Legislature would not budge till that proclamation was modified; and Gen. Anderson telegraphed me that on the news of Gen. Fremont having actually issued deeds of manumission, a whole company of our Volunteers threw down their arms and disbanded. I was so assured, as to think it probable, that the very arms we had furnished Kentucky would be turned against us. I think to lose Kentucky is nearly the same as to lose the whole game. Kentucky gone, we can not hold Missouri, nor, as I think, Maryland. These all against us, and the job on our hands is too large for us.
>
> You must not understand I took my course on the proclamation *because* of Kentucky. I took the same ground in a private letter to General Fremont before I heard from Kentucky.[96]

Presumably, Lincoln meant that he had larger reasons, and the only reason explained in the letter up to that point was constitutional — such a proclamation constituted "dictatorship." But we know, as Browning could not at the time, that Lincoln had told Frémont too that he endangered the securing of Kentucky by his proclamation, and Lincoln did not use the word "Constitution" in his letter to Frémont.

Kentucky, then, was more important than Lincoln wanted to admit, and he wanted to admit none of this in public, of course. His revocation of General Frémont's emancipation proclamation for Missouri also included revocation of an order to summarily execute rebels in Missouri found with weapons in their hands. Lincoln explained to Browning that such a drastic measure would only lead to retaliation by the enemy on Union men. But, Lincoln cautioned, "I did not say this in the public letter, because it is a subject I prefer not to discuss in the hearing of our enemies."[97] He did not want the Confederates to know that he had forbidden summary executions. It was better they should fear that possibility. Likewise, he certainly did not want them to know how important Kentucky was to the Union cause or how fragile was the Union's grip on the state. Nevertheless, if we compare only the private and confidential letters to Browning and to Frémont, they are not entirely consistent on Kentucky and leave us not knowing for certain how important was the calculation between military advantage and constitutional scruple.

Racism and the Problem of the Emancipation Proclamation

When we add racism to the context, the historical evaluation is even more difficult. But, of course, we must add it. It is simply impossible to understand the Emancipation Proclamation without it. There are at least two problems: one, Lincoln's estimate of the extent and intensity of the racist beliefs of the electorate, and second, Lincoln's own racism. The president's own views were in evidence fewer than six weeks before he chose to issue the Proclamation already sitting, written in draft, in his desk, when he met with an African American delegation in the White House on August 14, 1862 (described earlier in this chapter).

The most important piece of evidence is Lincoln's firm feeling that American racism was "a fact with which we have to deal" and something he could not alter even if he wanted to. Lincoln was not the only one to notice the problem, of course. The African American abolitionist Frederick Douglass, who was disgusted by Lincoln's address to the White House delegation, did also note, after the Emancipation Proclamation was issued, exactly what Lincoln had noted and feared all along: white men who did not want to fight to liberate the black race might well throw down their guns, as General Anderson's Kentucky recruits had done. Douglass wrote:

> But will not this measure be frowned upon by our officers and men in the field? We have heard of many thousands who have resolved that they will throw up their commissions and lay down their arms, just so soon as they are required to carry on a war against slavery. Making all allowances for exaggeration there are doubtless far too many of this

sort in the loyal army. Putting this kind of loyalty and patriotism to the test, will be one of the best collateral effects of the measure. Any man who leaves the field on such a ground will be an argument in favor of the proclamation, and will prove that his heart has been more with slavery than with his country. Let the army be cleansed from all such pro-slavery vermin, and its health and strength will be greatly improved. But there can be no reason to fear the loss of many officers or men by resignation or desertion.[98]

Was there reason to fear or not? For his part, Lincoln was afraid. In his loose interview with the Chicago churchmen less than two weeks before the issuance of the preliminary Emancipation Proclamation, he said that the appearance of such a proclamation would threaten the loyalty of the fifty thousand soldiers from the border slave states fighting for the Union side.[99] At least one shrewd observer at the time quickly noted that Lincoln's fears proved wrong. The *New York Times* on September 28 recalled the fear expressed by the president to the Chicago delegation, that, as the *Times* expressed it, the Proclamation "would be the occasion of a large defection of support that the Government . . . hitherto received from Border State Volunteers." But, the paper declared flatly: "There is as yet no demonstration of anything of the kind."[100] The *Times*, in this instance, understood the Northern people better than Lincoln did.

We have available to us a surprisingly good test of loyalty and the Proclamation.[101] The Proclamation was announced in the autumn of 1862 and finalized that winter, and the timing made for maximum scrutiny by the nation's fighting men. The date of issuance, January 1, made emancipation a newsworthy item at precisely the moment when Union soldiers all up and down the line were streaming into winter quarters to settle down in log huts by a warm fire to read the newspapers from home until the thaw and military campaigning could begin again on unobstructed roads. As he commented on the preliminary Proclamation, Douglass noted: "A month or two will put an end to general fighting for the winter. When the leaves fall we shall hear again of bad roads, winter quarters and spring campaigns."[102] Officers looked upon that period with some uneasiness. For example, from Nashville on November 26, 1862, General John M. Palmer wrote: "All the disorders now attributable to the army may be traced to idleness. . . . Men and officers lie in camps[,] read the Newspapers and discuss questions of policy[.] Demagogues spring up."[103] The inaction of the soldiers in winter quarters had an important effect on the popular press: with little military action to report, the papers from home were filled more than ever with news of political events, like the issuance of the final Emancipation Proclamation on New Year's Day. This was the time for racist demagogues to strike.

The Union army consisted mostly of mature citizen-soldiers, voters in civilian life and newspaper readers, too. The minimum enlistment age without parental consent was eighteen, and the average age of a soldier when he enlisted was almost twenty-six.[104] Most soldiers had voted — a majority, even, in a presidential election. When they opened the pages of their newspapers in the winter of 1862–63 they read about emancipation, but that was not all. More exciting political news soon crowded emancipation out of the picture.

The Democrats had performed better than expected in the previous autumn, and they had gained control of the legislatures of Indiana and Illinois. In January 1863 they entered upon their new legislative sessions. For the first time since the war commenced, important state governments fell under the authority of the opposition party. But the Democrats followed up their electoral success with a terrible misreading of the voting results.[105] They assumed that their political gains came from Northern weariness of the war. In fact, Northerners were not tired of war at all; they were tired of losing. The Democrats decided on a peace strategy for future electoral success. As soon as they took office they began making noisy gestures toward armistice and peace negotiations. They proposed resolutions in various state legislatures calling for an armistice and a convention of commissioners from the states to meet in Kentucky and negotiate a peace. The Democrats also drafted laws to shift control of the state militias from Republican governors Oliver P. Morton, in Indiana, and Richard Yates, in Illinois, to boards created by the Democratic legislatures. Republicans naturally depicted these as essentially treasonous movements to undermine the war effort. "Loyalty" became their political watchword.[106]

When soldiers read the news, they were, as perhaps Lincoln and Douglass feared, moved to speak out. But they did not voice the racist sentiments Lincoln assumed as "fact." On the contrary, largely ignoring the Emancipation Proclamation, the soldiers voiced a rabid nationalism aimed at quelling the seeming treason of their state legislatures. Beginning on January 30, 1863, and running almost to the end of April, regiments from Illinois, Indiana, and other states gathered at the direction of their officers, in dress parade and under military discipline, to hear and vote on political resolutions to be sent to their home newspapers.

The resolutions generally denounced the rise of "partisan spirit" in their state, rejected any notion of compromise or armistice with the Confederacy, and sometimes threatened to "return and crush out Treason" in their legislatures if ordered there by the governor or the president.[107] I have elsewhere dubbed this movement the near-revolt of the Illinois line. I discovered resolutions from 55 Illinois infantry regiments, 4 cavalry regiments, and 4 batteries of artillery. That is the size of a whole army in the Civil War. Such a number of regiments might add up to more than the 50,000 bayonets Lincoln feared might be lost with the premature issuance of the Emancipation Proclamation.

But the soldiers did not throw down their arms. The officers did not throw up their commissions. Instead, they gathered, under arms, and vowed revenge on the Copperhead legislatures back home. Emancipation was not on their minds and was rarely mentioned in their resolutions. When it was mentioned, it was favorably. Treason, not race, was on their minds. Nationalism simply trumped racism. If the soldiers had constitutional doubts, nationalism triumphed over them as well. When the soldiers returned to campaign in the summer, their political preoccupations were replaced by military ones, and the crisis — if there was one — had passed.

Since I wrote about the near-revolt of the Illinois line, other sets of soldiers' resolutions have been discovered. Historian Timothy J. Orr located many from Pennsylvania regiments, and Matthew Warshauer found resolutions from eight Connecticut regiments.[108] From all appearances, the nationalism of the Union soldiers was never more intense. Their racism was never less in evidence.

Why did Lincoln underestimate them? Why did he let imagined fears hold back the Proclamation? There is no obvious answer, but here is a possible one. Lincoln, like the Democrats in 1862–63, had made a political miscalculation, but he had done so on the basis of his disappointing loss of the Senate race to Stephen A. Douglas in 1858. Only two years before he won the presidency, Lincoln had lost to a desperate politician who invented the political strategy of stating boldly and snarlingly the idea that the United States was a white man's country. American politicians before Douglas did not ordinarily say that, but then not many American politicians in free states lived within boundaries that forbade African Americans from settling in their states by constitutional provision. Illinois had been the nation's leader in constitutionalizing racism, excluding African Americans from their state by constitutional provision years before any other state did.

Once again, it is important to recall constitutional history — especially that neglected constitutional history of the states. The Illinois Constitution of 1848 barred African Americans from settling in the state. Douglas's articulation of the racist ideas and slogans was also a product of the peculiar circumstance of the Illinois Senate race in 1858. At any other time and place in America up to then, Douglas would never have said such things in public. He would not have needed to, for senators were not popularly elected. They were chosen by joint ballot of the state legislature and the talents required to win were horse-trading ones, not oratorical and demagogic. But the Illinois race of 1858 took a peculiar turn with Lincoln's selection as a candidate by a party convention, and the subsequent canvass was conducted as a popular "beauty contest" between the pair, though the actual voting for senator would be by members of the legislature.

Douglas knew that Lincoln was an able opponent on the stump and that the Democratic Party in the state was split, with the minority of James Buchanan stalwarts adamantly opposed to Douglas's candidacy. So when Douglas first spoke in Chicago after Lincoln's "nomination" by the Republicans, he answered Lincoln's keynote speech for the campaign, the celebrated House Divided Speech. The Democratic keynote in Chicago stated in part: "I am free to say to you that in my opinion this government of ours is founded on the white basis. It was made by the white man, for the benefit of the white man, to be administered by white men, in such manner as they should determine."[109] Racism was not the whole of Douglas's platform, but it was the freshest part of it.

What Douglas said in the debates with Lincoln spread far and wide — well beyond what would in ordinary circumstances have been confined to the corridors of the Illinois state capitol. Democrats all over the country read his declaration that "this government was established on the white basis. It was made by white men, for the benefit of white men and their posterity forever and never should be administered by any except white men."[110]

Lincoln heard the words, too, of course. He heard them and then lost the election. Having fallen political victim to such race-baiting tactics only two years before winning the presidency, he may well have been oversensitive to the "fact" of racism. In a fragment of Lincoln's writing usually dated to 1859, the year after the failed campaign against Douglas, Lincoln exclaimed with unusual fervor: "Negro equality! Fudge!! How long, in the government of a God, great enough to make and maintain this Universe, shall there continue knaves to vend, and fools to gulp, so low a piece of demagougeism [*sic*] as this."[111]

In the end, then, we must conclude that the Constitution was a problem for emancipation but only one of several, and the last obstacle to be overcome was racism. Nationalism overcame that.

Racism Tried and Found Wanting

The initial impulse of the Democrats late in 1862 and early in 1863 was to follow where Douglas had led them before and to exploit the race issue implicit in the Emancipation Proclamation — and how better to do that than by agitating in the state legislatures for exclusion laws on the models of Indiana and Illinois? That would raise the bogey of a great northward migration of desperately impoverished African Americans. It was a strategy best pursued in those legislatures where Democrats enjoyed new power after the off-year elections. New Jersey and Pennsylvania led the way. These were moves for legislation, not constitutional amendments, but legislation had preceded constitutional amendments in Illinois and Indiana.

Democrats gained firm control of the New Jersey legislature, previously dominated by a patriotic bipartisan Unionism, in the elections of 1862. Although New Jersey neither shared a land border with any slave state nor was proximate to a slave state affected by the Emancipation Proclamation, the Democrats managed to get an exclusion bill through the lower house in March 1863, but it died in the upper house. Republicans opposed the measures with their votes.[112] Pennsylvania Democrats also performed well in 1862 and controlled a joint ballot of the two houses of the legislature by one vote. After extreme political measures were taken to guarantee a Democratic seat in the U.S. Senate, the Democrats moved early in February 1863 to introduce a bill to exclude African Americans from entering the state.[113] Without Democratic control of both houses, the measure never passed, and by spring the issues had changed. Everywhere in May 1863 Democrats were swept up in protests against the military arrest and trial of Clement L. Vallandigham, which seemed to have great possibilities for exploitation in political campaigns.

The campaign to introduce new exclusion laws or to invigorate ones already on the books peaked in late 1862 to early 1863 and receded quickly thereafter, hurried along by the rapid developments of war, nationalism, and emancipation. In Iowa, for example, a federal district court in 1863 declared the 1851 legislation excluding African Americans from settlement in the state unconstitutional.[114] The Iowa legislature repealed the law in 1864.[115] The struggles to remove the ban lasted longer in Illinois and Indiana, of course, because the provisions carried constitutional authority. In fact, the subsequent constitutional history of both states followed a baffling course. The Indiana Supreme Court, we are told, declared the provisions for black prohibition "null and void in 1866, because they were repugnant to the U.S. Constitution." Yet the reversal of the 1851 constitutional provision was not achieved until 1881.[116] In Illinois a revised constitution in 1862 included exclusion provisions submitted separately to the people, and they passed, but the rest of the constitution did not, and so the lot failed, apparently. The laws passed to implement the prohibition in the 1848 constitution were repealed in 1865.[117]

The response of politics to war issues was the driving force. Democratic gubernatorial candidates lost in the 1863 elections, including the martyr Vallandigham himself in Ohio by a great margin. When preparations for 1864's presidential canvass began, the issues of 1863 showed no clear promise for the Democrats. Civil liberties had not been enough to send Vallandigham to the governor's mansion in Ohio. Racist fears had not caused the legislatures to renew efforts to pass laws excluding African Americans from settlement in their states. The economy of the North, for a great nation in war, was performing well, and employment was high with so many men in the army. Democrats were certainly not restrained by conscience from exploiting racial issues, as their eager leap to exclude blacks in 1863 revealed. Appeals to racial prejudice would be a regular part of their campaign for the presidency in 1864, but they gained no concentrated focus then because of the Democratic failures at the polls in 1863, when the issue was prominent, especially in Pennsylvania. There was considerable temptation for the Democrats in 1864 to imitate the tactics of the victorious Republicans in 1860 and run a "hurrah" campaign with little focus on specific issues. The Democrats ran a diffuse campaign that has always been difficult to characterize. Meanwhile, the Republican appeals to nationalism pushed the racist messages off center stage. Prejudice among Democratic voters was surely a steady presence, but the circumstances of electoral politics and of war caused its presence to abate from the level reached in the Stephen A. Douglas campaign for the Illinois Senate seat in 1858. It would not rise in intensity again until after the war, when Reconstruction encouraged the aggressive race-baiting of the Democratic candidate for vice president in 1868, Francis P. Blair Jr.

The stubborn threat of racism is more visible in the fears expressed in public statements by Republicans in 1863 than in any electoral successes or in any relentless focus on race issues by the Democrats, who in this beleaguered period tried one issue after another — race, peace, civil liberties, and finally loyalty (with the nomination of military hero George B. McClellan in 1864) — in a desperate attempt to recapture the power they held before the Civil War. The point of this chapter is not to belittle the steady presence of racism, especially among Democrats, but to make clear by contrast with it the underestimated power of nationalism. Had Stephen A. Douglas lived to lead the party in the direction of constitutional racism, that movement might not have been halted by the war.[118] As it turned out, the leaderless Democrats floundered from issue to issue while the Republicans discovered the issue that brought their adherents in full turnout to the polls: nationalism.

Part 2

The Courts and the Nation

Whoever attentively considers the different
departments of power must perceive that, in a
government in which they are separated from
each other, the judiciary, from the nature of its
functions, will always be the least dangerous
to the political rights of the Constitution. . . .
The judiciary . . . can take no active resolution
whatever. It may be truly said to have neither
FORCE nor WILL but merely judgment.

— *The Federalist*, no. 78 (Alexander Hamilton)

Soldiers in the Courtroom

The Union enjoyed the luxury of a great advantage in manpower in the Civil War. We can see the effects of that advantage almost as much on the home-front as on the battlefields of the war. The Union authorities hoped for voluntarism. They encouraged voluntarism. When that failed they threatened conscription and occasionally actually used it, but as it turned out the draft was notoriously easy to evade — on appeal for health reasons, particularly.[1] But once a man was in the ranks, the attitude of the Union authorities was completely different. They fought tooth and nail to keep him there.

Lincoln went to what many regarded as dangerous lengths in suspending traditional civil liberties mostly to make desertion and encouraging desertion more difficult. As is often the case, such presidential policies are taken as a green light for men in lower positions of authority to exert force well beyond what the law allows. The army, in its zeal to stop the hemorrhage from its ranks by desertion, resorted to torture. The commonest practice, used in the Central Guard House in Washington, D.C., in 1864, fell short of what is called "water boarding" today, but it did involve the application of water to extract confessions. Naked prisoners, suspected of desertion, were sprayed with a stream of water from a small rubber hose to the point, in at least one well-documented case, where the skin broke. The prison authorities referred to the procedure as a "shower bath." As some of the prisoners were men from Ireland and thus British subjects, British authorities in Washington protested the euphemistic explanation of the shower baths, in one case observing: "This explanation does not show that the cold water was applied . . . in conformity with any law or regulations as a punishment for a known and proved offense: on the contrary it ten[d]s to confirm the statement that it is used . . . for the purpose of extorting, by the infliction of bodily pain, confessions from persons suspected of being Deserters."[2]

Horace Binney, though a defender of the president's power to suspend the writ of habeas corpus, was shocked even at practices of the authorities that stopped well short of the application of torture to suspected deserters. He had never contemplated the use of suspension of the writ to prevent a soldier or his parents from going to court when the boy was unlawfully enlisted.[3] Binney valued the heritage of individual liberty and trusted the judiciary too much to countenance such uses of the Constitution. Here he could hardly have found himself further from the government's attitude. The administration proved largely indifferent to individual rights on that point and so distrustful of the judiciary that it came close to provoking a constitutional crisis in 1863. When youths, who may have been plied with liquor and impressed into service, appealed to courts of justice to get out, the government sent in its attorneys to fight the appeal.

Nationalism proved victorious in courts faced with such questions. It thus triumphed over the value of the family. That was true in three respects. First, despite a two-year struggle in which many disillusioned (or, in some cases, disillusioning) youths escaped the ranks by habeas corpus, in the end the army put an end to the hemorrhage. Second, although family members — usually fathers but sometimes also mothers, especially widowed ones — made appeals for their sons, and the judges answered them and routinely freed the boys from the ranks, in fact, the judges never affirmed family values in doing so. The judges made decisions based entirely on considerations of power — namely, whether the judiciary had the power to remove a person from the clutches of the military. They never — not a single time in all the cases I have found — mentioned the rightful claims of the family to these unfortunate individuals. They never mentioned the role of the family in creating national feeling and inculcating national obligation. Third, the cases betrayed the surprisingly callous attitude toward youth embraced by a nation before the era of child labor laws and other welfare legislation. If the boys were too young for military service, it was generally explained in terms of their want of usefulness for military campaigning: they simply were not durable enough yet. There was no other tenderness of conscience about the decision. After all, the culture readily accepted sending boys as young as twelve into the danger zone as drummer boys. Musicians were also used as stretcher bearers once battle began, and that meant that drummers would not be spared the grimmest sights of carnage, not to mention the notoriously corrupting vices of the military camp. But drummer boys were of little use in combat. In other words, the general attitude was not one of sheltering tender minds and bodies but rather of waiting for the under-ripe to age. Then the state owned their services along with those of everyone else. In this realm, nationalism and the law revealed their tough, masculine side.

Oddly, the standard study of children during the Civil War ignored the problem of underage soldiers on purpose, but to do so risks considerable distortion of the society's conception of the role of children in the nation. Civil War society proves to have been more uncomfortably close to the modern era of child soldiers than we might expect in a sentimental Victorian culture.[4]

As for the actual nature of the conflicts over underage soldiers that were adjudicated in the courts and eventually dealt with decisively by the Lincoln administration, these revealed an arena of contested nationalism that was intensely fought but that has been ignored to date. For example, Stephen C. Neff's *Justice in Blue and Gray: A Legal History of the Civil War* does not mention the issue, nor does the work that blazed the trail for considering the legal history of the war, Harold M. Hyman's *A More Perfect Union: The Impact of the Civil War and Reconstruction on the Constitution*. People at the time, on the other hand, noticed — from observers in the popular press to distinguished jurists like Horace Binney.

The issue had a long and contentious history, with the notorious Hartford Convention making special mention of the attempts of the Madison administration to enlist young soldiers for the War of 1812 without their parents' consent. Previous to the Hartford Convention's consideration of the problem, New England courts had had their say, resisting the national administration's ambitions for mobilizing the American soldiery beyond traditional militia limits. Such serious conflicts over the defense of the nation in the past meant that there was a tradition of conflicts between the national and state governments over the power to mobilize the citizenry. This tradition continued and, for a time, accelerated during the Civil War.

These conflicts occurred where constitutional historians are likely to overlook them, not in the Supreme Court of the United States but in the lower courts of the states. The lower the judge, the higher his chances of encountering war issues in his courtroom. Of course, it would be ridiculous to expect the Northern appellate judiciary to be preoccupied with legal and constitutional questions arising only from military mobilization, war taxation, and liberties restricted by difficult national circumstance. The war did not come near absorbing all of the North's prodigious energies and resources, and the preoccupation of the courts with the ordinary questions of business was proof of that. Still, it might surprise the average Civil War historian to pull down the volumes of state reports, for example, and see case after case dealing with contracts and divorce and estates. I can recall my own surprise when first I looked, expecting to find so much having to do with great national issues of war and freedom, and coming instead to find so little that concerned anything outside the ordinary realm of a prewar lawyer's practice.

It is sobering to Civil War historians and to constitutional historians as well to examine a book like Carl B. Swisher's thorough, lucid, and lengthy *Oliver Wendell Homes Devise History of the Supreme Court of the United States, Volume V: The Taney Period, 1836–1864.* Chapter XXX, which deals with the Civil War period, begins this way: "While the nation was engaged in the Civil War, and Congress and the executive were giving most of their attention to the war, the Supreme Court, though it decided some war cases, was giving much of its time to controversies over land titles in faraway California."[5] Indeed, the principal consideration of the president himself in making one of his appointments to the Supreme Court during the war — Justice Stephen J. Field — was the appointee's expertise in the peculiar land laws of California, not issues associated with the war.[6] That reminds us to look to the president and Congress and even politicians on the stump for constitutional history in the mid-nineteenth century — and not so much to the U.S. Supreme Court.

The table of cases on which the standard history of the Constitution is based lists 733 cases, of which only 3 bear dates from the Civil War. The war was the central question in the *Prize Cases* of 1863, but the other two cases of war vintage are *Gelpke v. Dubuque* and *Ex parte Vallandigham*, both decided in 1864.[7] The *Dubuque* case dealt with quintessentially prewar issues of economic development: municipal bonds issued to fund railroad building. The *Vallandigham* case featured the most celebrated martyr to civil liberty in the war and raised the exciting general question of freedom of speech during the war. Early in 1864 Vallandigham appealed his conviction by a military commission to the Supreme Court, which ruled that it could not review the decision of a military commission.[8] The Court discussed only jurisdiction, not the exciting substance. Thus the *Prize Cases* stand as the only Supreme Court decision of any note about the war issued during the war. These cases, involving ships captured as prizes on the blockade early in the war, raised the question of whether and when war was properly declared or recognized (a state of war being a necessary precondition for the imposition of a blockade). The decision will be treated more fully in the next chapter, which highlights the war questions in the high courts. The justices, in a closely split decision, concluded that there was a war, that the president did not need Congress to declare it as such first, and that was all.[9]

The state court systems offered the greatest number of venues to hear citizens, and the judges, most of them, could issue writs of habeas corpus to examine cases of wrongful restraint of their states' citizens. Day to day, the real constitutional history of the Civil War in the North was fought at levels well below the appellate. Indeed, it was fought at the level of actual military service where nationalism tested the citizen's willingness to fight for his country.

The United States had the most powerful judiciary on earth. In theory, judges could halt armies in their tracks. A judge could require a general to appear in court; Roger B. Taney did, and so would others on rare occasions. Judges could and did frequently pluck uniformed men out of the ranks and restore them to mufti. Judges did not at all admire and occasionally expressed open disdain for the cowardly and scheming youths who appeared in their courtrooms looking for release from the army, but the judges thought they knew the demands of the law and they wanted to assert the ability of the judicial branch to correct the excesses of the executive.

The Problem of Underage Soldiers

The writ of habeas corpus, which we think of as a device to give the judiciary opportunity to review the cause of a person's arrest, had also long been used to look into why the army held certain soldiers in its ranks, as though such exercise of military authority resembled arrest and imprisonment by the executive branch. Remarkably, it did not matter that the soldier had likely volunteered to enter the army (prisoners in jails do not do that). The writ was used to look into both kinds of cases and had been so used throughout American history. It must be remembered that recruitment, for all the halo of democratic voluntarism surrounding it in American myth, could in fact be a rough-and-tumble process made notorious by the army and navy's practice of getting young men drunk and signing them up when they did not know what they were doing.[10]

The courts did not often interfere except in the case of underage soldiers. They rarely dealt with soldiers who had been impressed into service. The writ of habeas corpus was regularly, even frequently, employed to gain judicial inquiry into the question of whether a soldier had been below the legal age to serve without his parents' consent. If he was, then a judge could discharge him from service.

By the time of the Civil War, there was a well-known body of reported cases on the question that seemed to most American judges at first to add up to accepted doctrine. From the earliest statutes governing the enlistment of soldiers in the U.S. Army, boys under eighteen years of age were considered too young to serve. An attempt by the desperate Republicans in the War of 1812 to permit underage enlistment without parental consent met with virtual nullification in New England.[11] A half century later, despite the increased manpower demands of the great Civil War, restrictions on age persisted and were generally observed in laws governing mobilization.

Boys under eighteen could not enlist without parental consent, but the law was vague on the subject. Apparently the army took the boy's word that he was of age, and underage soldiers, boys eager to follow in their older brothers' footsteps to excitement and glory or boys eager to leave unhappy home situations where fathers beat them and exploited their labor, soon showed up in the Union ranks. Military life could be sobering, however, and after a time some of these youths had second thoughts, or parents found their runaway sons and sought their release from the army to return home and work on the farm. Then they sought a judge and a writ of habeas corpus.

Adequate record keeping would have eliminated this problem, as apparently it does today. But the United States of the mid-nineteenth century was an individualistic paradise free from bureaucracy and forms. There was then no official record of birth, and determining age was no simple matter. Some people did not know how old they were, and it was easy for those who did know to lie about it and get away with it. Testimony of close relatives and references to handwritten entries in a family Bible were the common resorts of lawyers and parents seeking to prove an enlistee was underage. They were the resort of those who wanted to defraud the government and escape irksome service, too. Thus in Pittsburgh in 1862 the father of one Patrick Carrigan Jr. sought a writ of habeas corpus for his son as an underage volunteer. He insisted that the boy had been born in 1845 and produced a Bible with the handwritten records to prove it. The judge grew suspicious of the entries in the book because the marriage of the parents and the birth of Patrick were written in the same hand and ink; he thought they might have been written at the same time. Carrigan Sr. explained that both entries were written by the parish priest. The judge examined the Bible more closely and discovered that this edition of the good book had been published in 1850, five years *after* the boy's alleged date of birth. The father was held for perjury, and the son was sent back to his regiment.[12]

The door to freedom for such reluctant enlistees as Patrick Carrigan was opened by the bias toward freedom in the American constitutional and legal system, a bias that made conscription seem unthinkable to some judges, despite the law of Congress and the plain wording of the Constitution on the power to raise armies. The legal expression of this attitude was to regard volunteering for military service as a contract. Thus Justice James Thompson of the Pennsylvania Supreme Court said in passing in *Kneedler v. Lane*: "Voluntary enlistment, as by contract, was the general method of raising armies there [in Great Britain] and with us, prior to and at the time the constitution was framed."[13] In common law, a child could not enter into a contract. Therefore, a judge might reason that the agreement of an underage enlistee was void because of his minority. By midcentury the doctrine usually cited was that a contract with a minor was voidable but not ipso facto void. That meant that some actions of an underage enlistee might be interpreted as tacit consent to a contract. Growing to proper majority in service, taking the government's pay all the while, sending the pay home to one's parents who were then as compromised as the boy, might make a difference. Most important, even an underage enlistee was a soldier until removed from the ranks by a court and might, given the peculiar dangers of that occupation, put other soldiers, legally enlisted, at risk by disobedience or cowardice. It was problematic to allow a soldier who endangered his comrades by deserting in the face of the enemy to go scot free and escape court-martial because, at a point perhaps now in the distant past, that soldier had been underage when he enlisted. Yet there would always be lawyers who would argue that although desertion from military service was not permissible, a youth should not be punished for desertion if he never legally enlisted in the first place.

Besides the bias of the American legal system toward individual liberty, there was a peculiar historical reason that the door was ajar for underage soldiers to escape the ranks. America's most unpopular war, the War of 1812, came early in the foundations of American law.[14] The Federalist Party, which bitterly opposed the war, was well represented on the bench while a Republican president and a Republican Congress led the country into war. That was especially true in New England, where the War of 1812 was particularly unpopular. Some widely cited precedents from that war still influenced judicial opinions at the time of the Civil War. The judicial practice of dealing authoritatively with underage soldiers in federal service appeared time-tested. Most judges regarded it as a duty to release underage soldiers from service in obedience to precedent and liberty.

The republic recognized concurrent jurisdiction of state and federal courts in many kinds of cases, including those of underage soldiers in U.S. service. Therefore, the established practice — little questioned and still followed at the time of the Civil War — was for state judges, by far the most numerous and therefore the most likely to encounter an appeal from the

parent of an underage soldier, to issue writs of habeas corpus and to discharge anyone who could prove he was underage.

In dealing with the many underage soldiers who came before them in
the first two years of the Civil War, judges worked off an existing body of
doctrine in court decisions that seems to have been generally familiar. In
one case stemming from the War of 1812, for example, the Supreme Judicial
Court of Massachusetts ruled in 1814 that a deserter from the U.S. service,
a young man named William Bull, could be discharged on habeas corpus
because he had enlisted as a minor. The case, *Commonwealth v. Cushing*,
focused on Bull, who was not only underage when he enlisted in the Sixth
Infantry in Boston, but was also an orphan, poor and desperate. Even so,
military service apparently proved worse than expected, and he deserted
while stationed in Vermont. He was arrested and was to be tried by court-
martial; by his own admission he had deserted the service.

Bull's lawyer argued that the contract into which the boy had entered
when he enlisted was void because he was a minor. The army's counsel
maintained that Congress could call up the militia, which itself included the
whole of the male population capable of bearing arms. Besides, "infants" (in
the law) could enter contracts under special circumstances, including one
of the most sacred and long-lasting: marriage. The contract for military
service must constitute a similar exception to the common-law rule.

Bull's lawyer had answers for the army's arguments, but the most important observation was this: "This being a case of personal liberty," one of
the judges said, "no argument was necessary" on many points. The decision
of the Supreme Judicial Court of Massachusetts embodied an almost cozy
feeling for local institutions in contrast to the cold and distant national
government. "The obligation to do duty with the militia at home," the court
ruled, "under officers generally deriving their commission from popular
elections, or at any rate appointed by the domestic authority of the state
government, is a very distinct thing from an enlistment into an army, subject to very different discipline, and to hardships and dangers unknown to
militia service." Infants' contracts were voidable, if not "*ipso facto* void." The
court concluded that a state court could release a youth from U.S. service on
habeas corpus.[15]

The same Massachusetts court ruled in 1814 in *Commonwealth v. Harrison* that the contract of Thomas Harrison, an underage soldier in the U.S.
service, was void, even though the soldier did not want to be released from
the army. He was apparently escaping his apprenticeship on a Russian ship,
and the Russian master was claiming the apprentice's release from the army
on habeas corpus in order to recover his labor on shipboard. The justices

did not much like it that the boy had been sworn to apprenticeship in a language (Russian) he did not understand, but they released him anyhow to take his chances with the life before the mast on a Russian vessel (perhaps, a worse fate than the army). The justices might have looked into the validity of the apprenticeship contract, but they were Federalists and bent on asserting the power of the state court against the national executive.[16]

Conflicting precedent did appear during the War of 1812, but such was the bias of American law toward personal freedom that the New England decisions reigned thereafter. In fact, Massachusetts's Federalist justices had to confront arguments to the contrary in their own day. But the Massachusetts justices refused to go along with an opinion of a fellow Federalist jurist, the renowned James Kent (known as Chancellor Kent), then chief judge of the New York Supreme Court. In a case called *In re Jeremiah Ferguson*, decided in the August term of 1812, Kent ruled that the state court had no jurisdiction over U.S. soldiers. Kent could find only one relevant precedent, a Maryland case from 1809, in which the judge expressed doubts about state jurisdiction but left room, depending on the peculiarities of the case. To Kent, "Our jurisdiction does not depend upon the greater or less degree of aggravation in the case, and . . . we have either no jurisdiction at all, or a completely concurrent jurisdiction." Though they did not reach consensus on the jurisdiction question, Kent and the other New York judges nonetheless remanded Ferguson to his regiment, the 13th U.S. Infantry.[17] In one instance, the New York court would go on to rule otherwise in a similar case. In *Grace v. Wilber* the Supreme Court of New York, following the customary analogy to the law of contract, ruled in 1813 that a boy under eighteen, and therefore below the age stipulated in New York law for liability to militia service, could not be held in the military.[18]

Precedents from the more popular, more victorious, and shorter Mexican-American War of 1846–48 were fewer and less well known, but they reinforced the legacy of freedom, despite the substantially different military experience for the nation. In *Commonwealth ex rel. Webster v. Fox*, the Pennsylvania Supreme Court in 1847 professed itself bound to protect individual liberty and discharged the underage soldier, even though the answer to the writ had stated that he was a deserter. The fact that he had deserted after enlistment was held to be immaterial, though the court admitted that if the army had answered the writ by saying the boy was being held in process for court-martial, "that might possibly make some difference." The decision affirmed that the state courts had concurrent jurisdiction with the U.S. courts over such matters and spurned Chancellor Kent's opinion on the question. The decision was notable for some clear thinking that would be echoed in later decisions in similar cases: if the desertion had taken place in the face of the enemy or while the army camped in enemy country, the court stated, that would make a difference, as even camp followers in such dangerous circumstances fell under military law.[19]

The Courts and the "Infant" Soldiers in the Civil War

Such precedents made dealing with the influx of unhappy underage soldiers or their parents into courtrooms during the Civil War a matter of business as usual. The precedents, because of the circumstances of American history up to that time, ran against national power and prerogative and in favor of individual liberty. No one seems to have taken into account that these precedents stemmed from an unpopular war and a factious section of the country. Precedents were the heart of the law, and history was seldom seen in context. No judge qualified the authority of precedent from the War of 1812 by observations on the unpopularity of the war among New England Federalists.

Months before the Civil War began, underage soldiers, perhaps fearing real war on the horizon, began to appear in courts seeking their discharge from the army on habeas corpus. The Republican press in New York City sneered at "The Babies Afraid of War Going Home." "Babies" made ironic reference to the technical status of underage soldiers as "infants" in the law. "Within the last week," reported the *New York Times* in January 1861, "something like a half dozen of Uncle Sam's soldiers have suddenly remembered that they were infants of tender years, and, therefore, not responsible for enlistment."[20] By August 1861, when there was war in earnest, the *Times* could complain that "The Plea of Infancy" constituted "An Epidemic."[21]

The Lincoln administration faced the issue early but interpreted it mainly as a problem of judicial loyalty rather than recruit retention. Such a definition of the problem meant, of course, that a judge could get in serious difficulties simply by following routine precedent in what appeared to be routine duties. The judge who did that was William M. Merrick, a federal circuit court jurist in Washington, D.C. A Democrat, he was not much bothered by the notion of causing trouble for the army or the administration even during this great war. According to constitutional historian Jonathan W. White, who has written the definitive work on Merrick, the judge issued some twenty writs of habeas corpus to release underage soldiers from the Army of the Potomac in the summer and autumn of 1861.[22] These took place in the period when Secretary of State William H. Seward oversaw the internal security system of the administration. Seward was more confrontational than Lincoln on such questions. On October 21, 1861, Seward ordered an armed guard to be placed around Merrick's residence in Washington. Merrick maintained that the conditions amounted to house arrest. The administration said only that he was under observation. The president ordered the judge's pay suspended — an unconstitutional act because Article III, section 1, of the U.S. Constitution protected the judiciary from executive or legislative pressure by guaranteeing that federal judges would serve during good behavior and that their "compensation . . . shall not be diminished during their continuance in office."

Judge Merrick's file at the State Department, which is printed in the *The War of the Rebellion: A Compilation of the Official Records*, makes no mention of his decisions in cases dealing with underage soldiers. Moreover, it contains an anonymous letter written to General Winfield Scott in January 1861, months before the firing on Fort Sumter, let alone the mobilization of young soldiers for the war, referring to a letter "received . . . from Judge Merrick, of your city, stating in effect that Washington would be in the hands of the secessionists by the 4th of March and that thousands of Marylanders that you are arming have a plot to desert all at once and fight on the other side."[23] Accusations of disloyalty were rife, and Congress eventually abolished the court and reorganized the judicial system of Washington to get rid of Merrick. He had life tenure, but it turned out that his court did not.[24]

If Seward's harassment of Merrick was meant as a warning shot over the bow of the Democratic judges, it was of no avail. Judges were stubbornly independent by trade and slaves to precedent by inclination. Republican and Democrat alike, the judges continued to apply the familiar practices in dealing with underage soldiers. The army took a different view. It did not regard the problem as one of loyalty but as one of retention of recruits. Although the policy may not have been stated in so many words in any set of general orders, it seems clear from the behavior of military officials that they believed a soldier once in the ranks was theirs to keep until the end of his term of service. They clearly regarded it as dangerous to discipline for soldiers to see any way out, once they were in, except at the end of the war, at the end of their term of service, or in a coffin. Federal attorneys and judge advocates were consistently made available to defend officers who were holding allegedly underage soldiers who had enlisted without the consent of their parents.

Yet, from all appearances, most judges marched in line with the precedent. In this instance, then, the law proved temporarily more powerful than the internalized sentiment of nationalism or the external application of the force of nationalism. However, Republican judges — there were not many of them as yet after years of Democratic domination of American politics and because the Republican Party only formed in the mid-1850s — were straining to find legal footing from which to resist the slide down the slippery slope of favoring the individuals over the army. Democratic judges, most of them, did not express squeamishness about releasing soldiers from the service.

In some instances, politics could make a circus of the legal disputes over underage soldiers. A good example was the case of Edward G. Maturin, arrested in New York City in March 1863 for desertion. Not only did Maturin come from a prominent Irish American family, but also his father, who sought a writ of habeas corpus to gain his son's release as an underage enlistee, hired a lawyer destined for fame. William F. Howe, who would become a founder of the criminal law firm of Howe and Hummel, kept an office across the street from the "Tombs," the New York City prison. Howe had recently served as a judge advocate in a New York cavalry unit, but the Maturin case represented his return to private law practice.[25]

Howe was on the road to a sordid prominence in his profession — as "Habeas Corpus" Howe. Apparently a recent immigrant from England, likely with a criminal record, Howe had a criminal practice at the beginning of the war. He was a solid Democrat in politics.[26] In the Maturin case, his view was that the boy was not merely unlawfully held by the army but that he had been kidnapped. To give the contentious lawyer his due, recruiters were often unscrupulous, and there was more than one allegation by an underage soldier that he had been led to drink too much alcohol before his unconscious enlistment. Howe encountered an unusually accommodating officer, one Colonel Loomis, who expressed a willingness to release Maturin if he was indeed underage and had enlisted without the permission of his parents. "That is not what we want," said Howe — according to the Republican *New York Tribune*, whose reporters interviewed several of the people involved in the case — "We want to maintain the majesty of the law of the State." "Well," replied the colonel, "do you want to maintain the majesty of the United States also? We have no desire to come into collision with the law of the State."[27] The idea of interposing state rights against federal power was growing in appeal among New York Democrats since Democrat Horatio Seymour ascended to the governorship at the beginning of 1863. Manton Marble, the editor of the *New York World*, a Democratic newspaper, expressed the idea as a desire to see the governor "interpose the arm and shield of the State of New York between Mr Lincoln & the oppressed within the circumference of the State."[28] "Interposition" was a term used during the War of 1812 to mean, essentially, "nullification."

Howe's interest in the Maturin case in 1863 seems markedly partisan, at least in the *Tribune*'s version of events, and all sources seem to agree on the extreme and virtually comic methods the lawyer employed. He had great difficulty getting a writ served on the military officers responsible for holding Maturin. The sheriff, who should have served it, proved reluctant to bother the military authorities; he thought the people issuing the writ deserved to be in prison themselves. Howe apparently persuaded a brother of the prisoner to request a pass to see his relative in jail, armed with a writ of habeas corpus to serve on Colonel Loomis. When that ruse failed, Howe employed someone, a perfect stranger to the colonel, to thrust an envelope through the officer's open carriage window while Loomis was attending a military funeral in the city. The wary colonel refused to accept the envelope.[29]

The Maturin affair had many other curiosities about it. For one thing, father and mother did not agree that the boy was underage, at least not until the mother learned that the unit in which her son enlisted was to be part of a force laying siege to Charleston, South Carolina. She was from Charleston originally and did not fancy that idea — so apparently she did not afterward counter her husband's attempt to get Maturin out of the army.

Yet, for all the peculiarly polarizing and seriocomic circumstances, this case came to a reasonable resolution. Loomis explained that he would have accepted a properly served writ of habeas corpus: "I always obey a civil process, properly served upon me, for I hold that military authority is subordinate to the civil."[30]

The court where this drama took place was the city's Court of General Sessions, a criminal court located on Wall Street, presided over by John H. McCunn, who heard the case in chambers. McCunn was a vociferous and extreme Democrat, a bête noire to Republicans, who thought his very presence besmirched the bench. Like "Habeas Corpus" Howe, McCunn was on the road to infamy. He was to be impeached as part of the Tweed Ring scandals after the war. At the time of the Maturin fiasco, the *Tribune* commented that "Judge McCunn . . . determined to have Col. Loomis arrested and push the case before the proper tribunal" as part of the scheme of "a few Copperheads . . . to bring about a collision between the State and Federal authorities."[31] Then, stepping out of the character imposed on him by the Republican press, McCunn accepted the colonel's explanation, decided not to attach him for defying his writ, and expressed a desire to avoid conflicts between the civil and military authorities. The Republican *Evening Post*, unlike the fractious *Tribune*, noted that this brought the "End of a Threatened Collision" and drew from the case the lesson of "the real harmony that exists between our civil and military authorities."[32] The press quickly lost interest in the case, and the eventual compromise solution was not reported. But no one had really learned any widely applicable lessons by avoiding the farcical collision. About two months later, after Judge McCunn released a man named Kirtland held as a spy or as a prisoner of war, the *New York Tribune* exclaimed in exasperation: "Seriously, is not the *habeas corpus* business, with regard to rebel spies, emissaries and Copperhead deserters, about 'run into the ground'?"[33]

The Maturin case of 1863 has pulled this narrative away from the beginning of the war and the origins of the conflicts over underage soldiers to make a point about the sometimes ridiculous extremes of partisanship in the judiciary, but from the beginning there were jurists of less confrontational temperament who would just as soon not have had to decide such difficult cases. John T. Hoffman, judge of the Superior Court of New York (located in New York City) and a rising Tammany Hall Democrat who would lend vigorous support to the war, had to determine the fate of a minor in April 1861. "I am ready," he stated, "to concede the power of the Congress of the United States to withdraw the consideration of cases of this description from the control of State courts."[34] Somewhat like this reluctant Democratic judge, federal judge Samuel R. Betts expressed a desire to avoid conflict with the executive at a time of crisis. Betts, an appointee of John Quincy Adams, lacked the powerful reigning partisan drives of Democrats and Republicans. Shortly before the war started he had begun to take a newly tough stance toward the illegal international slave trade (most of the cases came into his New York City federal court). In July 1861 Betts granted a writ of habeas corpus to one Purcell McQuillen. When the response to the writ proved inadequate, Betts allowed the officer holding the prisoner more time because he "thought that the judicial and military arms of the Government should support each other instead of seeking occasion of conflict."[35]

Betts's behavior, it is worth remembering, presented a marked contrast to the behavior of Chief Justice Roger B. Taney in the case he dealt with in Maryland, *Ex parte Merryman* (to be discussed in the next chapter). The officer in question in Maryland had sent an aide with the message that he was authorized to suspend the writ of habeas corpus in the case of *Merryman* and asked for time to consult the president of the United States on the matter. The aide told the Court, "He most respectfully submits for your consideration, that those who should co-operate in the present trying and painful position in which our country is placed, should not, by reason of any unnecessary want of confidence in each other, increase our embarrassments." Taney did not grant more time.[36] Some wanted to avoid collisions and some did not.

There were Republican judges who hewed reluctantly to their duty as well. The career of Judge William J. Bacon best illustrates the self-conscious conflict between judicial duty and national sentiment. Bacon was first elected as a Whig to the New York Supreme Court, Fifth District, in 1855 and reelected in 1861 as a Republican.[37] Serving one of eight district state courts in New York (despite its name the New York Supreme Court was not the state's highest appellate court), he was looking for ways to uphold the war effort while at the same time maintaining respect for precedent, but it proved difficult.

In June 1863 Bacon ruled for the government in *In re Beswick*, the sort of complicated case that could arise only after the war had been prosecuted for a long time. John D. Beswick had enlisted in a New York regiment in 1861, when he was only fifteen years old. He remained in the service for over a year, receiving his pay through July 1862 and sending some of it to his mother, who was poor. (She was widowed while her son was stationed in Virginia.) On September 14, 1862, Beswick deserted and returned to his mother in Utica, where he lived until arrested for desertion in March 1863. Only now did his mother seek a writ of habeas corpus to have her son discharged from the army because he was under the minimum age when he enlisted without the consent of his parents. Bacon ruled that "all discipline" would be "at an end" if a parent could "lie by for months, and even years, and make no effort to reclaim a minor child, and then, when by his misconduct he has made himself amenable to the punishment provided for desertion, step in and withdraw the subject of the writ from the action of the tribunal." Taking the mother's poverty into account, the judge said: "If after the fact of desertion, and before arrest, this application had been made, I am not prepared to say the mother might not have successfully urged her claim to the service of her son."[38] Bacon was uncomfortable failing to shield the soldier from the national government. He went on to mention what surely he did not need to under the circumstances: "If the maxim '*silent leges inter arma*' has in some connections a doubtful and dangerous aspect, I think in such a case as this it may be fairly invoked."[39] That rough-and-ready Latin maxim ("in war the law is silent") was more an argument from desperation than from law. Judge Bacon could only hope the Constitution was "adequate" for the crisis; he felt the need to leave room for the ultimate plea of military necessity.[40]

Two months later Bacon found the solution to his desperate problem in a most unlikely place: an opinion of Chief Justice Roger B. Taney. Bacon concluded in a case he decided in chambers, *In re Hopson*, that state courts like his had no power over soldiers held by federal authority. He had been haunted in the *Beswick* decision by the sense that his state court did have jurisdiction and had to find other reasons, stemming from the nature of military service itself, the need for discipline, and the necessity to prevent desertion in the face of the enemy under any circumstances, to remand the deserter to his regiment. In this new case he recalled, "The proceeding by habeas corpus had become so common it had been uniformly obeyed by the production of the prisoner, and I had myself, in common with scores of other judicial officers, often had alleged volunteers brought before me, and inquired into the validity of the enlistment, that it did not occur to me that a case existed, or could arise where the mandate of the writ to produce the body and set forth the cause of detention . . . could legally be disobeyed."[41]

The U.S. government's provost marshal general had been doing his legal homework and issued instructions to provost marshals holding deserters to refuse to obey the writ to produce them in court. He ordered them not to render prisoners if served a writ of habeas corpus and to state "that the law governing the instructions furnished him by the provost marshal general, and controlling his action in this and like cases, might be found in the language of Chief Justice Taney, in the decision of the supreme court of the United States, in the case of *Ableman v Booth*." That plea caused Bacon to go back and look again at *Ableman*, of which he had only a "general recollection." He admitted that "the full purport" of the opinion "was at first misconceived by me."[42]

The reason for the misconception is obvious. Taney's decision, issued before the war to meet problems characteristic of the prewar period, had the effect of clearing the path for federal officials enforcing the Fugitive Slave Act to seize the fugitives without hindrance from state officials in the North. In other words, Bacon suddenly discovered in 1863 the deliciously ironic applicability of an opinion meant to strengthen the Fugitive Slave Act of 1850 to the war against the Slave Power. Now he had precedent on his side and presumably no longer had to leave room for *inter arma silent leges*. It was a "singular fact," he noted drily, "that in some of the extreme southern states the power to interfere with the action of the United States had been repeatedly disclaimed, while in some of the northern states, and particularly New York and Massachusetts, 'reproached, obnoxious, but ever loyal Massachusetts,' it had been strongly maintained." He found precedents for federal power in Georgia and, to his surprise, even in South Carolina, "the very hot-bed where the extreme doctrines of state independence and state sovereignty have had their rankest growth . . . and culminating at last . . . in the horrible and accursed rebellion that has deluged the land in blood." The case of Charles E. Hopson involved able counsel on both sides: the up-and-coming Democratic lawyer from Utica, Francis Kernan, for Hopson's father and Republican Roscoe Conkling for the provost marshal.[43]

Since the discovery of *Ableman v. Booth* figured so prominently in *Hopson* and marked the turning point of the legal and constitutional history of the Civil War in the North, it is important to return briefly to the prewar period and examine that case.[44] It was a unanimous ruling of the Taney Court issued in 1859. Despite the fact that *Ableman* dealt with the question of fugitive slaves only two years after the *Dred Scott* decision, it has received surprisingly little treatment. The case affirmed federal power over state power in remanding fugitive slaves to their putative owners. The opinion involved an abolitionist named Sherman Booth, but it stemmed from two different events. The first arose in the early agitation over the Kansas-Nebraska Act in 1854. A mob broke into the Milwaukee jail and freed Joshua Glover, an escaped slave who had lived and worked for two years near Racine, Wisconsin. The abolitionists put Glover aboard a ship to Canada. A U.S. commissioner arrested Booth for aiding the fugitive's escape, but Booth's request for a writ of habeas corpus to a Wisconsin State Supreme Court justice led to his release on the ground that the Fugitive Slave Law of 1850 was unconstitutional.[45] Booth was rearrested on indictment by a federal grand jury and convicted. Once again the state supreme court released him on a habeas corpus appeal. Both this and the earlier decision were appealed to the U.S. Supreme Court.

Legal confusion arose from Taney's decision to combine the two cases. In one, Booth had been held under orders from a federal fugitive slave commissioner. In the other, he had found release after a guilty verdict in federal court.[46] The Taney Court now affirmed the incompetence of a state court to discharge a person held by federal authority, but in the first instance the federal authority was a commissioner and in the second a federal court.

The case of the commissioner was of real interest to perplexed judges in the Civil War, for that seemed to represent a form of federal authority short of a court and legal process — like a military officer, perhaps. William Bacon thus focused on the part of the decision dealing with the commissioner. "I deny that the commissioner was in any sense a judicial officer," Bacon said. In other words, the federal commissioner appointed under the Fugitive Slave Act of 1850 was analogous to the provost marshal who was holding the underage soldier as a deserter. Bacon defended his decision from possible objections that it too readily undermined state power and judicial independence and thus played into the hands "of a grasping national supremacy that seeks to override the authority of state tribunals, to break down all protection to individual freedom, and to found upon the shattered fragments of state sovereignty a great central despotism." Some who held such views were doubtless sincere and loyal, he admitted, but "on the other hand, I am persuaded that with a large number of those who united in these expressed apprehensions, it is nothing but the cry of the political demagogue ambitious for regaining power, or the howl of faction famishing for its accustomed spoils."[47]

Despite the discovery of *Ableman v. Booth* to save the day for the judge and the republic, Bacon went further in the opinion than he needed to. He brought up the demands of "this hour" for upholding the national government "in the exercise of the most rigorous powers with which it has been or can be clothed." Up to now in the nation's history, danger had come from the other direction, from "unduly magnifying state authority," to the point that "centrifugal force" was threatening to spin the country into "bewildering chaos." It was time to halt that trend and to lean in the other direction, toward national or central power. Bacon did not feel that the government was alien and needed "watchful scrutiny and jealous fear." It was "unwise" and "unmanly . . . to be filled with perpetual alarm, lest the government should grow too strong." Bacon invoked as his "creed" the doctrine of liberty and Union embodied in Daniel Webster's famous reply to Robert Y. Hayne back in 1830. Nor did he fear increasing the exclusive jurisdiction of the judges of the federal bench, as they were themselves citizens of both state and nation.[48] In decisions like these, we can detect the beginnings of a fundamental change in attitude toward government in the United States. Bacon was moving away from ages-old republican fears of power as always threatening and toward an attitude of trust. It would take a long time for such attitudes to replace republican paranoid dread of government power. But Civil War nationalism saw their birth.

In the end, Bacon could not quite restrain his nationalism in service to legalism. He invoked "a supreme rule of public safety" against "preserving the constitution in its minutest letter and most straightforward construction" at a time when "traitorous hands are mining beneath the citadel." He invoked "a spirit which looks to the conservation of national life, higher than the mere letter of parchment constitutions."[49] With the discovery of the federal powers underwritten in the opinion in *Ableman v. Booth*, Bacon had found his "adequate" Constitution, but it was not enough. Somehow, he could not resist looking beyond the parchment Constitution. Democrats found the Constitution entirely adequate. Republicans sometimes did not. Nationalism over and above useful Supreme Court precedent was controlling Bacon's opinion in 1863.

Hopson sought to have the decision reversed in October in the general term of the Court when two more judges would be present, but by that time Roscoe Conkling could fittingly point to the proclamation of President Lincoln suspending the writ of habeas corpus, issued on September 15, 1863 (to be discussed later in this chapter), to halt any further inquiry into Hopson's case. Because of the proclamation, the Court decided not to hear the case further.[50]

Another New York judge who came to embrace the new solution to the problem of minors in the army was E. Darwin Smith, of the Seventh Judicial Circuit, in Rochester, also a Republican.[51] Smith grouped several cases together and in a hearing at chambers on August 8, 1863, concluded that *Ableman v. Booth* meant that he could not inquire about prisoners held by federal authority as long as the officer responded to the writ and explained that the soldier was held under the conditions of the president's proclamation.[52] Smith explained:

It seems to me that the doctrine in this case of *Ableman* v *Booth* is very essential to the maintenance of the national authority, especially in a time of war. No government could maintain and exercise its powers in their full vigor when its acts could be controlled by the Judiciary of another sovereignty, or by a Judiciary owing its appointment and authority to another government. If every act of the general Government affecting the personal liberty of the citizen can be overhauled upon *habeas corpus* by the Judges of the State Courts, incalculable embarrassments and mischief might be the inevitable result. . . .

It is notorious that there are some evil-disposed persons in sympathy with the enemies of the country, who are opposed to the war, and who evince a spirit of hostility to the Government by hindering enlistments and volunteering — by enticing enlisted men to desert — in secreting deserters — and resisting by force their arrest and return to the army, and who by opposition to the draft and various other modes of procceding [*sic*] are seeking to defeat the operations of the Government in conducting the war. It would be surprising if such men could not find some convenient Judge who should issue writs of *habeas corpus* and by this process discharge all persons brought before them, on the ground that the laws of Congress authorizing enlistments, or the draft and the arrest of deserters, and perhaps the war itself, was unconstitutional, and thus give the color of law to their disloyal acts and proceedings.[53]

In a moment of ardent patriotism, typical of the Republican judiciary in wartime, Smith added: "But if it were doubtful whether the returns in these cases were sufficient to oust me of jurisdiction, as such jurisdiction could only be asserted by proceedings which would involve a conflict between the State and national Governments, I should be quite unwilling, and should hardly think it my duty, to initiate such proceedings at a time of great national peril, and when the Government is struggling for existence with a gigantic rebellion."[54]

If we look elsewhere in the nation's courts, it becomes clear that the summer of 1863 was the time when the judiciary discovered the uses of *Ableman v. Booth*. It had been available at least since early 1860. The law required publication of the Supreme Court reports within six months of the end of a term, and *Ableman* was decided in March 1859. But it looked like a fugitive slave case then. Who could have foreseen its relevance to wartime disputes over underage soldiers? No doubt Republican judges took one look at the opinion and dismissed it as more proslavery intervention from the notorious Taney Court — before the outbreak of the war.

We can trace a similar path of judicial discovery in Pennsylvania, where Republican judges reluctantly did their apparent duty and issued writs to soldiers and released them on good cause.[55] Judges, even Republicans like John J. Pearson of the Court of Common Pleas in Harrisburg, regularly issued such writs to underage soldiers and others through the spring.[56] Then an unusually scholarly judge in the Court of Common Pleas for Centre, Clearfield, and Clinton counties came to the rescue. He discovered the applicability of *Ableman v. Booth*. Judge Samuel Linn ruled that a state court could not release someone arrested as a deserter. The case was that of James Shirk, an appropriately named minor, arrested by the provost marshal as a deserter from the 45th Pennsylvania. The unfortunate Shirk had run away from home to enlist in 1861 but fell ill a year later and became a patient in a Washington military hospital. His father Jacob removed him from the hospital and took him home to Bellefonte, Pennsylvania. Jacob sought a writ of habeas corpus and claimed his entitlement to the boy's services until his majority. The sheriff, who was holding Shirk in jail for the provost marshal, answered Linn's writ by saying that he could not produce the prisoner because he was in federal custody. The judge heard from the boy's grandmother that he was born on July 11, 1847, and was thus only fourteen when he enlisted and only sixteen at the time of his arrest for desertion.

Judge Linn professed himself "clearly of the opinion that the State Courts have power to discharge, on habeas corpus, minors who are held to service under invalid contracts of enlistment," but in this instance the lawyer for the government argued that Shirk was under arrest as a deserter and was subject to court-martial. Had the return to the writ stated only that Shirk was detained by virtue of his enlistment, the judge would have released him, but how far could a state court go in exercising "jurisdiction over the person of a criminal arrested for an offence against the United States and of which the Courts of the United States have exclusive jurisdiction?" He adopted from Taney's ruling in *Ableman* the view that cases were divided "between two distinct sovereignties."[57]

Judge Pearson noticed and welcomed Linn's opinion, but it was a little too late to allow the army to hold on to Shirk. After Linn's decision, Shirk was sent to Camp Curtin, in Harrisburg, where his father attempted again, this time in Judge Pearson's Court of Quarter Sessions, to gain his son's discharge from the army. Pearson, apparently unaware of Shirk's recent experience and as yet unaware of *Ableman*, discharged him.[58]

Days later, Pearson discovered the new doctrine. A man named Richard Jones obtained a writ of habeas corpus for his son James, who had deserted from the 11th Pennsylvania Infantry. James was seventeen when he enlisted in November 1861. Neither his father nor his mother consented, but his mother had agreed to his serving as a civilian teamster contracted to the army. While away driving wagons, the boy enlisted in the field. "I should not hesitate to discharge James Jones from his contract for enlistment," said Pearson, affirming that the evidence that he was underage was convincing. But did the judge have jurisdiction? No, Pearson reasoned, because it was a "legal axiom, that whatever tribunal, having jurisdiction of the offense, first obtains custody of the person of the offender, under legal process, has the first right of trial and punishment." Once Pearson knew that James Jones was in custody under a criminal charge, he could not look at the facts behind the case. Pearson said that *Ableman* was controlling in Jones's case, but he did not say that the state lacked jurisdiction in every instance in which the federal government had custody of the citizen.[59] Still, Pearson must have looked upon the discovery of *Ableman v. Booth* as a godsend, for he was a thundering and aggressive nationalist.

Reviving the Charge to the Grand Jury as a Political Institution

Although some judges professed reluctance to place considerations of the law before the life of the nation and thus cultivated a passive image fitting a branch of the government lacking "force" or "will," as Alexander Hamilton had expressed it in *The Federalist*, no. 78, others felt denied their proper place as opinion leaders in American society.[60] They could help speed appeals along, but even then the subject of the case might not be appropriate for wartime issues or the timing might not fit the fast-moving context of wartime events. There was another way to have their say. They could revive the custom of the broadly political charge to the grand jury. Every judge whose court employed grand juries had and used the power to give the jurors a charge each time a jury was impaneled for the new session of the court. In fact, the charge to the grand jury was a time-honored custom. As historian Ralph Lerner described it, the judge explained to the new men "the statutes" for the federal grand juries and "the common law relevant to the performance of their duty" in state courts.[61] By custom, grand juries not only made decisions about prosecuting malefactors but also had certain responsibilities to inspect and evaluate important local public institutions. They looked at public buildings and infrastructure and at public nuisances and even at threats to the morals of the people.[62]

Therefore the judge's charge might naturally comprehend more than the statutes and the technicalities of the common law. It might even reach the realm of the political. After bitter conflict over this practice in the Early Republic, the judiciary generally pulled in its horns and stuck closely to the law, but the approach of the Civil War brought the judges out of their apolitical shells once more. For any person with a normal level of political interest, the Civil War was an irresistible subject to hold forth on, and judges had more than normal interest in politics. From beginning to end, then, the subject of the political conflict over the Civil War was a lure that some members of the judiciary could not resist.

In general, the urge to speak about the war from the bench proved to be a threat to civil liberties in the North. Though some Democratic judges also abused the institution of the charge to the grand jury, the biggest offenders appear to have been Republicans.

After a few initial charges of patriotic ardor early on, the prominent instances of making aggressive charges to grand juries came in the summer of testing loyalty, 1863. From high and low, the judiciary weighed in on national issues. When Justice David Davis, recently appointed by President Lincoln to the U.S. Supreme Court, went out on his federal circuit court duty in the spring of 1863, he found himself charging grand juries in the states of the Old Northwest, where there were exaggerated and sensational rumors of some sort of Great Northwest Conspiracy against the Union cause. In Indianapolis, Davis began his charge with a reminder of the "great national peril" and then offered this admonition to the grand jurors: "We may, and will differ, in any great war, on the right manner of conducting it, and the wisdom of the policy pursued, but no man, who is not a traitor at heart, will ever suffer that difference to lead him by speech or writing to counsel resistance to law." He proceeded to arouse fears rather than to allay them. "It is charged," the justice warned, "that there are secret organizations . . . with 'grips, signs, and passwords' having for their objects . . . resistance to Law, and the overthrow of the Government. . . . If anywhere in this State bad men have combined together for such wicked purposes, I pray you, bring them to light and let them receive the punishment due to their crime." He did not say what statute was violated by such behavior.[63]

When, like David Davis, Samuel Freeman Miller, a Republican and another recent Lincoln appointee to the U.S. Supreme Court, left Washington for duty on his federal circuit, he had the same idea in mind. Miller charged the grand jury of the circuit court in Des Moines to enforce treason laws, adding: "Most who are loudest in their complaints against the Government at the present time, profess to be peculiar champions of the law and the constitution. They surely should unite with us in the effort to enforce vigorously in this hour of our national calamity, the laws which are made for the security of all, and for the preservation of the government in which all are so vitally interested."[64]

At the level of the Court of Quarter Sessions in Harrisburg, Pennsylvania, the message from the bench was similarly stern. Late in April 1863 Judge Pearson gave a rousing charge to the grand jury in his court. "The exigency of the times," he told the assembled men, "and my great anxiety to benefit the country and shelter the community from impending evil, must be my apology for traveling out of the ordinary descriptions of crimes and misdemeanors, and calling your attention, and through you that of the people at large, to the danger of violating certain recently enacted laws of Congress."

Pearson encouraged the people to pay their war taxes "cheerfully and . . . honestly" because the war was an expensive but worthwhile endeavor. He noted that conscription must be enforced and reminded the people that the penalties for aiding desertion were severe. Moreover, if newspapers "counseled resistance to the draft and people took action afterward, then the newspapers were liable for treason as well." Pearson maintained that "at times like this, when the struggle is for national existence, words become things." He warned specifically against the Knights of the Golden Circle, the organization with its grips, signs, and passwords that had so stirred Justice David Davis, saying it "was very confidently asserted" that the organization was treasonous and gaining strength.

"There is an evil," Pearson warned, "of very considerable magnitude at the present time, and of almost daily occurrence, for which it is supposed there is no adequate remedy. I allude to that of persons reviling and railing against the Government under which we live, and praising and expressing a preference for that of the rebels." Such language often provoked violence against the speaker himself. The resulting vigilante behavior was not surprising, he said, though he admitted it was against the law. "The proper course," he suggested, "is to have the parties so reviling the government arrested and taken before a magistrate, where they may be bound over for their good behavior until the next session of this court, when the cause can be fully heard." He continued:

> We have no doubt that such seditious and traitorous expressions at a time like the present, if not indictable, afford good ground for binding the perpetrator for his good behavior, if for no other reason because it tends to breaches of the public peace by exciting others to break it, but numerous additional legal reasons may be adduced to justify such a course. Do not misunderstand me on this subject. Men have the most unlimited right to condemn, and if you please, rail at the *National Administration*, and object to the manner in which it conducts public affairs, but not to decry the Government under which we live, or express hopes or wishes for a dissolution of the Union, the destruction or defeat of our armies, the success of the rebels or the rebellion.

"It may be thought by some," he added, "that we are introducing a mere question of party politics into court, which we entirely disclaim." His explanation would hardly have satisfied many Democrats: "In a contest like that now waging in this country all whose feelings, wishes and sympathies are with the rebels, are traitors in their hearts, and all who render them aid or comfort, directly or indirectly, are traitors in their acts. All who are not for the government are against it. In this struggle for national existence there can be but two parties, true men and traitors; there can be no neutrals." Pearson did affirm that "parties will always exist in every free country," but he thought it was easy to distinguish their sphere of legitimate comment on, and criticism of the contemporary administration of affairs, from what was off limits: the government itself.[65]

These grand jury charges, it must be remembered, came from the bench, not from the hustings, and began to be heard before the occurrence of the military arrest, military trial, and candidacy-in-exile of Clement Vallandigham. They cannot be contextualized, as President Lincoln's sternest statements on restricting liberty (which were considered in Chapter 2) can be, by the aftermath of the defeat at Chancellorsville, and they were not nervous reactions to a party nomination — Vallandigham's for governor — which had not yet occurred.

The most circumstantially determined of the charges to the grand jury in 1863 may have been made in Philadelphia in January. The political context was this: Democrats had performed well in the elections the previous November, and Republicans were reeling in shock. On January 24, 1863, General Robert Schenck, the commander of the Middle Department, which included Baltimore and Philadelphia, ordered the arrest of the editor of the Democratic newspaper, the *Philadelphia Evening Journal*, for publishing an editorial that compared President Lincoln's recent annual message unfavorably with Jefferson Davis's address. James R. Ludlow, the judge of the Court of Quarter Sessions in the city and a Democrat, learned of the general's action on the last day of the court session. Ludlow immediately charged the grand jury with bringing about the arrest of the military officials who had apprehended the editor. The grand jury proved reluctant and the court's session ended on a Saturday night. That circumstance was important because the court was served by three judges who rotated responsibility for the sessions. Next in line was a Republican named Joseph Allison, who, on the next Monday, gave a very different charge to the grand jury. In fact, Allison's grand jury charge was more technical and less like a stump speech than that given by the Democrat Ludlow. But the reversal of direction — in the space of a weekend — made a mockery of impartial justice. A later reversal by the Pennsylvania Supreme Court in an important conscription case the same year — a matter of weeks — seemed almost patiently judicious by comparison.[66]

On the few occasions when Democratic judges gave political charges to grand juries, their message was almost always the same. They likened military arrests of civilians in their state, followed by incarceration in federal prisons outside the state, as "kidnapping," and they urged the enforcement of the laws against kidnapping by federal officers. The first and most famous conflict over grand jury charges hostile to the administration came in 1861 in the case of Judge Richard B. Carmichael, whose court was in Talbot County, on Maryland's isolated Eastern Shore. When Secretary of State Seward learned from a Maryland resident that Judge Carmichael was charging grand juries to indict federal officers for arresting civilians, he wrote the military commander who was in charge of the troublesome district, General John A. Dix, on October 3, 1861, and said, "It seems to me that that functionary should be arrested even in his court if need be and sent to Fort Lafayette." He added, "You may proceed accordingly."[67] That was not exactly an order, though Seward, who was at the time the cabinet officer responsible for overseeing military arrests of civilians, had the authority to order such arrests and was not shy about using it.

General Dix, a prewar Democrat given the difficult Maryland assignment in part because of his credentials for political reconciliation, seems to have held off from arresting Carmichael until early in 1862. By that time so many reports about the judge had reached him that Dix wrote the governor of the state for advice. The nature of his charges to the grand jury was prominent among the allegations against Carmichael:

> Hon. R. B. Carmichael has for many months been one of the prime movers of disaffection and disloyalty on the Eastern Shore of Maryland. He was the author of a treasonable memorial to the legislature, published and circulated under his own signature while holding a place on the bench. His charges to the grand juries in his district have been inflammatory and insulting to the Federal Government. He has caused military officers to be indicted and has charged grand juries that it was their duty to find bills against all persons who had given information on which arrests had been made by order of the Government. Under his instructions Brigadier-General Lockwood—whose conduct has been marked by the most prudent and discreet forbearance in the execution of my orders which have been by many regarded as too lenient—was subjected to the indignity of an indictment. This man is a dishonor to the bench. He is a dishonor to the loyal State of Maryland.[68]

General Dix was ready to banish Carmichael to the Confederacy.

Apparently the Maryland governor placed no obstacle in Dix's path, and in May the general dispatched the deputy provost marshal and four policemen from Baltimore to arrest the judge in his court, as Seward had originally suggested. When confronted by the officers, Carmichael denied the authority of the U.S. government to arrest him and resisted. In the ensuing melee he was struck on the head. Later, Maryland's senators went to work to gain his release, appealed in person to President Lincoln, and left him a newspaper copy of one of Carmichael's charges to the grand jury. Lincoln read it and "was not very favorably impressed towards the judge." Lincoln did focus on the substance of the matter and not merely the ideology expressed. "The object of the charge, I understand, was to procure prossecutions [sic], and punishment of some men for arresting, or doing violence to some secessionists—that is, the Judge was trying to help a little, by giving the protection of law to those who were endeavoring to overthrow the Supreme law—trying if he could find a safe place for certain men to stand on the constitution, whilst they should stab it in another place."[69] He recommended that the judge be required to take the oath of allegiance and then be released. By early December Carmichael was free.

One cannot imagine Lincoln initiating the arrest of a judge at work in his own courtroom and risking the scuffling that might ensue. That had the mark of Seward's more confrontational nationalism about it. Such noisy conflicts could be heard far and wide. Thus the antiadministration *Dubuque Herald*, when it reported another charge to the grand jury against kidnapping citizens, added: "For making precisely such a charge as this, Judge Carmichael of Maryland was by Federal minions torn from the bench while in actual discharge of duties."[70] Carmichael might have escaped arrest by Seward or Dix or Lincoln if he had not gone so far as to gain a grand jury indictment of Henry H. Goldsborough, president of the Maryland Senate, for his role in aiding and abetting the arrest of some Maryland civilians by Union military authorities. The pro-Union *Baltimore American* was aghast at that move: what Carmichael was urging was "unheard of in any other court in the State." He had maneuvered the grand jury into finding presentments against eighteen military officers for arresting civilians on orders. The newspaper also pointed out, what only the local press would be likely to notice, that Judge Carmichael omitted an obligatory charge to the grand jury on the "treason bill," which the Maryland legislature had "expressly required" of its judiciary.[71]

To understand the issue of the charge to the grand jury, the newspaper's observation about the treason bill is useful. First, it is a reminder that the charges to the grand jury of such Democrats as Carmichael were the parallel equivalents of the Republican charges and as notable for their lack of national sentiment as the Republican ones were for their injection of national sentiment. Second, it brings to our attention for the first time the true nature of the grand jury system. It was not the bulwark of liberty it was sometimes depicted to be. That was especially true in a slave state. In prewar Maryland, the legislature had required that there be a statement in the jury's charge about enforcing "certain sections of the Code relating to the circulation among the negroes of certain publications calculated to stir up insurrection."[72] During the war, control of the legislature changed, and now legislation required charging the grand juries on treason. Beyond the biases of the grand jury system itself, there loomed the further excesses of judges in using the charge to the grand jury to hold forth from the bench on political questions.

The headstrong Judge Carmichael certainly did not learn his lesson. By the spring of 1863, he was provoking conflict again and by the same means: the aggressive use of the charge to the grand jury. A letter to the editor of a Baltimore newspaper denounced the "gratuitous and uncalled for charge to the Grand Jury, on the subject of the action of the Government in arresting traitors. . . . The charge was entirely a one-sided affair. Not a word was said against the accursed Southern traitors . . . the Judge has made his political speech from the sacred seat of justice."[73]

Conscription

Only at the level of the Judge Pearsons of the country was the constitutionality of the mobilization measures of the Lincoln administration put to a full test, one that led, first — as perhaps judicial interpretation is supposed to lead — to a resolution of conflict based on precedent. In the end, the precedent of *Ableman v. Booth* was not altogether adequate, and presidential power had to be used to put a stop to the prolonged conflict over the bodies of soldiers brought into courtrooms across the country.

Although the U.S. Supreme Court never tested conscription, it was not Roger B. Taney's fault. He was itching to weigh in on it. He had already composed his "Thoughts on the Conscription Law of the United States," in, as even Taney's apologetic biographer admitted, "the form of court opinions."[74] The doctrines he had developed in *Ableman* took him in an entirely different direction from where it was leading Republicans on the bench. What he now emphasized was the idea of dual sovereignty, but in the case of the Conscription Act he did not lavish much attention on the sovereignty of the United States. Rather, he worried about the sovereignty of the states and declared that the Conscription Act threatened its destruction by making the militia, the embodiment of state sovereign power, the subject of conscription by the federal power.[75] Taney never got to put these "thoughts" to use in court.

There is an oddly parallel memorandum to Taney's on conscription in the Papers of Abraham Lincoln. Like Taney's "Thoughts," the Lincoln document is of uncertain date, and the author's intentions in drafting the document are unclear. It was not, however, improper for the commander in chief to assemble his thoughts on conscription, as it was for Taney to reach in advance of the arrival of a case before him the decision in the case. We know that in other instances the president drafted documents on explosive topics and held them for what he considered the right moment for their use.[76] In the case of his "Opinion on the Draft," a title given to the document by the editors of Lincoln's Papers and not by the president himself, the doctrine is entirely irreconcilable with the doctrine in Taney's document. Lincoln was so convinced of the constitutionality of conscription that he could only, as it were, stab his finger on the text of the U.S. Constitution. People "who desire the rebellion to succeed" and others who hoped to benefit politically by arguing in the same vexatious way "tell us the law is unconstitutional." Lincoln then stated bluntly, "It is the first instance, I believe, in which the power of congress to do a thing has ever been questioned, in a case when the power is given by the constitution in express terms." This idea of constitutional interpretation was a steady theme with Abraham Lincoln. In his First Inaugural Address over two years previously, before the firing on Fort Sumter, he had said:

> All profess to be content in the Union, if all constitutional rights can be maintained. Is it true, then, that any right, plainly written in the Constitution, has been denied? I think not. Happily the human mind is so constituted, that no party can reach to the audacity of doing this. Think, if you can, of a single instance in which a plainly written provision of the Constitution has ever been denied. If, by the mere force of numbers, a majority should deprive a minority of any clearly written constitutional right, it might, in a moral point of view, justify revolution — certainly would, if such right were a vital one. But such is not our case. All the vital rights of minorities, and of individuals, are so plainly assured to them, by affirmations and negations, guarranties [*sic*] and prohibitions, in the Constitution, that controversies never arise concerning them.[77]

Faced with such unreasoning opposition, Lincoln could be tempted by the explanation of conspiracy and evil motivation, not for him customary explanations for political opposition. But in the manuscript on conscription, he suggested that people who wanted the rebellion to succeed called the constitutionality of conscription into question. That was unfair in this case, of course. But the essentially rationalistic outlook of Lincoln's political thought — with little room in it for mystical expressions of nationalism or anything else — was nowhere more evident than in his standards for constitutional interpretation. He could understand conflict when, as he put it in his First Inaugural Address, the Constitution does not say, but denying the power to raise armies boggled his mind. "Whether a power can be implied," he went on, "when it is not expressed, has often been the subject of controversy; but this is the first case in which the degree of effrontery has been ventured upon, of denying a power which is plainly and distinctly written down in the constitution."[78]

In the 1863 document Lincoln eventually regained his political composure and offered an unusually clear-eyed, unsentimental view of military service:

> At the beginning of the war, and ever since, a variety of motives pressing, some in one direction and some in the other, would be presented to the mind of each man physically fit for a soldier, upon the combined effect of which motives, he would, or would not, voluntarily enter the service. Among these motives would be patriotism, political bias, ambition, personal courage, love of adventure, want of employment, and convenience, or the opposites of some of these. We already have, and have had in the service, as appears, substantially all that can be obtained upon this voluntary weighing of motives. And yet we must somehow obtain more, or relinquish the original object of the contest, together with all the blood and treasure already expended in the effort to secure it. To meet this necessity the law for the draft has been enacted. You who do not wish to be soldiers, do not like this law. This is natural; nor does it imply want of patriotism. Nothing can be so just, and necessary, as to make us like it, if it is disagreeable to us. We are prone, too, to find false arguments with which to excuse ourselves for opposing such disagreeable things.[79]

Congress raised armies because the Constitution said it could, and the Constitution was the supreme law of the land. That was the case, simply put. Lincoln realized that the provision for a $300 commutation was an objection on the grounds of equality and not of constitutionality. He went on to defend even that obnoxious provision as traditional and as putting a ceiling on the price of substitutes to be hired by the conscripted men who could not go. He did not cast aspersions on the patriotism of the men who thus wished to avoid service — as he did on the men who devised the arguments that the draft was unconstitutional. But the latter aroused his ire: "The principle of the draft is not new. . . . It has been used, just before, in establishing our independence; and it was also used under the constitution in 1812. Wherein is the peculiar hardship now? Shall we shrink from the necessary means to maintain our free government, which our grand-fathers employed to establish it, and our own fathers have already employed once to maintain it? Are we degenerate? Has the manhood of our race run out?"[80] If this document had actually been issued, and if Taney's secret opinion on conscription had been given in a case on appeal, what would have happened? We would certainly feature these two opinions in every compilation of documents on the constitutional history of the United States — if the United States still existed as one country.

We cannot really imagine how serious the constitutional conflict might have been had Taney found the opportunity to issue his opinion as a majority opinion of the U.S. Supreme Court and those ideas had come into conflict with Lincoln's, but we can gain a sense of the seriousness of the conflict in the less sharply delineated constitutional conflict that really did occur in 1863.

Wilson McCandless, a Democrat appointed to the federal court in Pittsburgh by President James Buchanan, released numerous minors from military service on habeas corpus.[81] In August 1863 McCandless heard the case of Joseph Will, of Cambria County, Pennsylvania, who had been arrested for obstructing the draft by refusing to have his name enrolled.[82] In *U.S. v. Joseph Will* McCandless ruled that enrollment and conscription were two different things, and resisting enrollment was not unlawful under the Enrollment Act of March 3, 1863 (the federal Conscription Act). The Republican members of Congress now paid the price of euphemism, having chosen to avoid the term "conscription" or "draft" in the name of the bill. Enrollment, McCandless argued, was a peaceful measure — like taking the census — whereas conscription was "peremptory in its character . . . requiring *force to support it*." The draft took men from home and family, and the census did not. Enrollment should not require penalties to enforce it. By that reasoning, McCandless somehow reached the conclusion that assaulting an enrolling officer was not a crime under the act of Congress.[83]

Meanwhile, Justice Walter H. Lowrie, of the Pennsylvania Supreme Court, who was on the verge of declaring conscription unconstitutional (in *Kneedler v. Lane*, to be discussed in the next chapter), issued a similarly obstructionist ruling. In mid-August Lowrie heard the case of a draftee named John T. Carney, from Indiana County, who had been declared unfit for service upon his medical examination but was arrested afterward, examined again, and pronounced fit. The enrollment board decided they had erred the first time. The government abandoned its original defense based on immunity from state jurisdiction and embraced a defense based on the finality of draft board decisions. Lowrie ruled that the board had no authority over Carney once they had exempted him.[84]

When another case of a similar nature came before Lowrie, the United States decided to challenge state court jurisdiction. Lowrie rose to the challenge. In *Commonwealth ex rel. McLain v. Wright*, decided in Pittsburgh on September 4, 1863, Lowrie clung to concurrent state jurisdiction in "cases of imprisonment under Federal authority, *not judicial.*"[85] In other words, his court would have to defer to federal authorities holding a prisoner for some judicial process, but merely being subject to military discipline did not rob the soldier of his right to have a state court review his status in the military on habeas corpus. *Ableman v. Booth*, in his view, applied only to judicial prisoners. The federal challenge to his jurisdiction had angered Lowrie. He insisted: "I feel bound to show that I have not been heretofore and am not now guilty of usurpation. Even some State judges have lately denied this jurisdiction to the State judiciary, and this makes its vindication the more important." Other state courts, in the hands of Republicans like Pearson and Linn, in other words, had declared themselves without juris-diction — and it was time to put a stop to that.

Chief Justice Lowrie invoked the traditional bias of American law to-ward freedom. He had on his side "the law of ourselves and our ancestors for several hundred years . . . always conducive to liberty, and [only] in very rare instance . . . used in a disorderly way." He could not "avoid thinking that, in the light of all our previous practice, this objection indicated an undue suspicion of the State courts":

> If the State courts are not to be trusted with any jurisdiction in cases involving acts done under federal laws, then our Federal union is greatly weakened by the loss of *moral* bond; mere legal force cannot hold the States together. There *is* a moral bond strong enough to hold them, made up of the moral fibres of respect and affection for the Constitution and laws, as heretofore usually understood, and of those of our social relations and intercourse, and I cannot contribute to the sundering of a single one of them. We have found . . . old paths to be paths of pleasantness and peace, and I cannot help to lead into new and untried or doubtful ones; not, at least, until the *moral* authority of social custom and usage has prepared the way and made the paths straight and ready for social travel. . . . Not more than one in many thousands of the transactions of social life requires the *force* of law for its protection or execution, when the stability of the law and of its administration, and its harmony with social usages are such that its *influence* is sufficient to suppress all question and dispute.

He concluded, "If our mutual alienation has gone so far that the State courts cannot be trusted to administer 'the Supreme law of the land,' it seems to me that it is quite time for us to begin to doubt our ability to maintain our federal Union; though very possibly I may over-estimate this danger."[86] Lowrie's bow in the direction of patriotism seemed weak: "I know that in the trying circumstances in which the Federal government is placed by the present rebellion, it is entitled within the Constitution and law, to the generous sympathy of all American citizens, and that all its measures ought to be liberally interpreted, and not narrowly criticized."[87]

When Lincoln got wind of the trend in state judicial decisions releasing soldiers on habeas corpus in Pennsylvania, he lost his temper — an uncommon occurrence. In a cabinet meeting held on September 14, 1863, the president, as Secretary of the Navy Gideon Welles reported, said "that he would not only enforce the law, but if Judge Lowry [*sic*] and others continued to interfere, and interrupt the draft he would send them after Vallandigham [that is, into exile]."[88] Edward Bates, the attorney general, also present at the cabinet meeting, recalled the president as saying, "It was a formed plan of the democratic copperheads, deliberately acted out to defeat the Govt., and aid the enemy. That no honest man did or could believe that the State Judges have any such power."[89]

Even in this suspenseful moment within the confines of the political concerns of the presidential administration, we can see a range of ways of thinking about constitutional questions. Secretary Welles was on the verge of realizing the remarkable power of the judiciary in the United States. In the cabinet meeting, he recalled in his diary:

I remarked that the subject was not new to me, — that I had two or three times experienced this interference by judges to release men from service, not in relation to the recent draft, but that we were and had been suffering constant annoyance. Vessels were delayed on the eve of sailing, by interference of State judges, who assumed jurisdiction and authority to discharge enlisted men in the national service in time of war, on *habeas corpus*. I had as high regard and reverence for that writ as any one, but it seemed to me there should be some way to prevent its abuse. A factious and evil-minded judge — and we had many such holding State appointments — could embarrass the Government, could delay the departure of a vessel on an important mission, involving perhaps war or peace, or interrupt great military movements by an abused exercise of this writ, — could stop armies on the march. I had questioned whether a local State or municipal judge should have this power to control national naval and military operations in a civil war, during the existence of hostilities, and suggested that, especially in time of war, United States judges were the only proper officers to decide these naval and military cases affecting the law and service of the United States.[90]

Welles was not a lawyer, and those in the cabinet who were reacted differently. Secretary of the Treasury Salmon P. Chase observed: "It has been generally conceded . . . or at least such has been the practice, that State Courts may issue Writs of Habeas Corpus for persons detained as enlisted soldiers, and to discharge them. Several cases of this kind have occurred in Ohio, and the proceeding of the State Court was never questioned, to my knowledge." Montgomery Blair, a famous lawyer and part of the team who had argued the *Dred Scott* case before the U.S. Supreme Court, said "that he had often, when a judge in Missouri, discharged soldiers on Habeas Corpus."[91]

After cabinet members cooled the president down a little, he issued a proclamation that satisfied Chase, who did not want it to seem that the writ was being done away with. The document was long and specific and aimed directly at the problem seen in this chapter:

> The privilege of the . . . writ shall now be suspended throughout the United States in the cases where, by the authority of the President . . . military, naval and civil officers of the United States . . . hold persons under their command or in their custody either as prisoners of war, spies, or aiders or abettors of the enemy; or officers, soldiers or seamen enrolled or drafted or mustered or enlisted in or belonging to the land or naval forces of the United States or as deserters therefrom or otherwise amenable to military law, or the Rules and Articles of War or the rules or regulations prescribed for the military or naval service by authority of the President . . . or for resisting a draft or for any other offense against the military or naval service.[92]

The proclamation changed the political and legal landscape for the rest of the war. In New York City, the Republican *Tribune*, commenting on a recent decision of the New York Supreme Court, wrote: "Since the suspension of the writ of habeas corpus the Court is not a coward's castle for the protection of disloyal men."[93] Lincoln "suspends the power of our McCunns and Leonards [Democratic judges in the city] to baffle, by habeas corpus, the National effort to fill the ranks of the Union armies."[94] The *Herald*, which always added the bite of cynicism and derision to its often shrewd observations, remarked: "The proclamation of President Lincoln is creating consternation among the youths who enlisted and have become 'tired of war's alarums.'" Citing the president's recent proclamation, Democratic Supreme Court judge Thomas W. Clerke remanded several young men (brought before his court on habeas corpus before the proclamation) to their regiments.[95] The old federal judge, Samuel Betts, was emboldened by the proclamation to declare, about the proposition that "the government cannot compel an infant to serve," that "our form of government has as much right to call to the field every man capable of bearing arms as any absolute monarchy on the face of the earth."[96] The *Herald* itself, incidentally, aware of the provocation in Pennsylvania, still doubted the wisdom of the proclamation but not its constitutionality.[97]

The Triumph of Nationalism in and over the Courts

After the September 1863 proclamation suspending the writ of habeas corpus, the legal history of the Civil War in the North subsided into irrelevance. Constitutional law in the North had been moving in a new nationalistic direction, with the crucial boost coming, ironically, from the pen of Roger B. Taney in *Ableman v. Booth*, but for now it stopped moving at all. Law had moved too slowly for the president, who had a nation to save. When he suspended the writ of habeas corpus in cases involving conscription and soldiers in the ranks, the effect was the constitutional equivalent of exiling the troublesome judges. Even the presidential election year of 1864 did not breathe much new life into the war between the courts.

Lincoln's actions remind us of the necessity of applying force or vigorous leadership in creating or maintaining nation-states even amid generally supportive national sentiment. Jefferson Davis and the Confederate Congress failed to take such steps to shore up conscription, and the judges in the Confederacy were left holding a bagful of difficult issues to sort out.

It is certainly true that judges were not immaculately conceived in the nineteenth century. Thus constitutional historian Don E. Fehrenbacher has described the justices of the U.S. Supreme Court under Roger B. Taney this way: "A constitution is as much a political as a legal document, and every constitutional decision is therefore to some extent a political act. Members of the Taney Court were predominantly politicians, appointed for political reasons in an intensely political age, and their partisanship, though it might be muted, was never entirely smothered by the proprieties of judicial office."[98] "The justices," he said in another memorable passage, "all political men in some degree, read their newspapers and probably followed the legislative debate in the *Congressional Globe*."[99]

In interpreting the work of the lower courts in the Civil War, if we combine all these images of the politically or ideologically motivated judges together, we can come up with perhaps as good a depiction of the judicial system as history can offer. On the problem of underage soldiers, the judges' political or nationalistic proclivities certainly directed their search for a solution. They read their newspapers, all right. And yet they did literally discover the law or, in the case of *Ableman v. Booth*, discovered the precedent and its applicability to a new situation unforeseen by the authors of the original decision. They did not actually "make" any law at all. They may not have discovered the uses of *Ableman* from the press necessarily, and the workings of the ordinary legal process — the research and arguments of the prosecutors and defenders — served its time-honored purpose. On the other hand, reporting was so imperfect, slow, and irregular that newspaper reports of opinions surely had some influence.

The result was politically predictable, but only within limits of legal precedent. In the case of the Civil War, historians have rare opportunities for understanding nineteenth-century society. The opportunity that lies in soldiers' letters home, an enormous national archive written by those who would not otherwise have left home to write letters and leave a written re-cord to be retained by those who might have thrown them away were they not generated in such historical circumstances, has been fully realized and often exploited. But the judicial record of the Civil War has been underes-timated. The sheer number of habeas corpus cases adjudicated in so com-pressed a period by so many judges to such a widespread extent has left us a rare opportunity to see the growth and development of judicial doctrine in detail, without great and imponderable variables of time elapsed, different contexts and conditions — in some instances, within the minds of the very same judges. As much as the development of nationalistic forces in the law, that ability to glimpse nineteenth-century legal minds at work is the point of this chapter.

The range of behavior and ideas was wide. It included the partisan com-edy of the Maturin case in New York City, but there were judges like Bacon and Smith who struggled conscientiously to keep their partisan inclinations within the customary boundaries of jurisprudence, reluctantly following precedent until they found a Supreme Court ruling that allowed them to rule the way they thought best for the republic. Nationalism was so power-ful a force, however, that Republican judges left the door open for invoking *inter arma silent leges* if somehow their interpretation of the law proved faulty. Democrats thought they had the law on their side, struggled against the new nationalist interpretation of *Ableman v. Booth*, and in the end rec-ognized their passive role in the face of the suspension of the writ of habeas corpus in most cases involving soldiers and conscripts. The revival of the political charge to the grand jury revealed that judges wanted to have their say, whether a case came their way or not, but that was more often used to stir nationalism than to put obstacles in its path or to protect individual liberty.

From the era of the Alien and Sedition Acts of 1798 to the wars of the courts over the soldiers in the Civil War, constitutional history was more concerned with power than with individual liberty. The Kentucky Resolutions of 1798 asserted the rights of the states to control speech, not the right of the individual, and the judges in the Civil War continued a struggle over the assertion of power by state judges as opposed to federal authority. Judges might on occasion invoke the liberty of the individual as a fundamental bias of American constitutional law, but as individuals, children counted for very little in the struggle for power. In the end, courtrooms were scenes of struggles for power, and the power of nationalism proved irresistible.

The Nation in the Courts

THE LEAST DANGEROUS BRANCH FIGHTS THE CIVIL WAR

Roger B. Taney hoped that the U.S. Supreme Court could play a configurative role in the Civil War. Providence had preserved him for this moment, he thought. With the departure of the Southern Democrats from Congress, only the courts stood in the path of fanatical Republicanism, which controlled the executive and legislative branches. But how could a judge make anything happen? Original jurisdiction in habeas corpus cases for federal prisoners gave Taney his chance, and he seized it eagerly in May 1861. But his opinion in this early case, called *Ex parte Merryman*, did not rally Democrats to frustrate the salvation of the nation or to mount a crusade for endangered civil liberties, or even to organize for the next elections. The opportunity of original jurisdiction now perhaps squandered — and it was not yet the first summer of the war — he had to wait. Evidence suggests that he occupied some of his time over the next two years in preparing opinions declaring unconstitutional both the Legal Tender Act and the Conscription Act, novel measures widely regarded as vital to the war effort. For want of appeals to the Supreme Court from lower court decisions involving these acts, his opinions languished unused in his desk. When another opportunity finally came his way early in 1864, he was too ill to participate in the consideration of the case, *Ex parte Vallandigham*, that might with his determined leadership have put the whole Court's stamp of approval on his *Merryman* decision on habeas corpus. The Court heard the case without him, and Justice James M. Wayne, of Georgia, a defender of slavery who remained loyal to the Union, writing for a narrow majority, decided the Court had no jurisdiction.[1]

Taney did not make the constitutional history of the Civil War. The president, Congress, and the political parties did more. The constitutional history of the Civil War was, in form, continuous with the previous history of the Constitution and quite unlike the modern era. In the first two-thirds of the nineteenth century, presidents and Congress made constitutional history as much as the Supreme Court of the United States did. The constitutional crises preceding the Civil War were not terminated or defined by court decisions. What is the U.S. Supreme Court's decision on the Alien and Sedition Acts? What is the Court's decision on nullification? There were none. The *Dred Scott* ruling of 1857 with its dramatic assertion of judicial review over the most important political questions of the day — the prohibition of slavery in the territories and the status of African Americans in the American legal order — might be viewed as the beginning of the modern constitutional era, ironically, with its prominent role for the U.S. Supreme Court. In other words, in content the *Dred Scott* case was backward looking, but in form it foretold the distant future.[2] Decisions of the Supreme Court after Taney's foray in *Ex parte Merryman* seem so insignificant that the standard modern history of the war, famed for its wide-ranging consideration of matters besides military campaigns, does not mention Court decisions made after the spring of 1861.[3]

It is true that in the Civil War–era vital cases concerning the national conflict were seldom considered in the nation's highest courts, federal or state. As appellate courts lacking original jurisdiction in most instances, they had to wait for the most important issues to wend their way up to them. That circumstance, rather than lack of force or will, explains Taney's failure to give the Supreme Court a major role in the war. The Civil War proved to be a long war by the standards of the mid-nineteenth century, but it was not long by the standards of the judicial appeals process. The war's length was not great enough for cases testing war powers to reach the highest courts. Consider the example of the most famous case from the era, *Dred Scott v. Sanford*. Dred Scott's search for freedom through the legal system began in Missouri in 1846. It ended with a U.S. Supreme Court decision in 1857. Eleven years was long even by the Dickensian standards of nineteenth-century justice, but the process was often long. The case most important to this book, *Ableman v. Booth*, another antebellum decision of the Taney Court, began with the arrest of abolitionist Sherman Booth in Wisconsin in the midst of the agitation over the Kansas-Nebraska Bill in Congress, early in 1854, and ended with Roger B. Taney's decision in the U.S. Supreme Court five years later, in 1859.[4] Neither of these cases, had they been initiated at the beginning of the Civil War, would have been decided by its end. The *Dred Scott* case, under such circumstances, would have commenced with the Lincoln administration and been decided well into Ulysses S. Grant's administration. One of the reasons habeas corpus became the focus of constitutional questions about the administration's conduct of the war is that such cases reached judicial resolution quickly, with a lawyer going to a single judge after his client's arrest and obtaining a ruling in chambers to hold or release in short order. What was true of the Civil War held true for cases stemming from other violent conflicts in the antebellum period. *Luther v. Borden*, which arose from an incident in Rhode Island's Dorr War of 1842, was decided only in 1849. The little-known Mexican-American War cases, *Mitchell v. Harmony* and *Cross v. Harrison*, were decided in 1851 and 1853 respectively, well past the Treaty of Guadalupe Hidalgo in 1848.

The necessity of judicial passivity was an agony for Chief Justice Taney, but for some other high judges, it was agony to be forced to decide questions fraught with significance for the future of the Union and the survival of the Constitution itself. The point is that the rather diminished importance of the courts in the political conflicts of the Civil War was a matter of process, not one of will. Some judges, like Taney, were itching to get their say. Some had their say whether they had a case before them or not. They used broadside charges to the grand jury.

The most neglected realm of constitutional history is the history of state constitutions. In the Confederacy, in the absence of a national supreme court, the state supreme courts played a more prominent role. Even in the North, where there were literally dozens of state supreme courts, some war-related issues were bound to reach their level. But the instances were rare: the Legal Tender Act was tested in the New York Court of Appeals (the state's supreme court) and conscription was tested in the Pennsylvania Supreme Court. Both cases were heard in 1863. Lower federal courts did not play a prominent role, and the judges of federal courts who heard cases involving important Civil War issues are hardly household names: Humphrey H. Leavitt (the case of Clement Vallandigham) and John Cadwalader (conscription). There were drummer boys in the army who emerged from the war more famous.

America's courts did struggle with considerations of nationalism, but most of the conflict occurred below the level at which constitutional history is traditionally written, the U.S. Supreme Court. At the level of the state supreme courts, both the Legal Tender Act of 1862 and the Conscription Act of 1863 underwent important judicial scrutiny. The constitutionality of the Legal Tender Act was at issue before the highest court in New York, the

Court of Appeals, in 1863. In the end, in *Metropolitan Bank v. Van Dyck*, the court upheld the constitutionality of the act.[5] Some of New York's finest lawyers were making their arguments in *Metropolitan Bank* while General Robert E. Lee was approaching Gettysburg, and it proved impossible for them to ignore that circumstance. John K. Porter, a part of the legal team making the case for the constitutionality of the measure, held that the Legal Tender Act was essential to the war effort and told the court: "It happens, by a singular coincidence, that the appeal to your Honors to declare the government impotent for its own defense, is made at a time, when the heels of the rebel soldiery are polluting the soil of a free state, between the capital of New York in which we hold our deliberations and the capitol of the nation where final judgment is to be pronounced."[6] How to decide a case during a great war became a serious question for many judges throughout the nation.

The *Prize Cases*

Roger B. Taney chose to ignore the great war as a circumstance conditioning interpretation of the law. In the *Merryman* case in 1861, he myopically ignored conditions in Maryland outside courtrooms, and it may well have required more than the arguments of counsel to make the judges on the bench acknowledge those circumstances. That was part of the importance of the *Prize Cases*, decided two years later, in which the U.S. Supreme Court (in a group of cases involving ships captured in the blockade) raised the question of the legality of the war itself (and thus of the naval blockade declared as a consequence of it).

As in Congress, the cooperation of some Democrats with the war effort was on occasion essential. They could have denied a quorum in Congress but did not. President Lincoln had not yet had an opportunity to appoint enough Republican justices to tip the old Taney Court balance, and holdover Democrats provided the crucial margin for a majority that recognized the war as legitimate in the *Prize Cases*. A Democrat, Robert C. Grier of Pennsylvania, wrote the majority opinion. He was an appointee of President James K. Polk, and modern Court historians identify him as a "dough-face"—a Northern man with Southern principles. Whatever his opinions on race, Justice Grier proved to be a nationalist when the chips were down. It is not easy to say why: like Taney, who proved not to be a nationalist and was a dissenter from Grier's opinion, Grier was old (born in 1794) and a graduate of the Dickinson School of Law. But, of course, he did not come from a slave state.[7] Likewise, Justice Wayne sided with the majority. He was a Jackson appointee, older than Grier, and a Georgia slaveholder, but he proved to be thoroughly supportive of the Union.[8]

The *Prize Cases* involved merchant vessels taken by the U.S. Navy on the blockade. The owners sued for the restoration of their property on the ground that the blockade was illegal because blockades were actions of war and no war had been declared. All the justices, Taney included, agreed with Justice Grier's majority opinion that a condition that could be described as war existed after July 13, 1861, when Congress, called into special session, recognized the situation as war. The dissenters said that no such condition existed before that date. The Court split 5-4. The differences beyond the technical date — that is, the constitutional reasons for their disagreement — boiled down to the following. Grier said the war could not be ignored as a fact. It was too large and destructive. The author of the minority opinion, Justice Samuel Nelson, a Democrat appointed by President John Tyler, insisted that the Court recognized as war only what the Constitution said a war was — and that was something declared by Congress. Grier's view has been widely quoted:

> A civil war is never solemnly declared; it becomes such by its accidents — the number, power, and organization of the persons who originate and carry it on. When the party in rebellion occupy and hold in a hostile manner a certain portion of territory; have declared their independence; have cast off their allegiance; have organized armies; have commenced hostilities against their former sovereign, the world acknowledges them as belligerents and the contest is *war*. *They* claim to be in arms to establish their liberty and independence in order to become a sovereign state, while the sovereign party treats them as insurgents and rebels who owe allegiance and should be punished with death for their treason. . . . As a civil war is never publicly proclaimed *eo nomine* against insurgents, its actual existence is a fact in our domestic history which the court is bound to notice and to know.[9]

What Justice Nelson said is not as familiar:

> An idea seemed to be entertained that all that was necessary to constitute a war was organized hostility in the district of country in a state of rebellion — that conflicts on land and on sea — the taking of towns and capture of fleets — in fine, the magnitude and dimensions of the resistance against the Government — constituted war with all the bel-

ligerent rights belonging to civil war. . . . It was said that war was to be ascertained by looking at the armies and navies or public force of the contending parties, and the battles lost and won. . . .

Now, in one sense, no doubt this is war, and may be a war of the most extensive and threatening dimensions and effects, but it is a statement simply of its existence in a material sense, and has no relevancy or weight when the question is what constitutes war in a legal sense, in the sense of the law of nations, and of the Constitution of the United States? [*sic*] For it must be a war in this sense to attach to it all the consequences that belong to belligerent rights. Instead, therefore, of inquiring after armies and navies, and victories lost and won, or organized rebellion against the general Government, the inquiry should be into the law of nations and into the municipal fundamental laws of the Government. For we find there that to constitute a civil war in the sense in which we are speaking, before it can exist, in contemplation of law, it must be recognized or declared by the sovereign power of the State, and which sovereign power by our Constitution is lodged in the Congress of the United States — civil war, therefore, under our system of government, can exist only by an act of Congress, which requires the assent of two of the great departments of the Government, the Executive and Legislative.[10]

Nelson found the Constitution entirely adequate to the nation's purpose. The tone of the opinion was thus typified by the assertion "that ample provision has been made under the Constitution and laws against any sudden and unexpected disturbance of the public peace from insurrection at home or invasion from abroad."[11] Nelson did not offer what Republicans were always seeking: abundant acknowledgment of the evil nature of the insurrection and patriotic encouragement to those whose job it was to put it down.

We know even this — the most important Supreme Court decision of the Civil War — imperfectly. The Supreme Court reporter, who saw to the publication of the decisions of the Court in bound volumes, held considerable sway over public knowledge, offering his own summary of the facts of the case preceding the opinions, and, in this case, selecting as representative arguments of counsel those of James M. Carlisle, for the shipowners, and Richard Henry Dana Jr., for the government (though the U.S. attorney general was in charge of the case).[12] There was no verbatim record made in the courtroom. The government was well served by its district attorney, Richard H. Dana, surely one of the Lincoln administration's wisest patronage appointments.[13] Dana was among the most famous lawyers of his day and had by the end of the Civil War a dozen of his arguments separately published as pamphlets. The argument in the *Prize Cases* was published as *Supreme Court of the United States: The Amy Warwick: Brief of R. H. Dana, Jr.*, one of those uncommon instances in which the arguments of counsel were saved for posterity. Such arguments might have made vigorous propaganda for the Union, and the failure of similar arguments to reach print is one of the subtle reasons that history has let the nationalism of the courts and lawyers go underestimated.[14]

James Carlisle focused on the extremes of Dana's arguments for the government. His own views were grounded in the idea of dual sovereignty, and he was not beyond the use of sleight of hand, a hallmark of legal arguments in the nineteenth century, with its ideal of extreme client loyalty. Thus he mentioned, by way of describing the limited powers of the president and the government in general, "the delegation of special and limited powers to the Federal Government, with the express reservation of all other powers 'to the States and the people thereof' who created the Union and established the Constitution."[15] But Carlisle's quotation from the Tenth Amendment was not exact and was quietly shaded toward the idea that the states were the fundamental unit. The amendment actually says, "The powers not delegated to the United States by the Constitution, nor prohibited by it to the States, are reserved to the States respectively, or to the people." The Constitution in reserving powers leaves them to the states or to the people, not to the people described as parts of the states (as in Carlisle's "thereof").

But for the most part, the shipowners' counsel took aim at Dana's broad arguments. Carlisle said:

> The counsel for the United States, speaking for the President, take very bold and very alarming positions upon this question. One of them testifies in well-considered rhetoric, his amazement that a judicial tribunal should be called upon to determine whether the political power was authorized to do what it has done. He is astounded that he should be required to "ask permission of your Honors for the whole political power of the Government to exercise the ordinary right of self-defence." He pictures to himself how the world will be appalled when it finds that *"one of our Courts"* has decided that "the war is at an end."[16]

Still another government lawyer had, as Carlisle noted sharply, played the loyalty card, saying at one point: "If 'the pure and simple function of the Prize Court be transcended, then the Court is no longer a Court of the sovereign, but an ally of the enemy.'"[17] Otherwise, the shipowners' case rested on the assertion that a war was something declared by Congress, period, and Congress had not declared war when the merchant vessels were taken in the blockade. That position was not without its political overtones, as it was based on a fundamentally Democratic view of the president and his powers in the Civil War. Carlisle said:

> The matter then comes back necessarily to the pure question of the power of the President under the Constitution. And this is, perhaps, the most extraordinary part of the argument for the United States. It is founded upon a figure of speech, which is repugnant to the genius of republican institutions, and, above all, to our written Constitution. It makes the President, in some sort, the impersonation of the country, and invokes for him the power and right to use all the forces he can command, to *"save the life of the nation."* The principle of self-defense is asserted and all power is claimed for the President. This is to assert that the Constitution contemplated and tacitly provided that the President should be dictator, and all Constitutional Government be at an end, whenever he should think that "the life of the nation" is in danger. To suppose that this Court would desire argument against such a notion, would be offensive.
>
> It comes to the plea of necessity. The Constitution knows no such word.[18]

The government's arguments — short of invocation of dictatorship — were all Carlisle said they were. Dana had indeed made the bold argument attributed to him. And Dana's pointing to the absurdity of a court of law declaring a war at an end stands startlingly alone in the period as questioning the astonishing powers of the judiciary in America. Much of the heart of Dana's argument was shrewd and intellectual. Unlike the shipowners' counsel, who began from the assertion that war was something declared by Congress, Dana started with the proposition that "war is simply the exercise of force by bodies politic." Therefore, there was nothing of justice about it. To confiscate the property of enemies was not a matter of punishing them for wrong but a matter of simple coercion. "For war," he went on, "is not upon the theory of punishing individuals for offences, on the contrary (except for violations of rules of war), it ignores jurisdiction, penalties and crimes, and is only a system of coercion of the power you are acting against."[19] He thoughtfully gave a philosophical explanation of the taking of private property on the high seas, a practice discouraged on land by the customary laws of war:

The hostile power has an interest in the private property of all persons living within its limits or control; for such property is a subject of taxation, contribution, confiscation and use, with or without compensation. But the humanity of modern times has abstained from the taking of private property not liable to use in war, when on land. Some of the reasons for this, are, the infinite varieties of its character, the difficulty of discriminating among these varieties, the need of much of it to support the life of non-combatant persons and animals, and, above all, the moral dangers attending searches and captures in households. But on the high seas, these reasons do not apply. Strictly personal effects are not taken. Merchandise sent to sea, is sent voluntarily, embarked by merchants on an enterprise of profit, taking the risks, is in the custody of men trained and paid for the business, and its value is usually capable of compensation in money.[20]

Dana had obviously thought deeply about the meaning of piracy and legitimate captures at sea. Indeed, in 1862 he had argued in defense of a marine insurance company attempting to escape payment for the destruction of a vessel by the Confederate commerce raider *Sumter*. Then his position had been that the acts of vessels with letters from Jefferson Davis sending them on their mission in fact constituted piracy and not belligerent captures of contraband of war.[21] The position taken there was, if not entirely the opposite, difficult to square with the position he took on the *Amy Warwick*, one of the *Prize Cases* before the U.S. Supreme Court later. That suggests the difficulties of interpretation involved in legal arguments, for they may not represent anyone's actual intellectual universe of beliefs and assumptions. Lawyers are paid to come up with clever arguments.

Aside from considerable intellectual ability and familiarity with affairs on the high seas (Dana was the author of the famed *Two Years before the Mast*), Dana had a gift for making the position of the opposition appear absurd. He thus characterized the position of the shipowners' counsel in the *Prize Cases* as forbidding the exercise of the war powers in a civil war by anyone but the enemy.[22] He insisted that war was "*a state of things*" and "not an act of legislative will," pointing out that Congress recognized rather than declared the foreign war on Mexico in 1846.[23] Dana's arguments, for all their dazzling brilliance, were not adopted wholesale by the majority opinion and actually may not have been necessary to persuade even the Democratic justices to support the government position. Certainly the Supreme Court did not join in ridiculing the idea of a court stopping a war. What ultimately swayed the pro-Union justices was nationalism.

The Legal Tender Act in the Courts

We can see the effects of Justice Grier's majority opinion in the *Prize Cases* in *Metropolitan Bank v. Van Dyck*. In this instance a state supreme court was considering an act of Congress passed on February 25, 1862, only a year and a half later, in the summer of 1863. It apparently required a streamlined path to the highest court in New York. Lawyer J. V. W. Doty had to explain to the justices that there was no written opinion from the lower court on this case and, indeed, that it had not even been argued there.[24] The case had been combined with another, *Meyer v. Roosevelt*. In the end, the act was upheld by a 5-3 vote.

The case arose from a requirement of the New York State Constitution that banks must redeem all their bills and notes in gold or silver upon demand. But on March 26, 1863, when a man named Valentine asked to redeem ten-dollar notes in specie at two New York banks, the banks offered Valentine only paper money, which the U.S. Congress had designated legal tender. Valentine protested to the superintendent of banks, the man named Van Dyck who was the respondent in the case, acting as though the banks were not in compliance with the law. The banks sued, wanting to pay in paper money rather than in specie.[25] They sued first in the state supreme court; then the decision was appealed to the state's highest court.

The New York Court of Appeals was made up of eight justices, four judges elected at large and four judges from the state supreme court with the shortest terms remaining. The opinions in *Metropolitan Bank v. Van Dyck* ran strictly along party lines, the two Democrats dissenting and the other six justices, elected on various anti-Democratic tickets over the years, upholding the authority of Congress in the matter.

Justice Henry E. Davies, elected to the court as a Republican in 1859, wrote the majority opinion.[26] Naturally eager to pronounce the Legal Tender Act constitutional, Davies was clearly relieved to find a judicial precedent for taking into account the condition of the nation in his opinion:

> We have abundant authority, if any were needed, for taking judicial notice of the existence of the present war, of its extent, and of the condition of the country. The Supreme Court of the United States, in the recent prize cases, say: "They cannot ask the court to affect a technical ignorance of the existence of a war which all the world acknowledges to be the greatest civil war known in the history of the human race, and thus cripple the arm of the government, and paralyze its powers by subtle definitions and ingenious sophisms." We take notice of the

fact that, to maintain armies and provide a navy for the prosecution of the war, more money is needed annually than all the specie within the United States, and that a resort by the government, to the use of its own credit, was not only a matter of necessity, but the result has demonstrated that it was a measure of prudence and wisdom. . . . Fortunate will it be for the government and the people, if, on a careful examination, it shall be ascertained by the courts that these measures which have produced such benign and important results, are in harmony with the letter and spirit of the Constitution, and authorized by it.[27]

Davies found in favor of the constitutionality of the congressional act in an opinion that thoroughly endorsed the power of the national government. He quoted the three times in the Articles of Confederation that the Union was declared perpetual (ignoring Article II, which declared the states sovereign). He then said that the Constitution meant to make that perpetual Union more perfect, and he noted that judges were sworn to obey the Constitution. "The omnipotence of the British Parliament," he asserted, "is not more absolute than is the supremacy of the Congress of the United States upon all subjects which are either expressly or impliedly delegated to it."[28] The supreme court of the first district had already held the notes of the government to be legal tender, and Davies piled on the nationalistic authorities to uphold the decision. He invoked *Ableman v. Booth*, by then emerging as a precedent for upholding federal authority over soldiers enlisted in the army under doubtful conditions. Now that opinion was finding broader uses in upholding federal power.[29]

Despite all these nationalistic sources of authority lined up neatly behind his opinion, Davies still had rough sailing ahead, for the Constitution did not expressly give Congress power to make legal tender of paper money. So he argued that the court could not construe the Constitution in such a way that it could not carry out its main objects. Ultimately, he relied on the historical practice of the Congress determining what was legal tender, and such long practice, unchallenged over the years, stood as proof of the power.[30]

One justice, Republican Ransom Balcom, found no particular need to invoke the U.S. Supreme Court.[31] Balcom reasoned that the law was constitutional because the power to make legal tender of the government paper was necessary and proper for maintaining and supporting an army and a navy to suppress the rebellion. He pointed out, as Davies did, that the measure was a success, and that "such a thing as pecuniary distress, in the loyal states, on account of the war, or by reason of the financial measures of the government, has not been heard of." The triumphalist tone of Balcom's opinion was dictated by overarching fear that the inflation of the Revolutionary War era might be repeated in the present war; thus it was not as triumphalist then as it sounds to us today. It was in fact defensive, an assurance that the greenbacks of the Civil War would not become as notoriously worthless as a Continental from the Revolution. Balcom was convinced that the country was facing "the wickedest and most groundless rebellion ever organized in any age or country" (he thereby supplied the sort of emotional comment that Republicans expected and the absence of which always made them suspicious).

As if all these assertions were not enough, Balcom carefully left room for the more nationalistic and entirely extraconstitutional authority for a legal decision, noting: "I will not say this law could not be sustained on the broad ground that the government of the United States has the right of self-preservation, and that it was necessary for that purpose."[32] Here the use of the term "broad" as in "broad construction" was as slippery and misleading as Carlisle's use of "thereof" had been. This was not a matter of construing some power broadly; it was a matter of invoking a power not mentioned at all. Regarding the measure as essentially a war measure, Balcom stated that it was "not probable such an act as this will ever be deemed necessary or proper in time of peace; and the one in question will undoubtedly be repealed, and the notes under it called in, and a metallic currency restored, as soon after the present rebellion shall have been suppressed."[33]

Justice William R. Wright, also a Republican, concluded his opinion affirming the constitutionality of the congressional act with this patriotic admonition to get priorities right:

> We have been admonished of the frightful consequences in the future, to result from an irredeemable paper currency, based on the credit of the nation; but if all the evils so strongly pictured, and which are mainly figments of the imagination, were to occur, how insignificant in comparison with a destruction of the government. If this magnificent governmental structure of ours falls, it will matter little that, in the effort to save it, disorder and ruin were brought on the commercial and monetary interests of the country.[34]

Justice James Emott, who came to the court on a ticket opposed to the Democrats in 1855, gave a concurring opinion that was unusually revealing about his personal motives. He said that he

approached the consideration of this great question with a desire to
sustain the act of Congress. . . . As much as this is due, in my judgment, to any and every act of the supreme legislature of the nation.
But this just repugnance to thwart that legislative will or prohibit its
exercise is enhanced in the present instance by the consideration of
the grave responsibility assumed by any citizen, who, in any way or
in any sphere of action, will interpose hindrances or obstacles to the
efforts of the government to suppress the great and wicked rebellion,
which has brought so much misery upon us — a rebellion as little justified in morals as in legal or constitutional right.

And yet, he noted, "the question for us, as judges, is simply one of law." He
had started from the assumption that the law was unconstitutional, but he
had discovered, happily, and "as a pure question of constitutional law," that
the act was within the powers of Congress.[35] Emott found the authority of
Congress in its power to "borrow money on the credit of the United States"
(Article I, section 8), which is essentially what the greenbacks did. Once that
power was granted, the ability of Congress to confer upon the government's
paper the qualities necessary to make it acceptable to the people was not
forbidden by the Constitution and was therefore an irresistible inference.[36]

Justice Richard Marvin, elected as an American Party candidate in 1855,
concurred, dwelling on the power of Congress over commerce and offering
no patriotic sentiment. Republican justice Enoch Rosekrans concurred as
well.[37]

Chief Justice Hiram Denio, a Democrat known for his judicial independence, dissented.[38] He was careful, however, to note the problem of the
national circumstance and, indeed, left a heartfelt lament that he could not
go where his Republican colleagues had gone in this case:

If my sense of duty would allow me to decide the case, as I should wish
the law under the circumstances of this moment temporarily to be, I
would unite in a judgment which should establish the validity of these
legal tender notes; for the preservation of the federal Union, which
is said to be involved, is the most ardent, I may say passionate desire
of my heart. . . . No man can have a stronger sense of the absolute
causelessness, nay, the utter wickedness of the insurrection than that
which I entertain — or of the duty of every citizen, whether in public
office or a private station, to yield to the constituted authorities upon
all questions of policy or expediency, not only implicit obedience, but
a sincere and generous confidence and cooperation.[39]

But Denio was "placed here to determine the law" as he understood it, and he could not see the constitutionality of the act. Without comment, Justice Samuel S. Selden, a fellow Democrat, agreed with him.[40]

History hung heavily over the decision. Most Americans were fearfully aware of the reputation of the financing of the American Revolution for ruinous inflation by paper currency. And Democrats in particular, since Andrew Jackson's day, leaned to hard money ideas. Thus it was for many loyal Democrats a hard dose to swallow: both a Republican policy and a soft money policy. The decision marked a triumph of nationalism in this instance of constitutional conflict, where the Constitution was not nearly as clear as in the case of conscription.

The Conscription Act in the Courts

Modern readers accustomed to thinking of constitutional issues in wartime mainly as matters of individual liberty at risk in a period when the state makes great demands upon its citizens will find it difficult to understand the arguments over conscription in the Civil War. Individual liberty had little to do with the issue: in that era of nationalism, judges focused on the question of which political entity had the higher claim to the citizen-soldier. At bottom, they assumed, some political entity did, and in the United States, either the federal government or the state government claimed that authority.

These days we might argue for a long time about conscription without ever mentioning the word "militia," but in the middle of the nineteenth century the issue of conscription was seldom discussed without reference to the militia. Both armies and militia were mentioned in the U.S. Constitution. But Americans apparently began to lose sight of this in the mid-twentieth century, when the draft was denounced as a totalitarian institution.[41] The important differences between the mindset of the nineteenth century and ours today are that nationalism then was not necessarily regarded as a near pathology, nor was the militia then viewed as a supplement to the army.[42] On the contrary, the militia was considered a balance to the army. Judges tended to think of the two institutions in the way they were described — somewhat misleadingly — in *The Federalist*. One or the other, or both, had a legitimate claim on the life of the citizen, for the idea of nationalism was that the citizen's life was not his own. It belonged to the nation.

Alexander Hamilton wrote the extremely able series of papers (nos. 23–29) in *The Federalist* making the case for the unlimited power of Congress to raise armies. As a onetime member of General George Washington's staff and an artillerist and member of the Continental Army in the Revolution,

Hamilton had few illusions about the utility of militias and nonprofessional soldiers for winning wars. He was perhaps the first and one of the most effective critics of the myth of the citizen-soldier in American history. In *The Federalist*, no. 25, after having argued for the power of Congress to raise armies, Hamilton paused and said:

> Here I expect we shall be told that the militia of the country is its natural bulwark, and would be at all times equal to the national defense. This doctrine, in substance, had like to have lost us our independence. It cost millions to the United States that might have been saved. The facts which from our own experience forbid a reliance of this kind are too recent to permit us to be the dupes of such a suggestion. The steady operation of war against a regular and disciplined army can only be successfully conducted by a force of the same kind. . . . The American militia, in the course of the late war, have, by their valor on numerous occasions, erected eternal monuments to their fame; but the bravest of them feel and know that the liberty of their country could not have been established by their efforts alone, however great and valuable they were. War, like most other things, is a science to be acquired and perfected by diligence, by perseverance, by time, and by practice.[43]

The Federalist had not only to explain the nationalist policies that lay behind the new Constitution but also to sell them to a people not as yet necessarily nationalized. Therefore, after arguing forcefully along the nationalist lines suggested by the quotation above, Hamilton near the end of his case, in paper no. 28, backed off a little and said there was no real danger of "usurpation" of the people's liberties by the U.S. Army because of the balance of the Constitution:

> Power being almost always the rival of power, the general government will at all times stand ready to check the usurpations of the state governments, and these will have the same disposition towards the general government. The people, by throwing themselves into either scale, will infallibly make it preponderate. If their rights are invaded by either, they can make use of the other as the instrument of redress. . . .
>
> It may safely be received as an axiom in our political system that the State governments will, in all possible contingencies, afford complete security against invasions of the public liberty by the national authority. . . . When will the time arrive that the federal government

can raise and maintain an army capable of erecting a despotism over the great body of the people of an immense empire, who are in a situation, through the medium of their State governments, to take measures for their own defense, with all the celerity, regularity, and system of independent nations? The apprehension may be considered as a disease, for which there can be found no cure in the resources of argument and reasoning.[44]

In the end, Hamilton felt compelled to say that the states had military power in the militias the equal of an independent nation and might need that power some day for protection from the national government.

Over the years after the ratification of the Constitution, the mythic prowess of the state militias recovered their reputation in America. The process began, of course, with the Bill of Rights. The Second Amendment was definitely the "militia amendment," not in the sense that it had no interest in an individual right to bear arms, but in the sense that it reaffirmed the importance of the militia after the arguments in *The Federalist* and in the nationalist ratification campaign had bolstered the power to raise armies. Thus the Bill of Rights reassured the people who needed such assurance that "a well regulated Militia" was "necessary to the security of a free State."[45] Hamilton's other arguments to the contrary faded from view.

Years later, when conscription became an issue in the courts, the clear thrust of the Federalist interpretation of the Constitution was no longer regnant in opinion. It was at first difficult for the question to enter the courts. But when it got there, it would be considered as a matter of maintaining a balance between state and national power.

After Abraham Lincoln suspended the writ of habeas corpus for the whole country, it required either an accelerated appeals path or some legal gymnastics to bring a war-related question quickly before a court. The draft riots in New York City in July 1863 caused Democrats to look for a way to bring the issue of conscription before the courts. George T. Curtis, one of the lawyers in the Legal Tender cases before the New York Court of Appeals, and Samuel J. Tilden, another prominent New York Democratic lawyer, contrived a case that would avoid the problem of the writ of habeas corpus. Just as the draft riots were ending, Curtis wrote Tilden and asked:

Does not the jurisdiction of our Supreme Court, in General Term, admit of a writ of prohibition, to be applied for on the ground that certain persons, etc., are about to enroll, summon, and subject to martial law A. B. and C. D., citizens of New York and members of its militia, etc., etc.? This would avoid all difficulty about the *habeas corpus*. If it be said that a prohibition out of a State court cannot control a Federal officer, I think it is sufficiently answered if the prohibition is founded on the allegation that the Federal officer is undertaking to act under color of a law constitutionally invalid. The process and the case may be afterwards drawn into the Federal judicial power for revision. But it may issue and may be served and then there is a Legal process and not a mere forcible resistance.

The Federal court, too, has probably the same jurisdiction, although I have not the means here of looking at that.[46]

This plan would employ arcane rules and procedures. The writ of prohibition was rarely used, and it was not at all clear that it could be used in this situation. Its only virtue was that serving this writ on an officer of the United States could not be answered by saying the writ of habeas corpus was suspended. In fact, the writ of prohibition was customarily served by one higher court on another to keep it from infringing jurisdiction; its application to an executive officer would raise questions about the separation of powers. The New York scheme, a desperate attempt to get around the suspension of the writ of habeas corpus, despite the able lawyers behind it, never came to fruition.

A Pennsylvania scheme, similarly desperate, actually worked for a brief time. Francis Hughes, the Democratic organizer who in 1862 had first championed the celebration of September 17 as Constitution Day, wrote Tilden shortly after the draft riots in New York to urge legal action there:

The suspense here to have the adjudication of your courts upon the constitutionality of the conscription act is painful. If the courts shall hold that this enactment is outside of and overrides the Constitution, our people in Penn'a will sustain that position. On the other hand, if the courts shall hold the act constitutional, rather than resist law and invoke anarchy, I do not think there will be any other opposition than sporadic outbreaks and a general fleeing to avoid the compulsory service. I write to ask you that for the sake of the public peace, and I may well add for the sake of republican liberty on this continent, you give your best efforts to obtain a *speedy* decision on this subject.[47]

Philadelphia lawyers George Wharton and Charles Ingersoll came up with the plan. Wharton was one of several lawyers who had answered Horace Binney with a pamphlet on habeas corpus. Ingersoll had also fallen victim to arrest for a speech he gave. Their idea was to get the constitutionality of conscription before a court by an injunction bill against the enrolling officers. They could then appeal directly to the state supreme court for injunctive relief, they thought. The gimmick was that the court would be acting as a court of equity (rather than a court of law) in order to issue an injunction. But equity (or chancery) courts traditionally dealt only with property, not with individual liberty. It would avoid the officer's invoking the suspension of the writ of habeas corpus all right, but the injunction was not meant to prevent harm to liberty, only to property that might be diminished in value before the court could decide the case.[48] Republican justices saw the move as simply substituting injunctive relief for the writ of habeas corpus and thus frustrating a clear power of the government under the Constitution by a highly irregular resort to a procedure customarily applied only to cases involving property.[49]

Nevertheless, the legal gambit worked well for the Democrats, because the justices rotated the duty of hearing pleas for injunctions and a Democratic justice was performing the duty when the Democratic lawyers appealed in the cases of the potential draftees. The men in question were Henry S. Kneedler and two other conscripts, and they filed the bill of injunction against the head of the conscription board, a man named David Lane.[50] In his opinion on the case, Justice James Thompson, a Democrat, stated simply: "Our jurisdiction of the case I think is plain. We have authority to restrain acts contrary to law, and prejudicial to the rights of individuals: Act of 16th June 1836."[51] Besides gaining direct access to a prestigious court controlled by a Democratic majority of 3-2, this strategy also avoided the habeas corpus problem. The strategy pursued an accelerated legal path because injunctions were immediate remedies for harm about to occur to the plaintiff. Wharton and Ingersoll also avoided another problem. Congress, on March 3, 1863, had not only authorized suspension of the writ of habeas corpus but also exempted arresting officers from suits for wrongful arrest in cases where habeas corpus figured. Though the damages to the conscripts, in other words, would be great, the remedy of a suit for damages seemed ruled out by the congressional act, which in part offered indemnity for officers making arrests of civilians. As Justice Thompson put it, "An action for damages would perhaps not be sustainable under a recent act of Congress, but if it should be, it would be against parties who intended no injury, and from whom, on account of obeying what they supposed to be law, in conducting the proceedings against him, but little could be recovered, although the soldier may have been carried to distant places, from his home, and may have undergone great hardships and vicissitudes."[52]

The scheme got the case before the Pennsylvania Supreme Court for an initial hearing on the request for a preliminary injunction on September 23, 1863; if the injunction was granted there would be a final hearing later. Unfortunately for the Democrats, 1863 was a gubernatorial election year in Pennsylvania, and the Democratic candidate for governor was a justice of the Supreme Court, George Washington Woodward. That circumstance perhaps induced caution, though customarily electoral politics produced the opposite behavior: brinkmanship. Election day was October 13, and the court postponed the hearing until after that date, to November 9. The majority opinion was written by Chief Justice Walter H. Lowrie, a Democrat who had just run for reelection to the court in October and lost. Because his term did not end until December, he had time to write the opinion as a parting shot.

Conscription would seem naturally to invite considerations of the national emergency, much more so than the money supply. But the Pennsylvania court was controlled by Democrats, and the arguments were not as shaped by overt nationalism as they were in *Metropolitan Bank v. Van Dyck*. In fact, if one stands back from the arguments as a whole, what is striking is the degree to which the Democrats controlled the tone of the courtroom debate. There was little sense of national emergency or struggle for existence. Surely that might have been different if the Confederates had won the Battle of Gettysburg four months earlier and Harrisburg, where the court was sitting, were besieged or even occupied by Robert E. Lee's troops. Justice Lowrie did express the "very real distress" that his mind was "forced into this conflict with an act of Congress of such very great importance in the present juncture of federal affairs." But, he said, he could not help it. The Conscription Act was unconstitutional.

In 1863 the arguments in Pennsylvania focused mostly on the role of the militia and therefore relied at times on *The Federalist*. Lowrie warned that conscription would destroy the state militias and thus leave "the states as defenseless as an ancient city with its walls broken down. Nothing is left that has any constitutional right to stand before the will of the federal government." That image of a state as a fortress walled off from the federal government speaks volumes about how different were the assumptions concerning state rights in the mid-nineteenth century from today.[53]

Lowrie did rely on historical arguments from both the British and the American past. His arguments cannot be characterized as inflammatory, but at one point they drew veiled parallels to the history of the English Civil War with its lessons for the dangers of the use of government power against liberty by the political party temporarily controlling the government:

Courts of High Commission . . . and Special Commissions of Oyer and Terminer . . . created for the purpose of trying and condemning acts which no law forbade — liberty of speech and of the press most cruelly punished by such courts when it ventured on too free a dissent from the policy of the dominant party — informations by the attorney-general substituted in such cases for indictments by the grand jury — members of parliament expelled because their opposition was offensive or dangerous to the ruling power — military officers dismissed because of their political opinions . . . — rumors of plots, real or fictitious, such as the Oates Conspiracy, the Meal Tub and Rye House Plots, raised and magnified in order to alarm the people against all opposition, and facilitate the downfall of dangerous rivals — patronage, pensions, and seats in parliament corruptly disposed of in opposition to public liberty — and the control of the militia so attempted to be usurped as to produce a revolution that resulted in the execution of Charles I.[54]

Lowrie recited all of these events as a warning against the excesses of party and the possibility of party use of the militia while under control of the federal government. On the other hand, some of the references might seem to have been aimed at unspoken topical parallels, most notably in the instances of the dismissal of military officers for political opinions (a parallel to George B. McClellan in the minds of Democrats) or the use of special commissions to try crimes unknown to the laws (military commissions in the American Civil War). A Democrat looking back on this opinion from the vantage point of 1864 might find its conspiratorial view of politics entirely vindicated by events subsequent to Lowrie's statement — the attempt to expel Ohio Democrat Alexander Long from the House of Representatives or the publication of the government's exaggerated report on the threat posed by the Knights of the Golden Circle, for example.

Because, in part, the government did not send counsel to argue its side of the case, Justice Lowrie chose to answer arguments he had learned about in other ways, most likely from the partisan press. "I have noticed the argument," he said, "that because the notorious Hartford Convention opposed the war of 1812, and with it Mr. Monroe's plan of recruiting the army [by conscription], therefore, opposition to a similar plan now ought to be suspected as unpatriotic." In other words, he was choosing to answer for the Democrats the partisan charge that their doctrines now echoed the old Hartford Convention with its supposedly treasonable and secessionist purposes. On the contrary, Lowrie said, the condemnation of the Hartford Convention was founded mainly on the undue and selfish prominence which it gave to, and the agitations it raised in favor of its own sectional interests, when the country was engaged in a dangerous war — its opposition to the admission of new states, for fear of losing the balance of power — its demand that negroes should be considered part of the militia — its opposition to persons of foreign birth being allowed to hold office, and to its real or supposed intention to produce a secession of the Eastern States, if it should not succeed in its measures.[55]

These had nothing to do with conscription, but they made neat parallels with modern politics in 1863. Lowrie was able to turn the tables and suggest that the Republicans ignored other objectionable features of the Hartford Convention. He thus made veiled parallels to Republican policies (opposition to foreigners, for instance, being a common Democratic allegation against the Republicans and their adherents who were former Know-Nothings).

It is interesting to note the quiet distortions of partisanship. The "demand that negroes should be considered part of the militia" was of a piece with the Hartford Convention's opposition to the three-fifths compromise in the Constitution and its swelling of the Southern states' electoral college vote for president of the United States. In fact, what the convention did, as historian James M. Banner Jr. expressed it, was to decry "the proposed apportionment of the conscripted militiamen on the basis of the white population alone," another measure that would have decreased the Southern states' burden of supplying manpower for the war at the expense of the New England states. The proposition on the racial basis of the militia was not one of the seven constitutional amendments recommended by the convention, which were well known. Lowrie had studied history closely to write his opinion.[56]

Finally, Lowrie dealt rather gingerly with the question of jurisdiction and the unusual route taken to the state supreme court via seeking an injunction, asserting: "No one denies that a federal, as well as a state officer, acting without constitutional authority, to the injury of any one, is liable to be sued for his acts in the state courts, and I am quite unable to discover that there is any distinction in such cases between preventive and redressive remedies."[57]

Fellow Democratic justice George Washington Woodward, the failed gubernatorial candidate, likewise showed a desire to criticize the politically vulnerable parts of the Republicans' conscription policy, even though election day in Pennsylvania was past. Referring to the provision in the conscription law for paying a $300 commutation fee in lieu of service, he said: "It is the first instance, in our history, of legislation forcing a great public burthen on the poor." But he had to admit, "This, however, is an objection to the spirit of the enactment rather than to its constitutionality."[58]

Woodward left the question of jurisdiction to Lowrie and focused his arguments on the constitutionality of the congressional act, particularly on the idea that the simple phrase at issue in the text of the U.S. Constitution — the power "to raise armies"— could possibly have been meant to include the power to raise them by conscription. Woodward argued that the Conscription Act merely renamed the militia of the states the "national forces" and then proceeded to assume powers over them inconsistent with the clauses of the Constitution governing the militia. (He did not allow for the persons liable to be raised in armies to be, inevitably, persons who were also members of state militias.) He also contended that the law was unconstitutional when it made draftees who failed to report to their rendezvous deserters, relying on Joseph Story's assertion that men could not be considered part of the armed services when called forth but only when in actual service. Finally, Woodward said that the only argument he had "ever heard suggested . . . which is applicable against all the views advanced in this opinion, is that called military necessity."[59] The government had not used any such contention in this case, since it had refused to argue the case (just as the government had not used the Hartford Convention–James Monroe conscription proposal argument). And we know that President Lincoln, for one, did not believe such a doctrine need be invoked. In his view, there simply should be no "denying a power which is plainly and distinctly written down in the constitution."[60] But Woodward provided his own interpretation of what "military necessity" might mean: "The country is involved in a great civil war, which can be brought to an honourable close only by an energetic use of all our resources, and no restraints should be tolerated, in such circumstances, save only those which Christian civilization has imposed on all warfare. Whatever is according to the constitution, the argument claims, may be done of course, whatever is over and beyond the constitution is justified as military necessity, and of that the president and Congress are exclusive judges."[61]

Justice Woodward then paraphrased his own paraphrase, saying that the "amount of the argument is, that the exigencies of the times justify the substitution of martial law for the constitution." He could then denounce martial law as no law at all. Finally, Woodward concluded that "the constitution anticipates and provides for . . . calamities" such as war and rebellion and therefore it was "a reproach to its wisdom to say that it is inadequate to such emergencies."[62] Students of the constitutional history of the Civil War will immediately recognize Woodward's argument for an "adequate constitution" as one of the leading interpretations of modern times, but they might be surprised to see its source in this case — a Democrat declaring conscription unconstitutional.[63] Woodward invoked it by way of refuting the common Republican argument of the day. "I do not," he said, "feel the force of the argument drawn from the distressing circumstance of the time."[64]

Justice James Thompson, the third Democrat on the Pennsylvania Supreme Court, was also on the side of pronouncing the law unconstitutional. He offered a clearly written and forceful reading of the Constitution and of *The Federalist* on this subject. He came the closest, perhaps, in all of the five opinions on the case, to considering the Constitution as a whole. All of the justices, but Thompson most notably, started from the assumption rather foreign to modern Americans, that the state militia was a balancing and not a supplemental force. "They are the security of the states," he stated flatly, "against the federal government, and their only security; for the states themselves are not allowed to support armies."[65] Therefore, the federal government could not be allowed to annihilate them under a conscription. He cited paper no. 28 of *The Federalist* to that effect. He also pointed out that the conflicting goals of the Constitution must be balanced — providing for the common defense as well as securing the blessing of liberty. Moreover, he was the only justice to note that the Second Amendment to the Constitution was meant to reaffirm that "a well-regulated militia" was "necessary to the security of a free state."[66] Thompson twice insisted that he strongly desired to "witness the suppression of this unjustifiable and monstrous rebellion," but he also had grown impatient with the dismissal of the rights of the states in the name of fighting rebellion. "What is to become of the states and their sovereignty, a matter often sneered at, but among the most distinct, clear and cherished principles in the whole body of the constitution?" he asked.[67]

Of course, the two Republican justices, William Strong and John M. Read, dissented. Strong relied on three simple points. First, it was "a confusion of ideas" to think the fact that the federal government "was one of limited powers" meant that the powers it was allowed to exercise were in themselves limited. They were limited in number but not in quality.[68] Second, he cited as precedents in practice the use of drafts by the governments of the states during the Revolution, albeit by reference to histories written by John Marshall and James Ramsay, not by citing the relevant statutes from original sources. Perhaps the necessary haste imposed by a request for a preliminary injunction (as well as the government's failure to supply counsel and argument) limited his research time. Third, he pointed out the obvious: the militia of the states included everyone liable to military service in the country and therefore when Congress raised armies from Americans, "Whether gathered by coercion or enlistment, they are equally taken out of those who form a part of the militia of the states."[69]

Justice Read supplied the crucial quotation from *The Federalist* that the Democratic justices ignored. In paper no. 23, Hamilton had written, famously, that the power to raise armies must

> exist without limitation; because it is impossible to foresee or to define the extent and variety of national exigencies, and the correspondent extent and variety of the means which may be necessary to satisfy them. The circumstances that endanger the safety of nations are infinite; and for this reason no constitutional shackles can wisely be imposed on the power to which the care of it is committed. This power ought to be co-extensive with all the possible combinations of such circumstances; and ought to be under the direction of the same councils which are appointed to preside over the common defence.[70]

To be sure, *The Federalist* was not the Constitution of the United States and Hamilton never mentioned conscription itself, but once the Democrats used it as authority, certainly the Republicans' use was fair and necessary for a balanced reading. On this question, because George Washington's old staff officer Alexander Hamilton wrote the relevant papers (nos. 23–28), *The Federalist* favored the Republican position of 1863. Justice Read also included a long section of his opinion on the peculiar history of the militia in Pennsylvania, a weak institution because of the importance and size of the community of Quakers in the state. That may not have advanced the Republican case greatly in the eyes of the greater world, but this was a decision by a state supreme court after all.

Read was as strong a partisan as his Democratic counterparts on the court and played the role parallel to that of Lowrie—of reading national history with partisan lessons for the present lurking behind his words. He dwelled at some length on the proposal for a draft devised by Secretary of War James Monroe in our "second war of independence." "It was opposed by the peace men of the day," Read said, "gentlemen who favoured the Hartford Convention, and who were entirely opposed to the general administration, and the further prosecution of the war." That was the point that Lowrie had argued against. Read then pointed to a measure devised in New York, a prowar state during the War of 1812, to raise twelve thousand men for the war by conscription—a measure devised by one of the founders of the Democratic Party, Martin Van Buren.[71] At that point Justice Read's nationalism took over his argument entirely, and he launched into a declaration of loyalty that made the affirmations of the Democrats on the court seem the tepid products of an obligatory patriotism:

> If there ever was an occasion to call every man into the service of his country, it is the present one, when we are engaged in combating the most formidable, wicked, and causeless rebellion known in history, of which the object of its traitorous leaders is to destroy the Union, to erect a purely slave confederacy, and to make Pennsylvania a border state, exposed to the annual inroads of unprincipled enemies. I am, therefore, for using the whole population, if necessary, of the loyal states to extinguish this treasonable rebellion. I have no idea of allowing northern sympathizers to stay at home, whilst loyal men fight their battles and protect their property. I would oblige all such men to render their full share of military service, and if I had the power I would place the New York rioters in the front ranks of the army.[72]

Read also tackled the issue of jurisdiction. "The proposition submitted to this court by the counsel of the plaintiffs," he said, "is that a state tribunal should prohibit an officer of the United States, acting in strict conformity to an act of Congress, from performing the duties imposed upon him by law. I cannot think we have any such power." The three plaintiffs were "in custody under the authority of the United States," and other judges and Republican lawyers had by this time discovered in *Ableman v. Booth* an assertion of the lack of power of a state court to bring the person within its jurisdiction.[73] "The doctrine contended for by the plaintiffs' counsel," he insisted, "is simply the Calhoun heresy of nullification . . . applied not by a convention or a state legislature, but by a state judiciary, who may, by preliminary injunctions, stop the raising of armies and the collection of taxes, duties, imposts, and excises, and thus paralyze the arm of government when stretched out to repel a foreign foe, or to suppress a rebellion, backed by several hundred thousand men in the field. I cannot agree that this court can nullify an act of Congress by any prohibitory writ."[74]

The court granted the preliminary injunctions, but the hearing on the final injunctions came only after Lowrie was replaced on the court by Justice Daniel Agnew, a Republican who had won election to the court in October. It was not an inspiring spectacle to see the same court, institutionally, overturn its own decision made less than two months earlier. Strong asserted that he never believed that a court of equity ever claimed to have authority in such a case.[75] In other words, the route to a quick decision and avoiding the problem of the suspension of the writ of habeas corpus was unique and, in the Republican's view, not really lawful. No court of equity could enjoin against an arrest, and now the hasty path to judicial consideration (really, reconsideration) was taken by the Republican interests. None of the customary steps in the arcane course of equity between the granting of a preliminary injunction and the final decision had been taken before this new hearing. Strong objected to these matters of "the minutest technicality."[76] He had nothing to add to his earlier considerations on the constitutionality of the draft.

Agnew likewise addressed the somewhat embarrassing reversal of judgment, elsewhere giving a vigorous nationalistic rationale for congressional power over the means of national defense. It seemed absurd to him that the defense of the realm would be vested in states, jurisdictions that were forbidden to raise armies or to conduct foreign policy or display many of the other essential qualities of national sovereignty.[77]

Democrats Woodward and Thompson united behind an opinion written by Woodward. It appears that the Democrats' legal gambit had by now backfired. In the first place, it was intended to be a fast track to the U.S. Supreme Court, but the defendants — the government — did not appeal. Instead, they turned the technicalities on the Democrats. Injunction bills were sought before one judge of the state supreme court (in this instance, he had called on all his colleagues to help him decide). The justice changed every month, and in this December the judge designated was the Republican Strong. He called for a rehearing on the preliminary injunction. The Democratic justices wrote paragraph after paragraph on the irregularity of this procedure, not dwelling, of course, on the irregularity of the injunction procedure in the first place (as a way to avoid habeas corpus).

They also seized the opportunity to answer the Republican arguments on the constitutionality of conscription. This process began with the lawyers for the plaintiffs, who included among them Sidney George Fisher's nemesis, Charles Ingersoll. Ingersoll's argument survives and makes very interesting reading. He objected sharply to the motion to dissolve the injunction, which he said was against the fifty-third rule of procedure for the state of Pennsylvania, if it was not irregular elsewhere.[78] Ingersoll was adept at historical argument. He said of conscription, "Nobody thought of such a thing. It is like the discovery of the President's right to suspend the *habeas corpus*. Both were discoveries made seventy-five years after the fact, after the world had been all that time unanimous to the contrary."[79]

Most effective was Ingersoll's dismissal of the alleged precedent for conscription found in a plan submitted by Secretary of War James Monroe to President James Madison during the War of 1812:

> The plan is said to have had the approbation of the Administration. . . . But Mr. Madison, the head of the Government, gave it none in his message to Congress, delivered on the 20th of the preceding month of September: he makes no allusion to it. It was a war message at a special session, just after the [British] capture of the capital, when the army and navy, and the means of strengthening them, were the only subjects treated in it, and addressed to a Congress sitting in the Post-Office building, because there was no longer a capitol — their own hall was a smoking ruin. It had been burned by the enemy. Was this a moment, if Mr. Madison supposed they were constitutionally entitled to make a draft, to hesitate to say so, when the armies of Great Britain, relieved by the treaty of Paris from their European enemies, were coming in renewed strength against us across the water? It appears to have been Mr. Monroe's project, who was a military man, and of nobody else connected with the Executive.[80]

On the other hand, Ingersoll, following the common practice of extreme client loyalty, utilizing any argument for his clients, put forward the United States's condemnation of impressment of sailors as though it presented the same issue as conscription. The question in impressments was not alone the right to force sailors into the navy, but the practice of impressing American nationals into the British navy. It was more an issue of nationalism than individual liberty.

Even Ingersoll retained the ultimate nationalist assumption of the nineteenth century: that some political unit had a right to the lives and fortunes of every single citizen:

> But governments have a power, beyond that of recruiting; they are *parens patriae*, and have the right to the personal service, if needed, of every citizen, just as they have to his estate and possessions. The citizen and all he has may be taken for the service of the country. God forbid the day should ever come when this power is denied or questioned. It is a right not only plain but familiar. Where, then, resides this final right of sovereignty, this right to call for and sacrifice the body of the citizen on the altar of the country? Where can it be but in the State, if it has not been expressly given away?[81]

The wisdom of Abraham Lincoln's version of American history devised for the sake of saving the Union was nowhere more apparent than it was in this courtroom. If one believed, as Ingersoll did, that the power of conscription did exist, it must have existed somewhere before the U.S. Constitution and that was in the states as independent sovereigns. In Lincoln's view, no state except Texas had ever been sovereign.

Ingersoll's argument was long and aimed everywhere to get at the fundamentals of constitutional interpretation. It is difficult at times to make oneself remember that it was only the argument of counsel — paid for and guided by the needs of clients. We know, of course, that there was more to the cause for Ingersoll than clients in this case, but still it was argument to a purpose determined by an adversarial system and not independent intellectual analysis. If it reminds us just how much talent was available for argument in the American legal system, it also must cause us to be cautious about lavishing too much attention and space on what, in some places, might have been throwaway lines, posturings, and cunning calculation. Still, the assumptions underlying the arguments could be revealing.

Ingersoll insisted on the necessity of interpreting the American Constitution in light of British experience, following the rule that it supplied the meaning of many otherwise difficult terms, but must always be interpreted so that when the meaning of the terms was discovered, it could not be the case that the American application of them was aimed at giving more power to government and less liberty to its citizens. In a way, this unconsciously revealed a weakness in Ingersoll's reasoning: to fix upon the importance of British experience in the case before him was to load the argument in favor of the influence of a nation whose history, because it was a secure island, meant that unlike other European powers it never had to resort to drastic means to enlist ground forces for its defense. For the sake of the argument at hand, however, Ingersoll was driven to a surprisingly antiracist interpretation of history:

> Sir, in the English law books we find much boast of English liberty, and well founded. . . . But when they go on to tell us they were always free, it is in their blood, in the Anglo-Saxon blood, as they call it, they are boasters and empty ones. Sir, did it ever occur to you that the reason why the English are free, and the only one, is because they do not keep an army among them, because they have no soldiers to keep them under? When the feudal days ended, England being an island, and early a naval power, and not in constant fear of invasion, did not set up an army. The representative bodies of the Continent of

Europe were as full of the spirit of encroachment on royal prerogative as ever the English parliaments were, and the blood of the Celtic and Romanic races is as liberty-loving as the Anglo-Saxon; but, unhappily, everywhere but in England there have been troops in pay from the time when the heads of fiefs ceased to follow the sovereign to the field.[82]

The arguments of Ingersoll's kinsman, Sidney George Fisher, were more profoundly and systematically racist, but Fisher came to support the Lincoln administration and the Emancipation Proclamation.

After this and other assertions of counsel, lost to us as usual, Woodward insisted that the Constitution was to be considered as a whole. The reason for that, of course, was that there were no qualifications in the grant of authority to Congress to raise and support armies. Embracing Woodward's rule of construction would mean that the method of raising and supporting armies would have to be compatible with the militia clauses of the Constitution and the Bill of Rights. "To call for the militia in a body," he insisted, "with their state officers at their head, is very unlike drafting them, man by man, into the federal armies, under such officers as the president may choose to appoint over them. The act does this latter thing, and therein it violates the constitution."[83] Thus the militia clauses provided Woodward's textual basis for argument. The theoretical basis, also a matter of considering the whole Constitution, letter and spirit, led to this admonition: "I think due attention has not been given to this argument — that all delegations of power are to be read in a manner consistent with the free and popular nature of the government."[84] That had been Ingersoll's main point about constitutional interpretation. Thus methods of raising armies typical of tyrannical governments would be ruled out. Another theoretical assumption lurked in Woodward's argument as well. "The state," he said, and he was referring to states of the Union, "is *parens patriae*."[85] The states did have the sovereign power to conscript every person for the ultimate defense, and the national government did not, in his view.

In the end, Woodward returned to the bitter dispute over the recourse to equity. He maintained that there was nothing wrong with seeking protection for individual rights through chancery courts if the writ of habeas corpus was no longer an available remedy to protect individual rights and liberty. Equity courts traditionally dealt only with civil law and property, not with rights and liberties. "Courts of equity," he said, "are accustomed to enjoin to prevent frauds, waste, nuisances, trespasses, obstructions, and diversion of watercourses, and in numerous other torts." Why should they not have jurisdiction "of torts which touch liberty"? He asked rhetorically, Did that mean "that property is better guarded with us than liberty?"[86] Woodward dismissed the applicability of the "much relied on" *Ableman v. Booth* decision because it referred to persons under process of a federal court, not persons restrained by a ministerial officer of the federal government.

Other Trials of the Constitution

In Indiana, where all four justices on the state's supreme court were Democrats, cases testing the constitutionality of the Legal Tender Act reached the appellate level in record time. The first required only three months from passage of the act on February 25, 1862, to a decision that was from all appearances adverse to the constitutionality of the act but that did not result in an order to the loser in the case, the State Bank of Indiana, to pay in specie.[87] Instead, the partisan Democratic chief justice, Samuel E. Perkins, appears grudgingly to have noticed the condition of the nation, admitting that "the disastrous consequences to the country that must follow a denial of the validity of that exercise of power, press hard upon the judiciary to sustain the violation of the constitution, if it be such, and thus create a precedent for further usurpations."[88] The Indiana Supreme Court stood as only the first court to hear the question, and, under the circumstances, he thought it best to acquiesce and await the necessary decision of the U.S. Supreme Court.

No such opinion came, of course, and Perkins had the chance to decide the important question again two years later in *Thayer v. Hedges*. Like the previous case, this one came to the state supreme court on appeal from a county circuit court. In other important respects, circumstances had changed. Although the Indiana Supreme Court was still composed of the same four Democrats, they had lost their seats in the state elections of October (they had only six-year terms). As lame ducks, the four were even less happy with the act of Congress than they had been earlier. Perkins's opinion was long and all but comic in its undisciplined jurisprudence. At one point in the opinion, he devoted some 300 words to the meaning of money in the Bible, noting the uses of silver and gold by the likes of Hanameel and Solomon and Abraham.[89] The opinion lacked discipline as well in the subjects it took up, though they were predictably Democratic in nature. Thus he dedicated another 250 words or so to asserting that the power to suspend the writ of habeas corpus lay with Congress and not the president.[90] The court found the legal tender law unconstitutional but once again deferred to a future U.S. Supreme Court decision thought to be in the works. The justices merely affirmed the judgment of the lower court. Otherwise, the opinion asserted the unconstitutionality of the act on the usual grounds, less constitutional than economic: money meant gold and silver coin. At one point in the opinion, Perkins even referred to "natural money."[91] The history of the issue in Indiana followed a herky-jerky path similar to the conscription issue in Pennsylvania. As soon as the new Republican personnel took over the supreme court benches, the judges, as historian Emma Lou Thornbrough expressed it, "dealt with the case as if it had never been considered."[92] Naturally, the Republicans found the law of Congress constitutional.

Nationalism in Constitutional Construction

The prestige of *The Federalist* was, on the whole, an advantage to nationalists in the Civil War era. For this work was a basically nationalist series of papers. It did not, it is true, make a specific case anywhere in the eighty-five numbered essays for a "perpetual Union," but that should not be our only measure. The papers were vigorously nationalistic, and only in recent times has that been adequately noticed, especially by the able constitutional historian, Akhil Reed Amar.[93] Certainly we can see it in Alexander Hamilton's arguments for the standing army that figured in *Kneedler v. Lane*. Though it was possible for Lowrie and Woodward to find promilitia support in *The Federalist*, such arguments did not represent the weight of the arguments in that source, and it was correspondingly easy for Strong, Read, and Agnew to make the case for the unlimited means of raising the national army. And though the Democrats became defenders of the militia during the Civil War, they did not particularly rely on the legacy of the Anti-Federalists on this subject, the second article of the Bill of Rights.

Increasingly, historians have been noting the nationalism of *The Federalist*. They have not yet gone far enough, and it is an important source of nationalism in the Civil War, especially among the judges of the day. In the series of eighty-five essays published over several months, Alexander Hamilton, James Madison, and John Jay put national defense and security first.[94] Historian Kenneth Stampp's influential essay describing the weakness and tardy appearance of the argument for perpetual Union simply underestimates the nationalism of *The Federalist*.[95] We have not come to expect sentiment and poetry in the arguments of Hamilton, Madison, and Jay, but there was even some of that evoked by the nation — for example, in paper no. 2, John Jay wrote:

It has often given me pleasure to observe that independent America was not composed of detached and distant territories, but that one connected, fertile, wide-spreading country was the portion of our western sons of liberty. Providence has in a particular manner blessed it with a variety of soils and productions and watered it with innumerable streams for the delight and accommodation of its inhabitants. A succession of navigable waters forms a kind of chain round its borders, as if to bind it together; while the most noble rivers in the world, running at convenient distances, present them with highways for the easy communication of friendly aids and the mutual transportation and exchange of their various commodities.

With equal pleasure I have as often taken notice that Providence has been pleased to give this one connected country to one united people — a people descended from the same ancestors, speaking the same language, professing the same religion, attached to the same principles of government, very similar in their manners and customs, and who, by their joint counsels, arms, and efforts, fighting side by side throughout a long and bloody war, have nobly established their general liberty and independence.

This country and this people seem to have been made for each other.[96]

The Federalist would surely have continued to be suffused with poetic nationalism had Jay not fallen ill. His loss to the intellectual legacy of *The Federalist* has been underestimated. Many of its other arguments are also nationalistic, but they lack the rhetorical nationalism of Jay.

In the fairly dignified realm of legal and constitutional argument, the Democrats were generally at a loss for traditions on which to draw. The Anti-Federalist legacy was the Bill of Rights, of course, and the Democrats certainly relied on that, but otherwise they quoted *The Federalist* and did not self-consciously invoke the Anti-Federalist writers such as Brutus and Centinel. I have never seen them quoted by Democratic judges in Civil War documents. Both Republicans and Democrats despised the anti–War of 1812 Federalists and the Hartford Convention, which was legendary for factious and treasonous opposition. In fact, both Democrats and Republicans sought to identify the other party with the Hartford Convention. Although politicians on the hustings readily seized on the so-called principles of 1798 — the Kentucky and Virginia Resolutions of 1798–99 — judges seem to have regarded those arguments as off-limits for their debates on the meaning of the Constitution. During the war they were not eager to cite South Carolina's John C. Calhoun as a learned expositor of the meaning of the document. Thus the intellectual advantage handed by tradition to the Civil War era lay entirely with the Republicans, as the constitutional theory (compact and state rights) that emerged within a decade of the ratification of the Constitution of 1787 was too readily identified with nullification and simply too Southern in origin — with the very names of "Kentucky" and "Virginia" Resolutions — to be of use in the courtroom. The standards of argument on the hustings were more freewheeling and, perhaps, more irresponsible than those that governed the nation's court system. It is simply untrue to say, as Kenneth Stampp did, that the argument for Union was at a disadvantage before or at the beginning of the Civil War. It enjoyed ample means and traditions, and the courtroom arguments demonstrate that.

The Democratic experiment of testing Republican war measures in state supreme courts failed. The Pennsylvania Supreme Court did get on the record its assertions of the unconstitutionality of the Conscription Act. But the act went forward in its operation, even for the three plaintiffs in the case. Kneedler and his fellow conscripts were apparently already in camp while the reversal of the preliminary findings was taking place. More to the point, conscription was not before the U.S. Supreme Court in late 1863 or early 1864. In fact, the Conscription Act of March 3, 1863, never got there. The assertion of the will and force of the judges would remain more a matter of judicial guerrilla warfare — sallies and attacks on the ability of the federal government to keep in its ranks individual soldiers in scattered regiments.

Together the Democrats and the Republicans had, in fighting the war in the higher courts, offered up a spectacle of nearly scandalous partisanship, quick legal research by courts of changed political complexion, and wrenching change in customary usages and procedures. On rare occasions a Democrat, moved by nationalism, broke ranks to prevent the courts from endangering the war effort. But on the whole, the nation was saved from violent confrontation with willful judges by the slowness with which the wheels of justice turned in the middle of the nineteenth century.

For the most part, the judiciary, like the rest of the North, was nationalistic. Of course, the experience of Judge Richard B. Carmichael in Talbot County, Maryland, served as a disincentive to those who were less so. Nationalism always involved force at some point. Judges usually sought nationalistic precedents, bolstered by nationalist traditions embodied particularly in *The Federalist*; these, in the end, reversed the legacy of the Federalist judiciary from the War of 1812.

The ineluctable assumption, perhaps the deepest one of the entire nineteenth century, was that nation-states did and should exist. In constitutional terms, that meant what Charles Ingersoll expressed starkly (but others as well), that ultimately the state could rightfully demand the lives and fortunes of its citizens. God forbid, said even this Copperhead opponent of the Union war effort, that that proposition should ever be denied.

Which particular nation-state could lay that rightful claim was a matter of contention many places in the world. That sense of nationalism was rather easy to create but could result in fierce temporary loyalties. It was analogous to the feeling of alumni loyalty to one's school. That is easily and quickly created in most people — every September of every year in each new group of freshmen — and once created is capable of unleashing considerable passion. Cheers, tears, song, and anger can all be aroused at a sports stadium or a pep rally the night before or at a graduation ceremony. The feeling lingers for years and can inspire considerable economic sacrifice — alumni giving. To be sure, an alma mater never demands the ultimate sacrifice of life, but the analogy is most instructive anyway. The nation-state could command all these things with an intensity to this day not fully understood from a psychological or social perspective.

What is deceptive about the powerful feeling in any particular case is the ease with which national sentiment can be aroused — hence the Confederate States of America. It is easy to create a nation (modeled on the idea of the sentiments felt by a great alumni group), but it is very difficult to create a nation-state. In the nineteenth century, a nation-state had to be carved out of the land and people of one or more already existing nation-states — hence the great American Civil War.

Constitutional history may be as good at revealing this powerful nationalist assumption to historians as any kind of history, because in the adversarial system, the arguments get ever sharper and reach for fundamental assumptions — such as ultimately the state can command the lives and fortunes of its citizens. In fact, constitutional history provides the most succinct and precise definition of nineteenth-century nationalism available: it was the belief that nation-states properly commanded the lives and fortunes of every person in the world.

Part 3

The Confederacy and Its Constitution

It may safely be received as an axiom in our political system that the State governments will, in all possible contingencies, afford complete security against invasions of the public liberty by the national authority. Projects of usurpation cannot be masked under pretenses so likely to escape the penetration of select bodies of men, as of the people at large. The legislatures will have better means of information. They can discover the danger at a distance; and possessing all the organs of civil power and the confidence of the people, they can at once adopt a regular plan of opposition, in which they can combine all the resources of the community.

— *The Federalist*, no. 28 (Alexander Hamilton)

Six

Secession DERATIFYING THE CONSTITUTION

Ira Berlin has introduced the distinction between a slave society and a society with slaves, attributing these stern qualities to the former: "In slave
societies . . . slavery stood at the center of economic production, and the
master-slave relationship provided the model for all social relations: husband and wife, parent and child, employer and employee. From the most
intimate connections between men and women to the most public ones
between ruler and ruled, all relationships mimicked those of slavery."[1] The
contrasting picture, also based on the centrality of slavery to the society that
became the Confederacy, was best delineated by J. Mills Thornton III in a
book about Alabama: "Antebellum Alabama was . . . a society obsessed with
the idea of slavery. In the first place, the fear of an imminent loss of freedom was a part of the inheritance which Alabama's citizens had received
from their Revolutionary forbears . . . this tradition was lent considerable
urgency by a daily familiarity with black slavery, which served as a constant
reminder of the terrible reality behind the politician's metaphor. . . . Finally,
slavery guaranteed, so it was believed, that very few white men would ever
have to depend directly upon other white men for their sustenance . . . the
existence of slavery quite naturally came to seem an essential bulwark of
freedom."[2] Neither of these views, though they could hardly differ more,
ignores or slights the importance of slavery. Both put it front and center in
their books. To know that the Confederacy was centrally concerned, even
obsessed, with preserving slavery obviously still leaves a lot of questions unanswered. What follows then, in pursuing the constitutional history of the
Confederate States of America, in no way calls into question the centrality
of slavery to that nation. But knowing that is only a beginning for understanding what the nation was like.

What did the secessionists have in mind? The Confederacy was a slave society by its own admission. Most white Southerners regarded the Confederacy as a slaveholding republic. When state secession conventions began to meet in the winter of 1860–61, their members anxiously consulted the secession feeling in other slaveholding states by sending commissioners to them. They did not, as Charles B. Dew points out, send commissioners to any free states.[3] The leaders of the first states to join together in the Confederacy knew what drew them together into a movement for a new republic.

For many Confederates that identity as a slave society persisted into the days of their republic's great struggle for survival. Thus on September 1, 1861, the *Mobile Register and Advertiser* announced to its readers: "We are a nation based on a 'peculiar institution' . . . [a] nation of one race which has transplanted from another clime a diverse and inferior race within its borders as a subordinate people of bondsmen."[4] They looked unblinkingly at the moral reputation such identity gave them in the world. "We are a 'peculiar people,' doomed to quasi-Ishmaelitism among the nations of the enlightened world," they admitted, and it was so because they were a "slave republic."[5] Thus slavery was an essential part of even the most sober Southerner's version of the Confederate nation.

But so was the republican ideal. The Mobile newspaper called the nation a "slave republic." There is no indication that the republican part of the description was less important than the slave part. Slavery held an essential place in most visions of the Confederate nation, but its presence there does not ipso facto tell the historian what the rest of the content of Confederate nationalism was. The protection and idealization of slavery did not dictate the rest of the content of Confederate nationalism. Slavery did not necessarily make the Confederacy authoritarian and undemocratic in politics. It played only one role in shaping the nation's abstract political ideas. Other ideals came from republicanism.

The Confederate States Constitution, the fundamental description of the relationship between rulers and ruled for their whole nation, did not mimic the master-slave relationship so visible in front of them in their local society. Instead, it mimicked the free Constitution of the United States. The most remarkable feature of the new nation's fundamental document was that it so nearly resembled the document that governed Abraham Lincoln and the rest of the United States. As Clement Eaton expressed it almost fifty years ago, "The Confederate blueprint of government drafted at Montgomery was largely a copy of the Constitution of the United States."[6] The characterization of the Confederate Constitution made by the succeeding generation's basic history of the Confederacy was about the same. Thus

Emory M. Thomas wrote, "Ironically, the most striking feature of the Confederate Constitution was not its Southern orientation. The permanent Constitution prescribed for the Confederacy much the same kind of union which the Southerners had dissolved."[7] A modern Civil War textbook is even more blunt: "Little originality went into framing the new instrument for the southern nation."[8] Except for lengthening the term of the president from four to six years, the essential republican features of Articles I and II of the U.S. Constitution were retained, closely and even lovingly copied. Elections were inexorably fixed by the length of term of the members of the Confederate Congress and of the president. Civilians controlled the military: the civilian president was the commander in chief. Military budgets could not exceed two years' duration and would thus regularly have to be renewed by a new Congress.

Circumstantial and politic reasons compelled the drafters of the Confederate Constitution to deviate as little as possible from the model of 1787. The Provisional Constitution drafted in Montgomery, Alabama, and adopted on February 8, 1861, was meant not only to govern the seven states that had seceded so far but also to attract into their confederation the eight slave states that had not seceded. That was best done by reassuring the potential members of the trustworthiness of the founding document of the new organization. There was no reason to scare off recruits from the new confederation by appearing to be unpredictable and despotic. They would be attracted to the confederation by seeing their old friend, the U.S. Constitution, there to greet them. The Southerners' antebellum quarrels had never been with the Constitution but rather with those in the North who ignored or perverted it, in Southerners' eyes. Yet, for all the compelling tactical reasons to adhere to the basic republican outlines of the old Constitution, the most powerful underlying reason was the sincere and continuing republicanism of the people who wrote the document and would live under it as Confederate citizens.

According to George Rable, the "most extensive exposition" of the new, Confederate Constitution was Robert H. Smith's *Address to the Citizens of Alabama, on the Constitution and Laws of the Confederate States of America, . . . at Temperance Hall, on the 30th of March, 1861*. Smith, a member of the Alabama secession convention himself, readily admitted from the start that "we have followed with almost literal fidelity the Constitution of the United States, and departed from its text only so far as experience had clearly proven that additional checks were required for the preservation of the Nation's interest."[9] Even so, a reader cannot help feeling that Smith was nationalistically proud of the modest constitutional innovations. Were the alterations from the U.S. model—which Smith called "additional checks"—actually aimed at imitating the master-slave relationship in the fundamental rules of the government of the white people of the Confederacy? Rable, for example, concludes: "Changes in the presidency and restrictions on the power of Congress reduced popular influence on public policy. Had they not had to worry about the reaction of the border states, the delegates at Montgomery and perhaps in some of the state conventions might have gone much farther toward creating an elitist government."[10]

The Confederate Constitution included a line-item veto for the president. It also gave the president forward-looking powers over the budget. Smith, in defending the document, bitterly denounced the legislative practices of logrolling and earmarking. "There is hardly a more flagrant abuse of it's [*sic*] power, by the Congress of the United States than the habitual practice of loading bills, which are necessary for Governmental operations with reprehensible, not to say venal dispositions of the public money, and which only obtain favor by a system of combinations among members interested in similar abuses upon the treasury."[11] The Confederate Congress could not make appropriations "from the treasury unless it be asked for by the President or some one of the heads of the Departments, except for the purpose of paying its own expenses and contingencies."[12] As for characterizing as "additional checks" other reform measures, that statement misrepresented the attempt to increase the "facility of communication between the Executive and Legislature."[13] The Confederate Constitution aimed at decreasing separation of powers by allowing Congress to "grant to the principal officer in each of the Executive Departments a seat upon the floor of either House, with the privilege of discussing any measures appertaining to his department."[14] All in all, it is difficult to say whether the new Constitution helped freedom or authority, but it is easier to see that it did not establish a society in imitation of the master-slave relationship. At least, it did not aim at creating a *legal* aristocracy. The Confederate Constitution retained the important Article I, section 9, provision forbidding the granting of titles of nobility.[15]

The States and Their Constitutions

The constitutions of the states in the Confederacy were of critical importance for measuring the extent of the new nation's adherence to republicanism. Belief in state rights lay at the theoretical foundation of the new republic, and the state constitutions are therefore perhaps the most important in evaluating the extent to which the Confederacy wanted to mimic the master-slave relationship of the plantation elsewhere in their polity. That is where the historians who have seen secession as a conservative coup have most often claimed to find their evidence. All of those documents had to be changed in some way to accommodate the new reality of belonging to a new republic with a different name. Did they also change their state constitutions in ways that mimicked the master-slave relationship for the Confederate citizens of their states? Like the provisional Congress of the Confederacy, which also operated as the constitutional convention, the secession conventions for a time operated as legislatures or extraordinary governing bodies, and that is where we must look for the all-important adjustments in governing relationships made by the states.

The work of the secession conventions holds the answer to the question of the "model of social relations" in the Southern slave society. For more than a century historians have argued over the fundamental ethos of secession: Was it a basically popular movement among Southern whites or a conservative coup by planters to protect their property and status? We need a fresh approach to the problem to untie the knot of disagreement. Should we interpret the six-year presidential term as an authoritarian and antirepublican innovation, or should we see the retention of a popularly elected president as basic fealty to republicanism (and the lengthened term, with its compensating ineligibility for reelection, as just the sort of improvement on republicanism that the great republican Thomas Jefferson himself had hoped to see in the original Constitution)?[16] Such debates could go on forever without satisfactory resolution, and we need some new way of evaluating secession and the resulting fundamental institutions of the Confederacy. Comparative constitutional history affords a solution, freeing the historian from the terms of the debate so far by reexamining the process as much as the political specifics of either side in the debate. The answer, in both process and content, lies in the secession conventions.

We can solve the initial problem of process by considering secession as the deratification of the Constitution of 1787. That supplies us with a useful analogy to the ratification of the U.S. Constitution of 1787. With that reconceptualization of the process we have at hand a ready standard to determine whether secession was a conservative coup, an attempt to put past the voters a reordering of Southern society in a more authoritarian and conservative hierarchy. After examining the process, we can apply our second test: an examination of the changes to the state constitutions made in the process of secession.

Southerners not only copied the Constitution of 1787, they also replicated the process by which the new government was ratified — only they were deratifying the Constitution. For them, secession was always a matter of practical and orderly parliamentary deliberation and action. It was accomplished by elections of delegates and arguments over the merits of the change and final decision by the ultimate sovereign in this republic: in their view, the people of the states in convention. Let us compare that process in the late eighteenth century with the one employed in the nineteenth century that has come to be called secession.

Despite the great time period intervening between the two constitutional movements, this is not a comparison of apples with oranges. In the first place, both the United States in 1787 and the Confederate States in 1861 were republics that included a vast interest in slave labor. Slaves constituted a much larger percentage of the population of the potential Confederate States of America in 1860 than they did in the potential Union of 1787, but they were a significant part of the earlier population, all the same. Of the nation's population at the first census, taken in 1790, only two years after ratification, of 3,929,214 people, 697,681 were slaves.[17] Slaves thus represented almost 18 percent of the country's population at the beginning of the republic. Slaves constituted about double that percentage of the Confederacy's population.[18] Nor is this necessarily a comparison of an illegal act (secession) with a legal one (ratification). Both processes had their critics from the standpoint of legality. We have already seen a lengthy exposition of the case against the legality of secession in President Lincoln's First Inaugural Address and his Message to the Special Session of Congress of July 4, 1861, described in the first chapter of this book. As for ratification, since the Articles of Confederation required unanimous approval of the states to alter them, the Constitution, which went into effect after only nine states ratified it, was also controversial and perhaps revolutionary. Constitutional commentator Richard A. Posner goes on to point out the controversial nature of the Reconstruction amendments by a similar comparison: "Both the original Constitution and the Reconstruction amendments were adopted irregularly, even illegally — the constitutional convention of 1787 exceeded its terms of reference from the Continental Congress, and the southern states were required to ratify the Reconstruction amendments as a condition of having their congressional representation restored — making those amendments, in [constitutional lawyer Bruce] Ackerman's words, merely 'amendment-simulacra.'"[19] In other words, the process of deratification of 1860–61 did not labor under such sharply different assumptions of legality as to alter the nature of the process.

The values associated with enslaving other human beings were not essential to the political process of 1787–89. And the attempt to set up a nation was not a conservative coup. It is true, of course, that the great historian Charles Beard considered the ratification of the Constitution of 1787 as essentially that very thing. Beard characterized the origins of the Constitution of the United States as an antidemocratic movement. In many states men seized the initiative and moved rapidly, he maintained. (In his view they did so to protect personal property, however, not slavery, which Beard hardly mentioned.)[20] In the century of scholarship that has followed Beard's lead in examining the process of drafting and adopting the Constitution of 1787, judgments have gone decidedly the other way. Great and painstaking documentary editing projects as well as extensive scholarly investigation in monographs in history and political science have, in fact, generally caused historians to marvel at the depth and breadth of the debate over the Constitution. Most recently, the editors of the exhaustive collection of documents surrounding that original process have concluded: "Taken together, the material . . . probably forms the greatest body of political writing in American history."[21]

No student of secession has ever spoken of the debate in the Southern states over the deratification question in such glowing terms, and yet were the processes of ratification and deratification not much the same? We can now have a way of measuring—by comparison—answers to the following questions, essential to determining whether secession could in any useful way be characterized as a "coup" and ultimately whether the values associated with the labor system of a "slave society" also determined the political culture and institutions of the Confederate States of America. Let us examine the problem with three questions: Was secession rushed? Was secession carefully and fully considered in rational political debate? Was secession a self-consciously antipopular movement or not?

Was secession rushed? It is true that some Southern states rushed to secede from the Union. In South Carolina and Alabama, conventions met for only four days before producing an ordinance of secession.[22] Yet that was longer than Georgia took to ratify back in 1788. Its ratification convention met for only three days, and one of those was a Sunday on which there were no official meetings of the eager group.[23]

The fact of the matter is that the states that saw it to their vital interest to be a part of the Union that emerged from the Constitution of 1787 wasted little time in signing on to the United States. Those included small states whose commerce was tied to seaports in adjoining states, Delaware and New Jersey, and the state most threatened by an Indian uprising and in need of immediate military aid, Georgia.[24]

The time that transpired from the drafting of the final version of the Constitution on September 17, 1787, to the ratification by the fifth state,

Connecticut, on January 9, 1788, was 115 days. We may consider that initial wave of ratifications as analogous to the first wave of secession (seven states) lasting from the calling of the South Carolina secession convention after the presidential election on November 6, 1860, through secession by Texas on February 1, 1861, a process that spanned 86 days. We should not allow the disparity in duration of process to deceive us into thinking the one markedly hastier than the other. The Southern deratifiers of the mid-nineteenth century were speedier, but they lived in the middle of the nineteenth century, after all. They enjoyed the advantages of railroads, the telegraph, and steam presses, among other advances in transportation and communication. The slowness of communications in 1787 was agonizing. After its signing in Philadelphia on September 17, 1787, a full week elapsed before the first commentary on the document appeared in a New York newspaper.[25] And it only appeared in New York that soon because the Constitution had to be sent to Congress to be approved for dispatching to the states for consideration. Still, there proved to be time enough afterward for extensive debate. In the period of the first wave of ratifications considered for comparison here, the first thirty-three papers of *The Federalist* were published. Those included, of course, the great paper no. 10. The period also saw the appearance of the first seven of the Anti-Federalist papers by Brutus as well as the first eight papers by Centinel and many other now-famous commentaries on the Constitution.[26] There had been plenty of time for developing thoughtful arguments.

Deratification benefited from three months of the most anxious public debate before the convention in Montgomery drafted a constitution. Altogether, the legislatures of eleven states called for elections to popular deratification conventions: South Carolina, Mississippi, Alabama, Florida, Georgia, Louisiana, and Texas (in the first wave of deratification) as well as more reluctant secessionists in Virginia, Arkansas, North Carolina, and Missouri (a state that never adopted a secession ordinance). Tennessee, Kentucky, Delaware, and Maryland never called conventions together, but the legislature of Tennessee decided for secession of that state.[27]

The process was repeated in reverse after the Confederate Constitution was drafted. Like the U.S. Constitution before it, the Confederate Constitution had a provision to go into effect without the ratification of all the states. After five states ratified, there would be elections for the president and the permanent Congress.[28] The conventions of Mississippi, Alabama, Florida, Georgia, Texas, and North Carolina met again to ratify the document. Among other things, that meant more consideration of the merits of secession. Tennessee had a referendum on ratification. Thus such documents as the statement of principles published by those who objected to secession in the Alabama convention could still have some effect.[29]

Was secession carefully and fully considered in rational political debate? If we measure debate by the quantity of documents making each side's arguments available, then secession was at least as carefully and fully considered in rational debate as formation of the original republic in the eighteenth century had been.

The extent of the political discussion in 1860–61 was much greater than in 1787. For a rough measure, compare, for example, two standard editions of the literature generated by the ratification of 1787–88 and the deratification of 1860–61. Bernard Bailyn's *The Debate on the Constitution* offers some 2,400 pages of documents, including the standard Anti-Federalist and Federalist series of commentaries by Publius, Brutus, the Federal Farmer, and Centinel. But he was forced to rely as well on private correspondence in which the Constitution was discussed and on speeches given in the ratifying conventions themselves. By comparison, Jon Wakelyn was able to locate 120 Southern pamphlets on secession, from which he published a selected number in *Southern Pamphlets on Secession, November 1860–April 1861*. He reprinted eighteen generated from the period November 26, 1860 to March 8, 1861, and they added up to over 300 pages. Had he aimed for more inclusive coverage, he could easily have multiplied that by six and filled 1,800 pages. His book includes pamphlets alone — not a single column inch of editorial coverage from the press. He condensed the pamphlets by excising long quotations, historical asides, and repetitious material. Wakelyn did not reprint speeches from the secession conventions.[30] Bailyn, by contrast, had to resort to newspaper coverage to recapture the eighteenth-century debate.

Wakelyn's collection of pamphlets on secession does include two (over and above the eighteen) that were published years before. But that serves only to remind us of a major difference in the two debates. The debate on the Constitution of 1787 was all new because the Constitution was new. It had actually been written in secret. Debate on it could begin only when the document left Philadelphia on September 17, 1787, and its somewhat startling contents were at last revealed to the public for comment. Previous documents were not relevant because the terms were substantially new. That was hardly the case in 1860–61. In fact, old pamphlets on the question of secession were republished while the secession conventions were meeting, in effect creating a discourse that was much richer than the one on ratification and reached back over at least a generation.

Here is one notable example of the ready recycling of old arguments still relevant to the secession issue. Christopher Memminger's 34-page pamphlet entitled *The Mission of South Carolina to Virginia* was written and first published in January 1860 in the wake of the alarming raid by John Brown at Harpers Ferry. After initial publication then, it was reprinted as an article in the December 1860 issue of *DeBow's Review*. It found new life as part of the attempt to get Maryland to secede from the Union in an edition published in Baltimore, most likely in early 1861.[31]

What historian Robert E. Bonner has described as the Confederate "equivalent to Thomas Paine's *Common Sense*," a sermon by Benjamin M. Palmer on *The South: Her Peril and Her Duty*, was printed in four separate pamphlet versions amounting to some 100,000 copies, not to mention republication in four Southern magazines and publication in whole or in part in numerous newspapers.[32]

One of the great advantages the politicians enjoyed in 1860–61 was the franking privilege and the ability to print and distribute speeches on secession delivered in Congress with the aid of the federal government itself. That factor helps account for many of the widely circulated pamphlets of the deratification period. Thus, of the eighteen pamphlets from the period reprinted by Jon L. Wakelyn, six—one-third of them—were published in Washington for members of Congress. The protagonists in the ratification debate had no such efficient printing and distribution organization behind them.

Was secession a self-consciously antipopular movement or not? From all indications, secession was everywhere a popular movement and to a certain degree self-consciously so. The educational reach of the initial debate proved great. At this point we must depart our parallel periods of ratification and deratification because the pamphlet literature from secession is not precisely enough dated. For this comparison of public debate, let us examine the Virginia secession convention, which met from February 17, 1861, until passing its secession ordinance on April 17. In that two-month period, convention members generated a tremendous amount of debate reported in the Virginia press. Moreover, they printed at least 105 pages of official documents of their own, reports of committees, and such.[33]

At one point the Virginians established a committee to confer with the editors of the *Richmond Enquirer* to ascertain whether the proceedings of the convention could be published on a separate sheet without any other matter—that is, as a broadside, to be posted and circulated beyond even the reach of newspaper circulation. Finally, when they published the secession ordinance itself, it was lithographed, a speedy technology unavailable for eighteenth-century documents.[34]

There is no comparing the quantity of materials available from the two periods, the one before the great communications revolution of the nineteenth century and the other after it.[35] Take pamphlets, for example. In Charleston, South Carolina, a merchant named Robert Gourdin organized other men of wealth into what was called the 1860 Association. In the months surrounding the presidential campaign of that year, Gourdin's association singlehanded printed and distributed 166,000 copies of some half dozen different secessionist pamphlets (by November 19).[36] Charles Beard's estimate of the total number of voters for the ratification conventions of the eighteenth century was 160,000.[37] Gourdin could have put a secessionist pamphlet into the hands of every single person who voted for a delegate to a ratification convention in 1787–88.

According to the *Documentary History of the Ratification of the Constitution*, edited by John P. Kaminski and Gaspare J. Saladino, in the period of ratification of the Constitution (1787–90) there were about 95 newspapers in America.[38] The population at the 1790 census was about 4 million, including nearly 700,000 slaves.[39] In April 1861 around 800 newspapers were being published in the eleven states that would form the Confederacy. Population growth since the ratification of the Constitution had not favored the South (except for the natural increase of slaves), and the population of the Confederacy, some 9 million, of whom about 3.5 million were slaves, thus saw its white population of 5.5 million served by about 800 newspapers. To compare the two populations, then, is to see that the number of people in the secessionist South did not double, but they were served by more than eight times the number of newspapers. In 1860 there were more papers in Virginia alone (still including western Virginia) — 117 — than were published in the whole country in 1787. Alabama's 89 newspapers almost equaled the number appearing nationwide at the time of the ratification of the Constitution, while they served a free population of only 529,164. Missouri had more than 140 newspapers debating secession in 1860. The Southern daily press produced acres of editorials on secession, but it could not be matched by the little weeklies of the late eighteenth century.[40]

Perhaps the most important point is this. There was no debating the Constitution of 1787 until it emerged from Philadelphia after September 17, 1787. The terms of the document — and hence the terms of the debate that followed — were unknown until that moment. Secession, on the other hand, was no secret. Southerners had threatened to secede and debated it among themselves and with Northerners for a generation, especially since the nullification crisis of 1832. Thus the true period of debate for secession was really twenty-nine years.

The Politics of Secession

Both ratification and deratification were products not only of ideas circulated by printing technology but also of the American political process and therefore involved a good deal more than stately, rational debate. In her recent work, *Confederate Reckoning: Power and Politics in the Civil War South*, Stephanie McCurry has dwelt on the rough-and-tumble practical politics in the election of delegates to the secession conventions in 1860–61. In part, her point is that white unity was mythical and brawling politics were proof of it, and in part, it is that thuggish repression of a concerned electorate was necessary to create an illusion of secessionist unanimity. Indeed, she characterizes the canvass in South Carolina as a "black shirt campaign." The underlying theme, of course, is that the victory of the secessionists was the triumph of a repressive and tyrannical minority. Of the election of South Carolina's secession convention, she says, "It took every trick in the political book to pull it off." In some other states, "the battle over the will of the people was open, direct, and violent, the divisions and fraudulent attempts to conceal them so apparent that in the end nothing resembling democratic legitimacy could be claimed." There is no room for misunderstanding the image of these elections left by *Confederate Reckoning*. Here is more of the telltale language McCurry uses to describe the secession elections: "a hybrid thing, evincing at once the character of an administrative coup and of an open-fisted brawl"; "a down-and-dirty political fight"; "violence was politics as usual"; "the fire-eaters' electoral strategy [was] a paramilitary one"; paramilitary groups were "empowered to accuse, harass, brutally beat, whip, shave, tar and feather, run out of town on a rail, and lynch."[41] But surely, as in all American elections before Reconstruction, both sides used the same political methods.[42]

There are no indications that the elections for the secession conventions were especially hard fought or that the politicians felt impelled to use "every trick in the political book" to win — let alone that rough-and-tumble methods were confined to one side. The true index of hard-fought elections is high voter turnout, a behavioral measure left unexamined in McCurry's treatment of secession. Turnout was notoriously low.[43] In fact, the elections for delegates were so quiet that they went by with scant notice in the press.

The key lay in the fact that the old parties were not competing as in the past, and they were the true experts at arousing the people (and also had the easiest consciences about fraud and trickery at the polls). Furthermore, the process of secession was nearly everywhere depicted as antipolitical and elevated above the corrupt ways of the old political parties. All of these factors point to an especially clean political campaign rather than an especially dirty one.

Politics in the cities of the nineteenth century were generally recognized as the most corrupt in an age with few regulations of elections anywhere. Yet if we look at the campaign in New Orleans to elect delegates to the Louisiana secession convention, it seems as legitimate as any ever seen there. The campaign, such as it was, was preceded by measures of the mayor — in the presidential election of November 1860 — to prevent corruption and violence at the polls. He closed the so-called coffee houses — which were apparently places to get liquor, generally regarded as the greatest corrupting factor on election day. As a result, according to press reports after the presidential election, despite "the most heated canvass" in twenty-four years, election day itself proved quiet.[44] That spirit of clean elections seems to have carried over to election day for convention delegates on January 7, 1861. From the forty-four polling places in New Orleans, each with four law enforcement officers assigned to it on election day, there was only one reported incident of attempted voter fraud on January 7. One voter — the newspaper reporter did not say whether the individual was an immediate secessionist or a cooperationist — attempted to vote registered under the name of a dead man, who had been well known in the area. The fraudulent voter was arrested for perjury.[45]

The antiparty tone of the Louisiana elections played a role as well. That tone marked both sides in the contest, even though the side least committed to immediate secession had adherents who basically thought that slavery was best protected by the national Democratic Party. Selection of candidates for delegates, which of necessity took place outside the traditional political party apparatus of nominating conventions, took place at meetings called to consult on the perilous condition of the country and "to express, through representatives to the State Convention, the will of the people," as the description of one such meeting in East Feliciana Parish put it. After the passage of resolutions on the crisis, candidates were chosen and it seemed that meeting organizers had the process in hand. One of the resolutions passed at the East Feliciana meeting declared "that this delicate question of our rights, our duties, and our remedies, has been too long the football of political quacks and demagogues," even though this turned out to be a cooperationist meeting.[46] The press warned against "thinly attended" nominating meetings, lest wire-pulling management of the selection process be possible.[47]

The special solemnity of constitutional decision-making definitely shaped the atmosphere of the convention elections. The canvass was marked by discussion of the issues in the press, but notices of parades and barbecues seem to have been scarce. The *New Orleans Times-Picayune* discussed the problems of separate state action for days and then published as a broadside extra, sometime after December 17, "AN APPEAL TO THINKING MEN," which featured the reflections of octogenarian Jacob Barker on the question "Have We Exhausted Constitutional Remedies?"[48]

The record for the amount of emotional ritual and parading, of course, is likely a mixed one, with more in some places than in others. But we have harder, more systematic and consistent proof that the process was not an especially corrupt one marred more than usual by political thuggery, trickery, or fraud. That proof lies in the scarcity of contested elections for delegates. In general, the secession conventions were conducted on the same system as the elections for Congress or for the state legislatures. The sheriff typically forwarded vote tallies to the secretary of state or the governor in exchange for a certificate of election for the winner.[49] When the convention gathered, the first business after prayer was calling the role of the delegates and the presentation of their credentials. At the South Carolina convention, the presentation of credentials was not followed by any contested election investigations, and the delegates proceeded quickly to the business of drafting a secession ordinance.[50] That accounted for 169 delegates elected, apparently without trickery or political incident serious enough for investigation by the customary parliamentary apparatus.[51]

Whether the election was dominated by cooperationists or by immediatists, whether the margin was narrow or wide, the delegates came to the conventions from elections that were seldom contested because of doubtful or illegal electoral tactics. Elections for delegates in Mississippi were apparently more "closely contested" than in South Carolina.[52] Still, the immediatists dominated the delegation, as they did in South Carolina. And more to the point here, of the one hundred delegates chosen, none was the product of a canvass resulting in a contested election when it came time to seat the delegates at the convention in Jackson.[53] Of Alabama's secession convention, McCurry says about the cooperationist delegates: "In every possible way they denied the legitimacy of the secessionists' claim to the mantle of the people."[54] But the way to challenge legitimacy lay open and unused because the elections were legitimate. In this state, not dominated by immediate secessionists, the process of electing the one hundred delegates resulted in no contested elections once they assembled and all one hundred answered the roll call.[55] Thus in three states among the fastest to secede, Southerners managed to select 369 delegates whose right to claim their seats went uncontested by disgruntled victims of electoral fraud. Presumably, fraud was not rampant.

Information is incomplete, but I could find only one contested election and two problematic election results in the six conventions I examined for this chapter. One, which proved very troublesome, was not the result of trickery but of a tie vote that was difficult to resolve. That occurred in Arkansas's Fulton County, and since the resolution of the case raised important constitutional issues, I will leave analysis of that problem to another place in this chapter. The other problematic elections occurred in Georgia, where the official election results from three counties — Chattahoochee, Glynn, and Lincoln — were never received by the governor, as required. The convention's certified members voted unanimously to seat the delegates who had shown up at the convention from those counties anyway.[56]

Virginia's secession convention presented a case of an officially contested election. When the delegates arrived for their initial session, M. B. D. Lane challenged the seating of John D. Sharp, though the election returns showed him to be the winner.[57] On February 21, 1861, the convention passed an ordinance on contested elections because the legislation calling the convention and providing for the method of dealing with such challenges as the House of Delegates handled them was deemed impractical. Instead, the convention asked the challenger to list the allegedly improper votes or the reasons the other candidate was unqualified for the position and submit these documents "in reasonable time."[58] In general, that was the problem of investigating electoral results for secession conventions: the time was so brief between election and the end of the convention's work that it was useless to investigate or implement a remedy by rescheduling the election. The problem in the single Virginia election remains unclear, but Sharp, a cooperationist, managed to keep his seat in the convention.

For those conventions that sat past the outbreak of war — a problem to be discussed later in this chapter — the question of the makeup of the delegation became complex, but not because of political trickery. In Virginia, for example, as the convention continued meeting well into wartime, some delegates (from western Virginia) joined the Union side and some were killed in battle (while the convention was in recess). But these losses were no reflection on the integrity of the process by which delegates to the conventions had been selected in the first place.

All in all, the six conventions investigated for this study — those of South Carolina, Mississippi, Alabama, Georgia, Arkansas, and Virginia — were represented by 899 delegates (adding to the 369 above, Virginia's 152, Arkansas's 77, and Georgia's 301). There was, apparently, only one contested election among these 899 — the Lane-Sharp dispute in Virginia. The elections for delegates to secession conventions do not appear by any measure to have been ones in which every trick in the political book was employed.

Could it possibly be said that the process in 1787–88 was any cleaner? In truth, there appears to be more firm evidence of strong-arm tactics and voter intimidation in 1787–88 than in 1860–61. Here are two examples from states that ratified the U.S. Constitution in the first wave. In Delaware, the already existing parties were called Tories and Whigs, and the Tories in the elections for delegates to the ratification convention used armed force to discourage Whig presence at the polls. A provision of the Delaware Constitution of 1776 forbade the presence of armed troops within one mile of the polling place. On election day in Delaware in 1787, Tory militia, apparently answering a secret call for a muster issued only to Tories, marched up to the polling place in Sussex County to the fife and drum and pitched camp just a mile away from the polls. Some of the militiamen would lay down their arms and vote while the remainder guarded the camp, then return so others could go cast their ballots. Fearing violence, Whigs stayed away from the polls and voting fell by 30 percent or more. Petitions protested this intimidation later, but in the end nothing was done about it. Men armed with clubs, swords, and pistols who were not a part of the militia camp were also present.[59]

In Pennsylvania, the use of mob violence to bring about the call for a ratification convention is well known. Pro-Constitution forces were temporarily in control of the Pennsylvania legislature, which was about to be dissolved for the annual state elections. The pro-Constitution forces did not know whether they would control the next legislature and wanted to move toward ratification before anti-Constitution forces in the western part of the state could organize. Opponents of the Constitution walked out and denied a quorum. Those in favor of ratification gathered a mob, evidently broke into a residence where the opponents who had walked out were hiding, captured two of them, and forced them into the chamber for the vote. By such methods Pennsylvania got its ratification convention.[60]

Finally, no reader of Forrest McDonald's revealing book about the interests behind ratification in 1787–88 could believe it was an antiseptic process. Here, for example, is McDonald's description of the crucial political maneuver for New Hampshire's ratification:

John Sullivan, a politician so methodical that he would soon be able to survey and classify and count every eligible voter in every town in New Hampshire, now surveyed the convention. At worst, the Federalists might fall two or three votes short. Taking no chances, they scheduled a final vote for the afternoon of June 21; and in the forenoon a pecunious citizen of Concord (where the convention was meeting) invited six impecunious anti-Federalists to lunch. The lunch was liquid and alcoholic, and a half dozen anti-Federalists failed to show up at the convention until later afternoon. By that time, the vote had been taken and the Federalists had won.[61]

The Sanctification of the Nation

If we turn from process to political content, deratification still holds its own compared to the era of the Founders. Even if there is no equal of *The Federalist*, no. 10, in the vast literature of secession, it can be said that there was not only more debate in 1860–61 but also at least one entirely new dimension of debate missing from the eighteenth century. A comparison of the discourse of 1787–88 with that of 1860–61 immediately reveals a striking difference: the absence of commentary by the clergy in the eighteenth century and the prominence of the clergy in the secession debate.

As far as we know from the printed record, not a single sermon was delivered on the proposed Constitution of 1787. In all the commentary painstakingly gathered for the *Documentary History of the Ratification of the Constitution*, there is only one minor public religious expression: the Philadelphia Baptist Association endorsed the new Constitution in a circular letter.[62] Apart from that endorsement, reported in a little newspaper notice, the clergy said nothing. That silence offers more than volumes of testimony might to prove the secular nature of the age in which the Constitution was drafted. Something important in the history of American nationalism had obviously occurred between the end of the eighteenth century and the onset of the secession crisis. It can be called the sanctification of the state. Americans in the eighteenth century expected the debate about the future shape of their nation to be largely secular. Americans in the mid-nineteenth century just as clearly expected the debate over the nation's future waged in the secession crisis to have a substantial religious dimension. In between had come the Second Great Awakening, the wave of religious revivals that converted great masses of Americans to evangelical religion. Expectations about the nation changed, and the changes were abundantly evident on the eve of the Civil War.

In the midst of the secession crisis, occurring in the waning days of his administration, President James Buchanan called for a national day of fasting and prayer to be observed on January 4, 1861. Buchanan's call *in the South* was an invitation to Southern clergymen, who often endorsed disunion, to weigh in on the secession crisis. As a Union-saving measure, the president's call was a failure. To Unionists countrywide, Buchanan's proclamation was so humble in tone that it seemed in itself a declaration of national failure. Kentucky's astute Presbyterian theologian, Robert Jefferson Breckinridge, said: "Let us bear in mind that the proclamation of the Chief Magistrate of the Republic which calls us to this service, asserts, in the first place, that ruin is impending over our national institutions; and asserts, in the second place, that so far as appears to him no human resources remain that are adequate to save them; and, in the third place, that the whole nation, according to his judgment, ought to prostrate itself before God and cry to him for deliverance."[63]

Buchanan's proclamation exemplified the changed expectations of the nation at a time of constitutional crisis. Now clergymen were invited to give their constitutional views, and all over the land they offered sermons about the crisis.

Immediate circumstances magnified the role of the clergy in deratification. Lincoln's election came on November 6, 1860. In the Southern states the feared outcome of the ballot launched debate on secession as a consequence. November 28 was observed in most places in the United States as a day of Thanksgiving. After the South Carolina convention passed a secession ordinance in late December, a beleaguered President Buchanan proclaimed his national day of fasting for January 4, 1861. Thus in the two months following the presidential election there were in most places in the nation two calls for public days of fasting, prayer, humiliation, or thanksgiving. The result in the South was a substantial production of sermons on secession. The modern compiler of Southern pamphlets on secession has observed that "a separate volume of sermon pamphlets could show the enormous impact of Southern churches on the secession movement."[64]

Although the proclamation of a national day of Thanksgiving would come only later and in the North during the Civil War, governors of individual states, North and South, customarily proclaimed a day. In November 1860, twenty-four states and territories observed the same day in November as a day of thanksgiving. These included the slave states of Kentucky, Louisiana, Missouri, Maryland, North Carolina, and Tennessee.

More Southern states had marked Thanksgiving the year before, and its decline in the South was a sign of worsening sectional tensions. But old habits died hard. In the past mayors had sometimes proclaimed a day for their municipalities, and in 1860 places that did not mark the New England festival could imitate it with their own local version. In Georgia, Governor Joseph Brown proclaimed a day of fasting and thanksgiving for November 28, 1860, and one of the results was a sermon on the secession crisis delivered on that day by the Reverend George H. Clark of Savannah; the sermon was later published as a pamphlet.[65] State proclamation or not, clergymen in the South spoke on national issues on the traditional Thanksgiving Day in late 1860. Thus James Henley Thornwell's famous Thanksgiving sermon, called *The Rights of the South Defended in the Pulpit*, reprinted as a pamphlet, was occasioned by Louisiana's observation of the day on November 29, 1860.[66]

The resulting literature written by clergymen on the deratification of the Constitution offers a surprisingly worthwhile body of reading. What it says about the enhanced veneration of nationhood generally, by offering so much speculation and advice on the future of the nation, is a consideration in itself for assessing the importance of nationalism in the mid-nineteenth century. But what it provides by way of original thought on constitutional questions and nationalism is also considerable and substantially neglected by historians who have read the literature only as theology and proslavery apologetics.[67]

Clergymen were not shy about speaking up. Theirs turned out to be as thoughtful a body of writings as any offered on the subject of secession. The standard production was the sermon — ideally, a work of pamphlet length that required thoughtfulness and ideas beyond the depth usually found in an ordinary newspaper column. There was an easy interchangeability among the clergy's thoughtful venues: articles for religious periodical reviews, sermons, and pamphlets. Thus the Reverend Charles Colcock Jones, of Georgia, wrote an article for the *Southern Presbyterian* answering the antisecession arguments of a fellow Presbyterian but Northerner, Charles Hodge. Hodge, a famous Old School Presbyterian theologian, wrote, "The State of the Country" for the *Princeton Review*. Jones answered it and received letters after the publication of the article urging its republication as a pamphlet. The Jones review was really too long for a newspaper to print, and the *Review* made two thousand extra copies.[68]

One of the most striking things to see in the sermons preached on secession in the South, whether they were occasioned by Buchanan's call or came independently of it, was their unembarrassed commentary on constitutional questions — having nothing to do with the relationship between church and state under the proposed constitutional order. The clergymen did not usually begin by disclaiming their own expertise on worldly questions: they waded in. Jones's path was made easy because his article answered a fellow clergyman and therefore dealt with the problem in the idiom of the theologian. We can tell from the reaction to the article that it provoked a mixture of theological and decidedly geopolitical considerations. Thus as one person who wrote to commend Jones for his work expressed it, Hodge had held up "secession as involving all the crimes of *perjury* and *covenant-breaking* and *treason* and *rebellion*" (at least one was a specifically religious problem in Calvinist language). But the letter to Jones dealt also with the practicalities of constitutional argument and geopolitical power, wishing that Jones had exposed Hodge's inconsistency in speaking "of withdrawing Canada from its allegiance and uniting it by revolution to the Northern confederacy." "No sin here!" he continued, "If the North propose[s] to aid in this *awful enormity*, Dr. Hodge thinks it would be a noble achievement, and he would open his arms to receive this perjured and covenant-breaking Canada!"[69]

The most famous of the Southern clergy's pamphlet offerings on secession is James Henley Thornwell's "The State of the Country." It began life not as a sermon on a Sunday in the pulpit but as an article written for the *Southern Presbyterian Review*, of which Thornwell was the editor. The very first sentence was a careful statement of the constitutional nature of South Carolina's secession: "It is now universally known that, on the twentieth day of last December, the people of South Carolina, in Convention assembled, solemnly annulled the ordinance by which they became members of the Federal Union, entitled the United States of America, and resumed to themselves the exercise of all the powers which they had delegated to the Federal Congress." The process, even in South Carolina, did not look flawed to Thornwell because of the prestige of the members of the convention especially. "Whatever else may be said of it, it certainly must be admitted that this solemn act of South Carolina was well considered," he concluded. It was also important both to the secession process and to the fact of Thornwell's endorsement of secession that he make clear that the movement was not one of political party, and that was a task perhaps best performed by the clergy. Certainly the image of secession he wanted to present was a process the precise opposite of what Stephanie McCurry claims was the case in fact. "Can any man believe," he asked, "that this is a factitious condition of the public mind of the South, produced by brawling politicians and disappointed demagogues, and not the calm, deliberate, profound utterance of a people who feel, in their inmost souls, that they have been deeply and flagrantly wronged?"[70]

It was also appropriate for a clergyman to deny that economic motivations lay behind the secession movement, and that Thornwell did as well:

> It has been suggested, by those who know as little of the people of the South as they do of the Constitution of their country, that all this ferment is nothing but the result of a mercenary spirit on the part of the cotton-growing States, fed by Utopian dreams of aggrandizement and wealth, to be realized under the auspices of free trade, in a separate Confederacy of their own. It has been gravely insinuated that they are willing to sell their faith for gold — that they have only made a pretext of recent events to accomplish a foregone scheme of deliberate treachery and fraud. That there is not the slightest ground in anything these States have ever said or done for this extraordinary slander, it is, of course, superfluous to add.[71]

Once we realize that the clergy assumed a significant role in the secession debate, it is hardly surprising that its members naturally discussed materialism and the moral rather than political motivations of the leaders of secession. Of course, Thornwell gave slavery his blessing, not exactly as an imperative moral right, but as a "natural" feature of humanity and history, and therefore not the mere creation of positive law.[72]

But the degree to which Thornwell focused on constitutional argument is striking. His authorities were figures like Joseph Story, not Joseph and Mary. He referred to *Prigg v. the Commonwealth of Pennsylvania* rather than the Book of Romans or Matthew, Mark, Luke, and John.[73] This preoccupation with secular issues of constitutional interpretation was not the ordinary direction the sermons took, but several did discuss power and law as much as morality and righteousness. Thornwell's pamphlet thus stands as an indication of the ready absorption of the clergy in questions of state not involving church and state, and with that absorption the underlying change of outlook on the nation that made its sermons acceptable, even desirable.

Sermons on secession, most commonly delivered on days of thanksgiving, humiliation, fasting, and prayer, seem naturally to have been cast more in a religious and less in a constitutional vein. Yet Kentucky's Robert Breckinridge, a Presbyterian minister and editor of the *Danville Quarterly Review*, still managed to devote considerable attention to constitutional arguments in his *Discourse Delivered on the Day of National Humiliation, January 4, 1861, at Lexington, Kentucky.* This sermon was notable for its secular themes. Instead of sticking to his moral specialties, Breckinridge aimed "to show . . . that our duties can never be made subordinate to our passions without involving us in ruin, and that our rights can never be set above our interests without destroying both."[74] Stressing the risks of the passions in governmental matters was no more than the authors of *The Federalist* had done back in the eighteenth century, when Reason reigned supreme, and to emphasize interests was decidedly secular.

Breckinridge offered a highly original constitutional argument. He distinguished between the theories of nullification and secession, justifying the first and rejecting the second. To do so he had to refer to the ideas of Thomas Jefferson as expressed in the Kentucky Resolutions of 1798. In the end Breckinridge came up with a novel piece of constitutional interpretation. He pointed out that the original ratification of the Constitution of 1787 depended only on the action of nine consenting states. The document would have gone into effect then, and the other four states "would have passed by common consent into a new condition, and for the first time have become separate sovereign States."[75] He was interested in these four states as precedents for Kentucky in case Kentucky did not secede. He drew an analogy to the present situation:

> What I make this statement for, is to show that, taking that principle as just and permanent, as clearly laid down in the Constitution, it requires at least eleven States out of the existing thirty-three States to destroy, or affect in the slightest degree, the question as to whether or not the remaining States are the United States of America, under the same Constitution. Twenty-two States, according to that principle, left after eleven had seceded, would be as really the United States of America under that Federal Constitution, as they were before, according to the fundamental principle involved in the original mode of giving validity to the Constitution. Kentucky would still be as really one of these United States of America, as when she was at first when, as a district of Virginia, who was one of the nine adopting States, she became, as such a district, a part thereof. And by consequence, a secession of less than eleven States, can in no event, and upon no hypothesis, even so much as embarrass Kentucky in determining for herself, what her duty, her honor, and her safety require her to do.[76]

It is an error that will lead to misunderstanding nationalism in mid-nineteenth-century America to say that there were secessionist sermons and there were Unionist sermons. Breckinridge was as interested in the fate of Kentucky to the exclusion of other states as any dedicated adherent of state rights and argued only partly for strict adherence to the old Union. In other words, to Breckinridge, the original proportion of ratifiers necessary to make the nation prescribed a critical mass required to form any country, and the Confederacy had not yet reached such a point of agreement. Nation-forming from states was not a piecemeal process, accumulating one state and then another and ceasing when states ceased to secede. There was a minimum proportion, Breckinridge argued.

Breckinridge had little use for the extremist states of the Deep South or for the fanatical states of New England; he thought the nation's salvation lay with "Ohio, Indiana, Illinois, Pennsylvania, New Jersey, on the one side; and Maryland, Delaware, Virginia, Kentucky, Missouri . . . on the other." As a matter of fact, it occurred to him, these states were great enough in extent and population "to constitute a great nation" by themselves.[77] So, in case the United States did fail, "then it belongs to this immense central power, to re-construct the nation, upon the slave line as its central idea; and thus perpetuate our institutions, our principles, and our hopes, with an unchanged nationality."[78] The thinking here was all geopolitical and not religious. If secession was driven by slavery, Unionism, of course, was by no means driven by antislavery sentiment, and Breckinridge would, if necessary, see the creation of a new nation, still half slave and half free, and perpetuating traditional American republicanism.

Mitchell Snay argues that "the sanctification of slavery was perhaps the most important element" in the "moral consensus" that religion helped create in the South.[79] Though defensive about slavery in the secession crisis, the clergymen who commented heavily on the Constitution were careful in what they said about the peculiar institution. Breckinridge wanted to save the old Union with slavery in it or create a new one with slavery still in it, but he did not approve of secession. By contrast, Benjamin Morgan Palmer, a Presbyterian minister in New Orleans, endorsed secession and insisted that the "providential trust" of the South was *to conserve and to perpetuate the institution of domestic slavery as now existing,* but he added:

> It is not necessary here to inquire whether this is precisely the best relation in which the hewer of wood and drawer of water can stand to his employer; although this proposition may perhaps be successfully sustained by those who choose to defend it. Still less are we required, dogmatically, to affirm that it will subsist through all time. Baffled as our wisdom may now be, in finding a solution of this intricate social problem, it would nevertheless be the height of arrogance to pronounce what changes may or may not occur in the distant future.[80]

Moreover, though Palmer certainly justified slavery as a civilized institution, he did not entirely rest his argument on its moral preservation: he rested his argument on the secular *"principle of self-preservation,"* which had to be invoked by Southerners because slavery was so inextricably "interwoven" with their society that their "material interests" and even family life were inseparable from it.[81] Perpetuity of slavery was seemingly unnecessary for Palmer's version of Southern nationalism.

Given the varieties of positions on secession taken by clergymen, given the different ideals of nationalism invoked by them, and given as well the subtle differences in their assertions about slavery, it seems somehow misleading and inadequate to assert, as Snay does, that "religion helped lead the South toward secession and the Civil War."[82] It is better to make a more cautious judgment: the degree to which the clergy felt impelled to discuss the secession crisis was proof that nationalism, the determination of what peoples would control what boundaries in the world, had become the most important question in the nineteenth century. Religion had to deal with nationalism, not the other way around.

Monsters and Secession

The creativity of the clergy's response to secession, as in the case of Breckinridge, is, next to its often secular preoccupations, its most surprising quality. Could the overall response to the secession crisis be termed equally creative in terms of constitution and nationalism? Except for the sampling of religious ideas on the subject, we have not examined the content of the debate, only its quantity and popularity. The quantity greatly exceeded that of the late eighteenth-century debate. With so much more to choose from, could we term the political arguments — the discourse surrounding the secession crisis — as impressive as the debate over the Constitution of 1787? The answer is, no one has to date, but in evaluating the quality and level of debate it must be kept in mind that the literature was not strictly Southern in origin. The debate over deratification could also include the Northern editorials and pamphlets and speeches urging the Southern states not to embark on secession. The quantity is impressive — overwhelming, in fact — and there is no comparing it with the earlier ratification process in terms of size, but the political ideas circulated in 1860–61 served a population eight times greater than that of the era of the Constitution of 1787. But, to put the question bluntly, was the debate any good? Did it in any way approach the level of discourse of the late eighteenth century?

Surely, it did not in some ways. For example, Gordon Wood credits the debate over the Constitution of 1787, particularly the arguments for ratification, with creating a "new science of American politics."[83] No such claim

could be made for secessionist ideas. Nor did the response to secession provoke a foreign and authoritarian theory of the state among Northerners, a
point discussed in the first chapter of this book. The hallmark and reputation of secessionist arguments are for clinging strictly to the old and rigid.
In fact, the ideas of the secessionists share some of the unattractive qualities
that Bernard Bailyn associated with the Anti-Federalists of 1787–88: rigid-
ity, paranoia, and mindless invocation of shopworn axioms.[84]

How paranoid was it? To be sure, secession fought an enemy that hardly
existed: fanatical, abolitionist Republicans. Republicans kept their distance
from abolitionists, carefully, and insisted on congressional legislation halting only the expansion of slavery. For their part, the Republicans rallied
their voters against a monolithic and aristocratic Slave Power that did not
really exist, either. To that degree, political movements of the period all
exhibited some "paranoid" tendencies. But what about the fear of secret
associations that did not really exist? Ironically, that proved to be a hallmark of secession in Texas. It is ironic, because the secessionist movement
in Texas was led initially by its supreme court, especially by Chief Justice
Oran Roberts, in a startling example of the aggressiveness of the so-called
least dangerous branch. In fact, the secession debate in Texas can be termed
a constitutional discourse, since the Unionist side of the formal intellectual debate was led by another Texas Supreme Court justice, James Bell.
Together Roberts and Bell offered, in a public debate in Austin early in December 1860, what William W. Freehling has termed a "high-powered exchange" providing "the best single-day debate anywhere in the Lower South
that fateful December."[85] They also demonstrated a shocking example of judicial impropriety, weighing in on popular public debate on highly charged
political questions — a forecast of the aggressive role increasingly taken by
the American judiciary in the crisis of the Civil War.

This, the only part of the secessionist movement of 1860–61 that actually constituted a coup d'état, was led by members of a state supreme court.
We can say of this astonishing movement in Texas that it was politically, if
not exactly constitutionally, creative. The Texas secessionists faced a vexing
problem. Only the state legislature could call a constitutional convention,
and the legislature was not in session that winter. The real problem was the
Unionist views of Governor Sam Houston, a hero of the Texas revolution.
He refused to call the legislature into session. This prompted the revolutionary move, by Chief Justice Roberts and by a fellow justice, Royall T.
Wheeler, to call elections to a convention to consider secession anyway.
Then, somehow realizing the possibility that such a movement resembled a
coup d'état, the justices also required that a secession ordinance would have

to be ratified by popular vote. In the end, Texas was the only seceding state so far to call a referendum on its secession ordinance. Thus the secessionist movement that most resembled a coup d'état was also the one least fearful of the voters.[86] This revolutionary movement was well considered — in some ways.

Secession in Texas also calls to mind the irrational element in the secession movement. In the summer of 1860 a series of fires consumed parts of Dallas and other North Texas towns. Today they are attributed to a period of extremely hot weather and to easily ignitable friction matches.[87] At the time the fires were widely attributed to antislavery Methodists and African Americans. They are now called the "Texas Troubles." But they were exploited by secessionists to stampede voters to disunion. It can be said that even moderates like John Reagan, who would become the postmaster general of the Confederacy, believed in them. He concluded a speech on secession he gave in Congress on January 15, 1861 — later circulated as a pamphlet — with reference to them:

> I must say that the very State from which I came, the very district which I represent, has had some painful experience during the last summer, growing out of the doctrines of abolitionism. We found, for the last two or three years, that the members of the Methodist Church North, and others, living in Texas, were propagating abolition doctrines there. We warned them not to carry on their schemes of producing disaffection among our negroes; but they persisted, and did not cease until they had organized a society called the "Mystic Red." Under its auspices, the night before the last of August election the towns were to be burned and the people murdered. There now lie in ashes near a dozen towns and villages in my district. Four of them were county seats, and two of them the best towns in the district. The poisonings were only arrested by information which came to light before the plan could be carried into execution. The citizens were forced to stand guard for months, so that no man could have passed through the towns between dark and daylight without making himself known. A portion of them paid the penalty of their crimes. Others were driven out of the country. These things had their effect on the public mind. They were the results of abolition teachings; a part of the irrepressible conflict; a part of the legitimate fruits of Republicanism.[88]

From the start, republicanism in America was characterized by near-paranoid fears of government power. And for all their admirers, the arguments of 1787–88 retained here and there some of these elements of irrationalism, as we can see, for instance, in *The Federalist*, no. 1, which ended with an image of disunionist conspiracy:

> The fact is that we already hear it whispered in the private circles of those who oppose the new Constitution, that the thirteen States are of too great extent for any general system, and that we must of necessity resort to separate confederacies of distinct portions of the whole. This doctrine will, in all probability, be gradually propagated, till it has votaries enough to countenance an open avowal of it. For nothing can be more evident to those who are able to take an enlarged view of the subject than the alternative of an adoption of the new Constitution or a dismemberment of the Union.[89]

The tendency accelerated in the nineteenth century with the rise of mass political parties and the growth of an increasingly pluralist society. It is not surprising to find such marplots as the "Mystic Red" featured in arguments over secession. What is surprising is the relatively small number of such references. They cannot be said to have dominated debate. Fears were raised about the possible impact of Republican policies on Southern society regularly in secessionist arguments, but they did not have to rely on the creation or exaggerated reporting of such imaginary conspiracies as the "Mystic Red."

The Soldiers' Vote

Finally, an account of the practical political content of the secession movement is imperative. Much of what has been written recently about Confederate nationalism would leave a reader with the impression not only of a coup d'état but of a thoroughly reactionary one. Take the influential example of Drew Gilpin Faust in *The Creation of Confederate Nationalism*. She focuses particularly on the secession conventions as illustrations of attempts to assert reactionary values in setting up the new republic. "The assembling of supralegislative bodies," she argues, "created the need for widespread political consensus on secession and other issues. Yet, in many states, the conventions also provided the opportunity for an oligarchy to take advantage of the crisis to advance its own antidemocratic ends in the process of state constitution making that followed withdrawal from the Union."[90]

First we should note that Faust has thus identified one of the most underestimated features of the constitutional history of the Confederacy—the expansion of authority of the secession conventions in several of the states beyond the act of severance from the Union and the continued government by ordinances from these conventions over important matters in the first year of the war. This further expands secession from a moment or even a movement with a sudden climax. In fact, the secessionists were at work in the conventions, here and there, well beyond the momentary issuance of their ordinances of secession. She realizes that in the emergency work of these conventions the "conservative tendencies within Confederate nationalism were profoundly altered and attenuated by the need to negotiate consensus," but the emphasis in her discussion is on "proponents of reaction," "conservative doctrines," "hierarchical political and social views," "oligarchic tendencies," and, in sum, "the conservative tendencies within Confederate nationalism."[91] This is a misrepresentation of the work of the secession conventions in the emergency of 1861–62. There was no conservative coup and no serious or widespread attempt at one — at any time in Confederate history from the secession conventions to the surrender at Appomattox. No one wanted to replicate the master-slave relationship in white society. But the Southern leaders *were* playing with political fire from the start.

This was a rare moment in Civil War history when political theory really mattered. The theory of secession, deriving one way or another from the works of John C. Calhoun, dictated that special conventions, embodying a sovereignty above that of the mere legislatures — a sovereignty of the originating sort that set up the very constitutions under which the state legislatures operated — had to be summoned to express the true will of the people on such an important question. For many, the idea was that this sovereign body was to act only on the question of secession. But a sovereign body has no political superior. Who could stop it if it continued acting? No one seems to have realized that there would inevitably be a sort of legislative spread in the work of the conventions. After all, the old state constitutions had to be squared with the new national reality. At least, the delegates had to change the wording from "United States" to "Confederate States" when the words occurred in the existing documents. And, especially because some of these conventions decided on secession only after war had broken out, there was a real reason for urgency and efficiency in getting the government under way.

As it turned out, not all the convention delegates confined themselves to this narrow focus. Instead, they wandered into general reform — to the methods of choosing the members of the state supreme court or to the ideal size of the legislature. In Virginia, Faust points out, "the convention presented to the people a constitution far less democratic than that which had been in force for the past decade, for it sharply reduced the number of elective offices and established a judiciary largely independent of the people."[92]

In the end, the people rejected the new proposed Virginia Constitution. Here is what Faust concludes, however, about the debates on such measures in these secession conventions:

> In terms of our concern with ideological strategies, the crucial issue is less the substantive political outcome than the dialogue that preceded actual political decisions. Proponents of reaction recognized war-born opportunities at the same time they confronted new wartime social and political constraints. . . . This was nationalism in creation — not a preconceived body of theories or abstractions, but ideas as rhetorical weapons, useful insofar as they could persuade, legitimate, or inspire. The forceful assertion of conservative doctrines as at once southern and sacred and the hegemonic effort to equate Yankeeism simultaneously with democracy and the Devil profoundly shaped the character of Confederate nationalism as it was promulgated from the pulpit, the stump, and the press. Those southerners who had embraced hierarchical political and social views in the antebellum years seized upon the changing situation as an occasion to advance these views and to associate them as closely as possible with the ongoing process of national self-definition.[93]

In truth, the work of the secession conventions was compatible with the popular democracy of the antebellum South and the Confederate experience afterward.[94] The most notable common theme in the work of the secession conventions, a problem that most of them tackled by way of making their state constitutions square with the new Confederate reality, was in fact to expand the franchise not to contract it. Put more properly, their task was to keep the ability to vote from being contracted by the advent of war. The Confederate States made certain, generally by legislation of the secession conventions, that soldiers could vote in the field. Soldiers in the Northern states did not necessarily enjoy similar accommodation. In that respect, the Confederacy proved more democratic than the North.

Let us examine Josiah Benton's book of 1915, still the standard work, on *Voting in the Field*. Before describing the protracted political battles over the soldiers' franchise in the North state by state, Benton included a brief chapter dispatching the question of the soldiers' vote in the Confederate states. "When the Southern States seceded," Benton wrote, they "nearly all dealt with the question of permitting soldiers to vote in the field. This they did in some cases by statutes, and in other cases, where the Constitution fixed the places of voting, by ordinances that were passed by the secession conventions, and were treated as amendments to the Constitution, or at least as having equal authority with the provisions of the Constitution."[95]

Benton went right to the heart of the matter in appraising that movement to enfranchise the Confederacy's soldiers:

> There does not seem to have been any reason for these Southern statutes, except the desire to preserve to soldiers who enlisted the rights which they had at home. There was no occasion for soldiers to vote to control the elections in any Southern States. After secession there was practically but one party in the South. There were no close states which it was thought might be carried by the soldiers' voting in the field, as was the case in the North. Soldiers' voting acts in the South must, therefore, all be regarded as having been passed solely for the purpose of preserving to the soldier his inalienable right to take part in the government of the country by voting.[96]

The movement was, simply put, profoundly democratic.

In that respect — and in others — the image of the secession conventions has been greatly distorted in writing the history of Confederate nationalism. In the first place, one does not derive from reading the journals of any of the conventions a feeling that this little group of men was a conservative junto bent on seizing their state government. Instead, one sees a gradual — but admittedly confident — assumption of power in small steps, from the administratively necessary and clarifying, to larger steps that represented intrusion on the control of military forces of the state, shaping of taxation, and modifications of its political rules and boundaries. Florida's convention even shortened the term of the governor from four to two years, though the new provision was not to go into effect until 1865.[97] The boundaries of counties came to be affected in some instances. Imbued with power, very great but surely temporary, some delegates sought what they thought was best for their state, without much thought, ostensibly, to the problem of sovereignty. In North Carolina, for instance, a delegate from Mecklenburg introduced an ordinance to amend the state constitution "to exclude atheists from office holding."[98]

North Carolina, as reluctant a seceder as any in the whole Confederacy, was in step with its more eager secessionist neighbors in making Confederate soldiers from their state eligible to vote in national and state elections. Their ordinance securing the right to vote for soldiers absent from their counties of residence passed the state convention on June 25, 1861.[99]

Virginia's delegates were careful to include soldiers already serving in the state militia in the vote to ratify secession. On April 20, 1861, a delegate recommended establishing a committee to "look into providing for voters, in the service of the State, to cast votes at the nearest place of election, on the question of ratification or rejection of secession." The resolution was adopted.[100] Virginians passed an ordinance permitting qualified voters who were absent from the state in Confederate service to vote for presidential electors and for members of the Confederate Congress on July 1, 1861, well before the Battle of Bull Run.[101] Virginia faced invasion and occupation as early as any state and more often than any other. Thus it proved to be important that its convention delegates moved early also to make provision for voting by refugees from occupied counties. The measure passed by a vote of 79 to 20 on November 19, 1861.[102] The late 1861 session of the convention voted to allow Virginians absent from the state in Confederate service to vote in state elections. The ordinance also included voting rights for citizens absent from their residence because of the presence of the enemy.[103]

These democratic measures passed energetically by the Virginia convention take on particular importance because that convention has been singled out by historians for its conservative activism. There were conservatives delegates in that convention, all right, and they urged various measures to limit the franchise and to ease the burden of taxation on the state's slaveholding elite. The measures did not pass, however, and, more important, it is clear that the conservatives were on the defensive in the Virginia convention. Early on, of course, the convention represented the whole state, including delegates from its Unionist western portions. Those delegates went on the attack first, urging various liberal measures. Well before secession, westerners moved — on March 2, 1861 — to impose an ad valorem tax on slaves.[104] The western delegates were politically threatening. One affirmed that there was no right of secession but that the right of revolution could apply as well to a part of a state that was oppressed "by others within the same state (as well as against [the] federal government)."[105] In other words, westerners were themselves threatening to secede from the state. Waitman T. Willey, who would later represent West Virginia in the U.S. Congress, moved early in the Virginia secession convention to equalize taxation and representation between the eastern and western portions of the state. He also stated a preference for apportioning senators in Virginia's legislature by the number of qualified voters.[106] Later, conservatives fought back, urging amendment of the state constitution to apportion representation in the state senate by population combined with the amount of taxes paid.[107] After the expulsion of the liberal western delegates on June 28, 1861, the measures assuring a democratic voice in wartime representation prevailed all the same.

Even in South Carolina, where the persistence of the secession convention became the principal question in state politics for more than a year after the war began, the record of the convention could not be easily characterized as antidemocratic. The convention passed ordinances in late 1861 that permitted South Carolinians from occupied areas of the state to vote outside their counties of residence and to enable South Carolinians in military service to vote in camp.[108]

These sweeping democratic movements to ensure that soldiers would have a say in choosing the governments that committed them to war could not be matched by the North. There the political party system impeded democracy. The Democrats fought the implementation of voting rights for soldiers, realizing that soldiers were likely to vote for the commander in chief when he ran for reelection in 1864.

The Problem of Sovereignty

The longer the conventions met, the more serious became the issue of secret sessions. Their operating in that fashion might well be grist for the mill of those historians who see in the conventions a conservative coup, working behind closed doors to accomplish changes in government the people would not like. Once again, comparison with the Philadelphia convention of 1787 is helpful. The delegates in Philadelphia worked entirely under a veil of secrecy. The veil was partial in the case of the secession conventions seventy-odd years later, but the most important difference was this: the secession conventions were in constant receipt of dispatches deemed sensitive in content that impinged on the public safety. They might have caused panic among the people, disrupted financial markets, and endangered the safety of a state if the state were to become an independent republic in a matter of hours. Typical was this telegram received by the Alabama convention. Dated January 12, 1861, and sent from Charleston, South Carolina, by Robert Barnwell Rhett Jr., it read: "Large steam ship off the bar, steaming up; supposed to be the Brooklyn. Expect a battle."[109] Of course, the Philadelphia convention did not work under the imminent threat of war or invasion and had other reasons for secrecy in its proceedings. The secession conventions did admit reporters for all but the secret sessions. The emergency conditions under which the secession conventions labored were greatest for those that took up their work after the firing on Fort Sumter. In the case of Virginia, war greatly complicated the process of maintaining a delegation. Some delegates went into rebellion (from western Virginia), and at least one was killed in action while on military duty.[110]

All along, and in most Confederate states, some delegates resisted the continuation in power of the bodies in which they sat as influential members. In Arkansas, a delegate proposed a resolution against the assumption of legislative powers "further than are necessary as incidents growing out of the change of our federal relations, and providing for the immediate defence of the state."[111] And some of the proponents of further sessions of the state conventions proved apologetic rather than grasping in describing their tasks. The president of the Florida secession convention, upon reconvening the delegates in 1862, said that he had thought they would never assemble again but now bowed to "circumstances of difficulty and embarrassment in the affairs of your commonwealth, which could not be relieved by any other than the sovereign power of the State." There was reason for apology. The original convention had adjourned sine die unless reconvened by the president before December 25, 1861. The Florida convention reconvened on January 14, 1862, because the state was in danger of bankruptcy. One of the problems this session took care of by invoking the sovereignty of the state was to allow soldiers to vote.[112]

There is a tendency to think of the secession conventions as the deliberative assemblies that took the Confederate States out of the Union. Some did, but one — Missouri's — did not. This was a convention called to consider secession too, but it was eventually dominated by Unionists. They acted to maintain their temporary power the same way the conventions acted that did take their states out of the Union. The tendency to find sovereign power alluring and comfortable was universal and not confined to regimes dominated by slaveholders.

Missouri was the only state in which the Unionists — Republicans — toppled the state government by a genuine coup d'état.[113] After Union military forces under Nathaniel Lyon, an army officer stationed in St. Louis, and St. Louis politician Francis P. Blair drove the prosecession government out of Jefferson City, Unionists reconvened the old secession convention, now lacking secessionists, who had fled. Because the elected governor of the state, Claiborne Jackson, fled to the Confederacy, the rump convention chose a new, Unionist governor, Hamilton R. Gamble.

Missouri was the only state in the Union to postpone major elections during the Civil War, putting off its gubernatorial election twice. First, the state convention meeting in the summer of 1861, after the initial coup, chose Gamble to fill the vacated governor's seat. It scheduled special elections to fill the vacated executive offices for November 1861, but in October postponed them until August 1862 (the first Monday in August was the traditional election day for the governorship and other offices except the presidency of the United States). Gamble remained in office. In June 1862 the Missouri state convention reconvened for a third session (its second session as the embodiment of Unionist sovereignty in Missouri). Among other things, the convention eventually decided not to force a popular election for governor later that summer and stipulated that Gamble's unelected term would extend to 1864. That would have constituted the normal term for a governor elected in 1860.[114] Then, in 1864, there would be a gubernatorial election, as usual.

The Unionist convention consciously abandoned the idea of having a referendum on its work. On the afternoon of July 29, 1861, Gamble asked the delegates: "Who are we that are here assembled? This is not a body assembled under the Constitution of the State by its direction. It is a body assembled by the people, directed by the people themselves in their original capacity." In the governor's mind, the convention was "an original, extra, and supra constitutional body . . . a body not mentioned in the Constitution, not contemplated in the Constitution . . . delegated by the people in their original sovereign capacity for the purpose of carrying out the will of the people."[115] Despite his repeated invocations in the people's name, Gamble was in fact finished with the people as having any further role in the workings of the convention. "Nobody ever heard of the Constitution of the United States being submitted to the people, or ratified by the voice of the people of the States," he insisted. Gamble had no doubt that "a Constitution, when adopted by a Convention elected by the people for the purpose of adopting a Constitution, is valid without any submission."[116]

Long before there was any election for governor, the state legislature began to meet again regularly as well. So Missouri had at times two legislatures, one sovereign and the other — the real legislature and not the convention — of limited sovereignty, theoretically. Despite all that abundance of legislative authority in the state, Governor Gamble, though conservatively legalistic in his outlook, as befit a former state supreme court justice, nevertheless enjoyed extraordinary powers because of the war. Not the least of these powers lay in his ability, as a convention member, to sit in and dominate the convention when he convened it again in 1862 to deal with the emancipation of slaves in Missouri.[117] Such was the history of a Unionist convention rather than a secessionist one. It is easy to see why the Founders of the American republic warned against the corrupting tendencies of power. The slaveholders held no monopoly on abuse of power. Yet in the end the Founders proved wrong on another point about power — it did not absolutely corrupt Americans anywhere. In the Union and the Confederacy alike, all states eventually returned to the antebellum style of republican government.

Surprisingly, many of the major dramas of Confederate constitutional history have barely been mentioned in standard histories. One of the greatest was the suspenseful existence of two governments at the same time within those states where the secession conventions met well past the time of drafting and adopting a secession ordinance. George Rable, for example, said that "because the legislatures continued to meet in all the Southern states, the conventions occupied a constitutionally anomalous position."[118] Surely it would make more sense to put it the other way around: because the conventions continued to meet well past the completion of their tasks of secession, a constitutionally anomalous situation developed. But "anomalous" is too mild a term. Here were the potential ingredients for constitutional crisis.

Even before secession was complete and it was clear that the conventions should be adjourned, the problem lurked. Ultimately, one might blame the difficulty on the inexorable logic of John C. Calhoun, the great theorist of nullification and widely regarded as the father of secession, who began his un-American political thought with the issue of sovereignty. By definition it was indivisible. Once identified, it was, as it turns out, very dangerous. That is why any serious conflict of authority in the secession conventions had explosive potential. Take the case of the problematic — not even contested — election from Fulton County, Arkansas. Two candidates for delegate, S. H. Cochran and S. H. Wren, got the same number of votes — 220. Local officials decided to award the convention seat to Cochran. The ballot asked the voter to vote for or against having a convention and to select delegates. The vote on the convention was not a tie — the county went for holding a convention. So the authorities gave the seat to the proconvention candidate Cochran.[119]

When Cochran got to Little Rock, other delegates objected to his selection. A committee on elections was appointed and ruled to seat no delegate from Fulton but to pay Cochran's mileage expenses to the convention. There should be another election, the committee's members said. But there was not necessarily time enough to hold another election and seat the new delegate before the work of the convention would be finished. Nevertheless, the call for a new election prevailed and Cochran returned home.[120]

When the convention asked Governor Henry M. Rector to issue an election proclamation for Fulton County, he refused, saying it would be unconstitutional and without law for him to call for such an election. The delegates did not much like to be lectured on the Arkansas Constitution and began their reply by noting that "His excellency" had "volunteered a disquisition on the nature of government." They informed the governor that "it appears to your committee that this convention being in legal contemplation, the whole people of the state . . . a resolution of this convention is as high a sanction as his excellency, or any other state officer, could have."[121] Arkansas was suddenly experiencing a constitutional crisis over the tied election in Fulton County in which all of 440 votes had been cast.

The convention itself then called for an election to be held in April, the president of the convention issuing the proclamation to the sheriff to proceed.[122] The crisis went no further, but the potential for constitutional conflict was fully revealed.

In South Carolina and Virginia the spectacle of two legislating bodies operating at the same time prevailed for a dangerously long time, but for a time the existence of two governments was inevitable in most seceded states. Declaring secession was not enough, anywhere. In general the conventions routinely established committees to tidy up such obvious problems as the former jurisdiction and role of the federal courts in the states, citizenship, and the appearance of the words "United States" in state constitutions and elsewhere.

Some conventions lingered longer than others, but it appears to have required special circumstances for a convention to loom as a threat to the simple resumption of the old state government, which was, after all, the ultimate answer to the charge that secession was anarchy. Still, circumstances could create a serious threat of having two governments—a sure invitation to anarchy. In South Carolina, the conflict between legislature and convention was the central issue in politics well into 1862.[123]

From this narrative comes this very important historical lesson: it required dramatic circumstances to perpetuate the life of the convention to positively dangerous lengths. In South Carolina the problems were three. First, the governor, Francis Pickens, was widely regarded as weak and unequal to the tasks of war. Second, and more important, a Union fleet captured Port Royal, South Carolina, on November 7, 1861, spreading alarm for the public safety of the state and establishing a Yankee outpost near the heart of the Confederacy that was never surrendered. Third, the Great Charleston Fire broke out on December 11, 1861, creating conditions for martial law in what was the most important city in the state and one of the more important ones in the Confederacy. The secession convention called itself back into session and created an executive council of five, consisting of a majority of three appointed members, the weak governor, and the lieutenant governor. This council essentially ran South Carolina's government until December 1862.

The convention was sovereign — in the view of some — and the council it created exercised what often seemed to be sovereign powers, including the imposition of martial law in the Charleston area on May 5, 1862, well past the time of the great fire. Before the end of the month, the *Charleston Courier*, which was not squeamish about the suspension of civil liberties on behalf of the Confederate war effort, was terming the executive council a "secret conclave of five dictators."[124] The conflict generated considerable constitutional argument. The *Courier*, which opposed the continuance of the secession convention, earlier wrote:

> We differ widely from the prevalent opinion in this State, as to the character and office of conventions. The general opinion in South Carolina is that they are the people, acting in their highest sovereign capacity, and are possessed of supreme and absolute power — supreme over law and constitution, over property, liberty and life. . . .
>
> The true theory of Conventions is that they are, not the people in the exercise of their highest sovereignty, but extraordinary delegates of the people, assembled on extraordinary occasions and emergencies, to discharge functions or perform acts, to which the ordinary departments of Government are incompetent, inadequate or unsuited. . . . Only representative bodies, responsible and amenable to the people themselves, [are] the true sovereign or source of legitimate authority.[125]

Consistency on constitutional questions was never possible because of political interests and habits, however. The *Courier* sharply criticized the executive council apparently because of the faction that controlled it. The newspaper eventually became one of the more ardent advocates of national power and Jacksonian firmness in meeting the challenge of the war.

The executive council imposed conscription, commandeered slaves to work on fortifications, and outlawed cotton exports unless the profits were used to purchase war materiel.[126] After months of relentless criticism, the council finally dissolved in December 1862. The pattern of constitutional history in South Carolina, then, is rather different from what one might expect. The greatest threat to liberty and the most authoritarian government (the executive council, the "conclave of five dictators") enjoyed power while the state was least threatened, early in the war. Subsequently, even though Charleston was under constant siege by a Union fleet from May 1862, and the state was finally invaded in 1865, the government of South Carolina was the state government of old, directed by a governor, a state legislature, and a supreme court. Through it all, the South Carolina State Supreme Court maintained a remarkable record of forbearance. The South Carolina State reports for the war years include only one case having to do with a war issue.

Virginia's secession convention, originally dominated by Unionists, reconvened in wartime to secede, and naturally its subsequent history was constitutionally controversial. Somehow, by the end of 1862, every state that witnessed the presence of two governments — a "sovereign" secession convention passing ordinances and a governor and state legislature enforcing and passing laws — resolved the potentially dangerous situation peaceably by dissolving the conventions and returning to familiar governments under slightly modified state constitutions of long standing. This constitutional history, general for much of the Confederacy, has been obscured by its treatment in the histories of single states only. Historians of the Confederacy as a whole have not described the overall pattern of averted constitutional crises in the Confederacy.

The resolution of the problem was a tribute to the nimbleness of Confederate political life despite the absence of political parties. South Carolina saw great rancor over the conflict of sovereignties, but in some states there was almost none. In the end, the familiar pattern of orderly creation of a nation emerged. The process was not as calm and seamless as that which had marked the original implementation of the U.S. Constitution back in 1787–89, but that ratification did not provoke or take place during a war.

In the Confederacy, tendencies to government by revolutionary convention appeared in many places, but they nowhere prevailed. That was one of its unheralded achievements. In the process, some states simply enjoyed the fruits of the emergency actions of the conventions, including the democratization of war by ensuring that the men who fought for the slaveholding republic, whether they owned slaves or not, could vote in camp. Overall, the record was democratic but not revolutionary or radical. Had the Confederacy prevailed on the battlefield and survived as a nation, it would doubtless celebrate that period of government by secession conventions as the United States does today the 1787 Philadelphia constitutional convention.

Seven

The Police State of Richmond

Had the Confederacy been allowed to establish a new nation without hindrance, it would surely have been a slave republic, as the United States was already, only with a greater proportion of slaves in it. There was nothing in the Confederate Constitution to suggest otherwise. There was nothing in the process of secession to suggest otherwise, either. In fact, that process seems in retrospect almost dreamily democratic, unfazed by the sure prospect of war that faced any new nation-state in the mid-nineteenth century, and unrealistic about assessing its chances of survival in a struggle against the rest of the United States.

Instead of a masters' dictatorship, even the possibility of war and the consequent need to put together a viably populous and prosperous nation dictated a free, democratic ethos for the hopeful nation's white people. The strategy, if it may be called that, for adding the rest of the slave states to the Confederate States of America was to lure them into a republic on the same model, with essentially the same constitution they were used to in the old United States, but with more accommodation to slavery.

War brought new pressures. Although secession was marked by its carefully debated, parliamentary, and orderly process—as well as by its solicitously democratic content for the white yeomen doomed to fighting the war that resulted from secession—it did initiate a nationalist revolution, unleashing and employing astonishing force. On the level of the individual Confederate citizen, the countervailing power of an organized loyal opposition was not present. The country's short history and long presidential term discouraged the vigorous organization of political parties for the great presidential contest. Had the Confederacy lasted one more year, parties would surely have been organized for the presidential election, and there were already signs of that movement, in Georgia and North Carolina particularly, in the very late days of the Confederacy. Still, there were no political parties with names and persistent organization. Did that leave dissenters without a voice? Did it cause them to take more readily to illegal forms of resistance? Was the Confederacy plagued by internal disorder and factious resistance?

Southerners did not foresee any special difficulties in adjusting to a major war. In fact, foresight was not a conspicuous characteristic of the secession debate. In all that discussion and debate that so completely outstripped the process of the founding of the United States in 1787–88, not much of the discussion concerned the military viability of the new Confederate nation. There was little focus on the war powers of the Constitution or the vigorous interpretation of them to be found in *The Federalist*. There was no discussion of a standing army or a more efficient militia organization. Once the nation was launched into what turned out to be a desperate, then fatal struggle for existence, there proved to be a short-term practical flexibility in Confederate constitutional arrangements that permitted a wide range of experience despite the nation's siege mentality. The naval blockade gave the Confederacy a national sense of being besieged, whatever the efficiency of the blockade in fact. The actual proximity of Union forces was not necessary to induce the feeling. And Southerners knew all too well that their defense of slavery was an anomaly in the world opinion they valued, that of England and France; they felt intellectually besieged. Some places were literally besieged. Newspapers printed in the great symbolic heart of secession, Charleston, each day counted up the days of their lengthy bombardment. Setting the tone for the whole nation, Richmond, the seat of the national government and of the most abundant and influential press, was more often beleaguered than Confederate authorities wanted to admit. Other areas, many of them rural, only imagined what the conflict was like and felt its strains mainly in sacrifice of youthful manhood to mobilization and in unwonted economic deprivation.

The constitutional experience that dawned on the slave republic with the advent of a great war cannot be accurately summed up by a monolithic interpretation. The Confederacy was not so rigid constitutionally that it died of state rights. It was not so flexibly modern that it threw over all North American experience and embraced state socialism. Instead, the Confederacy had a range of experiences, reaching from siege precautions to rather unrealistic persistence of peacetime liberties. Perhaps the most authoritarian experience, reaching the most Confederate white citizens for the longest stretches of time, came in the nation's capital. The experience of Richmond will provide the focus for a close-up examination of the effects that strains on the Constitution placed on the people and the courts. But before this chapter takes a look at Richmond, let us first consider the broad context of views on the Constitution in the Confederacy.

The Pamphlet Literature

President Jefferson Davis enjoyed the advantage of official status for pronouncements that were published separately at government expense and widely reported and reprinted in the press. It is surprising to look at the parallel documents to Lincoln's First Inaugural Address and his address to the special session of Congress of July 4, 1861 — the one given before and the other written after the war began. Davis literally gave two inaugural addresses — one on February 18, 1861, as provisional president before the war began and one on February 22, 1862, as president under the permanent Confederate Constitution, given well after the fighting was under way. Comparing the Lincoln and Davis addresses would make one think that Lincoln was the stickler for constitutional rectitude and not Davis, a reminder of how circumstantial were their differences on many constitutional questions.

Jefferson Davis's address of February 18, 1861, to mark his inauguration as provisional president of the Confederacy, differed from Lincoln's inaugural address in that Davis never quoted any text from the Constitution. It was an awkward fact that Davis as yet could refer only to a Provisional Constitution, a document cobbled together in Montgomery, Alabama, in five days, by a convention of six of the seven states that had seceded so far.[1] Of necessity, it substantially copied the U.S. Constitution. Davis was in Montgomery himself and could see the Constitution. In the inaugural address, Davis made clear that the Constitution was meant to be largely the same as the old one and that that familiarity stood as an assurance that the rest of the slave states — eight remained in the Union at that point — could join their new confederation without fear of loss of familiar liberties. "With a Constitution differing only from that of our fathers in so far as it is explanatory of their well-known intent, freed from sectional conflicts, which have interfered with the pursuit of the general welfare, it is not unreasonable to expect that States from which we have recently parted may seek to unite their fortunes to ours under the Government which we have instituted," he said blandly.[2] He took Confederate independence as a fact from which to start and wasted surprisingly little time on detailed and specific constitutional arguments. He quoted from the Declaration of Independence of

1776 (the word "inalienable" to describe the Confederates' rights), and he referred to the "right solemnly proclaimed at the birth of the United States," which was "affirmed and reaffirmed in the Bills of Rights of the States." But he did not actually quote from any constitution, new or old

Davis said it was "an abuse of language" to call the resumption of authority by the "sovereign States here represented" a "revolution."[3] He could even say that the Confederates had "changed the constituent parts, but not the system of government." He expressed confidence not only in the "Constitution framed by our fathers" but also "in the judicial construction it has received," surely meant as an expression of satisfaction with the Supreme Court of Roger B. Taney rather than John Marshall, though he did not say so expressly.[4] He did not offer a detailed and legalistic description of the process of secession: the address was short, thirteen paragraphs.

The inaugural address of the president under the permanent Constitution, given on February 22, 1862, talked a good deal more about the U.S. Constitution and its violations by the Lincoln administration than about the Confederate Constitution. Again, Davis did not quote any particular text from either Constitution but instead denounced "the disregard" that the North had "recently exhibited for all the time-honored bulwarks of civil and religious liberty," reminding his audience of the suspension of the writ of habeas corpus there and its attendant arrests, incarcerations, and other threats to political liberty.[5]

It is difficult to interpret the second address, given after the permanent Constitution was in place, because five days after the speech President Davis himself suspended the writ of habeas corpus in Norfolk and Portsmouth, Virginia. The military situation did not alter abruptly in that brief period, and the immediate provocation for suspending the writ of habeas corpus again, in Richmond on March 1, is not evident. There was no clear train of dramatically alarming events in northern Virginia preceding Davis's suspension like those in Baltimore preceding Lincoln's first suspension.[6] In short, it might be said that Davis's proclamations were prompted by lesser immediate and proximate provocation than Lincoln's at first.

The Confederate Congress renewed the authority to suspend the writ, and the period in which Davis clearly had the authority stretched to February 13, 1863. Eventually, opposition arose to these measures of Davis and to others. Indeed, the political opposition was felt so strongly that the Congress granted Davis the authorization only one more time. The politicians did not want to take on the habeas corpus issue in an election year — which was 1863 for the Confederate congressmen. There was substantial turnover in the Congress after the elections, but still the new Congress granted Davis the authority on February 15, 1864. When that authority expired on August 1, 1864, the Congress refused to renew it, despite the obviously beleaguered condition of the Confederacy.[7]

To look at the history books, one would say that the constitutional history of the Confederacy certainly got off to a more favorable start than that of the North. The route of troops to the northern frontier did not necessarily pass through contested territory, as the route to the District of Columbia did. The Battle of Bull Run of July 21, 1861, was not preceded by riots as troops changed trains to reach the Virginia front. Historians are increasingly coming to the realization that the Battle of Bull Run was important, not merely a sobering tactical setback for the North, but a great psychological windfall for the Confederacy. In addition to boosting military confidence in the South and undermining the confidence of the Union army, it did other things not previously noted, some of them of political and even constitutional significance.[8] It created heroes with which the people of the Confederacy could identify their national cause, one of whom, Stonewall Jackson, would ever after remain a heroic figure. It allowed the Confederate government to act as a victor does, from confidence, and not as a loser does, with cautious hesitation or desperation. There was no need in Richmond, on which all eyes now fell and to which many throughout the Confederacy looked for news, to restrict civil liberties or make threats against dissenters. The government could pose as the champion of liberty, inviting other slave states to join it and asking the world to compare the records of the Northern and Southern governments on civil liberty. President Davis did not feel the need to suspend the privilege of the writ of habeas corpus in the summer of 1861.

When Davis did finally feel the necessity the next winter, he, unlike Lincoln, asked his Congress for authority to do so — or so the story goes in the customary telling. In truth, the key was a difference in circumstance. When Lincoln felt the necessity to suspend the writ, after the Baltimore riots and the burning of the railroad bridges on the route to Washington, Congress was not in session. The president did not wait. When Davis moved to suspend the writ of habeas corpus, the Confederate Congress *was* in session. It is not clear that in a similar circumstance, Lincoln would have acted differently. And what a difference to Lincoln's reputation it would have made had Congress authorized the suspension first. There would have been no *Ex parte Merryman* and thus no rebuke from anyone on the U.S. Supreme Court.

Pamphlets and Political Culture

The most striking feature of the pamphlet literature generated by constitutional questions in the Confederacy was its scarcity. There were many
reasons for it, only one of them constitutional. The essential constitutional
context for publications of political literature was the same in the Confederacy as in the Union: the guarantees of freedom of speech and freedom
of the press. Slave states had for a generation practiced self-censorship of
abolitionist literature, and that de facto ban certainly persisted. Otherwise, the air was free for wide-open and loud debate. Davis never gained a
reputation for suppressing the opposition press, as Lincoln did. Shortages
of ink and paper were serious impediments in the Confederacy, but there
were more important institutional factors limiting pamphlet dialogue. As
is often the case with political literature in the United States, quantity depends on the proximity of the presidential contest. The Confederacy never
got close to a presidential election after the first uncontested one, because
of the six-year term, and that certainly decreased eagerness to publish polemical literature on politico-constitutional questions. The U.S. president
himself was a major producer of political literature in the North. Abraham
Lincoln had his Corning letter — on the franking privilege of his secretary
John G. Nicolay — printed and then distributed to key opinion leaders in the
Republican Party. When Roscoe Conkling of New York received a copy, he
responded naturally: "It makes the best Campaign document we can have
in this state." From New York another recipient informed the president:
"There has at this time been ordered 50,000 copies of your letter in pam-
phlet form from the 'Tribune' and before the present week closes there will
have been printed and circulated of this letter at least 500,000 copies. . . .
Your friends in New York are taking steps to give every Soldier in the field
a copy of it." After he received his copy, Francis Lieber proposed that the
Loyal Publication Society publish ten thousand copies.[9]

Mention of the Loyal Publication Society suggests another important
institutional contrast between the Union and the Confederacy. The Confederacy had no parallel organizations to the U.S. Sanitary Commission
(which organized great patriotic spectacles and festivals but did not deal in
constitutional questions) or the Loyal Publication Society, the New England
Loyal Publication Society, the National Union Congressional Committee,
the Society for the Diffusion of Political Knowledge, or the Union League
Clubs (all of which did address constitutional controversies in their polemical pamphlet literature). The Republican committees alone published more
than three pamphlets for every Republican voter in 1864.[10] Some of these

societies were party organizations, and most of them worked to the benefit of party. But the Confederacy had no political parties. Jefferson Davis, who was therefore neither the head of a political party nor eligible for reelection in 1867, had little reason to broadcast pamphlets in defense of the constitutional positions taken by the Confederate government. The president's messages to Congress were widely circulated in the press in the Confederacy (and in the North). They sometimes contained, in addition to routine reports, able defenses of administration policy. Yet they were lumbered up with reports on subjects across a broad spectrum and had no focused message. They offered Congress and people information from Davis's point of view but not really a polemical pamphlet or broadside literature. President Davis's only apparent foray into such confrontational and contentious publication was the 1862 *Correspondence between the President and the Governor of Georgia, relative to the Law Usually Known as the Conscription Law*, a twenty-page pamphlet containing both ends of the correspondence.[11] When President Lincoln answered his critics on habeas corpus in the summer of 1863, he did not publish in full the critical letters from the Albany Democrats or the Ohio Democratic Convention members to whom he chose to respond. He spun out his own arguments in answer to carefully selected charges from the critics.

Jefferson Davis also offered some "hurrah" documents, aimed at bucking up military and civilian morale, such as the 1863 broadside, *The President's Address to the Soldiers of the Confederate States! After Two years of Warfare Scarcely Equalled . . . Your Enemies Continue a Struggle in Which Our Final Triumph Must Be Inevitable*.[12] These were of necessity filled with heartfelt sentiment but not with complex content on policy, let alone, constitutional problems.

Davis's arguments for the constitutionality of conscription were circulated mainly courtesy of Georgia's Governor Joseph E. Brown, with whom the president had an acrimonious correspondence over the issue. Brown published the correspondence as government of Georgia messages. The state printers in Richmond also published the 1862 correspondence. Davis's ideas thus gained circulation but not without Brown's refutation of them right there in the document, too. Several versions were printed by the Georgia government. Davis never really got to answer in print the governor's later complaints about conscription and the suspension of the writ of habeas corpus, printed as official messages by the Georgia government. Davis's own reasoning for the suspension of the writ in widely circulated public documents came late — in a special message to Congress of February 3, 1864.

As for the output of Davis's critics, it was not great either. In fact, at the level of the political pamphlet, Roger B. Taney supplied 10 percent of the Confederate material on the issue of civil liberties: two editions of the *Merryman* opinion circulated in the Confederacy, *The Merryman Habeas Corpus Case, Baltimore: The Proceedings in Full and Opinion of Chief Justice Taney: The United States Government a Military Despotism*, published in Mississippi in 1861, and *Opinion of Chief Justice Taney, in the Case of Ex Parte Merryman, Applying for a Writ of Habeas Corpus*, published in New Orleans in 1861.[13] To that ironic Northern contribution to the Confederate literature might be added a pamphlet edition of S. Teackle Wallis's letter to Senator John Sherman about military arrests in Maryland, first published in Baltimore but later in a Confederate printing by the First Maryland Regiment in Richmond in 1863.[14]

An examination of T. Michael Parrish and Robert M. Willingham Jr.'s definitive *Confederate Imprints: A Bibliography of Southern Publications from Secession to Surrender* uncovers seventeen pamphlets on constitutional questions published in the Confederacy (besides the copies of Taney's opinion).[15] These include four different pamphlets containing Albert Pike's contentious correspondence with Generals Theophilus Holmes and Thomas Hindman over martial law in Arkansas. As constitutional issues are not mentioned in the titles of these pamphlets, there would be no way for a Confederate citizen to know what the subject of them was or for a bookseller to be able to comply with a request for any pamphlet literature on habeas corpus unless the bookseller himself had examined the contents of Pike's pamphlets (or was an Arkansan and knew of the political controversy firsthand). John H. Gilmer's opinion on the Conscription Act was developed in a pamphlet published in Richmond in 1862. Virginia state senator Robert R. Collier was responsible for two pamphlets on martial law, both published from 1863 speeches he gave in the senate. There was a speech by John P. Murray, of Tennessee, a member of the Confederate House of Representatives, and six pamphlets containing Georgia governor Brown's correspondence with Davis about conscription and messages to the legislature focusing on constitutional issues with the Richmond government. Two pamphlets reproduced Alexander H. Stephens's caustic criticism of the Confederate president, also dealing with constitutional issues, in 1864. Finally, there was a "statement" from twelve citizens imprisoned in Huntsville, Alabama, published in 1862. That brief list appears to exhaust the subject.

By contrast and by way of comment on the relative vigor of the political culture of the Confederacy and that of the Union, at least fifteen pamphlets were published in Philadelphia alone on habeas corpus and martial law, in addition to Sidney George Fisher's book, *The Trial of the Constitution*. No *book* on the Constitution was published in the Confederacy throughout its entire history. In that respect, Philadelphia alone proved visibly more interested in the Constitution than the whole Confederacy was. Thus one Northern city almost equaled the production of the entire Confederacy in pamphlets on war-related constitutional issues and exceeded its book production.[16]

There was no Confederate edition of *The Federalist*, despite its critical bearing on American constitutional interpretation, and no Confederate editions of important constitutional commentaries like that of Joseph Story. The standard bibliography of Confederate imprints includes sections on military, political, economic, business, scientific, and medical works as well as belles lettres and, of course, religion, but nothing on law and constitutional commentary. The Confederate Congress did publish a digest of the military laws of the Confederacy in 1862, and two editions of *The Judge Advocate's Vade Mecum, Embracing a General View of Military Law, and the Practice before Courts Martial*. These were more like manuals for a military lawyer than works for civilian lawyers and statesmen.[17]

The absence of constitutional law books from the bibliographies of Confederate imprints speaks volumes about the allegedly brittle constitutionalism of the Confederacy. Even the North saw a new edition of *The Federalist*, published because of the new outlook on constitutional issues raised by the war.[18] The fashionableness of state rights interpretation in the Confederacy naturally provided an intellectual animus against reproducing the arguments of men who had built and expanded federal authority. We can feel this patriotic intellectual resistance in the speech of Arkansas representative Augustus Hill Garland before the Confederate Congress on a bill to create a supreme court. Garland supported the creation (which never came about), but he felt the necessity of avoiding criticism that the U.S. Supreme Court in the days of John Marshall (rather than in the latter days of Roger B. Taney) had been the bête noire of advocates of Southern rights. "I do not care to trammel or circumscribe this discussion," Garland assured his listeners,

> by ideas and doctrines agreed upon, and engrafted on our institutions in days gone by. I will not undertake to control the decision of this question by what Hamilton, Marshall, Story, Kent or Webster may have said, nor what may have been published to the world in the *Federalist*, a work once [that is, at one time considered to be an] authority

I believe, but now in the hurried march of improvement and advancement is rejected, and none so mean as to open its musty leaves. . . . I prefer to look on our Constitution itself, and let it spider like draw from its own bosom the material for its work. I prefer to appeal to it as its own and best exposition, and shall only seek now and then to throw some light upon it, and I hope without offending, from the acknowledged leaders of what is called the *strict construction school*.[19]

Yet Marshall and *The Federalist* remained unchallenged authorities in court decisions in the Confederacy. For example, as we shall see in Chapter 8, Chief Justice John J. Allen, of the Virginia Supreme Court, readily invoked *The Federalist*, no. 23, in 1864 in upholding the power of the Confederate Congress to raise armies by conscription. The Confederates, in short, needed these books, but they had to rely on their old and worn copies purchased for their law libraries when they practiced law in the Union.

Moreover, the constitutional principles self-consciously invoked by many Confederates — the so-called strict construction school — were no more available than the alien authorities. There was no Confederate edition of the works of John C. Calhoun. There was no Confederate edition of the *South Carolina Exposition and Protest*. The Kentucky and Virginia Resolutions of 1798 and 1799, the centerpieces of state rights ideals, had to be recalled from memory or from old texts published in the Union.

The meagerness of the pamphlet literature does not tell the whole tale, for a substantial part of the Confederate literature of constitutional controversy that does exist was the product of friendless eccentrics of doubtful representative character. These marginal figures could hardly have replicated the sentiments of the average Confederate citizen. Albert Pike, after all, was a mystic Freemason, who once wandered off into the woods for a substantial period of his life. Alexander Stephens, despite his ability to win election to public office, was an eccentric and outspoken loner given to blunt and impolitic invective, whose only intellectual associate was his brother Linton Stephens. Robert R. Collier, the Virginia state senator from Petersburg, gave voice to almost absurd constitutional interpretation and spent his practical energies liberating liquor sellers who had been banished and arrested by the Confederate army.

Lack of organized political parties did rather marginalize and minimize the systematic literature of criticism. But probably the rarity of such literature stemmed as much from the basic unity behind the Confederate national effort and fundamental agreement on constitutional developments, as well as practical forbearance dictating postponement of disagreements on such matters until the war was won. Dissent on political-constitutional questions in the Confederacy was marginal or so expressed as to make allowance for the circumstance of desperate warfare. Complaints were generally muted, and efforts to meet dissent were limited, too.[20]

Voicing opposition was entirely possible, of course. Robert Collier played a major role in ensuring that civilians would not be tried by courts-martial in the Confederacy. He also probed the weaknesses of internal security arrests by defending prisoners who were held for selling liquor to soldiers in camp—hardly a direct threat to national security. Such positions were certainly sane enough, and Collier does not appear to have suffered the personality problems some other Confederate libertarians did. He was none the less prone to take absurd constitutional positions. He held the extreme state rights view that allegiance to the states was not only "primary" but also "in the last resort exclusive." And he would simply have erased part of the Confederate Constitution by interpretation. "No exigency to justify the suspension of the privilege [of the writ of habeas corpus], is possible," he wrote in one of his pamphlets, *Correspondence and Remarks on Two Occasions in the Senate of Virginia, on the Subject of Martial Law and Arrests and Confinement of Civilians by Military Orders*.[21] Article I, section 9, paragraph 3, of the Confederate Constitution provided for the suspension of the privilege of the writ of habeas corpus in case of rebellion or invasion, just as the U.S. Constitution did.

The mainstream vested its faith, for the time being until the Confederate presidential election anticipated for 1867, in the policies of the Davis administration. It seems hardly possible, surveying the pamphlet literature of political controversy, that the Confederacy could have died of internal divisions, as many historians now assert. There does not appear to have been enough political literature reflecting ideological division to be symptomatic of a fatal case of lack of nationalism and of want of agreement on constitutional fundamentals. Moreover, the small number of pamphlet subjects tends to exaggerate the importance of the few that survive, without any reason to rely on them as representative. Thus conscription looms as perhaps the greatest issue in the Confederacy, in part because the governor of Georgia challenged it and he had the resources of the state at hand to publish his complaints.

The introduction to this book prepared the ground for the considerable reliance on pamphlet literature as a characteristic form of expression in the political life of the Civil War era. Pamphlets were distinctly prominent in the process of secession, as Chapter 6 and the work of historian-editor Jon Wakelyn reveal. But pamphlets are not a distinguishing quality in any way of the political life of the Confederacy. The brief political life of that nation was distinguished by its lack of them. No historian could write even a short, warped, and spotty history of the Confederacy from the surviving political pamphlets. Nor can the constitutional scholar chart the course of the Confederacy's constitutional history from such literature. There are many reasons for the scarcity of pamphlets in the Confederacy, but the most important one is simply this: there was not as much to write about. The constitutional conflicts were not numerous or great. It was not a matter of greater adherence to the Constitution on the part of the Confederate government — the old myth of constitutionalism — for dogged adherence would have generated great conflict. Rather, it was a matter of nationalism, pervasive national feeling, and, it must be said, preoccupation with survival.

An overlooked reason was the considerable constitutional flexibility of Confederate institutions and the adaptability of state rights principles — especially in the hands of their self-appointed guardians, the state judiciaries. "Flexibility" and "adaptability" are not terms often applied in the past to Confederate constitutional and political history, but they do describe its character in fact.

The Case of Richmond

Except for cities undergoing regular bombardment and shelling, the capital of the Confederacy, Richmond, Virginia, likely suffered under the greatest restrictions of ordinary liberties among Confederate communities. Constitutional law professor Geoffrey Stone reminds us that in evaluating any internal security system we should apply several tests, of which one might be called the "victims test." He warns that any internal security regime might well be used by "us" against "them" and ultimately victimize the most vulnerable members of society in attempting to make the nation secure.[22] Much of this book so far has been concerned with the actions and ideas of the elites who imposed and resisted internal security measures during the Civil War — especially judges, scholarly lawyers, and the two presidents, North and South. It is important to reserve some space for depiction of the society that lived under the Constitution as shaped by the Civil War. The judges, lawyers, and politicians who argued about the policies tended to foretell ultimate disaster, such as dictatorship, should the wrong policy be carried to the extreme. They warned against its possible or eventual consequences. In the short run, of course, none of these was realized in full. But there were some unhappy consequences for some even in the short run.

Few people, if any, wanted to replicate the social order of the plantation for white people anywhere in Confederate society, but liberty was not the only ideal of Confederate citizens. Most Confederates also valued order in society, and, as it turned out, most citizens generally tolerated and sometimes urged the imposition of force to maintain the unity necessary to fight a determined foe that enjoyed, notoriously, great material and population advantages and that appeared to encircle and besiege their whole nation. As much as the U.S. Constitution, on which it was closely modeled, the Confederate Constitution allowed for enough exertion of force to permit a massive and effective mobilization of the nation for the war effort.

The capital of the Confederacy, Richmond, symbolized the history of the whole nation, though its history was not exactly typical of Confederate towns. It was virtually under siege for much of the war. As Union military pressure grew on Virginia cities, Congress and President Davis acted. He first suspended the writ of habeas corpus in Norfolk and Portsmouth. The provisions of that initial proclamation remind us of the difference in proximate threat of violent destruction that provided the imperative context of the proclamations of Jefferson Davis as opposed to those of Abraham Lincoln:

Whereas the Congress of the Confederate States has by law vested in the President the power to suspend the writ of *habeas corpus* in cities in danger of attack by the enemy:

Now, therefore, I, Jefferson Davis, President of the Confederate States of America, do hereby proclaim that martial law is extended over the cities of Norfolk and Portsmouth and the surrounding country to the distance of 10 miles from said cities, and all civil jurisdiction and the privilege of the writ of *habeas corpus* are hereby declared to be suspended within the limits aforesaid. . . .

Jefferson Davis.

War Department, . . . March 5, 1862

Maj. Gen. B. Huger, Norfolk, Va.

Sir: Martial law having been declared in Norfolk under the President's proclamation, he desires me to call your attention to the various measures which he hopes will at once be vigorously executed:

First. Some leading and reliable citizen to be appointed provost marshal in Norfolk and another in Portsmouth. . . .

Second. All arms to be required to be given up by the citizens; private arms to be paid for.

Third. The whole male population to be enrolled for military service; all stores and shops to be closed at 12 or 1 o'clock and the whole of the citizens forced to drill. . . .

Fourth. The citizens so enrolled to be armed with the arms given up and with those of infantry now in service at batteries.

Fifth. Send away as rapidly as can be done, without exciting panic, all women and children and reduce your population to such as can aid in defense.

Sixth. Give notice that all merchandise, cotton, tobacco, etc., not wanted for military use be sent away within the given time, or it will be destroyed.

Seventh. Imprison all persons against whom there is well-grounded suspicion of disloyalty.

Eighth. Purchase all supplies in the district that can be made useful for your army, allowing none to be carried away that you might want in the event that the city is beleaguered.

In executing these orders you will of course use your own discretion so to act as to avoid creating panic as far as possible. . . .

J. P. Benjamin, *Secretary of War*[23]

Compared with these orders in the Confederate president's proclamation, Lincoln's problems can be seen to have been much more political than military. The president of the United States issued no proclamation of similar desperation.

The pressure of General George B. McClellan's offensive on the Virginia Peninsula, which began organizing in the late winter and early spring of 1862 and culminated in a series of great battles at the end of June, brought about a declaration of martial law in Richmond on March 1, 1862:

By virtue of the power vested in me by law to declare the suspension of the privilege of the writ of *habeas corpus* in cities threatened with invasion:

I, Jefferson Davis, President of the Confederate States of America, do proclaim that martial law is hereby extended over the city of Richmond and the adjoining and surrounding country to the distance of ten miles; and I do proclaim the suspension of all civil jurisdiction, with the exception of that of the Mayor of the city, and the suspension of the privilege of the writ of *habeas corpus* within the said city and surrounding country to the distance aforesaid . . . .

Jefferson Davis.

II. Brigadier J. H. Winder, commanding Department of Henrico, is charged with the due execution of the foregoing proclamation. He will forthwith establish an efficient military police, and will enforce the following orders:

All distillation of spirituous liquors is positively prohibited, and the distilleries will forthwith be closed. The sale of spirituous liquors of any kind is also prohibited, and the establishments for the sale thereof will be closed.

III. All persons infringing the above prohibition will suffer such punishment as shall be ordered by the sentence of a court-martial, *provided* that no sentence to hard labor for more than one month shall be inflicted by the sentence of a regimental court-martial, . . .

S. Cooper, *Adjutant and Inspector General.*[24]

Presumably, the conditions in Richmond under martial law were as dire as those in Portsmouth and Norfolk, but the president's proclamation indicates drastic measures only in the matter of alcohol (and those measures of prohibition would have suited many reform-minded Confederates in times of peace).

But just how dire the practical realities of restrictions of constitutional freedom were in the Confederacy deserves further examination.[25] What happened in the capital of the Confederacy stands as a reminder that nationalism may be full and complete enough to sustain a nation-state for years and still require the employment of force on some of its citizens to maintain national existence.

In fact, many residents of Richmond welcomed martial law as the solution to their internal urban problems. Military authority helped the old ruling elite, accustomed to governing the antebellum town of 38,000, lash out with stern authority against the new city of 100,000 that Richmond was fast becoming as the center of the Confederate government.[26] The provost marshal also pursued the presumed aims of the law, tracking down the allegedly disloyal and dangerous, as well as spies purported to be lurking among the many strangers in the swollen administrative and military center.

None of the histories of Richmond goes into detail, and one can almost invoke the cliché that the devil is in the details in this instance. Records of dozens of arrests are available. For this chapter, I compiled records of arrest of 111 persons for the year 1862 by name from the Richmond newspapers, supplemented by records that appear in the Letters Received by the Confederate Secretary of War, 1861–65 (RG 109, National Archives, Washington, D.C., microcopy 437), and from the *Message of the President . . . Feb. 11, 1863 . . . Listing Civilians in Custody in Richmond*, a published government document. Another 75 persons arrested, whose records appear in the same sources, were prisoners sent into Richmond by military authorities outside the city and nearer enemy lines. In keeping with the spirit of Jefferson Davis's proclamations, which imposed martial law on an area ten miles around the city, these are included as well. Finally, newspapers noted several mass arrests without bothering to list the names of the prisoners.

Suspected Unionists were the earliest targets of arrest. The principles at work in their selection went beyond overt behavior that might betray disloyalty, such as expressions of pro-Union sentiments, reputations for having opposed secession in the elections on the question, or even hearsay about notorious individuals. Often the people were not Virginia natives. That clearly mattered to officials, because interrogators asked political prisoners about their place of birth and length of residence in the state. After a week of martial law the *Richmond Whig* commented reassuringly, "Nearly all the persons arrested on the charge of disloyalty were born outside of the limits of the Southern Confederacy."[27]

During the first week of martial law in Richmond, Confederate soldiers raided the German Turner Society in the Monticello House; they found a thirteen-star U.S. flag in a cupboard and the image of a goddess bearing a Union shield painted on the wall. The mural had likely been painted to suit the historic name of the house, and the flag was surely a symbol of prewar patriotism and dramatized the assimilationist goals of the immigrant society. Under martial law hysteria, however, such innocent items, even when tucked away, seemed proof of disloyalty. To arresting authorities, the real evidence of disloyalty was the German heritage of the club's members — their identity as "foreigners" in the Southern town. Ominously, the military authorities seized the club's list of its eighty-one members.[28]

Daniel Bitter, Heinrich Frisshorn, Charles Mueller, Julius Roth, and William Thom, identified as men of German heritage, were arrested in the early weeks of martial law.[29] Later in the summer, when tradesmen evaded the governor's order to close their markets by two o'clock in the afternoon, the provost marshal's detectives arrested sixteen men identified by the press as German tradesmen.[30] Stereotyping came easily in the nationalistic nineteenth century, and attitudes that help explain the early focus on German Americans in Richmond were displayed when a group of forty-odd German Baptists or "Dunkards" were released from military prison. They had been arrested by General Thomas J. "Stonewall" Jackson in the Shenandoah Valley and sent into Richmond, where military authorities steered twenty-five members of this peace sect into enlistment in the Confederate army. The Richmond newspapermen commented on their long beards and the fact that they smelled like sauerkraut — unlikely prison fare in the Eastern District Military Prison of Richmond.[31]

Many of these German Americans were of foreign birth but were not foreign to Richmond, where they had lived long enough to form a Turner gymnastic society. Suspicion quickly fell on real strangers, not imagined ones like the men of German heritage. And there were now plenty of those in Richmond. "We scarcely meet a familiar face in the streets, or in any case of the public places of amusement and resort," complained the *Richmond Dispatch* about the time the martial law regime was imposed. "The old population has been completely submerged by the tide which has set in since a year ago. . . . The consequence has been not only an amount of ruffianism, drunkenness, and bloodshed, unprecedented in our annals, but emissaries of Lincoln have had full sweep amongst a crowd where all were strangers to each other, and spies and traitors have held high holiday." The "old population," as the newspaper expressed it, could now control the new without customary constitutional or legal restraints. Jefferson Davis's order, declared the *Dispatch*, "makes us almost wish that cities were always governed by martial law."[32]

As Morton Grodzins has shrewdly observed, nationalism always contains specific social content.[33] That content is generally not inclusive of the criminal element. The nation is a social ideal, not a comprehensive sociological description of society with its criminal as well as law-abiding elements. A torrent of hatred was unleashed on the purveyors and partakers of vice in the transformed city. In May the editors of the *Dispatch* asserted: "As we are infested with hosts of thieves, blacklegs, prostitutes, and others, who daily offend the nostrils with their obnoxious and polluting presence, we deem it fitting to remind and request our worthy Marshal, that the public thoroughfares be no longer blockaded by such disreputable characters."[34]

Before the proclamation of martial law, all four of Richmond's major newspapers complained about the city's descent into dissipation. In January 1862 the *Examiner* observed that Richmond, "once a quiet city," had become a "noisy, reckless, and bloated metropolis of vice"; the editors especially blamed unlicensed grog shops.[35] The obsession of the *Whig* was gambling, which the newspaper repeatedly denounced the same month.[36] The moderate *Dispatch* grew exercised over "rowdyism" and looked upon control of the groggeries as "a measure of public safety and military discipline."[37] The *Enquirer*, presenting the fewest complaints of a moralistic sort, seemed most concerned about disloyalty among the citizenry, though the editors did join the chorus in an article entitled "Drunk and Disorderly," a phrase they characterized as a "now-a-days familiar accusation."[38] These problems might have appeared less urgent in the spring, when the improved weather brought news of military campaigns to fill the papers' daily columns. For now, they were urgent enough to override civil libertarian concerns.

It helped Richmond's citizens to foist the blame on outsiders, but many of those arrested were not really new to the Confederate capital: they were outsiders only in the imaginations of insiders. Thus, along with the political outsider John Minor Botts (a Virginia Unionist politician) and the Maine-born Universalist clergyman Alden Bosserman, the earliest individuals apprehended included Louis G. Smelmann, who might be termed a "moral outsider." A liquor merchant, Smelmann was arrested for selling cider.[39]

For some, liquor sellers were foreign to Richmond's true character. Like other Confederate towns that abutted military camps, Richmond seemed to have been invaded early in the war, not by Yankees but by binge-drinking hellions from the Southern countryside. To hear the newspapers tell it, brawling anarchy reigned in the streets as soldiers crowded the grog shops and ran amok. Freed at last from supervision by rural pastors, parents, and wives, young recruits garrisoning or on furlough in Richmond had a chance for the first time to enjoy themselves unrestrainedly. Richmond was "crowded with re-enlisted soldiers on furlough. A hundred whiskey shops are in operation on Main-street and the side alleys. Drunken men reel in and reel out, tumble into the gutters, sprawl over the sidewalks, brandish knives and pistols, and oftentimes indulge in those deadly conflicts which fill our prisons with candidates for the gallows."[40] Complaints like these must have reached President Davis, or perhaps he observed such behavior himself or read about it in the newspapers with the rest of the city's population, because his martial law proclamation for Richmond provided explicitly for prohibition. The immediate context seems important even for policies that aroused grand philosophical questions about liberty and order.

Martial law also served the vigilante impulse well. The provost marshal and other military authorities willingly lent themselves to the effort to restore Richmond to the prim community it had been before it was transformed into a roaring Confederate city of sin. Armed with the sweeping authority of martial law, the provost marshal's men on March 20, 1862, swept down on a notorious neighborhood at Seventeenth and Carey, in a low-lying area near the James River. The moral tone of the establishments there was regarded as sinking to the level of the land contours. The authorities went house by house, looking for "obscene conduct produced mostly by intemperance." They arrested eighty-nine people for offenses ranging from seditious language, disloyalty, or suspected Unionism to drunkenness and selling liquor. The *Dispatch* described the persons swept up in the raids as deserters, shirkers, and bad characters. "Many," it said, "were provided with British Consul papers; these were released after being identified." Most likely, such persons were Irish immigrants who had obtained papers from their consul to protect them from being forced into military service, though such registration was not required by the Confederacy until conscription was imposed in April. The *Dispatch* proclaimed the raids a success: they had done "much toward keeping the lower part of the city more quiet and peaceable than it ever was before."[41]

Martial law also proved useful in quelling labor unrest in Richmond. When lithographers employed by Blanton Duncan and Company refused to work in April, the provost marshal had them arrested. Their refusal to work was a serious matter, as Duncan and Company printed money for the Treasury Department used to fund the war effort. Throughout the conflict the Confederate government was desperate for skilled tradesmen who could print the currency. Before the war, most engraving and lithography firms were located in the North or in Border State cities that did not secede. According to Duncan, the Richmond firm contracted to produce small-denomination notes, and President Davis wanted apprentices to learn the trade; Duncan hired the new men at the suggestion of Secretary of the Treasury Christopher G. Memminger.[42] Thereupon, journeymen lithographers walked off the job and were summarily arrested; they spent the night in jail and returned to work the next day. Afterward, Blanton Duncan and the Confederate government turned to running Scottish lithographers through the blockade to to print Confederate currency.[43]

Evidence is fragmentary, but some of it indicates that martial law helped keep Richmond's white laborers in line. Public workers of all kinds, like those who worked in armories and in the city's gasworks, were apparently required to take an oath of allegiance to the Confederacy. Occasionally, the provost marshal arrested workers who refused the oath. Among them were Charles Murray and Franklin Sherman, operatives at Samson and Poe's Foundry on Byrd Street.[44] Free African Americans lived in conditions roughly equivalent to martial law at all times, in peace or war, and it is no surprise that the records of their arrests or imprisonment did not make the newspapers. Ten of the 724 prisoners in the Eastern District Military Prison on April 8, 1862, were identified as "negroes," but we know nothing else about them. Of the remainder, 213 were citizens.[45]

Untrammeled by party dictation, the vigorous Richmond press, though it carried traces of former long-standing identification with the old political parties of the Union, at first endorsed martial law. The sober *Dispatch* had cried out for internal security measures before the Confederate Congress acted to authorize President Davis to suspend the privilege of the writ of habeas corpus. On January 17, 1862, the paper warned against "Disloyal and Dangerous Inhabitants," declaring that dangerous men "should be placed under the surveillance of a vigilant police, and, when detected, punished as their crimes deserve. . . . A corpus of secret agents ought to be appointed."[46] The *Dispatch* likewise endorsed military seizure of corn used for distilling whiskey, labeling as "intelligent" the view of a reader that "in ordinary times I am opposed to all interference with trade; but in times like these, ordinary rules do not apply."[47] The editors noted the menace posed to ordinary citizens by drunken soldiers thronging the city's drinking hells, as they were called, and pleaded in the paper published the day before Jefferson Davis's proclamation that nothing could "meet the exigency but the proclamation of MARTIAL LAW in Richmond." Once the order was issued, the editors predicted that it would "be hailed with satisfaction by our people."[48]

Well before the president issued the proclamation, the pro-administration *Enquirer*, which had been Democratic in sentiment before the war and which received the printing contract of the Davis administration during the conflict, regularly reported, without condemnation, the imprisonment and interrogation of "Tories," mostly citizens from western Virginia.[49] After the imposition of martial law, the *Enquirer* echoed the *Dispatch* in predicting that "this action of our Government will be applauded by all good citizens as being no less wise than virtuous."[50]

The maverick *Examiner* pursued a similar course on the issue, essentially wishing for Davis's proclamation of martial law. The editors reported without protest the detention of political prisoners before the impositions of martial law in Richmond, complaining steadily that Richmond needed stronger city government and police, and criticizing the government's leniency in dealing with alleged traitors. They declared that the initial proclamation of martial law in Norfolk and Portsmouth would "be hailed with delight by every patriot."[51] Yet when the order for Richmond followed, the flighty *Examiner*, alone among the four major Richmond newspapers, greeted the news with some reservation: "The Proclamation of Martial Law is a measure of evident propriety in itself; but it may become a most fatal source of weakness to the Confederate Government if the powers it confers are abused."[52]

The *Richmond Whig*, as its name suggests, had supported the Whig and then Constitutional Union parties before the war, and it remained suspicious of old Democrats. It did not bend over backward to be kind to the administration of the old Democrat Jefferson Davis.[53] Even so, the *Whig* initially praised the imposition of martial law in Portsmouth and Norfolk as models for Richmond, and when their wish for martial law in their own city was fulfilled, the editors asserted: "It would probably have been well, if this had been done long ago."[54]

Perhaps it is not surprising to find universal acquiescence in the proclamation of martial law early in 1862. Richmond was threatened, the threat was new, and time would tell how steadily the press adhered to its policy of praise for limiting freedoms in the Confederacy. Nevertheless, it is useful to see that we cannot accept without reservation the ideas, once widespread among historians, that, as William M. Robinson expressed it, "the Confederate people . . . by nature were lovers of constitutional forms." Such assertions have come too easily from the pens of Confederate historians and have been too little subjected to close scrutiny. Even the modern Davis biographer, William Cooper, has said that the administration's security measures went against "the ingrained southern commitment to the individual liberty of whites." Emory M. Thomas, in his standard history of the Confederacy, referred to the difficulties internal security measures encountered in "the Old South's fundamental attachment to individualism and its jealous regard for civil liberties."[55] On the other hand, modern historians of slavery clearly go too far in asserting, likewise without examination of the Confederacy's constitutional history, that slave societies saw the master-slave relationship as the model for the whole society. Richmond's citizens may have gone without drink or dice for a time, but no one was working seriously to enslave them.

Authoritarianism?

The toleration for martial law withered. The successes of the Davis administration's war were too few for an independent press (even one not as given to habitual party criticism) to maintain universal and steady praise of these sometimes unpleasant measures. Martial law could become irksome in daily life and not be simply a matter of clearing drunken soldiers out of the gutter. The Confederacy's politicians steered away from internal security measures in the election year of 1863. Congress denied President Davis renewal of authority to suspend the writ of habeas corpus.[56]

The *Examiner*, suspicious from the start, managed to support the policy only for a brief time. The paper did not bat an eye at the broader uses of martial law for vigilante ends. "By closing the grog-shops, shutting up the most malignant Union men, and sweeping the streets of thieves and deserters," its editors commented, martial law had "thus far proved a great and genuine blessing." But they became bitterly critical of Jefferson Davis and censured him for almost everything his administration did. Though constitutionalism was not their focus, he lost their confidence in that realm as in all others.[57]

When Richmond's provost marshal, John H. Winder, unwisely threatened to suppress the *Whig*, the old opposition newspaper turned sharply against the suspension of the writ of habeas corpus.[58] Its editors now criticized martial law, but their criticism was hardly bitter, and the authorities in Richmond enjoyed long periods of silence on this issue on the part of the *Whig*, especially in the summer of 1862 as General McClellan approached ever closer to Richmond on the Peninsula. Eventually the *Whig* could be found praising President Davis's foremost critics of the state rights school: Joseph E. Brown of Georgia and Zebulon B. Vance of North Carolina.[59] Yet it is not clear that a consistently delicate constitutional conscience lay at the bottom of the *Whig*'s point of view. With roots in the constitutional philosophy of the Whig Party, the newspaper never claimed to be wed to strict construction. During the war, the editors urged making legal tender of Confederate money. "Whether constitutional or not," they wrote in 1862, "the issues of the Confederate Government must be made a legal tender. The salvation of the cause is dependent on it — and self-preservation is the first law of nature."[60]

When the question of suspending the writ of habeas corpus arose again in Richmond early in 1864, after the lapse of the first laws permitting Davis to suspend, the *Dispatch* followed a more libertarian line. "We should before this have indicated our opposition to the passage of the resolution . . . proposed in the Senate, which suspends the writ of *habeas corpus*," said the editors in regard to the legislation Davis requested, "had we not felt assured that it would never pass through Congress." Displaying some alarm at signs it was not doomed in fact, the *Dispatch* sounded a warning: "To suspend this law is to make the President a Dictator." No man "ought to be entrusted" with such power, "not even Washington himself, were he alive." The editors could "see no necessity for the grant of any such power at this time, or at any time."[61]

Yet final passage of the bill in Congress brought no direct censure from the newspaper. When in 1864 harsher critics of the power of the Richmond government began to coalesce into opposition political movements outside Virginia, the *Dispatch* backed off from criticism. Reacting to speeches by Governors Brown and Vance and Vice President Alexander H. Stephens, the *Dispatch* belittled the dangers of military encroachment on civilian authority and reminded its readers of the contrast the Confederate government still posed to William H. Seward and the autocrat "Abraham I."[62] Later that month the editors admitted that the power to suspend the writ of habeas corpus was "dangerous," but they insisted that "Congress knew the man" when they conferred the power on President Davis in February "and had no fear of its abuse for the very limited period during which it was conferred, and deeming it important for the public welfare."[63] The incessant criticism coming from Governor Brown provoked firmer responses from the *Dispatch*. "With regard to the law of last session," the editors pointed out in the spring, "nothing can be plainer than the power of Congress to pass it. That power is given in the Constitution in terms as plain and unmistakable as the power to declare war. . . . A man who disputes so plain a provision, expressed in such accurate terms, must be very far gone with the disease of fault-finding."[64] By May 1864, the newspaper was defending the suspension from attack generally.[65]

The *Enquirer*, whose editors were comfortable with Jefferson Davis's power from the start, moved smoothly from martial law to a more authoritarian political philosophy. In an article written after the president's authority to suspend lapsed in February 1863, the editors distinguished two meanings of "liberty," national independence and equality before the law, and stressed the greater importance of the former. The article made mostly reasonable assertions:

> The vast majority . . . of the Confederate people will . . . certainly acknowledge the necessity — if we would really and in very deed save the independence of the country from foreign rule — to invest their central agency, for the time being, with certain powers, both military and civil, which, in the times of peace and security, would be needless and injurious; and in all this, they will see no attack upon liberty in either of the two senses now defined. — Provided always that such powers be regularly conferred by the Confederate Congress, and limited by the temporary exigency of the case.

But the editors closed with a less circumspect statement: "Give us national independence first. National independence under a crowned king, rather than under our enemies' king. National independence under an absolute monarch, rather than the finest of Constitutional liberty under a Yankee majority."[66]

The *Enquirer* pleaded for martial law throughout 1863, when the Confederate Congress denied the president authority to suspend the writ of habeas corpus. By mid-July the exasperated editors depicted the Confederacy as a society under siege and recommended drastic measures:

> All exigencies of life ought to give way to the military exigency; all laws ought to be silent except military law. We regard all Judges and Courts, State and Confederate, all Congresses and Legislatures, as a nuisance, save insofar as they help us to strengthen the hands of the Commander-in Chief of the Confederacy. . . .
>
> This journal has always advocated the fullest measure of Democratic liberty, and the strongest guaranties for the civil rights of every citizen. When the war is over we shall stand on the same ground. But while the war is pending—and such a war—while the whole Confederacy is truly besieged, and every energy of every citizen is called . . . to save us from the final loss of all our rights in one common ruin together, we hold that society should be nothing but a camp; and its law should be the General orders.[67]

Thus far launched on the road to new political doctrines that would make the whole Confederacy an armed camp presumably governed by orders rather than laws, the *Enquirer* soon found itself bristling with the slogans of a warfare state:

> Speaking only for ourselves, but firmly believing we represent the people, we boldly avow that we would tear up the Constitution as waste paper, rather than suffer it to impede the public defence, or embarrass the government in the conflict for independence.
>
> If this Congress before it adjourns, or the next, when it meets, . . . will strip off all clogs, and break all fetters, and place the country on a war footing, and carry out the maxim, *"inter arma silent leges"* our sacrifices will not have been in vain, nor our independence much longer unacknowledged.[68]

The *Enquirer* has been described as the "fairest and most sensible" of Richmond's wartime newspapers, the "foremost daily" in the South, noted for its "restrained and balanced" editorials.[69] It therefore comes as a surprise to learn that George Fitzhugh, the extremist philosopher of authoritarianism in the 1850s, reemerged in the columns of the *Enquirer* in 1864 as a political apologist for emergency power for the Richmond government. Such a development, though perhaps later than might be expected, is surely grist for the mill of those who argue that the slave society modeled its social institutions throughout on the master-slave relationship from the plantation.

Fitzhugh arrived in Richmond as a refugee in 1862, abandoning exposed Front Royal, Virginia, and seeking a patronage job in the Confederate capital. President Davis endorsed the idea of finding a position for "friend Fitzhugh," and he became a clerk in the Treasury Department.[70] Along the way, as he incurred obligations to the Davis government, Fitzhugh's political philosophy had become more confused than ever. It might have been easy for a conservative political thinker to endorse the exercise of greater presidential authority in a war. But the invocation of state rights in secession, the ultimate foundation of the new nation, posed problems.

It is difficult to take all of Fitzhugh's assertions seriously, but the most important part of this new argument was its conclusion: Fitzhugh now defended the reauthorization of the suspension of the writ of habeas corpus by the president. In the course of reaching that practical position, fully permitted by the Confederate Constitution in a case of invasion such as the South was suffering then, Fitzhugh nevertheless assayed to dismiss constitutions and constitutionalism with a cavalier disdain. Unlike most Americans in the Confederacy or in the North, Fitzhugh was always ready to cut loose from the moorings of the familiar political philosophy of the Founders. "The great error of our predecessors," he announced blithely, was to think that a "little pen, ink and paper was all that was needed to construct the most perfect governments the world had ever seen." But "the fate of such beautiful machinery in France, in half a dozen other countries in Europe, in South America and Mexico, in its impending fate here, is fast awakening us from our delusions, and we begin to discover that written constitutions, or governments on paper, are the most ephemeral, weak and worthless things in the world."[71]

Fitzhugh also proved willing to jettison the widely accepted foundations of secession. "The insufficiency of the State Rights doctrines of '98, and of the Calhoun school of a later date, have begotten fears of Executive usurpation, that now sadly trammel the action of our Confederate Government and impair its strength and usefulness," he wrote. But a purely authoritarian philosophy of government, inspired by the master-slave relationship, was not compatible with state rights, and few Confederates thought that state rights could be jettisoned and still have a Confederate identity. Fitzhugh now argued laboriously that the sound institutions of the South lay in the states. The "prescriptive, God-made government, that began with the birth of mankind, and has grown up by gradual imprescriptible accretions to its present dimension," he maintained, lay in the separate states. To Fitzhugh, a state — meaning a state of the Confederacy like Virginia — was "a great physical being or existence, palpable to the senses." On the other hand, "a Union or Confederacy" constituted "a mere moral being . . . a non-entity, a legal fiction, or government on paper." It was inconceivable that "great physical realities, like the States," could be "oppressed or conquered by a metaphysical abstraction — such as the Confederate Government or league." Therefore, he concluded, "Let no one fear to entrust the Confederate Government with plenary powers during the pending war. There is not the remotest danger or possibility that such powers will be continued and exercised after the war is over."[72]

We might almost term the underpinnings of Fitzhugh's strange argument the "organic theory of state rights." What it reveals, besides the generally muddled state of mind in which Fitzhugh addressed society, history, and politics, is the approach of Southern authoritarians to the halfway accommodation with state rights and traditional liberal theory in the South. On the other side, as we shall see in the upcoming chapter on state rights, the mainstream thinkers in the Confederacy were attempting to accommodate their commitment to state rights to an expanded federal authority needed to fight the war for independence.

There was little resemblance between the political thought of Jefferson Davis and George Fitzhugh — which may help explain the absence of significant references to Fitzhugh in Davis's papers. Moreover, as a practicing politician and not an ivory-tower political philosopher, Davis could not afford to spurn the founding document of his nation, from which his office and powers were derived. Yet by early 1864, when Fitzhugh wrote his article, Davis did share with Fitzhugh a belief that he must give up for the short term maintaining some of the liberties promised by the Confederate Constitution in peacetime.

Davis said so flatly at about the same time Fitzhugh was writing. In a special message to Congress seeking authority to suspend the writ of habeas corpus, Davis more or less gave up on liberty for the time being:

> It has been our cherished hope — and hitherto justified by the generous self-devotion of our citizens — that when the great struggle in which we are engaged was passed we might exhibit to the world the proud spectacle of a people unanimous in the assertion and defense of their rights and achieving their liberty and independence after the bloodiest war of modern times without the necessity of a single sacrifice of civil right to military necessity. But it can no longer be doubted that the zeal with which the people sprang to arms at the beginning of the contest has, in some parts of the Confederacy, been impaired by the long continuance and magnitude of the struggle.[73]

Now he found "discontent, disaffection, and disloyalty" abroad in the land, and civil rights must now be sacrificed to military necessity. We might well think of this message as Jefferson Davis's Corning letter, though its sad and rather confessional tone did not properly match its tough message. It was hardly inspiring even to Confederate partisans.

Unlike Fitzhugh, however, Davis could never embrace extremist ideas. The Confederate president provided a constitutional argument buttressing his position: suspension of the writ of habeas corpus was "a remedy plainly contemplated by the Constitution." He insisted that all the powers of that document, "extraordinary as well as ordinary," were intended to be used when the situation required them. A "suspension of the writ," Davis pointed out, "when demanded by the public safety is as much a duty as to levy taxes for the support of the Government." Davis focused especially on the dangers in Richmond. "The Capital of the Government is the object of peculiar attention to the enemy," and Davis had "satisfactory reason for believing" that spies were "continually coming and going in our midst." Davis added ominously, "Apprehensions have more than once been entertained of a servile insurrection in Richmond," likely to be fomented by the hated Union general Benjamin F. Butler, now stationed in Virginia.[74] Once more Congress authorized the president to suspend the writ of habeas corpus but stipulated that the authority would expire in six months, in August 1864.

Jefferson Davis presented a history of disloyalty in the Confederacy that differed in pattern from the history of disloyalty in the North that Lincoln had offered in the Corning letter. In Lincoln's scheme, enunciated in 1863, the disloyal elements had been planted in the Union from the start of his administration, left behind in key places by the Southerners as they departed. In Davis's view, the Confederacy enjoyed unanimity at the start, but then war weariness had bred discontent and impatience with the experiment.

The Record of the Richmond Judiciary

Richmond was perhaps overserved by judiciary despite its spectacular growth in population during the war, and the availability of judges was one of the most important factors in the use and abuse of the writ of habeas corpus. In addition to the Confederate States District Court, there were the Virginia Supreme Court of Appeals, the Richmond Circuit Court in the state system, the Hustings Court (which heard civil cases and criminal ones not carrying the death penalty), and the Mayor's Court (which dealt with numerous offenses said to have been committed by slaves and with other minor crimes). All but the Mayor's Court saw some habeas corpus appeals.

Lawyers were abundant—congressmen and former political generals and others looking for work in times when many potential litigants were away in military service.

It is unclear what difference the restoration of the writ of habeas corpus made in Richmond in 1863. The notorious domestic passport system, for example, did not disappear with the change in the law. Travel by rail or other means required obtaining a passport, and documents were generally carefully examined. When the Confederate Congress investigated the system in January 1864, it discovered that the system had functioned steadily since its creation, which occurred well before the initial imposition of martial law in the city in 1862. "There was no law for it," testified the clerk in charge of the office early on.[75]

Were other aspects of martial law steady features of Richmond life, law or not? Press coverage of the provocations in everyday life, the gambling hells and intoxication, subsided, though there was a period known as the "era of garroting." Order seems to have been maintained at a level acceptable to the city fathers. These fathers remained a steady presence in Richmond's government until the end of the war. Thus when the Union army finally arrived to occupy the city, the delegation that met it represented the old Richmond elite. It included Mayor Joseph Mayo and three judges, John A. Meredith, James D. Halyburton, and William H. Lyons, along with two other prominent citizens. Mayo was a fixture from antebellum days, and the grand jury of the Hustings Court, presided over by Lyons, consisted of the same "gentlemen" for the whole period. The judges of Richmond's three courts, a generally neglected group in history, carried considerable prestige and power. Mayo himself presided over a court that dealt with violations of city ordinances and minor crimes.[76]

The persistent prominence of the judges to the very end of the Confederate experiment in Richmond reminds us of one obvious change that did come with the final restoration of the writ of habeas corpus in August 1864: the dockets of the city's courts grew suddenly crowded with applications from Confederate soldiers and draftees seeking writs of habeas corpus to release them from service for one reason or another. A brief examination of the record of the three Richmond courts from July through September 1864 is revealing of the legal status of civil liberty in the Confederate capital after its martial law experience and in the midst of the direst military circumstances.[77]

In July 1864, shortly before Davis's suspension ended, a couple of new habeas corpus cases reached nearly sensational reputation. The first, tried before James D. Halyburton of the Confederate States District Court for the Eastern District of Virginia, involved the well-known Richard D'Orsay Ogden, manager of the popular Richmond Theater. Halyburton, a former U.S. judge,[78] upheld the suspension of the writ of habeas corpus in the spring of 1864.[79] But just as the suspension was nearing the end of its term, in July, the Ogden case arose. Born in Britain, Ogden had come to the United States with his parents at the age of eight; by 1864 he had been a resident of Richmond about twenty years. Nevertheless, he sought exemption from military service on the grounds of being an unnaturalized British citizen and an undomiciled alien. The protracted trial was regarded as important, not only because of the celebrity of the plaintiff but also because the decision would affect the status of other foreign-born residents of the Confederacy. Ogden could afford excellent counsel and procured the services of George W. Randolph, the former Confederate secretary of war, and James Lyons, a former member of the Confederate Congress. The Confederate States attorney for the district, Patrick Henry Aylett, represented the government.[80]

Aylett argued that the Confederate major who claimed Ogden's services had adequately responded to the writ of habeas corpus and had put the burden of proof on Ogden. But Aylett presented his argument anyway. Because the plaintiff and his father were actors after their arrival in the United States, Ogden changed residence often, and that complicated the determination of his resident status. But Aylett discovered that when Ogden lived in Mobile, Alabama, he had voted for sheriff, and only residents could vote in that state. Ogden's answer to that part of the government's case was that he was drunk when he voted. Despite his client's inept response, James Lyons proved to be a formidable lawyer. He argued that if Ogden had become a citizen while living in Alabama, that was when Alabama was part of the United States and so he now qualified as an alien enemy. Alien enemies were never required to serve in the military because they likely faced execution if captured.

Judge Halyburton deliberated carefully and decided, in part because Ogden had exercised the franchise in Alabama, that Ogden was domiciled and liable to conscription. After giving his opinion, however, there was a dramatic development. Lyons introduced a treaty of 1794 between the United States and Great Britain that, he contended, determined Ogden's draft-exempt status. Halyburton agreed to hear the point and delay turning Ogden over to the enrolling officer. Lyons later held that the treaty with Great Britain applied now to the Confederacy just as it had to the United States, and that one of its provisions was that Britons could come to the

United States and remain for an unlimited time without any change in their national status. Halyburton reconsidered the case and ruled, four days after his original decision, that the treaty did not apply to this case.

The resourceful Lyons asked for bail for his client until the Confederate States Supreme Court decided the issue. Halyburton had reached the limit of his patience with the raising of this argument and pointed out to the attorney that there was no such court and he well knew it. Then, in a revealing aside, Halyburton said, as the press reported it: "It was a source of great regret to him that there was not such a body, for if there was he would not then have the entire responsibility resting on his shoulders."[81]

Halyburton might have added a lament about other difficulties he faced. With inadequate reporting of federal cases in the Confederacy, he apparently did not know that a fellow Confederate States District judge, Andrew G. Magrath of Charleston, had already decided a similar case a year earlier that Halyburton might have followed as precedent for his own opinion. In *Ex parte Henry Spincken* Magrath affirmed conscription and ruled on foreigners' status. Spincken had once enlisted in the German Artillery Company (a unit raised in Charleston) and had fought at Port Royal, but by 1863 his original term of service had expired. The revised conscription law extended soldiers' terms of service for the war's duration. Spincken contended that he was a resident alien, having come from Hanover seven years earlier. Judge Magrath insisted that residents had a duty to defend the country in which they resided against any enemy but the country of their origin. International law, he said, did not apply in Spincken's case.[82]

The responsibility that rested on the shoulders of the judiciary grew only heavier as the war made greater and greater demands on the Confederate people. In the autumn of 1864 some Marylanders who were living in Virginia sought exemption from conscription as citizens who had sought asylum in the Confederacy. Robert F. Hobbs had moved to Virginia in 1861 and now argued that his asylum ought not to be "disturbed" by a Confederate enrolling officer. The government maintained that Hobbs was a resident of the Confederacy. Hobbs employed able counsel, including former Confederate general Humphrey Marshall. Aylett presented the government's case. The press noted, once again, that the outcome would affect a substantial number of people in Richmond and in the Confederacy generally, for many Marylanders had arrived in the early part of the war. Halyburton sustained Humphrey's argument that exiles were never ordered to fight against the nation they had fled and ruled that Hobbs be discharged.[83]

It was the kind of decision that was likely to have wide consequences. Other men from Maryland now understood their position, including some already serving in Confederate army units. The men in question, over thirty-three of them, were not shirkers. They were members of a unit called Dement's Battery and had served since 1861. Their original term of enlistment had been three years, but the Confederate Congress had extended the enlistments of people already in the army. When these Marylanders were not allowed to leave the army, they sued for a writ of habeas corpus, arguing that they were wrongfully held to service. The men engaged opposition politician John H. Gilmer as counsel, and Halyburton apparently agreed to make a ruling applicable to all. The judge decided they were not liable to conscription and should be discharged.[84] Thus Halyburton, though a Confederate States judge, was responsible for the exodus of dozens of Marylanders from the Confederate ranks.

The state court system faced appeals for the writ as well. The case of N. Tinsley Pate came before William H. Lyons of the Hustings Court. Pate, a prominent citizen, had sought a writ of habeas corpus for release from militia duty. He was a Confederate detailed by the War Department to work in his own concrete factory because it was deemed a crucial defense industry. Since Virginia militia duty interfered with his duties in the concrete factory, Pate sued for release from the militia on the ground that state duty was interfering with his work for the Confederate nation. The judge ruled in Pate's favor.

In the Pate case, the government's position seems clear. Richmond's court watchers — and there were many — were treated to the anomaly of the Confederate States attorney appearing for the plaintiff in a habeas corpus case. Colonel Patrick H. Aylett usually represented the Confederacy against men seeking to escape Confederate service by appealing to the writ, but here the Confederate authorities wanted to be sure that state service did not supersede national service. Judge Lyons sided with Aylett, ruling that to hold Pate to militia duty "would be to disregard the paramount claim of the Confederate States, which should be most seriously guarded for many important reasons." The irony was that the state of Virginia could argue against the Confederacy in the name of military necessity, as the need to enlist all Virginians to defend their soil was never higher, and Pate was serving the Confederacy as a plant manager and not as a combatant. According to the local press, "This decision will materially affect the condition of those companies of the first and nineteenth regiments, which are composed almost exclusively of detailed conscripts, who are performing duties of the most varied and important character for the Confederate States."[85] The *Dispatch* noted the wider political significance of the ruling, commenting that Lyons's decision took "precisely the position of the Bureau of Conscription in its correspondence with Gov. Brown, of Georgia."[86]

After authority to suspend the writ expired on August 1, 1864, the Richmond courts apparently accomplished little other business except dealing with these applications and subsequent hearings. A rough calculation based on the reports in the *Dispatch* to the end of the year shows that the Confederate States District Court handled 75 such habeas corpus cases. The Hustings Court heard another 22, and Judge Meredith's circuit court saw 13. The total from Richmond's courts altogether was at least 110. The Confederate States District Court dealt with only 22 other cases in the same period. Unlike the work of the Confederate Congress, the courts worked in the open and sometimes drew crowds of interested observers.

The meaning of all this legal activity for liberty and national survival in the Confederacy has never been clear. Some at the time thought it a scandal and a libel on Confederate patriotism. *Richmond Dispatch* editor Edward A. Pollard later complained that "the demands for military service were cheated in a way and to an extent unexampled in the case of any brave and honorable nation engaged in a war for its own existence." The writ of habeas corpus, Pollard maintained, "became the vilest instrument of the most undeserving men; and there is attached to it a record of shame for the South that we would smilingly spare."[87] Decades later historian Frank L. Owsley essentially agreed, considering habeas corpus cases part of a hemorrhage that bled the Confederate States to death for the sake of state rights. In 1925 he declared, "After August 1, 1864, when the last act suspending the writ had expired, the fortunes of the South never rose again."[88]

Although editor Pollard had a point about the men who evaded service through court action, the cases tried in Richmond were not completely one-sided in meaning. Judge Lyons's decision in the Pate case was everything the War Department could have wanted, though it did not put more men in the ranks. The record of Judge Meredith of the Richmond Circuit Court may have come closest to fitting the pattern of abuse of habeas corpus. He faced in his courtroom men who claimed exemption from conscription on grounds of being ministers of the gospel, schoolteachers, and, most frequently, state officials. Meredith had to deal with a bevy of state officials elected in the spring, such as justices of the peace.

Most attention focused on the case of A. J. Camp, who claimed exemption from service under the conscription law because he had been elected a justice of the peace. The problem was that he had won the election while he was in the army — in effect, contended the Confederacy, he was seeking not exemption but discharge. The Confederate authorities argued the case strenuously, fearing a precedent. "They claimed," reported the *Dispatch*, "that after a man has once got into the service, there was no human power, except that which put him there, that could take him out." Nevertheless, the judge decided for Camp's discharge, as he did in most of these cases.[89]

The record is in fact mixed, even for individual judges. Judge Halyburton, though he had a hand in releasing some men from service, made important decisions in favor of the Confederate States. In the Ogden case, he had ruled that the plaintiff had voted in Mobile in 1861, as only a domiciled citizen could.[90] For Marylanders seeking to escape continued service in the Confederate army, Halyburton rendered a different kind of decision. He ruled that men from Maryland who moved to Virginia at the beginning of the war were undomiciled aliens — refugees, who were not liable for Confederate conscription.[91]

Escape from service even on a judge's order was not always easy or complete. After Halyburton's initial decision to discharge a Marylander from Dement's Battery, the prosecution had a good idea how future decisions in such cases would go. As more of the thirty-two Maryland artillerists came into court to claim their discharges from Confederate service, District Attorney Aylett planned a surprise for them. He arranged with Virginia governor William Smith to have state militia authorities at the door of the courthouse, and as five discharged Maryland men headed out the door, a guard stopped them for assignment to the state reserve forces. Faced with that fate, the Marylanders opted for the devil they knew and decided to stay in their Confederate unit, Dement's Battery.[92] One way or the other, the Marylanders in the Confederacy were going to have to fight in the war, either as Confederates or as Virginia militiamen.

Indeed, in the case of Frederick W. Boyd, Halyburton concluded that Richmond — and perhaps the whole Confederacy — had become a military camp. Boyd was a Marylander too, one of several detectives employed by the provost marshal's office to enforce military rules in the city. When accused of bribing an official, Boyd landed in the Eastern District Military Prison, popularly known as "Castle Thunder," and Confederate authorities prepared to try him by court-martial. Boyd sought a writ of habeas corpus to escape trial by military authority because, he claimed, he was a civilian. The government contended that although he was a civilian, he was employed in military duties and could be tried under the sixtieth article of war. That article made "sutlers and retainers to the camp, and all persons whatsoever, serving with the armies of the Confederate States in the field, though not enlisted soldiers" liable to court-martial, according to historian William M. Robinson Jr.[93]

Early in September Halyburton issued an elaborate opinion in the Boyd case, ruling that the detective was subject to military jurisdiction. "Boyd," he was reported to have said, "as a person in the employment of the Provost-Marshal of Richmond, was held to be a person connected with an army in the field, as Richmond is regarded as a military post for many purposes, and the authority of the Provost-Marshal extends to the camps within ten miles of Richmond."[94] Thus in Confederate law, Richmond had become, with or without the writ of habeas corpus, what it had been, in fact, for many: an armed camp substantially governed by military regulations and by military authorities.

These judicial decisions illustrate the meandering and pragmatic course of law and the relative freedom to denounce it. Sometimes the Confederate States judiciary upheld the rules that made Richmond a police state. Sometimes judges thought the freedom of the plaintiffs needed defense. On occasion, judges could rob state militias of men they wanted by retaining them in Confederate service, even when that service did not entail a combat role. State and Confederate authorities could cooperate, on occasion, to be certain that there was no net loss to the nation's defensive capabilities by putting those who escaped Confederate service into the state militia. The record was mixed and, apparently, a matter of law, judgment, and practical adjustment.

The Confederates attempted to reconcile a jurisprudence consciously grounded in state rights with military mobilization for independence. In general, they succeeded better than history has acknowledged.

Eight

State Rights in the Confederacy

The critical study of Confederate history began only in 1925 with Frank L. Owsley's *State Rights in the Confederacy*. Up to that time a nostalgic celebration of Confederate nationalism reigned in the South in the form of the Lost Cause myth. Owsley found fault with the myth, especially in its affirmation of unity among whites behind the Confederate cause from 1861 to 1865. In the preface to his groundbreaking study, he said:

> For sixty years the student and casual reader of Civil War history have labored under the impression that the South was "overpowered by superior numbers." This volume attempts to present a different point of view, namely that the Confederacy failed from internal, political causes, mainly state rights. Having lectured on this theme before southern audiences, I know that this new aspect of the question, as I present it, is sometimes misunderstood as being an unfriendly attack upon the people who fought for the idea of state rights. To those who are inclined to feel that I am making such an attack, I wish to say that, by way of explanation, this is largely because I do not dwell upon the heroism and unselfishness in the Confederacy which has been the theme of countless volumes and is, therefore, common knowledge. I assume that knowledge and hasten on to take up certain political phases which may well be called "the seamy side" of Confederate history.[1]

Owsley found fatal disunity where the Lost Cause myth had found romantic unity. The internal conflict, Owsley said, was rooted in the constitutional ideology that underwrote secession in the first place: state rights.

It apparently did not occur to Owsley to investigate the view of the Confederate Constitution that underlay his argument. So that myth — of obdurate Confederate constitutionalism — survived. Or to put it another way, Owsley failed to realize that the idea of fixed constitutionalism was as much a part of the Lost Cause myth as were white unity, the loyal slave, and the loss of the war to superior numbers and resources. As always, nation and constitution were intertwined though not identical.

After Owsley, the dam of Confederate historiography broke, and the field was flooded with historians who pursued the theme of internal dissent and collapse. State rights faded as an organizing principle for studying the political and constitutional history of the Confederacy. Historians pointed out that Jefferson Davis's central government in Richmond had trouble with only a couple of governors, and that in fact centralization to the point of state socialism was the most startling development in the Confederacy's history. In general, those historians who pursued Owsley's internal collapse theory now looked to class conflict rather than to state rights for an explanation.[2]

State rights was regarded as the merest rationalization ever after. Underlying social grievances might gain a voice under the rubric of state rights.[3] State rights had its last stand, so to speak, in the 1986 book, *Why the South Lost the Civil War*. The authors — Herman Hattaway, Richard E. Beringer, William N. Still Jr., and Archer Jones — argued that state rights proved somewhat beneficial to the Confederate war effort as a substitute for two-party competition in politics. Following the trail blazed by Paul Escott, these authors said: "Manifestations of opposition to the Confederacy on the grounds of violated state rights . . . constituted a safety valve for anger fed by resentment, discontent, and fear of ultimate failure by the government."[4] In other words, the authors of *Why the South Lost* assumed that two-party competition was helpful to a war effort, and the Confederacy, lacking political parties, needed some substitute for it — that is, state rights.[5] The whole idea of state rights has all but disappeared from recent histories of the Confederacy. In Stephanie McCurry's *Confederate Reckoning: Power and Politics in the Civil War South*, "state rights" receives but one mention. Discussing the issue of impressment of slaves to work on Confederate fortifications, McCurry says: "What looked like a struggle between state and federal power was really a struggle over the right of the central state to abrogate the sovereign rights of slave holders."[6]

What has been overlooked in historians' flight from study of the doctrine of state rights is the possibility that state rights and nationalism could and did coexist in the Confederate nation. In other words, the Confederacy did not founder on state rights nor did the Confederates survive for four long years because they discarded state rights theory. Instead, state rights theory was artfully adapted to the war effort. State rights provided a major statement of Confederate nationalism for many Southerners from the secession crisis right through the whole four-year attempt to build a nation. It was not the only vision of the Confederate nation by any means, but it was more important than its virtual disappearance from serious consideration in recent academic literature might suggest.

The Historic Meaning of State Rights

The idea of state rights, dismissed in recent times as merely a "fetish," amounted to a good deal more than local pride to Confederates.[7] In fact, state rights enjoyed a long history in America and at various times found ardent champions in New England as well as the South, among libertarians and champions of fugitive slaves as well as slaveholders, and political thinkers like Thomas Jefferson and James Madison as well as John C. Calhoun. It had roots in the very origins of republicanism. It was an American doctrine.

The idea that it was vital to liberty to keep representation rooted in the local lay at the philosophical heart of state rights doctrine. That idea, in turn, was ultimately rooted in the vital colonial experience of actual representation as the superior of virtual representation. First articulated in the Stamp Act crisis of 1765, the idea became important that people and interests had actually to be represented in popular assemblies and could not be virtually represented by statesmen legislating for the whole realm from Parliament.[8] Well before that revolutionary articulation, a vigorous republican tradition and practical colonial experience had tied legislators closely to their districts by residence and instructions. Liberty in the United States was vitally linked to the local.[9]

When they supported the new national Constitution in 1787–88, the Federalists moved away as far as they could from such ideas, but there was only so far they could go. The Anti-Federalist essayist who wrote under the name "Brutus" thus complained of the Constitution proposed in 1787:

> The people of this state will have very little acquaintance with those who may be chosen to represent them; a great part of them will, probably, not know the characters of their own members, much less that of a majority of those who will compose the federal assembly; they will consist of men, whose names they have never heard, and whose talents and regard for the public good, they are total strangers to; and they will have no persons so immediately of their choice so near them, of their neighbours and of their own rank in life, that they can

feel themselves secure in trusting their interests in their hands. The representatives of the people cannot, as they now do, after they have passed laws, mix with the people, and explain to them the motives which induced the adoption of any measure, point out its utility, and remove objections or silence unreasonable clamours against it.[10]

After arguing against "actual" representation in Congress of all social classes and for representation by merchants, landlords, and professional men, Alexander Hamilton in *The Federalist* explained:

If we take into the account the momentary humors or dispositions which may happen to prevail in particular parts of the society, and to which a wise administration will never be inattentive, is the man whose situation leads to extensive inquiry and information less likely to be a competent judge of their nature, extent, and foundation than one whose observation does not travel beyond the circle of his neighbors and acquaintances? Is it not natural that a man who is a candidate for the favor of the people, and who is dependent on the suffrages of his fellow-citizens for the continuance of his public honors, should take care to inform himself of their dispositions and inclinations and should be willing to allow them their proper degree of influence upon his conduct? This dependence, and the necessity of being bound, himself and his posterity, by the laws to which he gives his assent are the true and they are the strong chords of sympathy between the representative and the constituent.[11]

All along, the idea associating the state with "neighbors and acquaintances" and with mindfulness of the liberties of the people was the fundamental assumption of state rights. Of course, federalism was a distinguishing characteristic of the American republic.

Soon state rights gained new life and vigor in the conflict over the Alien and Sedition Acts of 1798.[12] As we saw in the introduction to this book, the answer of the Jeffersonian Republicans to the Sedition Act was the Kentucky and Virginia Resolutions of 1798–99. The compact theory of the Constitution and state sovereignty in U.S. history were thus first articulated to rescue individual liberty and a loyal opposition, not to protect slavery. The authors of the doctrine, Thomas Jefferson and James Madison, were among America's greatest political thinkers. Republicans in the South found much to like in the ideas then, but only a little over a decade later, New England Federalists found much to like in the ideas as well, embracing state rights ideals in their protests against the War of 1812. For much of its life and for many of its previous uses, the ideal of state rights had nothing to do with slavery and much to do with liberty or with minority rights. In 1812 state rights were embraced as antiwar and not bellicose. It was not so much a Southern idea as an American idea — hence its power.[13]

State rights had been around a long time, almost the length of the life of the republic, before John C. Calhoun and South Carolina's nullifiers made the ideas extremely dangerous, sectional, and closely associated with slavery. Even afterward, in disputes over fugitive slaves on the eve of the Civil War, liberal Northern judges and some Republicans embraced state rights as a protection for fugitives from slave catchers coming over state lines after their prey and from federal commissioners enforcing their claims under the Fugitive Slave Act of 1850.[14]

Without understanding the role of state rights in the Confederacy, there is no way to understand Confederate nationalism, with its contradictory appeals to order and liberty and with its mutually compelling appeals to yeomen and great slaveholders alike. The widespread invocation of state rights accounts in part for the loyalty of nonslaveholding yeomen to the cause of Southern nationalism because state rights were closely associated with local liberty. It helps account as well for the generally orderly quality of secession, from the actual process of adopting secession ordinances to the configuration of political boundaries on the map and the continuity of authoritative apparatuses of the state governments. States seceded, not merely slaveholders, and that made a very great difference.[15] South Carolina's Reverend James Henley Thornwell had been more intent on justifying slavery in his explanation of the wisdom of South Carolina's secession in January 1861 than on explaining the constitutional doctrine of state rights, but he could see the importance of state secession as more than a mere revolt of slaveholders:

> The separation changes nothing but the external relations of the sections. Such a dismemberment of the Union is not like the revolution of a State, where the internal system of Government is subverted, where laws are suspended, and where anarchy reigns. The country might divide into two great nations tomorrow, without a jostle or a jar; the Government of each State might go on as regularly as before, the law be as supreme, and order as perfect, if the passions of the people could be kept from getting the better of their judgments. It is a great advantage in the form of our Confederacy, that a radical revolution can take

place without confusion, and without anarchy. Every State has a perfect internal system at work already, and that undergoes no change, except in adjusting it to its altered external relations. . . . We do not see, therefore, that anything will be lost to freedom by the union of the South under a separate Government. She will carry into it every institution that she had before — her State Constitutions, her Legislatures, her Courts of Justice, her halls of learning — every thing that she now possesses. She will put these precious interests under a Government embodying every principle which gave value to the old one, and amply adequate to protect them. What will she lose of real freedom? We confess that we cannot understand the declamation, that with the American Union, American institutions are gone. Each section of the Union will preserve them and cherish them.[16]

The *Charleston Mercury*: State Rights and Race in Confederate Nationalism

It is not possible to comprehend the role of the *Charleston Mercury*, the most influential and prominent Confederate newspaper printed outside Richmond, without understanding the role of state rights. The *Mercury* has become legendary for its prickly dissent. Historian George Rable thought that other historians' illusions of party conflict in the Confederacy were derived from relying too heavily on the *Mercury* (as well as the readable and feisty *Richmond Examiner*) in their research. Likewise, Paul Escott cited the *Mercury* as "a major source of extreme states' rights theory" but did not go on to examine systematically the ideology of the newspaper as enunciated through the four years of the Confederacy's existence.[17] The fact is that the *Mercury* tempered and adjusted its enthusiasm for state rights during the Civil War.

The history of the *Charleston Mercury* reveals that there were "contested" visions of the Confederate nation, but that these conflicting views proved not to be debilitating to the war effort and did not force the idea of state rights to be repudiated, abandoned, or hypocritically ignored. The *Mercury*'s editors, especially Robert Barnwell Rhett Jr., self-consciously saw their outlook as consistent over the course of South Carolina history for a generation:

The *Mercury* was established in 1832. It has ever been the organ of the State Rights Republican Party of South Carolina, of which John C. Calhoun was the leader, which since the issue of the *Mercury* has predominated in this State, and whose policy has been carried out in the secession of these Southern States, and the erection of a Southern Confederacy. . . . It has always supported the true principles of the Republican or Democratic Party as laid down by Jefferson. The principles of the paper have been the same throughout its career.[18]

In sum, "the principle of State Rights" was the one "by which this Confederacy was formed." The *Mercury* was famous for criticizing the government and for its state rights views. But, as it turned out, even fervent belief in state rights was compatible with Confederate national self-determination.

Casual criticism from abroad early in 1863 provoked a key moment of definition of the *Mercury*'s philosophy. It is a sign of the prickly conception of the journalistic enterprise held by the editors that they rose so belligerently to the bait. Henry Hotze, the editor of the Confederacy's European propaganda newspaper, called the *Index* and published in London, once decided to fill the columns of his paper with a chatty guide for Englishmen to the Confederate press. Hotze was perceptive but a little too sharptongued. He accurately described the *Richmond Examiner* as "the Ishmael of the Southern press, so far as it is against everybody." He characterized the *Mercury* as being "almost rabid on the question of State Rights."[19] Hotze laid out the great variety of opinion found in the Confederate press by way of proving, in the end, that "in the South the press is not only free, but its freedom is abundantly used. . . . Such liberty would have been impossible in a revolution."[20]

Hotze went a little too far when he cited as proof of the *Mercury*'s extremism part of the political philosophy voiced by the paper on the eve of the Civil War. He pointed out "that at the time of secession this journal opposed the formation of a Confederate Government, and suggested in lieu thereof a kind of Diet, to which was to be delegated rather less authority than is enjoyed by the German Diet." The editors of the *Mercury* angrily characterized Hotze's assertion as "a falsehood." The Charlestonians laid claim to being the first to propose Montgomery, Alabama, as a site for the central Confederate government, and, more important, they supported the work of the convention there in drafting a constitution for the Confederacy. Their only criticism at the time concerned powers of taxation and the failure to close the door "against the admission of any non-slaveholding State," a position the paper maintained consistently throughout the war. The *Mercury* was never fond of executive power exercised from afar in general or by Jefferson Davis in particular; in the fall of 1861 the editors showed some interest in a proposal to have the presidential office held by the oldest member of the Senate and only for a two-year term.[21] Their principles were, on the whole, steady from the founding, and the quotation above describing the history of the paper going back to the nullification crisis was elicited by this conflict with Hotze. The editors said, fairly enough, that "we have criticized the policy of the Administration, chiefly as being too temporizing and timid. . . . We have endeavored to stimulate, strengthen, and support the Administration in decisive, energetic measures — on every vigorous policy."[22]

Henry Hotze was, even for a Confederate, obsessed with race. A Swiss immigrant who lived in Alabama before the war, Hotze had exploited his language abilities to translate into English from the French Arthur de Gobineau's *Moral and Intellectual Diversity of Races*.[23] We are indebted to the brilliant work in intellectual history of Robert E. Bonner for our awareness of Hotze. Bonner, a careful and wide-ranging student of Confederate nationalism, sometimes finds that racism lay at the heart of Confederate nationalist ideas, as in the case of Hotze. Bonner has also made us aware of the work of Leonidas W. Spratt, and other marginal intellectuals of the Confederacy, who saw even the white people of America divided into "races": Cavaliers and Puritans. The white field in the Confederate flags, Bonner has asserted, carried racial significance to some Confederates.[24] Conversely, Bonner reserves less room for state rights doctrines in his view of Confederate nationalism.[25]

The flag was, of course, a central national symbol, but Spratt and Hotze were not as clearly central to Confederate thinking. Surely the *Charleston Mercury* was at least as important as Hotze's little paper published in Europe to influence Europeans. The *Mercury* did not see eye to eye with the *Index* in emphasizing race. State rights held a place side by side with white racism in the *Mercury*'s view of Confederate nationalism.

That is not to say that the *Mercury* did not conscientiously affirm what most white Southerners regarded as the verities of racism. For most of the war, the paper sought to make slavery seem an advantage to the Confederacy and not the weakness the North had assumed it would be. One way was to argue that the existence of slavery made the white race better at waging war, imbuing it with a sense of nobility and honor that suited martial exploits.[26] The editors contended that the "fixed and regulated contact of the dominant race with the servile necessarily brings out in the white man those qualities fitted for predominance. . . . Whether in the military commandant, the political governor, the civic judge, the husband, parent or master, the tendency and effect is similar. . . . Authority and the exercise of command tend strongly to engender self-respect, dignity, decision of character, and the feeling of self-reliant power." These assertions may sound like admiration of master-slave relationships extended to the rest of society, but authoritarianism was not the aim of this state rights newspaper. Rather, its purpose was to counter the notion that the Southern elite was lazy and addicted to luxury, a common stereotype of the planter aristocracy. The "manly pride" engendered by constant contact with acknowledged inferiors was, they said, "more influential than the love of ease, more potent than the love of gain." The newspaper's editors were so infatuated with their editorial on "Race and the Sense of Honor at the South" that they ran it twice: once in June and again in November 1862.[27]

The *Mercury* also believed that the North had deluded itself with expectations of slave disloyalty in the Confederacy. The editors boasted that there had not been a slave insurrection since 1776, ignoring Virginia history (Nat Turner in 1831) and the disturbance over Denmark Vesey in Charleston itself in 1822 — which William W. Freehling has described as traumatic for South Carolinians.[28] During the summer of 1863, the *Mercury* reminded its readers that "the most extraordinary" lesson of the Civil War was that the slaves "have exhibited a fidelity that must be the astonishment of the world."[29] In 1865 the paper was moved to almost hysterical opposition to the proposition to enroll slaves in the Confederate army, a movement that provoked its first ranting and raving racist editorials of the whole war.[30]

Bonner suggests that Hotze had shrewdly figured out that Europeans were more likely to agree with the Confederates on race than on slavery, and that is true. But the two ideas were inextricably linked at the time. After all, racism also linked the North and the South, but such agreement by no means kept the two sections from trying to kill as many men from the other section as they could. Conversely, there is no understanding the popular character of Confederate nationalism without considering issues other than race and slavery.

Take the case of the "Address of the Confederate Clergy to the World," an international appeal signed by numerous Southern preachers. The allusions to slavery in that document, which was intended principally to arouse European sympathy for the South's endurance of wrong and destruction, provoked a sharp response from Scots clergy in a widely circulated "Reply to the Address of the Confederate Clergy" early in 1864. After this incident Hotze, we are told by Bonner, accelerated his move toward racism and away from proslavery discussions, but the response of the *Charleston Mercury* seems equally instructive. "The lesson is continually inculcated upon us," observed the editors, "not to put the cause of the South upon a proslavery crusade. We are battling for *the right of self government*. . . . The less said about slavery the better."[31] For the *Charleston Mercury*, in the American context, self-determination was a function of asserting state rights against an imperial federalism. Though thoroughgoing racists, of course, the editors did not turn from slavery to race but consistently kept the focus on state rights or national self-determination.

We find ourselves back to the problem of Confederate nationalism, as stated so brilliantly by Owsley long ago: Was that doctrine to which the *Mercury*'s editors clung, state rights, genuinely compatible with a national self-determination that had to be forged in a great war? The editors thought so, and their approach to the doctrine was more practical than "rabid."

The position of the *Mercury* on conscription is critical to our understanding, although its view has not always been accurately described. The paper's editorial on the first Conscription Act was entitled "Better Late Than Never."[32] To the new conscription law of July 1862 the editors gave more than grudging adherence, saying they could never understand why the upper age had been restricted to thirty-five years.[33] "Even Rhett [Jr.]," wrote George Rable, "refused to nitpick the details" of the second Conscription Act.[34] But a good deal more than that needs to be said about the subject.

The *Mercury*'s editors, like most Southerners at the time, viewed conscription as unconstitutional because it posed a threat to state militias and state rights. Indeed, they felt that the very existence of the states was endangered if the central government could make state government officials subject to the draft — a point often dwelled on by Governor Joseph E. Brown, of Georgia. The *Mercury* lumped conscription with two other policies of the Confederate government the editors considered nearly intolerable. They thought it unconstitutional for the central government to fund internal improvements (specifically, the railroads much needed for the mobilization of troops and supplies for the war effort). They also felt it was unconstitutional for the Confederacy to impose direct taxes on the states, believing that the power to put a direct tax on slaves was equivalent to the power to abolish slavery. The editors urged the states to call for a constitutional convention to deal with all three matters; they were grateful that a provision peculiar to the Confederate Constitution required only three states to "summon the convention." But, the editors insisted, "we deprecate any action by the States upon the important matters we have adverted to, until the war is over."[35]

As significant as these opinions was the treatment by the *Mercury*'s outspoken editors of the North Carolina Supreme Court's resistance to the new conscription law. They did not report the initial decision of its notorious chief justice, Richmond M. Pearson, who declared the new law unconstitutional. Rather, they noted that when the full court met to reconsider the question, the other justices overruled Pearson's decision.[36]

This sensible but still self-consciously pro–state rights position was not confined to the *Mercury*. The governor of South Carolina, likewise an advocate of state rights, wholeheartedly endorsed Confederate conscription. In 1863, the Richmond *Dispatch* identified Governor Milledge Bonham as the "chief Executive officer of the State which, above all others, perhaps, is most jealous of State rights." Nonetheless, he supported conscription. Conscription in South Carolina preceded Confederate conscription and came into conflict with some of Richmond's provisions. South Carolina authorities quarreled with President Davis, but Bonham reconciled the two conscription systems by reference to a judicial body. The *Dispatch* added firmly, "This is no time for making nice distinctions between the laws of the Confederate Government and the laws of any State. We want soldiers to fight, not lawyers to talk. We want State Governments that will conform their laws to those of the Confederate Government, not raise opposition to them."[37]

The Confederacy in the State Supreme Courts

The *Charleston Mercury* stood behind most of the judicial interpretations of conscription that upheld the draft in the courts of the Confederate states. A review of the decisions will serve to call attention to the steady support of conscription not only by the *Mercury* but also by the judiciary of those states. Historians from Albert Moore on have been struck by the endorsement of conscription by the supreme courts of the various Confederate states. But they have not been duly impressed by the intellectual underpinnings of that support. The judiciaries of those states were imbued, as much as any institution in the Confederacy, with the view that what was distinctive about the Confederate version of government was state rights. In other words, the courts probably provided the toughest potential test for conscription, even tougher than that posed by governors jealously guarding their militias. In judicial decisions on conscription, historians can find the most systematic and effective statements of state rights, but articulated without damaging Confederate nationalism and the effort to make the Confederate States of America a lasting nation-state.

As early as November 15, 1862, the *Mercury* reported in full one of the first state supreme court decisions upholding the constitutionality of conscription. Later the newspaper praised Judge Andrew Magrath's 1863 decision sustaining a revised Conscription Act. It is important to examine the

Confederate judges' record on conscription. As much as the editors of the *Mercury*, the judiciary of the Confederacy — both state and federal (a term Confederates would not have used) — was remarkable for (1) upholding conscription and (2) generally taking into consideration state rights doctrine in doing so. Thus, in the case of both the *Mercury* and the courts, those most conscious of the alleged state rights foundations of the Confederacy also upheld conscription. The founding principle, as they saw it, was compatible with mobilization for a war of independence even if that mobilization required conscription.

Though the Confederacy never organized a national supreme court, the judiciary remained as powerful as it had been in the antebellum South. Judges generally viewed state rights as the distinguishing feature of Confederate jurisprudence and yet, with the exception of one judge in North Carolina (Chief Justice Pearson), none of the thirty-seven state supreme court justices in the Confederacy made trouble for the centralizing Richmond government. Below the appellate level, there could be found more variety and more troublemakers, though most judges did not make trouble.

The Confederate States courts, which usually upheld the powers of the Confederate government, lacked the influence the federal judiciary might otherwise have had toward strengthening the central government for a simple institutional reason: as we have seen in the tribulations of Richmond's Judge Halyburton, the Confederate courts seem never to have organized a reporting system.[38] Historians cannot now go to the shelves of a law library and take down a volume or two of the Confederate States of America Courts Reports or the Confederate States Federal Cases. The state supreme courts continued their reporting in annual volumes as nearly as they could under the disrupting circumstance of war, and a visit to the law library shelves finds volumes of the Confederate period in series with the state reports before and after the war — South Carolina, Alabama, Virginia, and others. But such is not true of the national courts, and without official reports they could not exert their proper influence on state decisions. A judicial decision cannot be controlling or influential unless it is known to the rest of the judiciary. The decisions of the national courts in the Confederacy had to be learned from newspaper reports of them, hit or miss. In other words, the court system, as it was constituted, militated against nationalism, but a nimble reconciliation of state rights ideals with nationalism proved nevertheless to be the distinguishing feature of the jurisprudence of the Confederacy. The state and not the national courts had the leading role. Their decisions received extended notice in the press.

Whenever tested, conscription was upheld in the state supreme courts of the Confederacy.[39] Even more so than in the North, the issues in the Confederacy centered on the idea of competing roles of the state militias and the national army. Naturally, a country that was identified with state rights was likely to guard its militias more jealously than one less centered on the states. Yet from beginning to end, the courts in the Confederate states reconciled their differences with a national conscription.

The first state supreme court case upholding conscription came from the most aggressively assertive supreme court in all of the Confederate states, that of Texas. That court took the leading role in Texas's movement to secession, not the state's Union-leaning governor Sam Houston or its legislature. Justice Oran Roberts and Chief Justice Royall T. Wheeler, according to William W. Freehling, helped ram secession through the state legislature and bypassed the foot-dragging Houston.[40] Eighteen months later, the court, with George F. Moore replacing the fiery Roberts, considered the Confederacy's resort to conscription to raise armies. In an 1862 decision named *Ex parte Coupland*, the eager Texas jurists asserted the constitutionality of conscription.

The opinion was consistent with the activist reputation of the Texas judiciary: the justices wrote a decision despite the fact that there was no need at all to issue one. The prisoner in question, an unhappy conscript named F. H. Coupland, had earlier appealed for a writ of habeas corpus, which was issued in chambers by Wheeler, but Coupland had since deserted and was nowhere to be found. There was no body to be brought into court; the prisoner was no longer in custody.

The supreme court, apparently still intent on controlling the state from the bench, decided to issue an opinion on the issues in the case anyway. The majority opinion came from Justice Moore, who managed to uphold conscription from a boldly expressed state rights point of view. He phrased the question this way: "Has the nationality of Texas (we speak of it as an individual sovereign community or state) conferred the power of doing this upon the Confederate States?" Such delegation of power was the point of having a Confederacy in the first place. Moore refused to regard the militia, a state institution, as being the body to be conscripted. Militiamen were also citizens of the Confederacy. The Confederate Constitution restricted the militia to repelling invasion and suppressing rebellion. Militiamen could not defend the national honor against foreign powers in a foreign war.

Moore did not say so, but he was offering a solution to a potential problem for the Confederate nation. In the War of 1812 the adherence of the New England states to the idea that the militia could be used only to repel invasion or suppress insurrection had led to serious disputes with the federal government. New England states withheld militia from federal control because, they argued, the war goals of the administration were not defensive and the administration wanted New England troops to invade Canada.[41] Surely the Confederacy, under the assumptions of extreme state rights interpretation of conscription and nationalization of the militias, might have run into similar trouble, with states withholding their militias from the invasion of Maryland and Kentucky in 1862 or Pennsylvania in 1863.

Moore dealt with fundamentals in clear language, admitting that ideally patriotism should voluntarily meet the war demands agreed upon by the nation. But volunteering did not take care of the issue of equity—that is, "making the burthens of war fall equally upon the willing and the unwilling." Conscription was necessary and proper for solving that problem.

Moore firmly concluded that the "theory of our government, when properly understood, does not militate against the constitutionality of the law." Justice James Bell, who had opposed the ardent secessionists on the court before the state seceded, dissented, arguing strenuously at length that conscription was unconstitutional. His reasoning was not based on the peculiar principles underlying the Confederate Constitution but relied to some extent on arguments borrowed from U.S. authorities of the past. Chief Justice Wheeler made clear his belief that conscription was constitutional.[42]

But Texas lay on the remote frontier of the Confederacy, and the earliest decision upholding conscription to gain widespread attention in the press was *Asa C. Jeffers v. John Fair*, heard late in 1862 in the Georgia Supreme Court reviewing a decision in a habeas corpus appeal from a judge named Baldwin. The counsel for the conscript Jeffers argued that the Confederate Congress had no authority to raise armies by coercion and could only call for volunteers; that all armies raised by the Congress except with volunteers were actually the state militias and had to be commanded by officers designated by state authorities; and that the power to raise armies by conscription could be used to "disband" and "annihilate the State government by conscription of all the State officers."

The Georgia court delivered a decision almost as stunning as the one from Texas for its assertion that state rights did not interfere with mobilization. Justice Charles J. Jenkins wrote the majority opinion. The statute, Jenkins said, acted on individuals and not on militiamen—that is, a citizen's status was not submerged in his status as a militiaman. Raising armies and calling out the militia were not one and the same thing. The Conscription Act simply did not have a tendency to destroy the state governments, and one must consider the whole point of forming a confederation, namely national strength. To be sure, Jenkins "tremble[d] at consolidation," as did nearly everyone in the Confederacy, but he made explicit the memory of the Hartford Convention and the New England states in the War of 1812 that properly hung over such decisions. That history from the old confederation proved that there could be "refractory Governors and too tardy Legislatures."[43]

The most important part of the ruling for many Southerners was the part dealing with the possibility of destroying state rights by destroying the states altogether. Jenkins had to acknowledge that that particular objection had been "pressed" in "high quarters" and with an "earnestness" that meant it could not be ignored. Jenkins's view was that it did not really deserve such serious consideration otherwise:

> It is maintained that if there is no limitation of this power, it may be carried to the obliteration of all State authority, including in its exactions the persons of Governors and officers of all the departments. There *is* a limitation to the power: It is two-fold: 1st. . . . that the creature may not destroy the creator. . . . Can we have *any* government in which it is not necessary to impose some confidence in its administration? Second, in the 4th clause of the 3d section of the Constitution, a republican form of government is guaranteed to every State. . . .
>
> These fears of the destruction of State authority and sovereignty . . . are "chimeras dire," phantoms of the imagination.[44]

Jenkins attempted to show that the reverse of the proposition might as plausibly be argued. "It seems not to have occurred to the objectors, who conceding that the power, as an incident to that of raising armies, must *ex necessitate rei*, exist somewhere, admit for the States, that they might enroll the corresponding officials of the Confederate Government, and thus, in the midst of war, annihilate the agency charged with its prosecution."[45] Jenkins made the contrast stark. On the one hand, without the power to raise armies by any method that did not itself destroy the Confederacy, the Confederate States of America had "but the shadow of a government, and the experiment of Confederated Republics must inevitably fail." On the other hand, fears that the power would somehow obliterate the states derived simply from "excited imagination" and "distrustful hypercriticism." "There are," he admitted, "certain first principles which underlie all governments." If the Confederate government drafted the very governments of the states, then it obviously violated the intention of the framers of the Confederate Constitution in giving them the war powers in the first place.

One of the most remarkable features of Jenkins's opinion was its steady reliance on analogy with the U.S. Constitution. "Our Constitution," he readily acknowledged, "(with a few exceptions not affecting this investigation) is a liberal copy of the Constitution of the United States. . . . The experience which induced its adoption was our experience."[46] Therefore he sought "whatever light . . . may be derived from American history, and whatever authority from eminent actors in the political arena, between the declaration of independence and our secession from the Union" as "legitimate aids in the further prosecution of our inquiry." There followed long quotations from George Washington. Then came, from the standard edition of the debates at the Philadelphia constitutional convention of 1787 and from the records of the ratifying conventions in the states, lengthy quotations from James Madison, John Marshall, Alexander Hamilton, Oliver Ellsworth, and Charles Pinckney. To support his view of the power to raise armies without limitation as to means, Jenkins cited *The Federalist*, nos. 15, 19, and 20.

In the end, however, Jenkins knew that he must deal with the question of state rights. He stated flatly that the power to raise armies by conscription was "compatible with the large residuum of sovereignty which the States intended to retain." He admitted that if the exercise of the power would subvert the state governments then it would be "violative of the spirit of the Constitution." But he thought "the existing happy mean, may be made to work safely and beneficently."[47] Jenkins obviously did considerable research for the case. He even cited articles in *Niles' Weekly Register* from 1814 describing James Monroe's plan for conscription and the support of it by George M. Troup, a famous Georgia statesman.[48]

Among the last of the state supreme courts to weigh in on the constitutionality of conscription was that of Virginia. In 1864 Chief Justice John J. Allen finally made the decision in *Burroughs v. Peyton* and *Abraham v. Peyton*, the cases of two men who had hired substitutes and were later conscripted and held by Major T. J. Peyton in Camp Lee, outside Richmond.

Historian Albert B. Moore stated that Allen's ruling "asserted the power of the Confederate Government with a baldness that must have caused painful reflections to the disciples of State sovereignty."[49] A close reading suggests otherwise. Allen announced his resolve to decide on conscription in the two cases with this statement: "Considerations of expediency and policy cannot be permitted to control our judgment." The court must decide on the law, "however disastrous may be the consequences of our decision." In reading the decision, members of the Davis administration and officers of the Conscript Bureau must have trembled when they reached this point, fearing a ruling against conscription of the righteous *"fiat justitia ruat coelum"* (let justice reign though the heavens fall) sort.[50]

But Allen ruled in favor of the unlimited power of Congress to raise armies, quoting among other authorities Alexander Hamilton's vigorous *The Federalist*, no. 23, and pointing out that the militia could not possibly be the sole reliance for mighty armies because the Constitution forbade the militia to be used in foreign wars. He noted that the Confederate government must be able to draw on militias for soldiers because the militias legally constituted the whole arms-bearing population of the states. Like Jenkins, Allen recognized that the power to raise armies might be abused, but when he identified the constitutional safeguards against its abuse, he added one that seems surprising: "The protection against its abuse . . . is to be found in the responsibility of Congress to the people, ensured by their short tenure of office; and in the reserved right of each state to resume the powers given to the Confederate government, whenever, in her judgment, they are perverted to the injury or oppression of her people." Far from being a bald assertion of the Richmond government's power, Allen's decision invoked the ultimate safeguard of nullification or secession from the Confederacy itself. In addressing the threat to states that lay in the possible conscription of state government officers, he declared: "Congress can have no such power over state officers. The state governments are an essential part of our political system; upon the separate and independent sovereignty of the states the foundation of our confederacy rests." He added that the states themselves enjoyed the power of deciding which state officers were essential.[51]

The mention of nullification, the doctrine based on the same compact theory of the Constitution that underlay secession in the 1860s, provides, ironically, a startling reminder of the strength of Confederate nationalism within the comfortable confines of Confederate constitutionalism. The Confederacy, despite the fact that South Carolina, the birthplace of nullification, was its charter member, seems never to have been in the least threatened by this Southern doctrine of state nullification. In Georgia, after the fall of Atlanta in 1864, defeatists embraced calling state conventions, but the threat went no further there, and these were aimed vaguely at peace negotiations — not nullification of specific obnoxious Confederate laws. North Carolina was similarly deeply disaffected and toyed with such ideas. However unhappy the citizenry may have been at times with the government in Richmond, their leaders never seem to have thought even of rallying them around the interposition or state nullification of unpopular laws. Moreover, the absence of threats of nullification in the Confederacy likewise points to the comfortable reconciliation of state rights with national mobilization for war. The courts and ardent state rights ideologues such as the *Mercury*'s editors could affirm state rights without going to the brink of nullification.[52]

Two years after his decision in *Jeffers v. Fair*, Justice Jenkins of the Georgia Supreme Court reaffirmed his opinion on the constitutionality of conscription in the face of a nearly hysterical challenge from the libertarian fringe of the Confederacy. *Barber v. Irwin* dealt with several habeas corpus cases involving men who had been detailed from Confederate service or exempted from service under revisions of the Conscription Act passed on February 17, 1864, in order to pursue vital civilian occupations in Georgia, such as plantation overseers or other essential workers. The most interesting feature of the case was the argument made by the lawyers for Georgia's militia officers. The lawyers were an obviously politically inspired group, including Robert Toombs and Linton Stephens, the brother of the disaffected Confederate vice president, Alexander Stephens. Part of their strategy was to assert that conscription was unconstitutional—in the face of the precedent from the very court in which they argued and the very same Justice Jenkins. They maintained that conscription violated the provision against illegal search and seizure, being an illegal seizure of a person.

Jenkins managed to restrain himself when faced with this unusual, not to say preposterous argument, and to put forth his customarily clear, commonsensical opinion on the question. He asked whether the power to raise armies was "incompatible with the sovereignty of the several states." Any power was susceptible to abuse, he acknowledged, but statesmen did the best they could. They "make the grant large enough to meet such contingencies, and to provide against abuse, in the structure of the government." Then he cited a litany of traditional American safeguards, such as a two-house legislature and limited terms of office. In the end, he had to admit, "Nothing is more absolutely certain than that the vast operations of government cannot be conducted, without more or less of trust."[53]

Jenkins also went to great lengths to explain why an unlimited power to raise armies was compatible, though not without risk, with a government based on state sovereignty. His argument focused on the protections that lay in the structure of constitutional government—popularly chosen legislators and checks and balances among the branches of government.

The decision, although the written part of it went to great lengths to defend conscription, in fact was a practical victory for Governor Brown of Georgia. Jenkins also ruled that the men were exempted from the Confederate army but not from the Georgia militia. Jenkins breezily dismissed the idea that the Confederacy's details were a real form of military service. The men in question were engaged in agricultural pursuits and not bearing arms. The state could claim their services, as they very much wanted to at the moment. Jenkins's decision came in the November term of the court, long after the fall of Atlanta. The Confederate army as a matter of fact was inadequate to protect Georgia in 1864, as General William T. Sherman was proving vividly every day, and the governor did need to call out the militia for defense. Jenkins did not say those things, and the decision could be taken as an affirmation of the powers of the Confederate national government even while giving Governor Brown the five men for the militia.

Jenkins's opinion, like many others written during the Civil War by judges North and South, contained a nationalistic assumption dictated by the mindset of the era and not by the words of the written instruments of government. In deciding cases having to do with military service, judges often simply affirmed the obligation of every citizen to defend the nation at its call. Jenkins wrote: "Publicists lay it down as a principle upon which all social organization rests, that each one owes to all his associates the duty of defending them against external dangers. Without this there can be neither government nor society. It is, then, an obligation older than any written constitution."[54]

The demands made on Georgia by the military campaigns of 1864 put severe stress on the courts, too. The men conscripted into Confederate service and then detailed to civilian occupations deemed crucial to the war effort by the Richmond government were eyed hungrily by Governor Brown and the Georgia militia officers, thinking now in desperate terms of militia resistance to Union invasion. Such thinking was necessary even before the Jenkins decision cited above. General Sherman was well north of Atlanta in May 1864, but his army was in Georgia and heading south. The Confederate army had not yet proved completely inadequate to defend the state, but Georgia was in obvious peril. Controlling decisions from the supreme court still mattered, of course. Thus a judge in Richmond County, where Augusta lay, noted that the revocation of substitutes by Confederate law was "no longer an open question in Georgia" because the higher court had decided the issue; accordingly, he ruled to dispatch some local men, who had sent substitutes to the army, to the Confederate enrolling officer.[55]

As the situation grew more serious in the summer, Governor Brown issued a proclamation that immediately put some distance between him and his previous record of obstruction of conscription and at the same time laid claim to able-bodied Georgians for defense of the state in cases where the

Confederacy had them in desk jobs behind the lines. On July 9, 1864, Brown proclaimed that "under our form of Government, each State is sovereign." Yet Georgia

> does not deny that, if the Confederate Government needs her citizens for an army or armies, her own right to their military service must, according to the Constitution, give place to the higher claim of the nation. But she has never agreed in the Constitution, and ought never to consent outside of it, that Congress may place her citizens where, while not required to do military service to the Confederate States, they are relieved, or prevented from siding, with their arms, in rescuing her from a barbarous and unrelenting foe.

Even with such doctrines in the air, Judge John T. Clark of the Patula District Superior Court, in Lumkin, exempted a man from the Georgia militia because he served on an advisory board for the Confederate Conscript Bureau and that was a necessary military service. On the other hand, Clark ruled that a Confederate tax collector and an assessor were liable to Georgia militia service because they were not in the military but in the civil service of the Confederacy.[56]

The proliferation of controversial cases of judges determining obligations of military service on habeas corpus hearings was a function of military desperation in besieged parts of the Confederacy, like Georgia and Richmond, Virginia, especially after the spring of 1864. In Georgia they were multiplied by the beginnings of the formation of a political opposition there, and by the defeatism embodied in the contention of such opposition newspapers as the *Augusta Chronicle and Sentinel* that the war could not be won by force by either side and must be settled by negotiations initiated by state conventions. Even so, Governor Brown continued to attempt to reconcile state sovereignty with the demands of the Confederate armies, and Georgia's judges looked carefully at behind-the-lines Confederate jobs to determine whether they really constituted army service or not. Those discriminations were made only to facilitate defense by the Georgia militia. The controlling nature of state supreme court decisions upholding Confederate draft laws was universally acknowledged in the lower courts as far as the patchy reporting of cases allows us to judge.

On the other hand, the Confederacy's state judges were laying claim to be able to judge controversial mobilization cases, and that was in itself somewhat obstructionist: the Confederate government had to respond, producing a prisoner with an officer in charge and employing a state's attorney for defense. As Jefferson Davis had warned on February 3, 1864, that might stop an army on the march in its tracks:

> In some of the States civil process has been brought to bear with disastrous efficiency upon the Army. Every judge has the power to issue the writ of *habeas corpus*, and if one manifests more facility in discharging petitioners than his associates the application is made to him, however remote he may be. In one instance a general on the eve of an important movement, when every man was needed, was embarrassed by the command of a judge — more than two hundred miles distant — to bring . . . or send . . . before him, on *habeas corpus*, some deserters who had been arrested and returned to his command. In another, a commandant of a camp of conscripts, who had a conscript in camp, was commanded to bring him before a judge more than a hundred miles distant, although there was a judge competent to hear and determine the cause resident in the place where the writ was executed. He consulted eminent counsel, and was advised that, from the known opinions of the judge selected, the conscript would undoubtedly be released, and the officer was therefore advised to discharge him at once, and return the facts informally; that such a return was not technically sufficient, but would be accepted as accomplishing the purpose of the writ. He acted on the advice of his counsel, and was immediately summoned by the judge to show cause why he should not be attached for a contempt in making an insufficient return, and was compelled to leave his command at a time when his services were pressingly needed by the Government and travel over a hundred miles and a considerable distance away from any railroad, to purge himself of the technical contempt.[57]

On the other hand, the judges in their courtrooms made what appeared to be careful decisions. Thus Judge Jaynes of the Petersburg Circuit Court in Virginia in the late autumn of 1864 decided that mail contractors already in the army were not to be discharged; they must be already out of the service when appointed. He decided that state officers mandated by the Virginia Constitution were exempt from Confederate service but withheld judgment on state officials created by the state legislature. He ruled that an underage soldier who enlisted with or without parental consent could not make a contract and was removable from the ranks. He ruled that soldiers already in the ranks were not entitled to discharge when they reached ages mentioned for eligibility limits to conscription in legislation — 45 for active service or 50 for reserves. All of these discriminating decisions came in a courtroom threatened by Union military campaigns in the Richmond-Petersburg area in late 1864.[58]

How Pressing Was Impressment?

Conscription was not the only important power of the Confederacy to pass the test of the state supreme courts. In Georgia, a much-watched case upheld the power to impress products for the Confederate army. In *Cunningham v. Campbell* Justice Jenkins once again sustained the power of the Richmond government, but it was not an unalloyed victory for the Confederate army. Under an act of Congress the Confederate Commissary in Macon in 1863 impressed large quantities of sugar belonging to various firms, including David L. Campbell's, whose name went on the case. The Confederate officers gave them seventy-five cents per pound compensation. The businessmen had themselves paid a dollar a pound, and they maintained that the sugar was worth a dollar twenty when seized. The Confederate government did not contest those facts. The businesses sued, saying that the law under which their property was taken without just compensation was unconstitutional. The Confederate authorities were unlucky, for they had seized the sugar in a district where the judge was not particularly disposed to sympathize with the authority of the central Confederate government. Judge O. A. Lochrane gave the plaintiffs possessory warrants and the property came before the court, where he awarded it to the plaintiffs (essentially, unless the Confederate government agreed to pay more).

The government appealed to the Georgia Supreme Court, where eventually the clear-thinking Chief Justice Jenkins upheld the Confederate statute allowing for impressments. But he was careful to ignore the pleas of necessity, which had been made much of, apparently, by government counsel and likewise much criticized by the lawyers for the businesses. Necessity, Jenkins insisted, "asserts itself in the inevitable *now*," but the sugars were impressed for depots from which they would be requisitioned for future use. Jenkins was not going to ignore the possibility of "'*extreme necessity*,' inducing and justifying action upon the principle '*salus populi, suprema lex*.'" But such dire conditions did not apply in this case. This was an appropriation of property for future public use according to a statute and thus only a matter of public utility. He thus shrewdly made his mark against the overuse and abuse of the plea of military necessity in circumscribing private rights and private property.

Jenkins nevertheless upheld the statute, except, of course, those parts of it that violated the Constitution. It was settled doctrine in the Georgia court itself that private property could be seized for public use with just compensation. And he cited Chancellor Kent on the necessity of the condition of just compensation. Therein lay the problems for the Confederate government, according to Jenkins. The mechanism for setting compensation was inadequate, and the resulting compensation in this case was not "just." When he discussed these economic questions, Jenkins skirted issues of price and profit that, in a lesser judge in similarly heated circumstances of inflation of currency and shortage of consumer goods, might have led to demagogic grandstanding. On the one hand, just compensation did not dictate paying "any price which the owner may demand" and certainly "not a price fixed by holders in conspiracy, not yet attained in commercial transactions; but which in the spirit of speculation they resolve to realize in the future, or force in the present, from the necessities of the Government." "Against all such exactions and conspiracies," he insisted, "impressment is a rightful remedy." On the other hand, the government appraisers fixed prices for large geographic areas for long periods of time, as much as sixty days, ignoring local conditions and rapidly changing market rates. It was "equally untrue, and unphilosophical to say that these fluctuations are produced by speculative operations," for the underlying causes were supply and demand. In the end, he said, impressment was a fair remedy, but the mechanism under the law for arriving at just compensation in fact resulted in violating the constitutional provision that private property could not be taken for public use without just compensation.[59]

State rights did not figure in the opinion, and Jenkins made no reference to the principles of construction he applied, whether strict or not. But he did allow for the condition of the country:

Much has been said, and eloquently said, of the imperiled condition of the country, and the fatal consequences likely to result from judicial interference with the *war* measures of the Government; but let it be remembered that by a provision of the instrument itself, Judges as well as legislators, are sworn "to support the Constitution"; and this they are to do in war, as well as in peace. We yield to none in respect for the Congress of the Confederate States; we would at all times, and especially in times like the present, most reluctantly dissent from their construction of the Constitution; we would, in cases of doubtful meaning, incline to give them the benefit of the doubt, for the safety of the country. Beyond this point of concession, not even war, with its attendant horrors, may rightfully impel the judiciary. Positive conviction of constitutional obligation may not be yielded under any circumstances.[60]

The press reported the opinion as a victory for the powers of the Confederate government, but the chief justice of the state supreme court had also reaffirmed the rights of his state.

The decision on the sugar case was not as much a victory for the Confederate government as it appeared to some. To the obstructionist Judge Lochrane, of Macon, there was room for doubt, and he proved more inclined to rule against impressments of property than against the demands of the Confederate government for manpower. He was, after all, of the nationalist persuasion on manpower, having ruled in one case that "all persons who are citizens of a Government may be used by the Government in time of war, and it was the duty of Courts to sustain the Government in the means exercised rightfully to protect the whole people from subjugation and ruin."[61] In impressment cases, however, Lochrane's guiding principle was "a man's house is his castle." Thus in *Home v. J. M. Green, Surgeon*, Lochrane embraced a stern doctrine, verging on ignoring the condition of the country. "In meeting . . . the questions of this case," he said, "we shall not look to the hardships that grow out of the proper and manly administration of the law of the land. It may leave soldiers unprovided with shelter. . . . With the consequences we have nothing to do." He issued an injunction against the Confederate surgeon who was in charge of military hospitals in Macon and the colonel commanding to prevent them from taking the Planter's Hotel and the stores adjoining that property for a Confederate hospital. Like Jenkins, Lochrane did not think that the military necessity contemplated by the Constitution was present. Battle lay in the future and one hundred miles away from Macon in midsummer 1864. It was not the case that 500–1,000 wounded soldiers were already in Macon needing shelter that would have to be impressed in the emergency. If the Confederate government contemplated a permanent hospital in Macon, it was obligated to purchase a building or build one from scratch.[62]

The careful assessment of "necessity" allowed for by Justice Jenkins gave Georgia judges room for decisions averse to the Confederate government. In the wretched autumn of 1864, a Georgia superior court judge named R. C. Clarke affirmed in *Joseph B. Ivey and Others v. Captain Benjamin F. White and Dr. Foster, Post Surgeon* the right of the judiciary to judge of the necessity. It was not known when the 2,400 patients being planned for by the surgeon and captain would come to Albany, and it was not a necessity requiring the impressment of houses. The judge referred not to Lochrane's decision but to information that the superior court in Atlanta "decided distinctly that the Courts were judges of the necessity upon a proper case made." He too affirmed that a man's home was his "castle." Government counsel argued that "the effect" of his judgment "would be to raise a question of every impressment of supplies or beasts of burden. I cannot say such a question might not arise, but he would be a weak Judge who would hesitate to affirm such a necessity within the limits of the acts of Congress."[63]

The Lower Courts, Grand Juries, and Confederate Nationalism

The historians, such as Albert B. Moore, who argued that state rights undermined the Confederate war effort, knew that the state supreme courts generally upheld conscription. They argued that lower courts caused trouble for the mobilization system. On balance, that does not appear to be true, especially so by comparison with the record of the courts in the Northern states during the war. Inadequate reporting of decisions in the Confederacy makes the historian's task especially difficult at this lower level, but a substantial number of cases were described or mentioned in scattered newspapers. These show a varied but not obstructionist record.

An early example came to the Charleston, South Carolina, City Court in the autumn of 1862. Alston Pringle, the recorder and judge of the court, had been asked to issue a writ of habeas corpus for Benjamin Sauls, a minor, whose father sought his release from the Confederate army. Pringle asked whether, as recorder, he had jurisdiction in a case in which the detainee was being held by the general government. The precedents in such cases from the old Union were mixed, and the U.S. Supreme Court had never ruled directly on such a case. South Carolina precedent was clear, however, according to Pringle. And he could invoke the famous jurist Langdon Cheves on the question. Pringle found this precedent by reading *Niles's Register* for 1817 (a case involving a federal prisoner but not a soldier). Pringle felt special confidence in the wisdom of his decision not to interfere when he recalled the antebellum record of Northern state courts in cases of federal prisoners who were fugitive slaves. The record of state courts' defiance of national authority to hold the prisoners under federal statute was proof of "a fatal local fanaticism." A Union could not be founded on such a want of confidence in the central government. Pringle said that he had no jurisdiction and that the application must be made before the Confederate States Court.[64]

There were contrary decisions. In that same season of initial tests of the constitutionality of conscription, Judge Thomas W. Thomas of the Superior Court of Elbert County, Georgia, located on the border with South Carolina, ruled firmly against conscription in a case involving a man who had twice failed physical examinations when attempting to volunteer and was subsequently conscripted. Thomas ruled the conscription law unconstitutional because Congress had no power "to create a militia of its own." "A strict construction gives this result," he insisted, "and strict construction is our settled policy and law." He pointed out that the states were sovereign and independent and made the government. If the central government could draft the state officers such as governor, it could destroy the states. If somehow the central government exempted them from conscription, it was still asserting its jurisdiction over them by assuming a power to exempt or include; if the government could draft with conditions, it could also do so without conditions.[65]

A previously unnoticed measure of the patriotism of the judiciary in the Confederacy can be seen in charges to the grand jury and in other questions that were not constitutional in nature. Still, these need to be weighed in making the overall assessment. The judiciary of the Confederate States appears to have been even more aggressive than the Northern judiciary. With no political parties to agitate public questions, the judges felt more call to weigh in themselves. They had from the colonial days of the county court system enjoyed great prestige in the South, and that does not seem to have disappeared by the time of the Civil War.[66] There was no reason to wait for the Supreme Court of the Confederate nation to speak, because it was never going to, as none existed.

When judges spoke to their grand juries beyond the obligatory explanation of laws to be enforced, their words appear to have been nationalistic. Sometimes these gratuitous harangues did deal with constitutional issues. Thus one Judge Gholson, in a charge to a grand jury in Petersburg, Virginia, railed against the despotism of the Lincoln administration. "In comparison with such tyranny," he concluded, "the Spanish Inquisition was tolerable."[67] Judge West H. Humphreys of the Confederate States Court in Knoxville, Tennessee, delivered a charge to the grand jury described by a Georgia newspaper as "one of the most able expositions of the wickedness of the abolition raid upon the South." Dwelling on specifics, Judge Humphreys noted that Confederate military authorities were being much annoyed by writs of habeas corpus and that people who professed allegiance to the Union were alien enemies and not entitled to the writ of habeas corpus. Only citizens had the right. Doubtless these were serious issues in East Tennessee, which was dominated by pro-Union majorities.[68]

It was more in keeping with the traditional role of the grand jury as a guardian of local morals and institutions for the charge to deal with extortionate prices. Judges throughout the Confederacy denounced the alleged practice. Some were high ranking. Andrew G. Magrath, of the Confederate States District Court in Charleston, charged the grand jury on extortion as early as the autumn of 1862. It was a revealing moment, for it showed the aggressiveness of the judiciary in a clear light. The grand jurors received the charge, but what, they asked, were they supposed to do?

> In reference to the matter of extortion in the prices of nearly all the necessaries of life, now practiced by dealers, vendors and manufacturers, the evil effects of which your Honor has so vividly depicted to the Jury, we are at a loss to devise or propose a remedy. The matter is said to be governed by the laws that regulate trade — "supply and demand." . . . These cormorants in human shape inflict more misery upon the people than the depredations of the enemy. If the Government could arrest this evil, it would be a blessing second only to peace. The Jury feels themselves incompetent to advise the mode.

The judge had left them another seemingly intractable problem as well.

> The other matter to which your Honor has called the attention of the Jury, is one that has attracted the notice of all patriotic citizens. We mean the great number of foreigners who have enjoyed all the privileges of natives, in times of peace, but who now turn their backs upon us and claim protection from the powers they formerly and solemnly abjured. . . . It behooves the Government to remedy this.[69]

Far from exercising his duty to address the laws that needed to be enforced during the term of court, Magrath had called attention — at least in the grand jury's estimation — to problems caused by the want of laws to regulate. In other words, Magrath had used his charge to the grand jury to air his views on political problems.

Georgia had on the books a statute punishing extortion, and the press there beat the drum loudly for its enforcement. Extortion was frequently the subject of charges to the grand jury.[70] In the spring of 1862, a man named Bull who was judge of the Fulton Superior Court, charged the grand jury there in much the same manner that Magrath would in Charleston. Bull urged the grand jury to enforce extortion laws and "recommended the prosecution of all foreign born citizens, who have exercised the right of citizenship, and now claim exemption from military service in the Confederate army."[71]

The difficulties in acting against foreigners seem obvious enough, and extortion, as a common-law crime, did not mean the same thing as was conveyed in the term charging "extortionate" prices. Extortion, according to *Black's Law Dictionary*, is the "offense committed by a public official who illegally obtains property under the color of office; esp., an official's collection of an unlawful fee."[72] The judges were making political points rather than good law, apparently. Hashing out disputes over extortion at the level of the local court and grand jury became so habitual in Georgia that the press reported the disputes as they might have political party contests of prewar days. Without naming any names, the Macon newspaper described the actions of a judge in "a county nearby" who charged the grand jury to "visit just deserts on extortioners and speculators" and then himself became the first victim. He was indicted for selling shoe leather at extortionate prices. The Macon paper explained that the grand jury was made up of planters. Now, complained the Macon newspaper, it was impossible to get provisions even for charitable institutions in that place because the same planters withheld them for unreasonable prices. The soldiers' wives suffered accordingly, it was reported.[73] The spirit of judges in imparting political content to the work of the grand jury infected the grand juries themselves with a willful political animus. A grand jury in Mobile, Alabama, insisted that the Confederacy's military adversaries could never defeat it but the love of money within the Confederacy could. The local newspaper complained that the grand jury pointed out the evil but did nothing about it — indeed, it "quailed before" influential people. The editors called for the organization of a committee that would publish the names of merchants who overpriced the provisions they sold.[74] Whatever the facts of the case, the interesting point is the prominence of the judiciary in this argument over patriotic sacrifice.

Citizens came to look to the grand juries for meting out justice to those who refused to take Confederate currency in payment for debts because it was not legal tender — a practice also widely equated with the lack of patriotism and with undermining the national currency's value. A citizen committee in Putnam County, Georgia, proposed taking the names of such selfish individuals and presenting them to the grand jury for action or publishing them abroad as a "Black Roll."[75] In the spring of 1864 the grand jury in Macon thus lashed out at the opposition to the Davis administration shown by the government of Georgia's Governor Brown. Its statement touched on a key constitutional question: "We feel it to be our duty to protest against the resolutions of the General Assembly of this State in reference to the late law of Congress suspending the writ of habeas Corpus. In this our struggle for liberty and independence, all the resources of our country should be brought into requisition, our people should be united, and everything that looks to division and dissension among ourselves should meet with our unqualified disapprobation."[76]

A grand jury in Tallapoosa, Alabama, declared the currency essential to the liberties of the Confederate people: "If it goes down, our army must melt away." The grand jurors urged the Confederate Congress to tax the "Shylocks and speculators" who depreciated the value of the currency by refusing to accept it as payment.[77] A Judge Cochran in Georgia used the occasion of the charge to the grand jury to offer essentially a patriotic address, reminding the people at home of their duty to provide subsistence for the soldiers. He denounced those who spoke of reconstructing the Union and said there was no real reason for despondency.[78]

The political points made were consistently nationalistic. The judges haranguing their largely helpless grand juries employed a conventional model of self-sacrifice for the nation to impugn the integrity if not the loyalty of those who charged high prices in the time of national shortages caused by war. The grand juries themselves eventually followed the lead of the politically demonstrative judiciary. I could find no charges to the grand jury in the Confederacy that could be construed as opposing the war effort — no charges to the grand jury to watch out for kidnapping of local citizens by Confederate officials making arrests or to insist on looking out for the common soldier in the ranks who was underage and enlisted without parental consent — or even to interfere with conscription officers.

The record shows no pattern of resistance on state rights principles by state courts in the Confederacy. There was, instead, a generally earnest attempt to wrestle with difficult questions posed by the shortage of manpower in a nation at war that was based on a federal system of states. The lack of manpower dictated the thorough military mobilization of a society that valued individual liberty. Nearly every single male of military age was classified by military authorities — soldier, exempt, detailed. By 1864, as we have seen in the decision of Justice Jenkins in Georgia and of Judge Halyburton in Richmond, two jurisdictions were claiming the military population at once: the Confederacy for its beleaguered armies and the states, like Georgia, for their militias, called out to defend local areas left otherwise defenseless by the overstretched Confederate armies. There was a tendency for military authorities to attempt to lay their hands on groups in society ordinarily considered outside the demands of military service: foreigners and even invalids. Increasingly, the courts stood as the only arbiters of these extraordinary demands on the people of the Confederacy. In other words, the courts did not intervene more and cause more trouble for the nation. Rather, the nation called on the courts more and more to render difficult decisions involving the liberties of the people.

It was almost the case that the lame and the blind were beginning to appear in courtrooms to seek refuge from the long arm of military authorities in the South. Judge Lochrane, of the superior court in Macon and often a thorn in the side of Confederate authorities, dealt in January 1865 with a man who had been found unfit for service because of the condition of his eyes by the medical examiner for the Confederate army. But he was assigned to hospital duty. Under a writ of habeas corpus the man sought discharge from illegal restraint by the Confederate States. Lochrane ruled that the power to raise armies was not unlimited and applied only to able-bodied men. "We fully appreciate and recognize the condition of the country," said the Georgia judge, but the power to raise armies applied only to men who could be soldiers.[79]

It would be a mistake to focus on the generally reasonable decisions of the courts at the expense of executive and political resistance that invoked the Constitution in order to frustrate attempts of the Richmond government to gain control of the available manpower resources of the Confederacy. There were such struggles all along in the history of the Confederacy, and in its waning and more desperate days they became very sharp indeed. Frank Owsley concentrated on such struggles because he had come to believe that the state rights ideology of the South actually caused its defeat; thus he logically and purposefully honed in on the important problem of putting soldiers in the field. He dedicated two long chapters of his short book to those problems. But in the end, the numbers of men lost to Confederate service through state selfishness and constitutional obstinacy perhaps did not seem enough to account for defeat, and he decided to direct attention to the problem of impressments of supplies, as exacerbated by the insistence of governors to supply their own troops in Confederate service (thus raising prices in competition for short supplies and making for inequalities in provisioning the fighting forces). In other words, Owsley came to have a sort of weakness for economic arguments for the Confederate defeat. Both problems would have been very great, however, regardless of state rights ideology.

All in all, modern historians of the Civil War, who live this side of the unpopular Vietnam War and who have witnessed stubborn reluctance to serve on the part of large portions of Americans of military age, are most impressed with the effectiveness of Confederate mobilization. Gary W. Gallagher puts the rate at 75–85 percent and calls it "an astonishing mobilization."[80] We can glimpse Jefferson Davis's anxiety in dealing with these problems late in the war when he made a whistle-stop tour across Alabama to the Carolinas in the autumn of 1864. It was not perhaps the best time to refer to the importance of state rights to the Confederacy, but in Columbus, Georgia, on September 30, he did. He managed to bring central themes of Confederate history together. "Inherent sovereignty remains in the States themselves," he insisted, and "this theory of government the Yankees could not comprehend." He went on: "Nor was this to be wondered at, for [the] simple reason that the great State institution of the South was the true basis for such a government. . . . In the South, a great law of nature pointed out a menial class, distinct from the governing class. . . . Here, then, and here only, every white man is truly, socially and politically equal to every other."[81] Republicanism, in its Southern version of combined state rights and slavery, remained the focus of the Confederate nation still.

When he reached South Carolina, the going got a little easier for the beleaguered president. In a speech at Columbia on October 4, Davis complimented South Carolinians on their political willingness to allow their sons to fight on distant fields for the independence of the Confederacy. "You understood the nature of the compact entered into by the sovereign States," he said. "Your battles are fought on other fields" (though it would not be true for long), "you have no constitutional scruples, like Governor Strong, of Massachusetts [in the War of 1812], against marching your militia from the borders of the State, to fight the battles of the cause in which you are engaged." Then Davis attempted to connect himself closely to the South Carolinians. "It is needless for me to argue questions here which I have discussed elsewhere," he said, "for here I am among the disciples of him from whom I learned my lessons of State Rights — the great, the immortal John C. Calhoun."[82] He was sincere about his debt to Calhoun, and, of course, he was shrewd to bring it up in Columbia. But he also revealed, even in the midst of his struggles with Governor Brown of Georgia, that he saw no need to concede the state rights position to the other side.

The Resilience of State Rights in the Confederacy

Frank Owsley, in *State Rights in the Confederacy*, wrote: "It is not a mere coincidence that . . . after August 1, 1864, when the last act suspending the writ [of habeas corpus] had expired, the fortunes of the South never rose again."[83] It is difficult to believe that the suspension of the writ in the summer of 1864 would have reversed the Confederates' military fortunes, but Owsley did make a point never adequately considered: that the failure to suspend the writ of habeas corpus after August 1 did leave the Confederate judiciary with a heap of problems to sort out.

It is easy to get the impression from reading the Richmond press for this period that restoration of the writ unleashed a flood of claims in the courts from men who were no longer committed to the Confederate nation. The legal scene in Richmond seemed in retrospect to journalist Edward A. Pollard, writing in 1869, a spectacle of selfishness and lack of dedication to the nation. Pollard was among the first — long before Owsley — to fault the people for want of commitment to the cause of Confederate nationalism. The people lacked "patriotic devotion to the South."

Pollard insisted on a point that the Lost Cause champions never much dwelt upon: "Only the utmost rigor of conscription forced a majority of its troops in the field; . . . half of these were disposed to desert on the first opportunities; and . . . the demands for military service were cheated in a way and to an extent unexampled in the case of any brave and honorable nation engaged in a war for its own existence." As proof, Pollard cited "the remarkable fact that in one year the Confederate States attorney in Richmond tried *eighteen hundred* cases in that city on writs of habeas corpus for relief from conscription!" "This honored writ," he declared, "became the vilest instrument of the most undeserving men; and there is attached to it a record of shame for the South that we would willingly spare. Mr. Humphrey Marshall, a member of the Confederate Congress . . . added to his pay as a legislator the fees of an attorney to get men out of the army; he became the famous advocate in Richmond in cases of habeas corpus; and he is reported to have boasted that this practice yielded him an average of two thousand dollars a day!"[84]

Pollard blamed the lawyers and the people but did not mention the judges. One suspects that he was wrong about the people and the lawyers, but his silence on the judiciary was merited. Certainly Judge Halyburton's record was not wanting in dedication to the Confederate nation or to the law.

Other commonly used sources for Confederate history naturally exaggerate the resistance to the nation's demands. In his diary Robert Garlick Hill Kean, a clerk in the War Department, definitely took the War Department's view of the conscription problems. Unlike Pollard, however, Kean singled out the judges as troublemakers. As early as May 20, 1863, Kean observed that "the local judiciary are doing what they can to defeat the conscription and encourage desertion in many places, especially Georgia, North Carolina, and Tennessee. These states have the largest infusion of dissatisfaction, the former source of Unionism, a great deal of faction, and the two latter [states] any quantity of Reconstructionism."[85] In other words, he accused them of wanting to reunite with the North.

Despite Pollard and Kean, the period beginning with the summer of 1864 and ending when the Confederacy ended a little less than a year later, considered as a whole, was one of continuity in conscientious judicial application to the problems of liberty and power in the Confederacy. Looking at cases decided after Owsley's fateful date, August 1, 1864, will illustrate the point. In Georgia especially, the demands of the obstreperous, longtime governor, Joseph Brown, for control of troops to defend his own state now made sense, with the invasion of the state by General Sherman and the inability of the Confederate government to offer any armies of adequate size to protect the state. Here judges were faced with a novel situation. Brown's militia for local defense was seeking to enlist men who were in Confederate service but detailed by the government to noncombat roles. The net loss of military persons in these cases was zero—if we ignore the amount of time spent by officers and men in the courtroom before the judge. By ruling for Brown at this time in Confederate history, judges were not undermining the defense of the South.

One can imagine the outrage aroused by such decisions in the average Georgian, who was prey to the authority of Confederate conscription officers who were themselves in desk jobs that offered no front-line aid to the state to repel the Union armies. As Sherman's "bummers" bore down on the citizens, agents of the Richmond government went into their offices in Georgia's towns and watched; at the same time they saw to it that Georgians were swept into Confederate service to be stationed by Jefferson Davis and the War Department anywhere Richmond thought best. Tax assessors, said the judges, could not follow that course, but those designated by the War Department could. Georgia's Judge Clark and others bowed to central authority only where they had to and devised workable principles for dividing up the precious manpower of the Confederacy between the militia and the national army.

In Virginia during the same period, Confederate judges were faced with a similarly large array of cases involving conflict between state and national jurisdictions. Virginia had been invaded years earlier than Georgia, and Richmond had been under siege, off and on, since the spring of 1862. To be sure, in the summer of 1864 the Virginians had not been left to their own devices by the Confederate army. But their situation was desperate.

Virginia wanted its militia for defense, there were numerous able lawyers available in the capital of the Confederacy, and major military prisons were located there. The pattern of conscientious decisions was roughly the same. No judge was entirely predictable as a tool of the central government or a troublemaker for the Confederacy.

The Confederacy did not die of state rights, but state rights never died, either.

Epilogue OTHER WARS

After the Union defeat at the Battle of Bull Run on July 21, 1861, the U.S. Congress hastened to pass a resolution disavowing any radical aims in the war and affirming that the country was fighting only for the Constitution and the Union (and not with any intent "of overthrowing or interfering with the rights or established institutions" of the states in rebellion).[1] After thus running away from any antislavery provocations, the congressmen next hastened to ask for divine help. A joint committee of the Congress went to the president to beg him to "recommend a day of public humiliation, prayer and fasting, to be observed by the people of the United States with religious solemnities." Perhaps in other times in the republic's history a president with religious convictions as coolly rational as Abraham Lincoln's might have refused, but these appeared to be desperate times for the republic, and Lincoln complied. On August 12, 1861, he issued a proclamation for such a day to be observed on the last Thursday in September:

> Whereas it is fit and becoming in all people, at all times, to acknowledge and revere the Supreme Government of God; to bow in humble submission to his chastisements; to confess and deplore their sins and transgressions in the full conviction that the fear of the Lord is the beginning of wisdom; and to pray, with all fervency and contrition, for the pardon of their past offences, and for a blessing upon their present and prospective action:
>
> And whereas, when our own beloved Country, once, by the blessing of God, united, prosperous and happy, is now afflicted with faction and civil war, it is peculiarly fit for us to recognize the hand of God in this terrible visitation, and in sorrowful remembrance of our own faults and crimes as a nation and as individuals, to humble our-

selves before Him, and to pray for His mercy, — to pray that we may be spared further punishment, though most justly deserved; that our arms may be blessed and made effectual for the re-establishment of law, order and peace, throughout the wide extent of our country; and that the inestimable boon of civil and religious liberty, earned under His guidance and blessing, by the labors and sufferings of our fathers, may be restored in all its original excellence.[2]

Jefferson Davis had long since invoked divine blessings on the Confederacy, though like Lincoln he was not then a member of any church. As early as May 28, 1861, Davis issued a proclamation that read:

When a people who recognize their dependence upon God, feel themselves surrounded by peril and difficulty, it becomes them to humble themselves under the dispensation of Divine Providence, to recognize his righteous government, to acknowledge his goodness in times past, and supplicate his merciful protection for the future.

The manifest proofs of the Divine blessing hitherto extended to the efforts of the people of the Confederate States of America, to maintain and perpetuate public liberty, individual rights, and national independence, demand their devout and heartfelt gratitude. It becomes them to give public manifestation of this gratitude, and of their dependence upon the Judge of all the earth, and to invoke the continuance of his favor. Knowing that none but a just and righteous cause can gain the Divine favor, we would implore the Lord of hosts to guide and direct our policy in the paths of right, duty, justice, and mercy, to unite our hearts and our efforts for the defense of our dearest rights; to strengthen our weakness, crown our arms with success, and enable us to secure a speedy, just, and honorable peace.

To these ends, and in conformity with the request of Congress, I invite the people of the Confederate States to the observance of a day of fasting and prayer by such religious services as may be suitable for the occasion, and I recommend Thursday, the 13th day of June next, for that purpose, and that we may all, on that day, with one accord, join in humble and reverential approach to him in whose hands we are, invoking him to inspire us with a proper spirit and temper of heart and mind to bear our evils, to bless us with his favor and protection, and to bestow his gracious benediction upon our Government and country.[3]

The Confederate president's proclamation recognized the long odds his nation faced, and he later, in 1863, invoked as text "the battle is not to the strong, but to whomsoever he willeth to exalt."[4]

The public fast days and days of thanksgiving called for in the North during the Civil War may seem like a Republican innovation born of the evangelical mid-nineteenth century. That theory comports with the evangelical Protestant base of voters imputed to the Republican Party of Lincoln. For some, the proclamation of special religious days seems to fit Lincoln's growing personal religiosity during the war as well as the shrinking influence of Jeffersonian principles of separation of church and state.[5] President Jefferson, who believed in "building a wall of separation between church and state," boasted, when he condemned "alliance between Church and State" in a letter to the Danbury Baptist Association, written on January 1, 1802, that he did "not proclaim fastings and thanksgivings, as my predecessors did."[6]

But such interpretations do not square exactly with the documentary record. Jefferson Davis deviated from the path of separation almost as soon as he could. James Buchanan had deviated, too, on the eve of the Civil War, recommending a day of humiliation and prayer to be observed on January 4, 1861, in the depths of the secession crisis. Unlike Lincoln, Buchanan could not be said to have been playing to his base, as he met a torrent of abuse in the sermons given by antislavery clergy on that day.[7] President Buchanan knew he might lose the nation, and so did Lincoln and Davis, later.

Throughout American history, presidents in trouble, whatever their political affiliation, and despite their personal weak religious identity, called for national days of fasting, prayer, and humiliation. President Thomas Jefferson issued no such proclamations, but Jefferson did not face invasion or civil war while he was president of the United States. Jefferson's close friend and fellow founder of the Republican Party of the Early Republic, James Madison, did confront an invasion, and Madison issued two calls to the beleaguered nation for fast days during the War of 1812.[8]

President Madison issued the first call on July 9, 1812, early in the war before American fortunes turned very bad. The second appeared on July 23, 1813. In part, it read:

> Whereas in times of public calamity such as that of the war brought on the United States by the injustice of a foreign government it is especially becoming that the hearts of all should be touched with the same and the eyes of all be turned to that Almighty Power in whose hand are the welfare and the destiny of nations:

I do therefore issue this my proclamation, recommending to all who shall be piously disposed to unite their hearts and voices in addressing at one and the same time their vows and adorations to the Great Parent and Sovereign of the Universe that they assemble on the second Thursday of September next in their respective religious congregations to render Him thanks for the many blessings He has bestowed on the people of the United States; . . . that in this season of trial and calamity He would preside in a particular manner over our public councils and inspire all citizens with a love of their country . . . and that . . . He would now be pleased . . . to bestow His blessing on our arms.[9]

Whatever their principles on the separation of church and state, and Madison was as ardent on that point as Jefferson, losing a country or a war drove politicians to prayer. Even for presidents, there are no atheists in foxholes. Here was a little-noticed strain put on the Constitution by war.[10]

In surprising ways, then, the records of Lincoln and Madison, of Jefferson Davis and the Confederacy, and of the United States in the War of 1812 and in the Civil War were similar. Though he found a need for public prayer and national humiliation, too, President Madison managed to lead the United States in his desperate war without resort to suspending the privilege of the writ of habeas corpus. Nevertheless, the role of the Constitution in war was sharply contested during that conflict. But it is crucial to see the role of the Constitution broadly and not as though the whole of its meaning were embodied in the First Amendment. Both the Civil War and what has only very recently been termed "The Civil War of 1812" challenged the Constitution or were challenged by it.[11] The Civil War ended, more or less, with the Thirteenth Amendment to the U.S. Constitution, but it is useful to recall that the War of 1812 ended with delegates from the Hartford Convention heading to Washington, D.C., with seven proposed constitutional amendments in their portmanteaus. Nothing came of them because of the abrupt conclusion of the war and the marvelous victory of Andrew Jackson at New Orleans. But constitutional ideas had obviously been profoundly stirred by the course of the war.

We should think of the War of 1812 and the Civil War as constitutionally similar and politically different. The Hartford Convention of 1814 was constantly referred to during the Civil War. It was a surefire negative political reference for nearly any politician. Republicans especially found it appealing to liken the Democrats to the potentially treasonous Federalists who met at the Hartford Convention. For their part, the Democrats likened the

Republicans to the Federalists who passed the Alien and Sedition Acts of 1798. *Yet despite all the political rhetoric, what is noticeable in retrospect is that there was no Hartford Convention during the Civil War.* Indeed, there was no such thing in either the North or the South. Despite all the scares about a Northwest Conspiracy and Clement Vallandigham's peace wing of the Democratic Party in the North, it is well nigh inconceivable to think that, as General George Gordon Meade was about to meet General Robert E. Lee at Gettysburg, a group of delegates might have been heading from states in the Old Northwest to Washington, their portmanteaus filled with constitutional amendments to propose to the Lincoln administration as ultimatums for the continuance of the membership of their states in the Union. It is nearly as difficult to imagine a similar group streaming out of Milledgeville or Raleigh, constitutional amendments in hand, to make similar demands on the Richmond government even in 1865.

Americans had, more or less, solved the practical problem of a loyal opposition in the aftermath of the War of 1812. Politicians had seen that there simply could not be a threat of another Hartford Convention looming in the future for every American war. They had come close enough to losing the War of 1812. Once the troops were in the field, the Congress had to vote supplies and both parties had best look as though they supported them with all necessary resources. That resolve became the most important part of America's unwritten constitution. Indeed, it proved vital to Abraham Lincoln's political survival, or his political career would have ended in 1849, well short of his presidency, the victim of opposition to the Mexican-American War. But he had kept his eye always upon it and therefore remained a viable candidate.

As for the written Constitution, Americans did not set about solving the problems it had posed during the War of 1812. The Federalists were seen as the problem, not the Constitution. Yet there were very serious constitutional problems then. One standard constitutional history of the United States, for example, says this:

> Bitterly opposed to the War of 1812, Federalists seized on the issue of federal control of the state militia to challenge the authority of the general government. The Constitution dealt with the problem in a seemingly clear way by giving Congress the power "To provide for calling forth the Militia to execute the Laws of the Union, suppress Insurrections, and repel Invasions." Congress was also authorized "To provide for organizing, arming, and disciplining the Militia, and for governing such Part of them as may be employed in the Service of

the United States." Against the manifest intention of these provisions, several New England states under Federalist control refused to permit their militia to be commanded by federal officers or to become an integral part of the army of the United States. Furthermore, all of the New England states attempted to ban service of their militia outside their borders and in effect built up separate state armies for their own defense against British attack.[12]

To historians looking back on the weaknesses of the United States in the War of 1812, the problem did not appear to be the Constitution but the military and economic backwardness of the infant United States. Because the dangerous constitutional conflicts of the War of 1812 have been substantially overlooked, the idea that the Constitution might pose difficulties for an administration fighting a war seemed somehow a new problem of the 1860s. But it was not. It was not new and, more important, *it may not have been any more a problem in 1861 than in 1812.* What we need is a book called "Constitutional Problems under Madison."

The modern *Encyclopedia of the War of 1812* has no article on the role of the Constitution in the war.[13] Likewise, a book-length annotated bibliography published in 1985 contains no entry for the Constitution in the index, and the section on "The Internal Scene" does not cite a single work on the Constitution.[14] The sense of profound, new, and unsolved constitutional problems that plagued the nation's war effort in 1812 has been substantially lost. For example, the heritage of protection for "infant" soldiers was left as a legacy of the War of 1812 and weighed as a burden on the conscientious judges of the Civil War period.

Because of the neglect of the War of 1812, the great modern historian of the Constitution in Civil War and Reconstruction, Harold M. Hyman, could write: "America's unusually happy domestic history during the War of 1812 and the Mexican War, as well as its Constitution, justified the assumption that armies were susceptible to civilians' controls and that soldiers need not gall civilian populations."[15] The problems in the War of 1812 ran in quite the other direction, with civilians in the New England states frustrating the demands of the commander in chief and the army. The unhappiness of the Federalists then verged on consideration of nullification and secession.[16] Neither the Confederate nor the Union opposition grew so frustrated, even though the wars were notably similar in offering little role to the opposition party in Congress, and the South had a strong nullification heritage to boot. Both the War of 1812 and the Civil War commenced roughly at the beginning of a presidential term, and for Federalists in the one and for Democrats in the other the four-year constitutionally mandated term stretched out as a period of frustrating powerlessness to determine strategy or policy for the war.

The trend to ignore constitutional problems in the War of 1812 and to overperceive them, perhaps, in the Civil War, is greatly accentuated by the tight focus on First Amendment freedoms and especially by the problem of free speech in wartime. I began with such a focus myself, writing in the 1980s and 1990s on Lincoln and civil liberties. Here is another example of the focus. Law professor Geoffrey R. Stone's influential *Perilous Times: Free Speech in Wartime from the Sedition Act of 1798 to the War on Terrorism*, later abridged under the broader title, *War and Liberty: An American Dilemma 1790 to the Present*, devotes its first chapter to the quasi-war with France, because of the importance of the Alien and Sedition Acts, which were a response to it, and the second chapter to the Civil War. The first chapter describes the Early Republic as "the time when the United States first faced the challenge of reconciling the Constitution with the perceived necessities of wartime."[17] The remainder of the book makes it seem as though the Constitution is the First Amendment only and hence something to be "reconciled" with war. But the relationship of the Constitution to war is greater and broader than issues of freedom of speech and the press. The Constitution identifies and defines war and types of war, describes the forces to be mobilized to fight, and says who shall mobilize and deploy them. It is true that the War of 1812 was relatively free of problems over free speech, but it is not true that it was waged in freedom from constitutional problems.[18]

I was convinced, when I completed this book, that it should be only the beginning and not the end. I hope it will be the beginning of something greater than renewed attention to the constitutional history of the Civil War. I would like to see it launch a new series of titles, beginning with "Constitutional Problems under Madison" and stretching through all of our wars until we have accumulated a shelf of volumes that reconsider the role of the Constitution in America's wars.

Notes

Prologue

1   See, e.g., Woden Teachout's *Capture the Flag*. Her title gave me the term used in the title of this prologue.
2   Weakly observed in scattered places today, "Constitution Day" is hardly the equal of the other famous holidays. For a time in the twentieth century it was touted as an anticommunist landmark on the calendar. On its conservative meaning, see Kammen, *A Machine That Would Go of Itself*, 220–23, 385.
3   *Harrisburg Patriot and Union*, August 16, 1862. Though noted in history for his insistent insertion of race as an issue into political rhetoric in Pennsylvania during the war, Hughes sought other resonant themes around which to revive the Democratic Party in the state. See Dusinberre, *Civil War Issues in Philadelphia*, 139, 179.
4   *Harrisburg Patriot and Union*, September 18, 1862.
5   *Pittsburgh Post*, September 19, 1862.
6   *Pittsburgh Post*, August 20, 1863.
7   *Pittsburgh Post*, September 18, 19, 21, 1863.
8   *Pittsburgh Post*, September 23, 1863.
9   *New York Herald*, September 19, 1864.
10 George B. McClellan to Samuel S. Cox, February 12, 1864, in Sears, *Civil War Papers of George B. McClellan*, 565.
11 *Pittsburgh Post*, September 26, 1868 (weekly ed.).
12 *Pittsburgh Post*, September 17, 18, 1868.
13 *Pittsburgh Post*, September 16, 17, 18, 1872.
14 This is the point of Kammen, *A Machine That Would Go of Itself*.
15 Silbey, *A Respectable Minority*, 72, 106.
16 Peterson, *Jefferson: Writings*, 449–56. I am indebted to Levy, *Jefferson and Civil Liberties*, esp. 56, for analysis of Jefferson's position.
17 Peterson, *Jefferson: Writings*, 449.
18 Schlesinger, *History of American Presidential Elections*, 2:953.
19 *Cleveland Plain Dealer*, March 24, 1864.
20 *Pittsburgh Post*, September 19, 1862.
21 Neely, *Boundaries of American Political Culture*, 88.
22 *Harrisburg Patriot and Union*, August 16, 1862.
23 *Pittsburgh Post*, September 23, 1863.
24 *National Intelligencer*, September 29, 1864.
25 That is substantially the point of Hyman, *A More Perfect Union*.
26 For the motto's first use during the war, see the report of the Union rally in the *New York Herald*, April 21, 1861.
27 For these distinctions, see Snay, *Fenians, Freedmen, and Southern Whites*, chaps. 4, 5.
28 For the use of that term, see Anderson, *Imagined Communities*.
29 Altschuler and Blumin, *Rude Republic*, 165.
30 Lawson, *Patriot Fires*, 164.

31   *New York Evening Post,* July 8, 1863. On loyalty scares, see Fredrickson, *Inner Civil War,* 130–50.
32   *New York Evening Post,* July 8, 1863.
33   On the importance of these somewhat neglected elections, see Holt, "An Elusive Synthesis," 123.
34   *Cleveland Plain Dealer,* June 30, 1864.
35   *Cleveland Plain Dealer,* July 5, 1864.
36   Ibid.
37   I myself made the mistake of so framing the question until I read Benedict Anderson's *Imagined Communities.* See, e.g., Neely, "Abraham Lincoln's Nationalism Reconsidered."
38   Anderson, *Imagined Communities,* 141.

Introduction

1   John W. Burgess's two-volume work comes immediately to mind, but it was actually a narrative history of the Civil War with one chapter in the second volume entitled "Interpretation of the Constitution under the Stress of the Military Events of 1862 and 1863" and another five-page chapter on "The President's Order Executing the Emancipation Proclamation." He devoted four paragraphs of the two-volume study to the Confederate Constitution, focusing most of his attention on the provision in the document forbidding the reopening of the African slave trade. See Burgess, *Civil War and the Constitution,* esp. 1:117–19. Nevins, Robertson, and Wiley, in *Civil War Books,* 1:107, accurately describe it as "heavy on the military and political history of the war."
2   Kelly, Harbison, and Belz, *American Constitution,* for example, a standard modern text and an exemplary one, devotes one of thirty-six chapters — fewer than thirty pages — to the Civil War. Within that space, the authors offer six paragraphs (pp. 186–87) on the provisions of the Confederate document but afterward simply nothing about its development over the eventful four-year history of the Confederacy. The text studies the "origin and development" of the "American Constitution." An excellent brief text, Benedict, *Blessings of Liberty,* treats the Confederacy only as an object of Union policies; it provides no discussion of America's "other" Constitution or its development.
3   Hyman, *A More Perfect Union,* 104.
4   Randall, *Constitutional Problems under Lincoln,* first appeared in 1926. Neff, *Justice in Blue and Gray,* the most recent history (2010), offers a "legal history of the Civil War." But by that the author means mainly a history of the war from the standpoint of international law, analyzing what was legal and illegal in the practices of the generals and statesmen. Only two of the ten chapters deal with constitutional history, and those are written from a standpoint innocent of political party considerations. Even in describing an instance in which the U.S. Supreme Court reversed a previous decision of its own because of changes in personnel on the court, Neff does not mention the party affiliations of the justices (see p. 50). On questions of the laws of war, however, the book is original, comprehensive, and of great value.
5   Stephens, *A Constitutional View of the Late War between the States,* was peculiarly animated by a desire to lay claim to a consistent constitutionalism in the South for the sake of resisting Reconstruction and thus minimized the constitutional conflicts within the Confederacy and between Jefferson Davis and Alexander Stephens himself. After a markedly brief discussion of what were, in fact, bitter differences between president

and vice president on constitutional and policy questions, Stephens hastened to say, "But enough on these subjects. . . . On all these points . . . the differences between Mr. Davis and myself were in no respect . . . unlike those differences which often occur between the several Members of the same Cabinet, where all are equally earnest and sincere in their efforts to promote a common object" (2:574–75). The book is cast in the form of a debate with an imaginary judge, and one standard bibliography of Civil War books characterizes it this way: "Like Davis, who might have delivered a reminiscence of real value, Stephens presents a defensive and illogical rationalization and apologia for the actions of the Confederacy." Eicher, *The Civil War in Books*, 61–62, from which I borrow the term "apologia."

6 Owsley, *State Rights in the Confederacy*, was published in 1925. Owsley did not mention the Confederate Constitution until well over a fourth of the way into the book (p. 84); he never described the Constitution, and he referred to only two state supreme court cases, identifying neither of them by name or date. The book is actually about political conflicts.

7 There are two books on the origin and writing of the Confederate Constitution: De-Rosa's *Confederate Constitution of 1861*, and Charles Robert Lee's *Confederate Constitutions*. They are not constitutional histories that describe at length the uses and development of the Confederate Constitution after it was written, though DeRosa offers a useful and compact survey of constitutional developments at pp. 112–19.

8 On the War of 1812, see the epilogue of this book. See also Tutorow, *The Mexican-American War: An Annotated Bibliography*.

9 This point is reinforced by Neff, *Justice in Blue and Gray*, esp. 52–55.

10 Widmer, *American Speeches*, 195.

11 Freidel, *Union Pamphlets*, 1:4–5. George M. Fredrickson, in his *Inner Civil War*, 130–33, similarly noted the rise of "the doctrine of loyalty" in the North in the first three months of 1863.

12 Neely, *Last Best Hope of Earth*, 172.

13 Silbey, *American Political Nation*, 144–45.

14 Perry, *Life and Letters of Francis Lieber*, 330.

15 Robert C. Grier to John Cadwalader, January 21, 1862, Cadwalader Collection, ser. 6 (Judge John Cadwalader), box 268, Historical Society of Pennsylvania, Philadelphia. This reference was generously supplied by Professor Jonathan W. White of Christopher Newport University.

16 *New York Evening Post*, April 7, 1863. An advertisement for the pamphlet appeared in the issue of February 13, 1863.

17 Silbey, *A Respectable Minority*, 257.

18 Silbey, *American Party Battle*, 1:xii.

19 Ibid., 1:xv.

20 Ibid., 1:xvi.

21 Dimunation and Engst, *Legacy of Ideas*. My thanks to Elaine D. Engst, Director of the Division of Rare and Manuscript Collections and University Archivist at Cornell, for personal help in understanding the place of the White pamphlets in the collection.

22 Thanks to James P. Quigel Jr., Associate Librarian, and Sandra Stelts, Curator of Rare Books and Manuscripts, of the Special Collections Library at Penn State University for a tour of the Pamphlets of the John M. Read Collection, which spanned perhaps three decades of collecting and specialized also in transportation law and constitutional discourse.

23   Crandall, *Confederate Imprints*, xii.

24   Freidel, *Union Pamphlets*, 1:1. Joel Silbey, who was a pioneer of the New Political History, was also keenly interested in pamphlets and edited a collection of them.

25   Ibid., 1:2.

26   Bailyn's ideas were later embodied in an extremely influential book, Bailyn, *Ideological Origins of the American Revolution*.

27   Orwell quoted in ibid., 2.

Chapter 1

1   Peterson, *Jefferson: Writings*, 1371.

2   Basler, *Collected Works of Abraham Lincoln*, 4:235–36.

3   Ibid., 1:488.

4   Ibid., 2:245.

5   See Boritt, *Lincoln and the Economics of the American Dream*, 38–39. Boritt's book revolutionized the study of Lincoln's life, pointing to the importance and coherence of his economic vision. Boritt was more interested in Lincoln's economic ideas than in how he viewed nationalism or the Constitution.

6   Holt, *Political Crisis of the 1850s*, 112.

7   Basler, *Collected Works of Abraham Lincoln*, 1:488.

8   Neely, "War and Partisanship," 207–8. Northern Whig leader Daniel Webster began as a Federalist in politics and thus, unlike Clay, opposed the War of 1812. It is important to remember that these positions preceded the formation of the Whig Party and that that party had no record or established positions on national wars before the Mexican-American War.

9   Basler, *Collected Works of Abraham Lincoln*, 1:476.

10   Ibid., 4:66.

11   Riddle, *Congressman Abraham Lincoln*, 42.

12   Basler, *Collected Works of Abraham Lincoln*, 4:66. These statements also appeared in the material supplied by Lincoln to a presidential campaign biographer in 1860.

13   Ibid., 1:451–52.

14   I follow the excellent treatment of this case in Stowell, *Papers of Abraham Lincoln*, 3:308–16.

15   Ibid., 3:342–43.

16   Ibid., 3:360.

17   Ibid., 3:376.

18   The case resulted in a hung jury. For a brilliant but very unfavorable view of the work the law accomplished for capitalism during that period, see Horwitz, *Transformation of American Law*. For a more favorable appraisal of the work of lawyers like Lincoln in enabling the growth of capitalism, see the argument relying on legal scholar J. Willard Hurst in Boritt, *Lincoln and the Economics of the American Dream*, 152. The most hostile view is taken by Sellers, *The Market Revolution*, esp. 47. None lays adequate emphasis on nationalism in cases like Lincoln's.

19   Stowell, *Papers of Abraham Lincoln*, 3:360.

20   Basler, *Collected Works of Abraham Lincoln*, 8:402–3.

21   Abraham Lincoln to Thurlow Weed, December 17, 1860, ibid., 4:154.

22   Abraham Lincoln to James Watson Webb, December 29, 1860, ibid., 4:164.

23   Stampp, "Concept of a Perpetual Union," 3–36.

24   Fehrenbacher, *Dred Scott Case*, 27.

25   Wilson and Davis, *Herndon's Lincoln*, 287.

26   Basler, *Collected Works of Abraham Lincoln*, 4:264.

27   Ibid., 4:265.

28   Ibid. Lincoln got the date of the Articles of Confederation wrong. They were accepted by Congress to be ratified by the states in 1777. In 1781 Maryland, the last to act positively, consented to the confederation.

29   Abraham Lincoln to James N. Brown, October 18, 1858, in Basler, *Collected Works of Abraham Lincoln*, 3:327.

30   Speech at Springfield, Ill., June 26, 1857, in ibid., 2:406.

31   Constitutional scholar Akhil Reed Amar says that "Lincoln . . . stood on rock-solid ground in the 1860s." Amar, *America's Constitution*, 472.

32   In his message to the special session of Congress of July 4, 1861, Lincoln asserted that "no one of our States, except Texas, ever was a sovereignty." Basler, *Collected Works of Abraham Lincoln*, 4:434.

33   Jensen, *Articles of Confederation*, 236–37.

34   On the origins of the speech, see Douglas Wilson, *Lincoln's Sword*, 44–70. Wilson is concerned only with the "tone" of the speech, not its arguments or policy content.

35   Wilson and Davis, *Herndon's Lincoln*, 287.

36   Goodwin, *Biography of Andrew Jackson*, 421.

37   Ibid., 433.

38   On the use of Daniel Webster as a source for the speech, see Douglas Wilson, *Lincoln's Sword*, 304n.

39   Stampp, "Concept of a Perpetual Union," 34–35. Lincoln's uses of the language of the U.S. Constitution caused the *London Times* to complain that the "speech takes up grounds strictly constitutional" and that Lincoln could not free himself from the "shackles of a merely legal mind." Quoted in *New York Times*, April 3, 1861.

40   Basler, *Collected Works of Abraham Lincoln*, 4:265–66.

41   Speech in the Senate, February 5, 6, 1850, in Hay, *Papers of Henry Clay*, 672. This important speech is only summarized in the volume of the Clay Papers cited here. For the complete text, see Widmer, *American Speeches*, 387–454.

42   Basler, *Collected Works of Abraham Lincoln*, 4:269.

43   Colton, *Speeches of Henry Clay*, 2:554.

44   Goodwin, *Biography of Andrew Jackson*, 429.

45   The reading of dictatorial tendencies into Lincoln's most noticeable early speech, the Address before the Young Men's Lyceum of Springfield, Ill., of January 27, 1838, is misleading and does not account for abundant contrary evidence. For the original statement of this wrongheaded view, see Edmund Wilson, *Patriotic Gore*, 106–8. Several historians have followed in Wilson's path of interpretation.

46   Basler, *Collected Works of Abraham Lincoln*, 4:268.

47   This is the heart of the argument in Bestor's famous article, "The American Civil War as a Constitutional Crisis."

48   Kenneth Stampp, for example, asserted: "He made no original contribution to the classical nationalist argument when he attempted to prove that 'the Union of these States is perpetual.'" Stampp, *And the War Came*, 200.

49   Actually the Constitution reads: "This Constitution, and the Laws of the United States which shall be made in Pursuance thereof; and all Treaties made, or which shall be made, under the Authority of the United States, shall be the supreme Law of the Land." For Webster's words, see Wiltse, *Papers of Daniel Webster*, 341. The judicial power in Article III is actually described thus in the Constitution: "The judicial Power shall

extend to all Cases, in Law and Equity, arising under this Constitution, the Laws of the United States, and Treaties made, or which shall be made, under their Authority."

50 Basler, *Collected Works of Abraham Lincoln*, 4:268. The language Lincoln used in his original draft was much stronger in its denunciation of the Court. See Douglas Wilson, *Lincoln's Sword*, 63–64.

51 The democratic nature of the content of the speech was particularly noted by the *London Star*; see *New York Times*, April 3, 1861.

52 I am grateful to constitutional historian Jonathan W. White for pointing out to me the relevance of Lincoln's speech in opposition to the *Dred Scott* decision.

53 The words are Lincoln's paraphrase of Douglas's accusations. See Basler, *Collected Works of Abraham Lincoln*, 2:400.

54 Ibid., 2:402.

55 Ibid., 2:401.

56 Kramer, *The People Themselves*.

57 Wiltse, *Papers of Daniel Webster*, 332.

58 Benedict, *Blessings of Liberty*, 172–73. Such ideas are compatible with the reigning paradigm for the intellectual developments of the Civil War as representing conservative reaction. That thesis was first argued by George M. Fredrickson in his *Inner Civil War* (1965).

59 The modern idea that nationalism was made and did not grow has led to a tendency to see nationalism and its traditions invented in very modern times by forceful leaders and by the press. See in addition to Benedict Anderson, *Imagined Communities* (1983), discussed below, two other influential books published the same year: Ernest Gellner, *Nations and Nationalism*, and Eric J. Hobsbawm and Terence Ranger, *The Invention of Tradition*. For application of the ideas to the American Civil War, see Melinda R. Lawson, *Patriot Fires*. "Agents of Civil War nation-building," says Lawson, "brought more European-style tools to their task, depicting the nation in more traditional, historical, and cultural terms" (p. 4).

60 Anderson, *Imagined Communities*, 141.

61 Basler, *Collected Works of Abraham Lincoln*, 4:271.

62 James G. Randall, in *Lincoln the President: Springfield to Gettysburg*, 1:301–2, appears to recognize the distinct difference in this last passage of Lincoln's address.

63 Nicolay and Hay, *Abraham Lincoln*, 3:321. See also Douglas Wilson, *Lincoln's Sword*, 64–65.

64 Ronald C. White Jr. says, "It is a fair question whether Lincoln trusted too much in the power of rational argument" in the First Inaugural Address. White, *The Eloquent President*, 97.

65 *New York Herald*, March 5, 1861.

66 *New York Tribune*, March 6, 1861.

67 Quoted in ibid. Among the numerous papers quoted on the address by the *Tribune*, the *Providence Post* also singled out the "argument against the right of secession" as one of the better parts.

68 Randall, *Lincoln the President: Springfield to Gettysburg*, 1:298–310. Even philosophically inclined historians like William Lee Miller do not show great interest in the nationalist arguments. See Miller, *President Lincoln*, 10–12, 19–28. Guelzo, in *Abraham Lincoln: Redeemer President*, dismisses the speech as a "mixture of the obvious and the hopeful" (p. 264).

69 Amar, *America's Constitution*, 627–28n.

70 Basler, *Collected Works of Abraham Lincoln*, 4:265.

71   Ibid., 4:195–96. David Potter first noticed the starkly unsentimental nature of that defi-
     nition of a state in *The Impending Crisis*, 560–61.
72   Basler, *Collected Works of Abraham Lincoln*, 4:195.
73   Foner and Taylor, *Frederick Douglass*, 438.
74   Even James Oakes, whose book deals directly with the relationship between Lincoln
     and Douglass, notes only that Douglass hated the address for its apparent moral indif-
     ference to slavery. See Oakes, *The Radical and the Republican*, 142. William Lee Miller
     quotes from it in a footnote in *President Lincoln*, 11n. Earlier Lincoln books generally
     did not seek Douglass's texts for comment on Lincoln. For example, Douglass receives
     one sentence in the first two volumes of Randall's *Lincoln the President: Springfield to
     Gettysburg*.
75   Foner and Taylor, *Frederick Douglass*, 433.
76   Oakes, *The Radical and the Republican*, 18–19.
77   Foner and Taylor, *Frederick Douglass*, 437.
78   Ibid.; Kramer, *The People Themselves*.
79   Donald, *Lincoln*, 283. William Lee Miller was struck by this able interpretation of the
     original draft, too. See Miller, *President Lincoln*, 21–22.
80   Foner and Taylor, *Frederick Douglass*, 438.
81   Douglas Wilson, *Lincoln's Sword*, 48.
82   Basler, *Collected Works of Abraham Lincoln*, 4:253, 265.
83   Schlesinger, *History of American Presidential Elections*, 2:1125.
84   Basler, *Collected Works of Abraham Lincoln*, 4:250, 262.
85   Lawson, *Patriot Fires*, 144.
86   Marx and Engels, *Civil War in the United States*, 258. For the opposite view of the power
     of words, see McPherson, *How Lincoln Won the War with Metaphors*. Douglas Wilson,
     Lincoln's Sword, supplies the image and lengthy and careful analysis of language.
87   Douglas Wilson, *Lincoln's Sword*, 76.
88   Basler, *Collected Works of Abraham Lincoln*, 4:440.
89   Ibid., 4:436.
90   Ibid.
91   Ibid., 4:432–33.
92   Ibid., 4:434–35.
93   Ibid., esp. 4:432–36.
94   *New York Times*, July 6, 1861.
95   *New York Tribune*, July 4, 1861.
96   *New York Herald*, July 6, 1861.
97   *Philadelphia Inquirer*, July 3, 1861.
98   *Philadelphia Inquirer*, July 6, 1861.
99   Jonathan W. White, *Philadelphia Perspective*, 102–3. Fisher's own eccentric ideas on
     the nation are discussed at length in Chapter 2.
100 *Chicago Tribune*, July 6, 1861.
101 Foner and Taylor, *Frederick Douglass*, 464–65.

Chapter 2

1   Basler, *Collected Works of Abraham Lincoln*, 5:49.
2   Indeed, by 1865 Lincoln regarded the question of the status of the states after secession
    as a "pernicious abstraction." See his last speech, in ibid., 8:402–3.
3   Ibid., 4:437.

4   Ibid., 5:51–52.

5   Ibid., 4:426.

6   Ibid., 4:430, 6:266.

7   Randall, *Constitutional Problems under Lincoln*, 118.

8   Farber, *Lincoln's Constitution*, 158.

9   Swisher, *Roger B. Taney*, 554. The question of the secession of Maryland was as yet a wide-open one, and there was therefore room in Taney's statement for his identification with a Confederate nationalism and his imagining himself, a Marylander, as a citizen of a Southern republic, in the eventuality of a successful separation, rather than as a citizen of a Northern republic looking across the Potomac at a Southern one.

10   For more on the conflict in the *Merryman* case, see Neely, "The Constitution and Civil Liberties."

11   Indeed, *Merryman* garnered little fame in the nineteenth century. John A. Marshall's *American Bastile*, an 858-page monument to the martyrs of the internal security policies of the Lincoln administration, did not feature the *Merryman* case among the 98 examples written about in the book, nor did it mention Taney's decision as a bulwark of individual liberty. In Alexander Johnston's entry on habeas corpus in a forerunner of the modern *Encyclopedia of the Social Sciences*, John J. Lalor's *Cyclopaedia of Political Science*, 2:43, *Merryman* is mentioned, but the article says only that Taney referred the case to the president once his writ was ignored (and does not describe or even refer to the written opinion).

12   Parker, *Habeas Corpus and Martial Law*, 19.

13   Ibid., 32.

14   Parker, *Habeas Corpus and Martial Law*, 35; Nicholas, *Martial Law*, 4.

15   For a brilliant article foreshadowing the historical realization of the importance of the Adams precedent, see David Donald, "Abraham Lincoln: Whig in the White House," in his *Lincoln Reconsidered*, 204–6.

16   Parker, *Habeas Corpus and Martial Law*, 44.

17   Paludan, *Covenant with Death*, 131.

18   Parker, *Habeas Corpus and Martial Law*, 20.

19   *Ex parte Merryman*, 17 F. Cas. 144 (1861), LexisNexis, p. 6.

20   Parker, *Habeas Corpus and Martial Law*, 3–4.

21   *Baltimore American*, May 14, 1861.

22   *Baltimore American*, May 2, 1861.

23   *Baltimore American*, May 6, 1861.

24   *Baltimore American*, May 22, 23, 24, 1861.

25   Basler, *Collected Works of Abraham Lincoln*, 6:265–66.

26   I have written about the message at greater length in Neely, *Fate of Liberty*, 11–14.

27   Constitutional and legal history hue too closely to the courtroom and fail to offer a political and intellectual context. Binney is mentioned only briefly in McGinty, *Lincoln and the Court*, 79–80, and not at all in Neff, *Justice in Blue and Gray*. McGinty does a nice job of tracing Binney's readership among high-ranking judges. The best treatment of Binney's ideas, as is often the case for such questions, remains Randall, *Constitutional Problems under Lincoln*, 124–27.

28   Fredrickson, *Inner Civil War*, 141.

29   "To the president of the United States," broadside, 35 X 22 cm, Philadelphia, April 15, 1861, American Antiquarian Society, American Broadsides and Ephemera, ser. I, no. 11050, read electronically, January 19, 2008; also quoted in Charles Chauncey Binney, *Life of Horace Binney*, 326.

30 Charles Chauncey Binney, *Life of Horace Binney*, 333.

31 Ibid., 334–35.

32 *National Intelligencer*, June 22, 1861.

33 Freidel, *Francis Lieber*, 310–11.

34 Lieber, *On Civil Liberty and Self-Government*, 1:31.

35 Donald, *Lincoln Reconsidered*, 205, long ago recognized the inconsistencies.

36 Basler, *Collected Works of Abraham Lincoln*, 4:430.

37 Horace Binney, *Privilege of the Writ of Habeas Corpus*, in Freidel, *Union Pamphlets*, 1:231.

38 Ibid., 1:230.

39 Swisher, *Oliver Wendell Holmes Devise History*, 917–18. Swisher, Taney's sympathetic modern biographer, does not mention Binney's pamphlet in his biography of the chief justice, nor does he explain its substantive arguments when he does refer to the pamphlet in his much longer history of the Taney court.

40 Horace Binney, *Privilege of the Writ of Habeas Corpus*, in Freidel, *Union Pamphlets*, 1:231.

41 Fredrickson, *Inner Civil War*, 77.

42 Charles Chauncey Binney, *Life of Horace Binney*, 299 (from a letter to Francis Lieber, February 18, 1860).

43 Ibid., 369.

44 Ibid., 321, 360.

45 Ibid., 382–83, 398.

46 Ibid., 98.

47 *National Intelligencer*, October 27, 1832. The paper was actually commenting on a speech by Daniel Webster as well.

48 Ibid.

49 On the issue of disobeying a court order, see Farber, *Lincoln's Constitution*, 188–92.

50 Horace Binney to Abraham Lincoln, April 5, 1861, Lincoln Papers, Library of Congress, reel 20.

51 Basler, *Collected Works of Abraham Lincoln*, 8:373.

52 Hyman, *A More Perfect Union*, 132n, 140.

53 See *Memoir of the Hon. William Whiting*, 7–8.

54 Whiting, *War Powers of the President*, i–ii.

55 Ibid., iii. Whiting was referring particularly to Article I, section 8, clause 1.

56 I have benefited from conversations on this subject with William A. Blair, of the Penn State History Department, who is writing a book about treason in the Civil War.

57 Whiting, *War Powers of the President*, 12.

58 Paludan, *Covenant with Death*, 145–46.

59 Ibid., 17.

60 Ibid., 46.

61 Ibid., 60.

62 Ibid., 68.

63 Basler, *Collected Works of Abraham Lincoln*, 5:329.

64 Ibid., 7:433.

65 Neff, *Justice in Blue and Gray*, 58.

66 Hyman, *A More Perfect Union*, 190. Neff quotes this claim in his book.

67 Freidel, *Francis Lieber*, 329–32.

68 *Memoir of the Hon. William Whiting*, 1–5.

69 Ibid., 9.

70   Neff, *Justice in Blue and Gray*, 31.
71   Douglas Wilson, *Lincoln's Sword*, 162–63.
72   Basler, *Collected Works of Abraham Lincoln*, 6:266–67.
73   Ibid., 6:263–65.
74   Ibid., 6:265.
75   Ibid., 6:263n.
76   [Welles], *Diary of Gideon Welles*, 1:470.
77   Basler, *Collected Works of Abraham Lincoln*, 6:302–3.
78   For more on the Corning letter, see Neely, "The Constitution and Civil Liberties," 45–51.
79   Basler, *Collected Works of Abraham Lincoln*, 6:301n.
80   Ibid., 2:60.
81   Ibid., 4:341.
82   The argument was apparently put forward by S. S. Nicholas, *Habeas Corpus: The Law of War and Confiscation.*
83   Charles Chauncey Binney, *Life of Horace Binney*, 354.
84   Basler, *Collected Works of Abraham Lincoln*, 5:436–37.
85   Ibid., 6:451.
86   Parker, *To the People of Massachusetts*, 6–7. For more on the Dexter-Parker dispute, see Paludan, *Covenant with Death*, 150–51.
87   Parker, *Revolution and Reconstruction*, 10.
88   Ibid., 28.
89   Ibid., 29.
90   Paludan, *Covenant with Death*, 145–47.
91   Parker, *Three Powers of Government*, 14.
92   Parker, *Revolution and Reconstruction*, 10.
93   Randall, *Constitutional Problems under Lincoln*, 163–64.
94   Charles Chauncey Binney, *Life of Horace Binney*, 389–90.
95   Horace Binney, *Privilege of the Writ of Habeas Corpus . . . Third Part*, 60–61.
96   Ibid., 62.
97   Ibid., 22.
98   *Presidential Power over Personal Liberty*, 2–3, 26.
99   I am indebted for this point to Jonathan W. White, "The Trials of John Merryman," consulted in June 2010, p. 57 (now published as *Abraham Lincoln and Treason*). See *Ex parte Bollman and Swartwout*, 4 Cranch 75 (1807), p. 8.
100 *Ex parte Vallandigham* (1864) saw the Supreme Court answer a request for a writ of habeas corpus and then deny its jurisdiction because Clement Vallandigham had been sentenced by a military court and the Supreme Court could not review its decisions.
101 See Jonathan W. White, *Abraham Lincoln and Treason*.
102 Warshauer, *Andrew Jackson and the Politics of Martial Law.*
103 Basler, *Collected Works of Abraham Lincoln*, 6:269.
104 Swisher, *Oliver Wendell Holmes Devise History*, 851–52.
105 Curtis, *Executive Power*, 1:456.
106 Ibid., 1:460.
107 Ibid., 1:461.
108 Ibid., 1:468.
109 Ibid., 1:467–68.
110 Ibid., 1:472.
111 Ingersoll, "Personal Liberty and Martial Law: A Review of Some Pamphlets of the Day," in Freidel, *Union Pamphlets*, 1:274.

112 Basler, *Collected Works of Abraham Lincoln*, 8:254.

113 Hyman edited a modern edition of Fisher's book and devoted considerable space to him as well in *A More Perfect Union*, esp. 111–15 and 120–21. Randall did not take the approach of supplying an intellectual context for the ideas about the Constitution. It is unclear that he saw them as *developing* through time.

114 In the end, if all three of Binney's pamphlets were considered as one work, they too would equal a book. Whiting's pamphlets defending the president added up to a book as well.

115 Francis Lieber had the time as well, for he was a law professor at Columbia, but he appears to have worked slowly and to have spent his force as a writer of substantial works in the texts he wrote before the war. He did signal service directly to the war effort by drafting brief codes for guerrilla warfare and for covering the laws of war in general during the war. He also was heavily involved in the Northern pamphleteering operations of the Loyal Publication Society. Surprisingly, then, Lieber played the most active role of all the constitutional intellectuals. Thus he was a forerunner of political science and a forerunner of the intellectual in service to the state in wartime—anticipating the Progressive Era in both capacities.

116 Fredrickson, *Black Image in the White Mind*, 69–70, 92–96.

117 Paludan, *Covenant with Death*, 193.

118 Fisher, *Trial of the Constitution*, 33–34.

119 He did read in it. See Jonathan W. White, *Philadelphia Perspective*, 72.

120 Fisher, *Trial of the Constitution*, 218.

121 Ibid., 237–38.

122 Ibid., 160–61.

123 Anderson, *Imagined Communities*, 9–10.

124 Charles Chauncey Binney, *Life of Horace Binney*, 375–76.

125 Nevins, *War for the Union*, 72.

126 Benedict, *Blessings of Liberty*, 187–89; Brock, *American Crisis*, 271–73.

127 Woodrow Wilson, *Congressional Government*.

128 Paludan, *Covenant with Death*, 44.

129 Hyman, *A More Perfect Union*, 551.

130 See Schneider, *Lincoln's Defense of Politics*, 125–44.

131 The best evidence for this comes from policies pursued in Missouri. See Neely, "The Constitution and Civil Liberties," 51–61.

132 Hyman, *A More Perfect Union*, notes Fisher's "distinguished mentorship in the law" (p. 110).

Chapter 3

1 That the Constitution was hijacked is the thesis of Don E. Fehrenbacher's brilliant book, *The Dred Scott Case: Its Significance in American Law and Politics*.

2 Urofsky and Finkelman, *Documents of American Constitutional and Legal History*, 1:378.

3 Berwanger, *Frontier against Slavery*, 45. See also Thornbrough, *The Negro in Indiana*, 58, 68.

4 Wubben, *Civil War Iowa*, 7.

5 Berwanger, *Frontier against Slavery*, 32.

6 Ibid., 45.

7 Ibid., 93.

8 Ibid., 95.

9 Fehrenbacher, *Dred Scott Case*, 347–48.

10 See Thornbrough, *The Negro in Indiana*, 58–63, 71–72, for cases reaching the Indiana Supreme Court. One of these cases was decided during the Civil War.

11 Basler, *Collected Works of Abraham Lincoln*, 3:9.

12 Ibid., 3:10–11.

13 See Holt, *Political Crisis of the 1850s*, 5, 152–54.

14 Basler, *Collected Works of Abraham Lincoln*, 2:467.

15 Fehrenbacher, *Dred Scott Case*, 438. "It was at most a potential danger," Fehrenbacher admitted.

16 Foner, *Free Soil, Free Labor, Free Men*, 97–98.

17 Basler, *Collected Works of Abraham Lincoln*, 3:53–54.

18 See Boucher, "In Re That Aggressive Slaveocracy." For a modern attempt to revive the Slave Power idea, see esp. Richards, *Slave Power*.

19 Thornbrough, *The Negro in Indiana*, 84.

20 Neely, "Colonization and the Myth," 57–60.

21 Basler, *Collected Works of Abraham Lincoln*, 2:231.

22 Ibid., 5:48.

23 Ibid.

24 Ibid., 2:268.

25 See Neely, *The Union Divided*, esp. 194–97.

26 Guelzo, *Lincoln's Emancipation Proclamation*, 22–23.

27 Randall, *Constitutional Problems under Lincoln*, 365.

28 Ibid., 370. Randall was careful to add, in the end, that Lincoln's "circumspection . . . should not be regarded as dimming his intense conviction as to the moral wrong and shameful social abuse of slavery. . . . These sentiments were among the deep fundamentals of Lincoln's liberal thought."

29 Basler, *Collected Works of Abraham Lincoln*, 2:268–69.

30 Ibid.

31 Ibid., 4:263.

32 Ibid., 4:518.

33 Ibid., 4:531.

34 Ibid., 5:222–23.

35 Ibid.

36 Ibid., 5:388.

37 Donald, *Lincoln*.

38 McPherson, "What Did He Really Think about Race?" 18–19.

39 Basler, *Collected Works of Abraham Lincoln*, 5:371–72, 374.

40 Ibid., 5:420. I have written about Lincoln's inept preparation of public opinion before the proclamation in "Colonization and the Myth That Lincoln Prepared the People for Emancipation."

41 I borrow the phrase from Peter Gay, *A Loss of Mastery: Puritan Historians in Colonial America* (Berkeley: University of California Press, 1966).

42 Neely, *Fate of Liberty*, 52–53.

43 Ibid., 61.

44 Some historians would point to a similar period while he was a member of Congress. See Riddle, *Congressman Abraham Lincoln*, and Beveridge, *Abraham Lincoln, 1809–1858*.

45 Basler, *Collected Works of Abraham Lincoln*, 5:437–38.

46 Ibid., 5:444. Although it is difficult to separate the effects of the Battle of Antietam from the effects of the Emancipation Proclamation, Lincoln's point about the stock market appears to be inaccurate.

47 Ibid., 5:530.

48 Ibid., 5:536.

49 [Welles], *Diary of Gideon Welles*, 1:150. Treasury secretary Chase did not mention the proclamation of September 24 in his diary. Niven, *Salmon P. Chase Papers*, 399–402.

50 Curtis, *Executive Power*, 1:451–52.

51 Ibid., 1:452–53.

52 Ibid., 1:451.

53 Basler, *Collected Works of Abraham Lincoln*, 6:408.

54 Curtis, *Executive Power*, 1:463.

55 Ibid.

56 *The Case of Dred Scott.*

57 Kirkland, *A Letter to the Hon. Benjamin R. Curtis*, 4.

58 Ibid., 3.

59 Ibid., 9–10.

60 Ibid., 6–7, 12.

61 Ibid., 12–13.

62 Ibid., 7.

63 Ibid., 15.

64 Lowrey, *The Commander-in-Chief.* The first edition was published by G. P. Putnam in 1862, and the second, three pages longer, came from the same publisher. I have used the second edition, which was reprinted in Freidel, *Union Pamphlets*, 474–502.

65 Ibid., 485.

66 Ibid., 493n–94n.

67 Ibid., 481–82.

68 Ibid., 492.

69 Ibid., 497.

70 Ibid.

71 Basler, *Collected Works of Abraham Lincoln*, 6:30.

72 Lowrey, *The Commander-in-Chief*, 499. The second edition of Lowrey's pamphlet included an answer to criticism of the president's suspension of the writ of habeas corpus. He confined it to a very long footnote and relied on quoting the War Department's solicitor, William Whiting.

73 Ibid., 488.

74 An exception, though not exactly a partisan use, is the reference to the example of the Mexican-American War in the *Prize Cases* discussed in the next chapter.

75 Basler, *Collected Works of Abraham Lincoln*, 2:472n.

76 Abraham Lincoln to Joseph Medill, June 25, 1858, in ibid., 2:474.

77 Ibid., 6:301n.

78 Ibid., 6:302.

79 *New York Times*, June 8, 1861. Thus New Yorkers like Kirkland and Lowrey might have read about these cases in the *Times*.

80 *Cross v. Harrison*, 16 How. 164 (1853), p. 14.

81 Ibid., p. 20.

82 Ibid.

83 Lowrey, *The Commander-in-Chief*, 485.

84 Curtis, *Executive Power*, 1:463–64n.

85 Ibid., 1:464n.

86 Lowrey, *The Commander-in-Chief*, 501.

87 *Mitchell v. Harmony*, 13 How. 115 (1851), p. 16.

88 Curtis, *Executive Power*, 1:467–68.

89 Ibid., 1:468.

90 Keegan, *Mask of Command*, 164–234.

91 Hyman, *A More Perfect Union*.

92 Guelzo, *Lincoln's Emancipation Proclamation*, 222.

93 Basler, *Collected Works of Abraham Lincoln*, 2:126.

94 Lyman Trumbull to Abraham Lincoln, September 7, 1862, Lincoln Papers, Library of Congress, reel 41.

95 Basler, *Collected Works of Abraham Lincoln*, 4:506.

96 Ibid., 4:532.

97 Ibid., 5:371–74.

98 Foner and Taylor, *Frederick Douglass*, 519.

99 Basler, *Collected Works of Abraham Lincoln*, 5:423.

100 *New York Times*, September 28, 1862. The *Times* had reported the president's reply to the Chicago clergymen two days earlier, on September 26.

101 Guelzo, in *Lincoln's Emancipation Proclamation*, 182–87, stresses the disloyalty provoked.

102 Foner and Taylor, *Frederick Douglass*, 519.

103 John M. Palmer to David Davis, November 26, 1862, Lincoln Papers, Library of Congress, reel 44.

104 McPherson, *For Cause and Comrades*, viii.

105 Holt, "An Elusive Synthesis," 124.

106 See Fredrickson, *Inner Civil War*, 130–50 (on loyalty).

107 Neely, *The Union Divided*, 41–47.

108 Timothy J. Orr, "'A Viler Enemy in Our Rear,'" 171–98. There were at least sixteen Pennsylvania regiments making resolutions. See also Warshauer, *Connecticut in the American Civil War*, 106–15.

109 Johannsen, *Stephen A. Douglas*, 642.

110 Ibid., 673.

111 Basler, *Collected Works of Abraham Lincoln*, 2:399.

112 Gillette, *Jersey Blue*, 203, 231–32.

113 *Harrisburg Telegraph*, February 7, 1863.

114 Wubben, *Civil War Iowa*, 7.

115 Voegli, *Free but Not Equal*, 166.

116 McLauchlan, *Indiana State Constitution*, 19.

117 Cole, *Era of the Civil War*, 271–72, 335.

118 Douglas, who died in 1861, also left a legacy of nationalism to his party with his statements of determination to quell rebellion first, save the country, and then resume arguments over partisan differences. "There can be no neutrals in this war, *only patriots — or traitors*," he said in Chicago on May 1, 1861. See Johannsen, *Stephen A. Douglas*, 862–68.

Chapter 4

1 Anbinder, "Which Poor Man's Fight?," 352.

2 Neely, *Fate of Liberty*, 109–12.

3   Horace Binney, *Privilege of the Writ of Habeas Corpus . . . : Third Part*, 62.

4   Marten, *The Children's Civil War*, 2.

5   Swisher, *Oliver Wendell Holmes Devise History*, 746.

6   Randall and Current, *Last Full Measure*, 268–69.

7   Kelly, Harbison, and Belz, *American Constitution*, 1:A115–A132 (I exclude *Merryman*).

8   Swisher, *Oliver Wendell Holmes Devise History*, 335–38, 929–30.

9   For a balanced assessment of the *Prize Cases* and the development of presidential power during the Civil War, see Kelly, Harbison, and Belz, *American Constitution*, 1:299–301.

10   On the notorious naval rendezvous in New York, see Lafayette Baker, *United States Secret Service*, 399.

11   Hickey, *War of 1812*, 243–44.

12   *Pittsburgh Gazette*, August 30, 1862.

13   *Kneedler v. Lane*, 45 Pa. 238 (1863), p. 22.

14   Morison, "Dissent in the War of 1812," 3, terms that war the most unpopular.

15   *Commonwealth v. Cushing*, 11 Mass. 67 (1814). See also *Commonwealth v. Harrison*, 11 Mass. 63 (1814). For a contrary opinion from James Kent in a New York case, see *In re Jeremiah Ferguson*, 9 Johns. 239 (1812). For an important Mexican-American War case, see *Commonwealth ex rel. Webster v. Fox*, 7 Pa. 336 (1847).

16   *Commonwealth v. Harrison*, 11 Mass. 63 (1814).

17   *In re Jeremiah Ferguson*, 9 Johns. 239 (1812).

18   *Grace v. Wilber*, 10 Johns. 453 (1813).

19   *Commonwealth ex rel. Webster v. Fox*, 7 Pa. 336 (1847).

20   *New York Times*, January 15, 1861. Judge Henry Hilton, of the Court of Common Pleas in New York City, the county court, had released an underage soldier the day before this report of the *Times* appeared. For Hilton, see Chester, *Courts and Lawyers*, 2:898.

21   *New York Times*, August 27, 1861. The newspaper referred in particular to the case of Stephen A. Spencer.

22   Jonathan W. White, "'Sweltering with Treason,'" 38. I follow very closely here White's excellent account of the Merrick problem.

23   *War of the Rebellion*, ser. 2, 2:1021.

24   Jonathan W. White, "Sweltering with Treason," 43–46.

25   *New York Tribune*, April 17, 1861.

26   Rovere, *Howe and Hummel*, 62–64; Burrows and Wallace, *Gotham*, 636, 1000–1001. Professor James Hitchcock of St. Louis University first alerted me to the existence of "Habeas Corpus" Howe and the Rovere book about him, which I have followed closely here.

27   *New York Tribune*, March 5, 1863.

28   See Neely, *The Union Divided*, 115. Marble was commenting on a case involving freedom of the press.

29   *New York Tribune*, March 5, 1863; *New York Herald*, March 6, 1863.

30   *New York Times*, March 5, 1863. Apparently, Loomis did not have control of the prisoner anyway.

31   *New York Tribune*, March 5, 1863.

32   *New York Evening Post*, March 6, 1863.

33   *New York Tribune*, June 9, 11, 1863.

34   *In re Dobbs* [*Dabbs?*], Superior Court, N.Y. (1861). Hoffman nevertheless discharged the underage soldier, Henry Dobbs, following the state supreme court's recognition of "the power and duty of State judges" in such matters. The soldier had enlisted on March

28, 1861, without his father's permission, but it is not clear on what day the judge announced his decision on habeas corpus in the case.

35   *New York Times*, July 30, 1861.

36   Swisher, *Oliver Wendell Holmes Devise History*, 846. In Betts's federal district court there was no question of asserting state jurisdiction over a federal soldier as there was in the state courts. Only the law of the matter, not the jurisdiction, was at issue there.

37   *New York Herald*, November 7, 1853, November 7, 1861.

38   *In re Beswick*, N.Y. Sup. (1863), p. 4.

39   Ibid., pp. 4–5.

40   The discovery of an "adequate" Constitution during the Civil War is a theme of Hyman, *A More Perfect Union*.

41   *In re Hopson*, 40 Barb. 34 (1863), p. 2.

42   Ibid.

43   Ibid., pp. 3, 5–6, 10. On Kernan, see Mitchell, *Horatio Seymour*, 237.

44   Despite its importance at the level where the legal battles of the Civil War were fought out in the North, *Ableman* is only briefly referred to in Randall, *Constitutional Problems under Lincoln*, 430–31. Likewise the reference in Neff, *Justice in Blue and Gray*, 160, is slight and vague about application of the precedent.

45   I follow closely the excellent description of the case in Swisher, *Oliver Wendell Holmes Devise History*, 653–57. It is mentioned briefly in the important work of Fehrenbacher, *Dred Scott Case*, which says that Taney "was on much more solid ground here than in the Dred Scott case" (p. 453).

46   Ibid., 658–69.

47   *In re Hopson*, 40 Barb. 34 (1863), pp. 13–14.

48   Ibid., 15.

49   Ibid.

50   Ibid., 15–16.

51   Smith was elected as a Republican in 1863. *New York Herald*, November 3, 1863.

52   *New York Tribune*, August 25, 1863. "Supreme Court of New York: In the Matter of William J. Jordan . . . Joseph Eck . . . John Hedges," *American Law Register* 11 (October 1863): 749–61, JSTOR, accessed July 10, 2006.

53   Ibid., 759–60.

54   Ibid., 761.

55   See *Harrisburg Telegraph*, July 27, August 13, 15, 1863, and *Case of Shirk*, 5 Phila. 333 (1863), pp. 3–5.

56   See, e.g., *Harrisburg Telegraph*, April 27, 1863.

57   *Harrisburg Telegraph*, July 27, 1863; *Case of Shirk*, 5 Phila. 333 (1963), p. 4.

58   *Harrisburg Telegraph*, August 13, 1863.

59   *Harrisburg Telegraph*, August 15, 1863.

60   Hamilton, Madison, and Jay, *Federalist Papers*, 433.

61   Lerner, "Supreme Court as Republican School Master."

62   For a fuller discussion of the problem of charges to the grand jury, see Neely, "'Seeking a Cause of Difficulty,'" 54–57, on which the discussion above is based.

63   Quoted in King, *Lincoln's Manager*, 210.

64   *Dubuque Herald*, June 3, 1863.

65   *Harrisburg Telegraph*, April 28, 1863.

66   Neely, "'Seeking a Cause of Difficulty.'"

67   *War of the Rebellion*, ser. 2, 2:85.

68   Ibid., ser. 2, 2:213.

69 Basler, *Collected Works of Abraham Lincoln*, 5:285–86.
70 *Dubuque Herald*, December 25, 1862. The judge was New York City Recorder John T. Hoffman.
71 *Baltimore American*, June 2, 1862.
72 *Baltimore American*, May 20, 1862. See also May 21, August 22, 1861, and January 16, 1862.
73 *Baltimore American*, April 29, 1863. For a New York instance, though less sensational, see the report of the charge of John T. Hoffman of the Recorder's Court in New York City in the *Dubuque Herald*, December 25, 1862.
74 Swisher, *Roger B. Taney*, 571.
75 Ibid.
76 Douglas Wilson, *Lincoln's Sword*, 162–63.
77 Basler, *Collected Works of Abraham Lincoln*, 4:267.
78 Ibid., 6:446.
79 Ibid., 6:445–46.
80 Ibid., 6:448. New York used conscription in 1814, but all federal attempts to authorize a federal system failed. Hickey, *War of 1812*, 241–43.
81 *Pittsburgh Post*, April 21, July 31, August 1, 17, 1863.
82 *Pittsburgh Post*, August 24, 1863.
83 *Pittsburgh Post*, August 17, 1863.
84 Ibid.
85 *Commonwealth ex rel. McLain v. Wright*, 3 Grant 437 (Pa. 1863), p. 5.
86 Ibid., p. 7.
87 Ibid.
88 Basler, *Collected Works of Abraham Lincoln*, 6:444–45n.
89 Neely, "Justice Embattled," 47.
90 [Welles], *Diary of Gideon Welles*, 1:432–33.
91 Niven, *Salmon P. Chase Papers*, 441–42.
92 Basler, *Collected Works of Abraham Lincoln*, 6:451.
93 *New York Tribune*, September 22, 1863.
94 *New York Tribune*, September 18, 1863. William H. Leonard ran in 1854 as a Hard Shell Democrat for the position of city judge in New York City. *New York Herald*, November 2, 1854. The Hard Shell Democrats were those uninclined to allow the bolting Free Soilers of 1848 back into the Democratic Party. See Gienapp, *Origins of the Republican Party*, 39.
95 *New York Herald*, September 17, 1863.
96 *New York Herald*, September 18, 1863.
97 *New York Herald*, September 19, 1863.
98 Fehrenbacher, *Dred Scott Case*, 233.
99 Ibid., 194.

Chapter 5

1 Klement, *Limits of Dissent*, 259.
2 That is the way Don E. Fehrenbacher saw the decision — as racist but embodying an attitude of "judicial sovereignty." See his *Dred Scott Case*, esp. 595.
3 McPherson, *Battle Cry of Freedom*.
4 Swisher, *Oliver Wendell Holmes Devise History*, 653–62.
5 The case included *Meyer v. Roosevelt*.

6   Porter, *Treasury Notes a Legal Tender*, 36.

7   McGinty, *Lincoln and the Court*, 26.

8   Ibid., 24, 101–2, 268–69.

9   Randall, *Constitutional Problems under Lincoln*, 53.

10   The *Prize Cases*, 2 Black 635 (1862 [*sic*]), p. 36.

11   Ibid., p. 37.

12   McGinty, *Lincoln and the Court*, 134–35.

13   Ibid., 27.

14   Dana, *Supreme Court of the United States: The Amy Warwick*. Of course, from its title this thirty-page pamphlet would not be recognizable as a stirring argument for the Union.

15   The *Prize Cases*, 2 Black 635 (1862 [*sic*]), p. 9.

16   Ibid., p. 11.

17   Ibid.

18   Ibid., p. 13.

19   Ibid., p. 15.

20   Ibid.

21   Charles F. Dole, *Argument for the Plaintiffs in the Case of the Golden Rocket*.

22   The *Prize Cases*, 2 Black 635 (1862 [*sic*]), p. 17.

23   Ibid., p. 19.

24   Lord, *Arguments of Counsel*, 9.

25   *Metropolitan Bank v. Van Dyck*, 13 E. P. Smith 400 (1863), p. 1.

26   *New York Tribune*, November 4, 1859. Apparently Davies was also the nominee of the Whig Party. See *New York Herald*, November 5, 1859.

27   *Metropolitan Bank v. Van Dyck*, 13 E. P. Smith 400 (1863), p. 18.

28   Ibid., p. 4.

29   Ibid., p. 6.

30   Ibid., pp. 14–15.

31   Balcom, a Republican, was elected to the New York Court of Apppeals in 1863. See *New York Herald*, November 4, 1863.

32   *Metropolitan Bank v. Van Dyck*, 13 E. P. Smith 400 (1863), pp. 35, 36, 37.

33   Ibid., p. 37.

34   Ibid., p. 44. Wright was elected to the New York Court of Appeals in 1861 as the candidate of the Republican, American, and People's Union parties. See *New York Herald*, November 1, 4, 1861.

35   *Metropolitan Bank v. Van Dyck*, 13 E. P. Smith 400 (1863), p. 52.

36   Ibid., p. 50. Emott was elected to the New York Court of Apppeals as a Whig in 1855. See *New York Herald*, November 6, 1855.

37   See *New York Herald*, November 6, 1855. Rosekrans, a Republican candidate, was elected to New York Court of Appeals in 1863. See *New York Herald*, November 3, 1863.

38   Mitchell, *Horatio Seymour*, 203. Denio was elected to the New York Court of Appeals in 1857. See *New York Herald*, November 1, 1857.

39   *Metropolitan Bank v. Van Dyck*, 13 E. P. Smith 400 (1863), p. 74.

40   Selden was elected to the New York Court of Appeals as a Democrat in 1855. See *New York Herald*, November 6, 1855.

41   Leach, *Conscription*, iv–v. Neff, in *Justice in Blue and Gray* (52–55), agrees that this was how the nineteenth century viewed the issue.

42   On the history after the Civil War that made the militia irrelevant, see Pauline Maier, "Justice Breyer's Sharp Aim," *New York Times*, December 22, 2010.

43   Hamilton, Madison, Jay, *Federalist Papers*, 162.

44   Ibid., 177–78.

45   Ibid., 558. See Amar, *America's Constitution*, 323–25, and *Bill of Rights*, 47, 51, 56–57, which provide essential insight into the "militia amendment."

46   Neely, "Justice Embattled," 51.

47   Ibid., 53.

48   On equity, see Friedman, *History of American Law*, 47–48, 130–31, 346–47.

49   Ibid., 2.

50   Leach, *Conscription*, 374.

51   *Kneedler v. Lane*, 3 Grant 465, 45 Pa. 238 (1863), p. 21.

52   Ibid.

53   Ibid., p. 9.

54   Ibid.

55   Ibid., p. 11.

56   Banner, *To the Hartford Convention*, 339–42.

57   *Kneedler v. Lane*, 3 Grant 465, 45 Pa. 238 (1863), p. 11.

58   Ibid., p. 13.

59   Ibid., p. 19.

60   Basler, *Collected Works of Abraham Lincoln*, 6:446.

61   *Kneedler v. Lane*, 3 Grant 465, 45 Pa. 238 (1863), 19–20.

62   Ibid., 20.

63   See Hyman, *A More Perfect Union*.

64   *Kneedler v. Lane*, 3 Grant 465, 45 Pa. 238 (1863), p. 20.

65   Ibid., p. 24.

66   Ibid., p. 26.

67   Ibid., pp. 27, 26.

68   Ibid., p. 29.

69   Ibid., p. 33.

70   Ibid., p. 34.

71   Ibid., p. 37.

72   Ibid., p. 38.

73   Ibid., p. 40.

74   Ibid., pp. 40–41.

75   Ibid., p. 42.

76   Ibid., p. 43.

77   Agnew, *Our National Constitution*.

78   Ingersoll, "Conscription. Argument before the Judges of the Supreme Court of Pennsylvania in the Case of Kneedler et al. vs. Lane et al.," 340. I am indebted to Professor Jonathan White, of Christopher Newport University, who generously provided this reference.

79   Ibid., 346.

80   Ibid., 351.

81   Ibid., 364. See also Hobsbawm, *Nations and Nationalism*, 5, 28.

82   Ingersoll, "Conscription. Argument before the Judges of the Supreme Court of Pennsylvania in the Case of Kneedler et al. vs. Lane et al.," 376.

83   *Kneedler v. Lane*, 3 Grant 465, 45 Pa. 238 (1863), p. 66.

84   Ibid., p. 67.

85   Ibid., p. 68.

86   Ibid., p. 70.

87 Both plaintiff and defendant, it was noted, desired a speedy ruling. *Reynolds v. State Bank of Indiana*, 18 Ind. 467 (1862), p. 2. See also Thornbrough, "Judge Perkins," 80n.

88 *Reynolds v. State Bank of Indiana*, 18 Ind. 467 (1862), p. 4.

89 *Thayer v. Hedges*, 22 Ind. 282 (1864), p. 11.

90 Ibid., p. 9.

91 Thornbrough, "Judge Perkins," 93.

92 Ibid., 94.

93 See Amar, *America's Constitution*, 43–48. Amar's nationalist interpretation is essential to understanding *The Federalist*, and I am heavily indebted to it.

94 Ibid., esp. 44.

95 Stampp, "Concept of a Perpetual Union."

96 Hamilton, Madison, and Jay, *Federalist Papers*, 32.

Chapter 6

1 Berlin, *Generations of Captivity*, 9.

2 Thornton, *Politics and Power*, xviii.

3 See Dew, *Apostles of Disunion*, 18.

4 *Mobile Register and Advertiser*, September 1, 1861.

5 *Mobile Register and Advertiser*, February 2, 1862.

6 Eaton, *History of the Southern Confederacy*, 51.

7 Thomas, *Confederate Nation*, 64.

8 Donald, Baker, and Holt, *Civil War and Reconstruction*, 142.

9 Rable, *Confederate Republic*, 59; Wakelyn, *Southern Pamphlets on Secession*, 199.

10 Rable, *Confederate Republic*, 63.

11 Wakelyn, *Southern Pamphlets on Secession*, 199–200.

12 Ibid., 200.

13 Ibid.

14 Ibid., 201.

15 DeRosa, *Confederate Constitution of 1861*, 141. Constitutional historian Donald Nieman rejects emphasis on state rights as a theme in the Confederate Constitution and explains that the Constitution was not antipopular but rather "republican," in the most old-fashioned sense, in its alterations from the U.S. document, embodying a hostility to political parties. See Nieman, "Republicanism, the Confederate Constitution, and the American Constitutional Tradition."

16 On Jefferson and the type of presidency proposed at the Philadelphia convention in 1787, see Peterson, *Jefferson: Writings*, 172, 913, 916–17, 942, 1153. The most cogent argument on the conservatism of secession conventions is Michael Johnson, *Toward a Patriarchal Republic*.

17 *Historical Statistics*, 25.

18 Donald, Baker, and Holt, *Civil War and Reconstruction*, 183–84.

19 Posner, *Overcoming Law*, 217.

20 See also Beard, *Economic Interpretation of the Constitution*, 218, where he describes ratification as a "*coup d'etat*."

21 Kaminski and Saladino, *Documentary History of the Ratification of the Constitution* (hereafter cited as *DHRC*), 13:xvii.

22 Wooster, *Secession Conventions*, 15–22, 52–58.

23 Edward J. Cashin, "Georgia: Searching for Security," in Gillespie and Lienesch, *Ratifying the Constitution*, 93.

24 The Federalists did move quickly to shortcut the opposition in Pennsylvania. For an interpretation of ratification that considers the *interests* and political makeup of the states as deciding factors, see McDonald, *Formation of the American Republic*. I rely heavily on his interpretation and accounts of the process for my treatment here. Though they are not as consistently focused on interests and politics as McDonald's account, the essays by different authors in Gillespie and Lienesch, *Ratifying the Constitution*, also inform my descriptions and analysis. The essays that stress politics and interests rather than ideology make the ultimate comparison of *process* with deratification in 1860–61 possible.

25 *DHRC*, 13:217.

26 The commentaries are usefully arranged in chronological order (rather than by ideological camp) in Bailyn, *Debates on the Constitution*.

27 McPherson, *Battle Cry of Freedom*, 254–55. Daniel Crofts, in *Reluctant Confederates*, dubbed the others "reluctant." Marshall DeRosa, in *Confederate Constitution of 1861*, shows little interest in process and focuses on the substantive differences between the U.S. and Confederate constitutions, arguing that the latter embodied Anti-Federalist ideals rather than those of the Federalists (p. 17). Ralph Wooster, *Secession Conventions*, 3, centers on the sociological profile of the 1,859 members of the conventions or state legislatures that considered secession.

28 DeRosa, *Confederate Constitution of 1861*, 150.

29 Wooster, *Secession Conventions*, 47–48, 60, 74, 92, 112, 135, 188n, 203. None of the conventions met long to consider the Constitution, in contrast to the lengthy ratification conventions of 1788 in closely contested states like New York and Virginia.

30 Wakelyn did include one speech, published as a pamphlet, made by a commissioner visiting the Virginia convention from another state and attempting to persuade it to secede. See Wakelyn, *Southern Pamphlets on Secession*, 387.

31 Memminger, *Mission of South Carolina to Virginia*.

32 Bonner, *Mastering America*, xii–xiii. Bonner estimates that fully 25 percent of all slaveholders in the South could have owned a pamphlet version of this one publication! Bonner does careful work on the versions of this document available during the secession crisis.

33 See Parrish and Willingham, *Confederate Imprints*. See also Freehling and Simpson, *Showdown in Virginia*, 381–86.

34 Parrish and Willingham, *Confederate Imprints*, 385–86 (item 4365). It was entitled "An Ordinance to Repeal the Ratification of the Constitution of the United States."

35 For a book that emphasizes the crucial role of the communications revolution in the Jacksonian period, see Howe, *What Hath God Wrought*, esp. 5.

36 Cauthen, *South Carolina Goes to War*, 43.

37 Beard, *Economic Interpretation of the Constitution*, 250.

38 *DHRC*, 13:xviii.

39 *Historical Statistics*, 25.

40 Statistics were compiled from Kennedy, *Preliminary Report on the Eighth Census* and *Population of the United States in 1860*.

41 McCurry, *Confederate Reckoning*, 39–40, 47, 53.

42 Ibid., 49, 53.

43 Thornton, *Politics and Power*, 407–8.

44 *New Orleans Times-Picayune*, November 6, 8, 1860. The election day details on the polls come from coverage of the presidential election in the November 9, 1860, issue of the paper.

45 *New Orleans Times-Picayune*, January 9, 1861.

46 *New Orleans Times-Picayune*, December 28, 1860.

47 *New Orleans Times-Picayune*, December 16, 1860.

48 Though not dated, the broadside appears around December 17, 1860, on the microfilm edition of the newspaper.

49 Bensel, *American Ballot Box*, 5–7.

50 *Journal of the Convention of the People of South Carolina*, 5.

51 Wooster, *Secession Conventions*, 16.

52 Ibid., 28.

53 *Journal of the State Convention*, Jackson, Miss.

54 McCurry, *Confederate Reckoning*, 60.

55 Ibid., 52; William Russell Smith, *History and Debates of the Convention of the People of Alabama*, 14.

56 *Confederate Records of the State of Georgia*, 213–17.

57 Document V, *Report of the Committee of Elections*, 6.

58 *An Ordinance Touching Contested Elections*.

59 *DHRC*, 3:92–104.

60 *DHRC*, 2:112–21.

61 McDonald, *Formation of the American Republic*, 223.

62 *DHRC*, 1:374.

63 Wakelyn, *Southern Pamphlets on Secession*, 248.

64 Ibid., 380.

65 George H. Clark, "A Sermon, Delivered in St. John's Church, Savannah, on Fast Day, Nov. 28, 1860," in Wakelyn, *Southern Pamphlets on Secession*, 55–62.

66 For lists of states observing the holiday, see *New York Herald*, November 24, 1859, November 29, 1860. On Thornwell's sermon, see Wakelyn, *Southern Pamphlets on Secession*, 157.

67 For a somewhat different view, see Snay, *Gospel of Disunion*, 174. In the 1830s, Snay argues, Southern clergymen had ignored constitutional arguments and focused exclusively on the aspects of the abolitionist threat that were regarded as moral questions. They left state rights to the Southern politicians. See pp. 47–48.

68 Myers, *Children of Pride*, 649–50, 652. OCLC locates only one copy under the title "State of the Country," or rather *The Princeton Review on the "State of the Country."* Archival survival rates and OCLC locations can offer only the roughest approximations of publications numbers, though we can say that they err on the side of underestimation.

69 Meyers, *Children of Pride*, 651.

70 James Henley Thornwell, "The State of the Country," in Wakelyn, *Southern Pamphlets on Secession*, 157–59.

71 Ibid., 160.

72 Ibid., esp. 165.

73 Ibid., 166 (Story), 168 (*Prigg*).

74 Robert Jefferson Breckinridge, "Discourse Delivered on the Day of National Humiliation, January 4, 1861, at Lexington, Kentucky," in Wakelyn, *Southern Pamphlets on Secession*, 248.

75 Ibid., 255. Breckinridge believed in the nationalist theory of American constitutional history, which posited that the original thirteen states had never existed as independent states but as states of the United States from the Declaration of Independence through the Revolution. Thus, based on his theory, nonratifying states would have entered independent statehood for the first time.

76 Ibid., 255–56.

77 Ibid., 259.

78 Ibid.

79 Snay, *Gospel of Disunion*, 215.

80 Quoted in Wakelyn, *Southern Pamphlets on Secession*, 67.

81 Ibid., 68.

82 Snay, *Gospel of Disunion*, 218.

83 Wood, *Creation of the American Republic*, chap. 15.

84 Bailyn, *Ideological Origins of the American Revolution*, 321–79.

85 Freehling, *Road to Disunion*, 450.

86 Ibid., 451–52.

87 Buenger, *Secession and the Union in Texas*, 55–57.

88 Wakelyn, *Southern Pamphlets on Secession*, 156.

89 Hamilton, Madison, and Jay, *Federalist Papers*, 30–31.

90 Faust, *Creation of Confederate Nationalism*, 34.

91 Ibid., 35–39.

92 Ibid., 38. See also Michael Johnson, *Toward a Patriarchal Republic*, on Georgia.

93 Faust, *Creation of Confederate Nationalism*, 39.

94 A commonly used term to describe societies "democratic for the master race but tyrannical for the subordinate groups" is *herrenvolk* democracy. Fredrickson thus quotes Pierre L. van den Berghe and discusses the concept in *Black Image in the White Mind*, 61.

95 Benton, *Voting in the Field*, 27.

96 Ibid., 29.

97 *Ordinances and Resolutions Passed by the State Conventions of the People of Florida*, 10.

98 *An Ordinance to Amend the Constitution*, May 28, 1861, single sheet (Syme and Hall).

99 Ibid.

100 *Journal of the Acts and Proceedings of the General Convention of . . . Virginia*, 170–71.

101 *Ordinances Adopted by the Convention of Virginia . . . in June and July 1861*, 46.

102 Ibid., 323, 334.

103 *Ordinances Adopted by the Convention of Virginia . . . in November and December 1861*, 65.

104 *Journal of the Acts and Proceedings of the General Convention of . . . Virginia*, 74.

105 Ibid., 103–4.

106 Ibid., 106–7.

107 Ibid., 172.

108 *Charleston Mercury*, January 14, 1862; *Journal of the Convention of the People of South Carolina . . . in 1860, 1861 and 1862*, 785–87.

109 William Russell Smith, *History and Debates of the Convention of the People of Alabama*, 14.

110 *Report of the Committee of Elections upon the Resolution of Mr. Wyser with Regard to Absent Members*.

111 *Journal of Both Sessions of the Convention of . . . Arkansas*, 257.

112 *Journal of the Convention of the People of Florida at a Called Session Begun . . . January 14, 1862*, 4–5, 98. The ordinance for the soldiers' vote passed 23 to 17 on January 25, 1862.

113 Michael Fellman deserves praise for his forthright description of the Unionist movement in Missouri in 1861. See Fellman, *Inside War*, 10.

114 Parrish, *History of Missouri*, 31, 43, 90–91. William E. Parrish suggests that although the convention did not fear popular elections, the delegates did not want to hurt the feelings of the incumbent governor and lieutenant governor. Gamble was a somewhat

reluctant public servant who had come out of retirement in Pennsylvania at the urging of his brother-in-law, Edward Bates (President Lincoln's attorney general), to become a member of the convention (see p. 9). In *Inside War* (p. 10), Fellman terms the action in Missouri a *"coup d'etat."*

115　*Proceedings of the Missouri State Convention*, 73.

116　Ibid., 74.

117　Parrish, *History of Missouri*, 94, 96.

118　Rable, *Confederate Republic*, 32.

119　*Journal of Both Sessions of the Convention of . . . Arkansas*, 10.

120　Ibid., 23–27.

121　Ibid., 56–58.

122　Ibid., 68–70. Because the convention called itself into a second session in May, Cochran was able to retake his seat. Ibid., 114, 120.

123　Edgar, *South Carolina: A History*, 360–62. I follow Edgar's account closely here.

124　*Charleston Courier*, May 22, 1862.

125　*Charleston Courier*, February 11, 1862.

126　Edgar, *South Carolina: A History*, 362.

Chapter 7

1　Thomas, *Confederate Nation*, 58.

2　James D. Richardson, *Messages and Papers of the Confederacy*, 1:35.

3　Ibid., 1:33.

4　Ibid., 1:36.

5　Ibid., 1:184.

6　For the rumors and advice Davis was receiving by letter and telegram during that period, see Crist, *Papers of Jefferson Davis*, 8:64–75.

7　Owsley, *State Rights in the Confederacy*, 171–202.

8　For the new appreciation of the Battle of Bull Run, see Adams, *Fighting for Defeat*, 71–86.

9　Neely, "Civil War and the Two-Party System," 93–94, 103n.

10　Ibid., 94.

11　Georgia's Governor Brown protested the publication of the letters. See Crist, *Papers of Jefferson Davis*, 7:262–63, 299. Yet the state of Georgia apparently saw to the publication of the correspondence in three different editions.

12　Parrish and Willingham, *Confederate Imprints*, 124 (item 923).

13　Ibid., 487, 513 (items 5609, 5935).

14　Ibid., 523 (item 6053).

15　I have excluded from the count reports of state supreme court cases. There were also perhaps five broadsides about martial law and habeas corpus, one of them containing John H. Gilmer's arguments before Judge J. B. Halyburton on a habeas corpus case in Richmond in 1864. Ibid., 472 (item 5423).

16　Most of this literature was the work of Philadelphians, but not all. Joel Parker's lecture appeared in its second and more widespread edition in a Philadelphia printing, and a printer in Philadelphia reprinted Kentuckian S. S. Nicholas's arguments on martial law.

17　Because it was new and somewhat different, the Constitution of the Confederacy was published in many different editions.

18　See Hamilton, *The Federalist . . . Reprinted from the Original*.

19 Quoted in Robinson, *Justice in Grey*, 477–78. Robinson discovered the document. Obviously there is room for irony in some of Garland's words, but the acknowledgment of the prevailing intellectual atmosphere is clear.

20 The effect was the opposite of that imputed to the lack of political parties in the Confederacy, which some said bred extremism and shrill and diffuse dissent. See, e.g., McKitrick, "Party Politics," and David M. Potter, "Jefferson Davis." The dissent was not particularly diffuse. It tended to follow state rights lines.

21 [Collier], *Correspondence and Remarks . . . in the Senate of Virginia*, 19, 22. Collier published another pamphlet on the same subject in the same year. On Collier, see Neely, *Southern Rights*, 49–51.

22 Stone, *War and Liberty*, 169.

23 James D. Richardson, *Messages and Papers of the Confederacy*, 1:219–20.

24 Ibid., 1:220–21.

25 Neely, *Southern Rights*, began such a description but did not give the capital of the Confederacy close scrutiny.

26 The title of this chapter derives from Thomas, *Confederate State of Richmond*. For population estimates, see ibid., 24, 128, and Stout and Grasso, "Civil War, Religion," 315.

27 *Richmond Whig*, March 8, 1862. Jefferson Davis himself was born outside what later became the actual limits of the Confederacy, in Kentucky, and had lived in Richmond only for some months in 1862.

28 *Richmond Whig*, March 8, 1862; *Richmond Enquirer*, March 7, 1862; *Richmond Dispatch*, March 8, 1862.

29 *Richmond Dispatch*, March 7, 21, April 3, 10, 26, 1862.

30 *Richmond Enquirer*, July 8, 1862.

31 *Richmond Dispatch*, April 19, 1862.

32 *Richmond Dispatch*, March 12, 1862.

33 Potter, "Historian's Use of Nationalism and Vice Versa," 48.

34 *Richmond Dispatch*, May 15, 1862.

35 *Richmond Examiner*, January 25, 1862.

36 *Richmond Whig*, January 9, 11, 13, 1862.

37 *Richmond Dispatch*, February 5, 13, 1862.

38 *Richmond Enquirer*, February 7, 1862.

39 For Botts and Bosserman, see Furgurson, *Ashes of Glory*, 115; for Smelmann, see *Richmond Dispatch*, March 3, 1862.

40 *Charleston Courier*, February 19, 1862.

41 *Richmond Dispatch*, March 21, 1862.

42 Jefferson Davis's direct connection with the labor dispute cannot be established except from newspaper hearsay, but he was still under pressure to produce Confederate currency in September 1862 and had the secretary of war reply to a congressional inquiry about requisitions on the Treasury that the reason for failure was the "impossibility of lithographing the notes with sufficient rapidity." See Crist, *Papers of Jefferson Davis*, 8:384.

43 *Richmond Dispatch*, April 11, 12, 1862; *Richmond Enquirer*, April 8, 1862. See also Neely, Holzer, and Boritt, *Confederate Image*, 6. The Scottish lithographers proved no more content than the Richmond journeymen and later attempted to run the blockade to escape the Confederacy. See, e.g., the cases of Thomas Cook (C956) and Edward McLaughlin (C959), Letters Received by the Confederate Secretary of War, 1861–65, microfilm, reel 88.

44 *Richmond Dispatch*, March 4, 1862; *Richmond Enquirer*, April 14, 18, 1862.

45 *Richmond Dispatch*, April 8, 1862.

46 *Richmond Dispatch*, January 17, 1862.

47 *Richmond Dispatch*, February 28, 1862.

48 *Richmond Dispatch*, February 28, March 3, 1862.

49 Trexler, "The Davis Administration and the Richmond Press"; Rable, *Confederate Republic*, 148; *Richmond Enquirer*, October 5, 7, November 8, 12, 19, 1861.

50 *Richmond Enquirer*, March 4, 1862. The newspaper had followed the work of habeas corpus commissioners James Lyons and Sydney S. Baxter, who interrogated the "state" or "political" prisoners and noted when those arrested for frivolous reasons had been released. See, e.g., *Richmond Enquirer*, January 10, 1862. The commissioners interrogated such prisoners even before the writ of habeas corpus was suspended in the Confederacy. On the commissioners, see Neely, *Southern Rights*, 80–98.

51 *Richmond Examiner*, January 7, 25, February 25, 28, 1862.

52 *Richmond Examiner*, March 4, 1862.

53 See Thomas, *Confederate State of Richmond*, 17–19; Andrews, *The South Reports the Civil War*, 28; Crist, *Papers of Jefferson Davis*, 8:103; and Trexler, "The Davis Administration and the Richmond Press," 187–88.

54 *Richmond Whig*, March 3, 1862.

55 Robinson, *Justice in Grey*, 383; Cooper, *Jefferson Davis*, 386; Thomas, *Confederate Nation*, 150.

56 For the legislative history, see Robbins, "The Confederacy and the Writ of Habeas Corpus."

57 Blair, *Virginia's Private War*, 106; *Richmond Examiner*, March 7, 1862.

58 Trexler, "The Davis Administration and the Richmond Press," 188.

59 Ibid., 190.

60 *Richmond Whig*, August 23, 1862.

61 *Richmond Dispatch*, January 12, 1864.

62 *Richmond Dispatch*, March 10, 1864.

63 *Richmond Dispatch*, March 26, 1864.

64 *Richmond Dispatch*, April 4, 1864.

65 *Richmond Dispatch*, April 22, May 23, 1864.

66 *Richmond Enquirer*, March 20, 1863.

67 *Richmond Enquirer*, July 15, 1863.

68 *Richmond Enquirer*, January 26, 1864.

69 Trexler, "The Davis Administration and the Richmond Press," 178, 181.

70 Wish, *George Fitzhugh*, 308–10; Crist, *Papers of Jefferson Davis*, 7:196, 355; 9:98. For the characterization of Fitzhugh as a consistently authoritarian political thinker, see Genovese, *The World the Slaveholders Made*. There is no systematic bibliography of Fitzhugh's work, and the article under discussion here is not cited in the secondary works on Fitzhugh.

71 *Richmond Enquirer*, February 2, 1864.

72 Ibid.

73 James D. Richardson, *Messages and Papers of the Confederacy*, 1:396.

74 Ibid., 1:399–400, 397.

75 Jones, *Rebel War Clerk's Diary*, 2:133; *Communication of the Secretary of War . . . Jan. 27, 1864* (on the domestic passport system); Thomas, *Confederate State of Richmond*, 19.

76 Furgurson, *Ashes of Glory*, 26, 332; Thomas, *Confederate State of Richmond*, 19. See also *Richmond Dispatch*, September 20, 1864.

77 This leaves out the Mayor's Court, which did not have authority to issue the writ of habeas corpus and the state supreme court, which dealt with many matters not having to do with Richmond.

78 On Halyburton, see Robinson, *Justice in Grey*, 18. On Ogden, see Thomas, *Confederate State of Richmond*, 115.

79 *Augusta Chronicle and Sentinel*, April 26, 1864.

80 *Richmond Dispatch*, July 29, August 2, 1864.

81 *Richmond Dispatch*, July 19, 26, August 2, 12, 16, 1864.

82 The decision, reported in the *Charleston Mercury* on June 30 and July 5, 1863, was pronounced "very able" by the editors.

83 *Richmond Dispatch*, August 17, 19, 1864.

84 *Richmond Dispatch*, September 14, 15, 20, 1864.

85 *Richmond Dispatch*, July 23, 25, August 6, 1864.

86 *Richmond Dispatch*, August 6, 1864.

87 Pollard, *Life of Jefferson Davis*, 310, 327.

88 Owsley, *State Rights in the Confederacy*, 202.

89 *Richmond Dispatch*, August 22, 1864.

90 *Richmond Dispatch*, August 12, 16, 1864.

91 *Richmond Dispatch*, August 17, 19, November 22, 1864.

92 *Richmond Dispatch*, October 4, 1864.

93 Robinson, *Justice in Grey*, 363–64. Actually, it made them "subject to orders, according to the rules and discipline of war." Confederates had avoided trying civilians by military courts. *Revised U.S. Army Regulations of 1861*, 494.

94 *Richmond Dispatch*, September 3, 1864.

Chapter 8

1 Owsley, *State Rights in the Confederacy*, vii.

2 On the internal collapse school, see Gallagher, *The Confederate War*, 18–28. For an extreme statement of the internal collapse viewpoint, see Williams, *Bitterly Divided*. For other observations on the historiography, see Neely, "Abraham Lincoln vs. Jefferson Davis," 99–103.

3 See Escott, *After Secession*, esp. 92–93.

4 Beringer, Hattaway, Jones, and Still, *Why the South Lost the Civil War*, 221.

5 Elsewhere I have argued that the two-party system was not an asset in Union victory. See Neely, *The Union Divided*.

6 McCurry, *Confederate Reckoning*, 276.

7 See Lewis O. Saum, "Schlesinger and 'The State Rights Fetish.'"

8 For emphasis on that point as the constitutional issue, if it may be called that, over which the American Revolution was fought, see Morgan and Morgan, *Stamp Act Crisis*, 99–119.

9 Bailyn, *Ideological Origins of the American Revolution*, 162–75.

10 Brutus Letters, no. IV, November 29, 1787, in Bailyn, *Debates on the Constitution*, 1:426.

11 Hamilton, Madison, and Jay, *Federalist Papers*, 212 (no. 35).

12 Stampp, "Concept of a Perpetual Union."

13 McCardell, *Idea of a Southern Nation*, 16; Banner, *To the Hartford Convention*; Hickey, *War of 1812*.

14   Swisher, *Oliver Wendell Holmes Devise History*, 668–69.

15   Bestor, "American Civil War as a Constitutional Crisis."

16   James Henley Thornwell, "The State of the Country," in Wakelyn, *Southern Pamphlets on Secession*, 175–76.

17   Escott, *After Secession*, 77; Rable, *Confederate Republic*, 133.

18   *Charleston Mercury*, January 29, 1863.

19   *Charleston Mercury*, January 28, 1863.

20   Ibid.

21   Escott, *After Secession*, 78.

22   *Charleston Mercury*, January 29, 1863.

23   Bonner, "Slavery, Confederate Diplomacy," 290–91.

24   Bonner, *Colors and Blood*, 115.

25   But he does not ignore them. See Bonner, *Mastering America*, 220–41.

26   *Charleston Mercury*, June 25, 1862.

27   *Charleston Mercury*, November 29, 1862.

28   *Charleston Mercury*, August 6, 1862; Freehling, *Prelude to Civil War*, 53–61.

29   *Charleston Mercury*, July 22, 1863.

30   *Charleston Mercury*, January 26, 1865.

31   *Charleston Mercury*, January 29, 1864; Bonner, "Slavery, Confederate Diplomacy," 299–300. Bonner also quotes this in *Mastering America*, 299.

32   *Charleston Mercury*, April 3, 1862.

33   *Charleston Mercury*, July 30, 1862. Paul Escott correctly notes that the *Mercury* later gave some notice to opinions, like that of Alexander Stephens's brother Linton, opposing conscription, but the paper more than once gave voice to ideas with which its editorial page was not in firm agreement. See Escott, *After Secession*, 86.

34   Rable, *Confederate Republic*, 140, 156. Of the first Conscription Act, the "hypercritical" Rhetts, father and son, according to Rable, "could only chide the president for not recognizing the necessity for a draft before Kentucky and Tennessee had been lost."

35   *Charleston Mercury*, March 4, 1864.

36   *Charleston Mercury*, March 8, 1864.

37   *Charleston Mercury*, December 5, 1863; Moore, *Conscription and Conflict*, 298–301.

38   Robinson, *Justice in Grey*, 169. On the organization and jurisdiction of the judiciary of the Confederacy, see also pp. 3–69.

39   That statement goes a long way toward correcting the impression given in Frank Owsley's *State Rights in the Confederacy* that "the state courts served as a vast 'leak' in the military system of the Confederacy" (p. 195).

40   Freehling, *Road to Disunion*, 450–52.

41   Hickey, *War of 1812*, 259–65.

42   *Ex parte Coupland*, 26 Tex. 386 (1862).

43   The decision was reported in the *Charleston Mercury*, November 15, 1862.

44   Ibid.; *Jeffers v. Fair*, 33 Ga. 347 (1862), pp. 11–12.

45   *Jeffers v. Fair*, 33 Ga. 347 (1862), p. 10.

46   Ibid., p. 5.

47   Ibid., p. 10.

48   Ibid., pp. 12–13.

49   Moore, *Conscription and Conflict*, 180.

50   Leonard Levy celebrates such decisions in his *Jefferson and Civil Liberties*, 25.

51   *Burroughs v. Peyton*, 57 Va. 470 (1864).

52 The term "nullification" does not appear in the index to Owsley, *State Rights in the Confederacy*.

53 *Barber v. Irwin*, 34 Ga. 27 (1864).

54 The *Mercury* printed the decision in full, without comment.

55 *Augusta Chronicle and Sentinel*, May 4, 1864. Justice Jenkins upheld the constitutionality of the new law of January 24, 1864, on substitutes. See press coverage in the *Augusta Chronicle and Sentinel*, June 23, 1864.

56 *Augusta Chronicle and Sentinel*, October 1, 1864.

57 James D. Richardson, *Messages and Papers of the Confederacy*, 1:398.

58 *Augusta Chronicle and Sentinel*, November 27, 1864.

59 *Cunningham v. Campbell*, 33 Ga. 625 (1863), pp. 3–4, 7.

60 Ibid., p. 6.

61 The case is identified in the press only as *D__y v. Fitzgerald*. In the case, in which he quoted his previous opinion, Lochrane discharged James F. Russell, who was not a citizen but a resident alien, born in Canada. See *Augusta Chronicle and Sentinel*, April 17, 1864. Within the bounds of the same thinking of universal eligibility for Confederate service, Lochrane also put the disabled out of bounds of those who could be considered liable for service. See *Augusta Chronicle and Sentinel*, February 22, 1865.

62 *Augusta Chronicle and Sentinel*, July 17, 1864.

63 *Augusta Chronicle and Sentinel*, November 3, 1864.

64 *Charleston Courier*, October 30, 1862. Neither Pringle nor any other Confederate judge discovered *Ableman v. Booth*.

65 *Charleston Courier*, September 30, 1862.

66 Ireland, *County Courts in Antebellum Kentucky*.

67 *Charleston Courier*, May 26, 1862.

68 *Augusta Chronicle and Sentinel*, January 18, 1862.

69 *Charleston Courier*, October 18, 1862.

70 *Macon (Ga.) Journal and Messenger*, April 2, 1862.

71 *Macon (Ga.) Journal and Messenger*, April 16, 1862.

72 Garner, *Black's Law Dictionary*, 623. Historians writing on the controversy over extortion in the Confederacy and people at the time have not carefully defined the term. See, e.g., Faust, *Creation of Confederate Nationalism*, 42. It was used to mean "greed," which was not against the law anywhere.

73 *Macon (Ga.) Journal and Messenger*, August 5, 1863.

74 *Mobile Register and Advertiser*, October 28, 1863.

75 *Macon (Ga.) Journal and Messenger*, September 2, 1863.

76 *Macon (Ga.) Journal and Messenger*, May 18, 1864.

77 *Augusta Chronicle and Sentinel*, October 27, 1863.

78 *Augusta Chronicle and Sentinel*, November 28, 1863.

79 *Augusta Chronicle and Sentinel*, January 15, 1865. Lochrane's decision was apparently upheld by the state supreme court.

80 Gallagher, *The Confederate War*, 28–29.

81 Crist, *Papers of Jefferson Davis*, 11:76.

82 Ibid., 1:86.

83 Owsley, *State Rights in the Confederacy*, 202.

84 Pollard, *Life of Jefferson Davis*, 310, 327.

85 Younger, *Inside the Confederate Government*, 64.

Epilogue

1   McPherson, *Battle Cry of Freedom*, 312.

2   Basler, *Collected Works of Abraham Lincoln*, 4:482.

3   James D. Richardson, *Messages and Papers of the Confederacy*, 1:103–4. The correct date for the proclamation is May 23 (not May 28), 1861, according to Crist, *Papers of Jefferson Davis*, 7:178.

4   Proclamation of February 27, 1863, in James D. Richardson, *Messages and Papers of the Confederacy*, 1:325.

5   See, e.g., Guelzo, *Abraham Lincoln: Redeemer President*, 322–23.

6   Quoted in Levy, *Jefferson and Civil Liberties*, 8. George M. Fredrickson sees in Thanksgiving and other wartime religious developments a sinister conservative theocratic assault on the values of Jefferson and American civil liberty. See Fredrickson, "Coming of the Lord," esp. 122.

7   See the sermons reported in the *New York Herald*, January 5, 1861. President Buchanan's proclamation is reproduced in Sickel, *Thanksgiving*, 144.

8   Sickel, *Thanksgiving*, 141–43.

9   Ibid., 142–43.

10 Among other things this strain led to a movement to insert "God" into the Constitution by amendment at the time of the Civil War. See Fredrickson, "Coming of the Lord," 122.

11 Alan Taylor, *Civil War of 1812*.

12 Kelly, Harbison, and Belz, *American Constitution*, 1:149.

13 Heidler and Heidler, *Encyclopedia of the War of 1812*.

14 Dwight L. Smith, *War of 1812: An Annotated Bibliography*.

15 Hyman, *A More Perfect Union*, 142. But see also pp. 12, 54.

16 For decades the trend in writing the history of the War of 1812 was to downplay the seriousness of the Federalist opposition. See Morison, "Dissent in the War of 1812," and Banner, *To the Hartford Convention*. For a recent argument pointing in the opposite direction, see Buel, *America on the Brink*. Constitutional history does not play a large part in the book, which is about political parties.

17 Stone, *War and Liberty*, 1.

18 See Stone, *Perilous Times* and *War and Liberty*.

Bibliography

Manuscripts

Letters Received by the Confederate Secretary of War, RG 109, National Archives,
microfilm
Abraham Lincoln Papers, Library of Congress, microfilm

Newspapers

Augusta (Ga.) Chronicle and Sentinel
Baltimore American
Bellefonte (Pa.) Watchman
Charleston (S.C.) Courier
Charleston (S.C.) Mercury
Chicago Tribune
Cleveland Plain Dealer
Dubuque Herald
Harrisburg Patriot and Union
Harrisburg Telegraph
Illinois State Register
Macon (Ga.) Journal and Messenger
Mobile Register and Advertiser
National Intelligencer (Washington, D.C.)
New Orleans Times-Picayune
New York Atlas
New York Day Book
New York Evening Post
New York Herald
New York Times
New York Tribune
New York World
Philadelphia Evening Bulletin
Philadelphia Inquirer
Philadelphia Public Ledger
Pittsburgh Gazette
Pittsburgh Post
Richmond (Va.) Dispatch
Richmond (Va.) Enquirer
Richmond (Va.) Examiner
Richmond (Va.) Whig
Savannah (Ga.) Daily News
South Carolinian (Columbia)
York (Pa.) Gazette

Court Cases

Ableman v. Booth, 21 How. 506 (1859).
Barber v. Irwin, 34 Ga. 27 (1864), WL 1156, Westlaw Campus.
Burroughs v. Peyton (with Abraham v. Peyton), 57 Va. 470 (1864), WL 1893,
Westlaw Campus.
Case of Shirk, 5 Phila. 333 (1863), WL 4561 (Pa. 1863), Westlaw Campus.
Cherokee Nation v. State of Georgia, 30 U.S. 1 (1831), WL 3974, Westlaw Campus.
Commonwealth ex rel. McLain v. Wright, 3 Grant 437 (Pa. 1863), Westlaw Campus.
Commonwealth ex rel. Webster v. Fox, 7 Pa. 336 (1847).
Commonwealth v. Cushing, 11 Mass. 67 (1814), WL 960, Westlaw Campus.
Commonwealth v. Harrison, 11 Mass. 63 (1814).
Thomas Cossman v. Captain W. K. Bradford (reported in Augusta Chronicle and Sentinel,
June 30, 1864).
Cross v. Harrison, 16 How. 164 (1853), WL 7678 (U.S.N.Y.), Westlaw Campus.
Cunningham v. Campbell, 33 Ga. 625 (1863), WL 1060 (Ga.), Westlaw Campus.

Dies v. Hurtel, 34 Ga. 109 (1864).

Ex parte Anderson, 16 Iowa 595 (1864).

Ex parte Bollman and Swartwout, 4 Cranch 75, 8 U.S. 75 (1807), WL 1261
(U.S. Dist. of Col.), Westlaw Campus.

Ex parte Bolling, in re Watts, 39 Ala. 609 (1865), WL 366, Westlaw Campus.

Ex parte Coupland, 26 Tex. 386 (1862), WL 2879, Westlaw Campus.

Ex parte Hill, in re Willis et al., 38 Ala. 429 (1863), WL 372, Westlaw Campus.

Ex parte Merryman, 17 F. Cas. 140 (No. 9487), LexisNexis Academic.

Ex parte Henry Spincken (Confederate District Court) (1863) (reported in *Charleston
Mercury*, June 30, July 5, 1863).

Ex parte Vallandigham, 1 Wall. 243 (1864), 925.

Daniel Fry and Eight Others v. Captain John Cunningham (reported in *Augusta Chronicle
and Sentinel*, July 16, 1864).

Grace v. Wilber, 10 Johns. 453 (1813), Westlaw Campus.

Horne v. J. M. Greer, Surgeon (reported in *Augusta Chronicle and Sentinel*, July 17, 1864).

Hurd et al. v. Rock Island Bridge, in *The Papers of Abraham Lincoln: Legal Documents
and Cases*, edited by Daniel W. Stowell, 3:308–83. Charlottesville: University of
Virginia Press, 2008.

In re Barrett, 25 How. Pr. 380, N.Y. Sup. (1863), WL 4254, Westlaw Campus.

In re Beswick, 25 How. Pr. 149, N.Y. Sup. (1863), WL 3675, Westlaw Campus.

In re Michael Boley (reported in *Augusta Chronicle and Sentinel*, August 17, 1864).

In re Collins, N.Y. Co. Ct. (1863), WL 3676, Westlaw Campus.

In re Dobbs [Dabbs?], N.Y. Superior Court (1861), WL 4893, Westlaw Campus.

In re Jeremiah Ferguson, 9 Johns. 239 (1812), Westlaw Campus.

In re Gregg, 15 Wis. 479 (1862).

In re Higgins, 16 Wis. 351 (1863).

In re Hopson, 40 Barb. 34, N.Y. Sup. (1863), Westlaw Campus.

In re Benjamin Sauls, City Court of Charleston, S.C. (1862) (reported in *Charleston
Courier*, October 30, 1862).

In re Webb, N.Y. (1862), WL 495; 137 A.L.R. 1467, Westlaw Campus.

In the Matter of William J. Jordan . . . Joseph Eck . . . John Hedges, American Law Register
11 (October 1863): 749. JSTOR.

In the Matter of Jacob Spangler, American Law Register, 11 (August 1863): 598–614.

Joseph B. Ivey and Others v. Captain Benjamin F. White and Dr. Foster, Post Surgeon
(reported in *Augusta Chronicle and Sentinel*, November 3, 1864).

Asa C. Jeffers v. John Fair, 33 Ga. 347 (1862), WL 937, Westlaw Campus.

King v. Daniel, 11 Fla. 91 (1864), WL 1119. Westlaw Campus.

Kneedler v. Lane, 3 Grant 465, 45 Pa. 238 (1863), WL 4874, Westlaw Campus.

Kneedler v. Lane, 3 Grant 523 (1863), WL 5095 (Pa.), Westlaw Campus.

Lanahan v. Birge, 30 Conn. 438 (1862), WL 702, Westlaw Campus.

Luther v. Borden, 7 How. 1 (1849), 522.

Metropolitan Bank v. Van Dyck, 13 E. P. Smith 400 (1863), Westlaw Campus.

Mitchell v. Harmony, 13 How. 115 (1851), WL 6662 (U.S.N.), Westlaw Campus.

The *Prize Cases*, 2 Black 635 (1862 [*sic*]), WL 6725, Westlaw Campus.

Reynolds v. State Bank of Indiana, 18 Ind. 467 (1862), WL 2259, Westlaw Campus.

Shirk's Case, 3 Grant 460 (1863), WL 4561 (Pa.), Westlaw Campus.

Simmons v. Miller, 40 Miss. 19 (1864), WL 2385, Westlaw Campus.

The State, ex rel. Dawson, in re Strawbridge and Mays, 39 Ala. 367 (1864), WL 511,
Westlaw Campus.

State v. Zulich, 5 Dutch. 409, Westlaw Campus.

Thayer v. Hedges, 22 Ind. 282 (1864), WL 1937 (Ind.), Westlaw Campus.

U.S. ex rel. Henderson v. Wright, 2 Pitts. 440 (1863).

U.S. ex rel. Turner v. Wright, 2 Pitts. 370 (1862), 137 A.L.R. 1467.

U.S. v. The F. W. Johnson, 25 Fed. Cas. 1232 (1861).

U.S. v. Joseph Will (reported in *Pittsburgh Post*, August 17, 1863).

Wantlan v. White, 19 Ind. 470 (1862).

Weems v. Farrell 33 Ga. 413 (1863), WL 1024, Westlaw Campus.

Worcester v. Georgia, 31 U.S. 515 (1832), WL 3389, Westlaw Campus.

Printed Primary Sources

Agnew, Daniel. *Our National Constitution: Its Adaptation to a State of War or Insurrection*. Philadelphia: C. Sherman and Son, 1863.

Bailyn, Bernard, ed. *The Debates on the Constitution: Federalist and Antifederalist Speeches, Articles, and Letters during the Struggle for Ratification*. 2 vols. New York: Library of America, 1993.

Baker, George E., ed. *The Works of William H. Seward*. 5 vols. Boston: Houghton Mifflin, 1884.

Baker, Lafayette. *History of the United States Secret Service*. Philadelphia: L. C. Baker, 1867.

Basler, Roy P., ed. *The Collected Works of Abraham Lincoln*. 9 vols. New Brunswick, N.J.: Rutgers University Press, 1953–55.

Binney, Horace. *The Privilege of the Writ of Habeas Corpus under the Constitution: Second Part*. Philadelphia: C. Sherman and Son, 1862.

———. *The Privilege of the Writ of Habeas Corpus under the Constitution: Third Part*. Philadelphia: Sherman and Co., 1865.

Breck, Robert L. *The Habeas Corpus, and Martial Law*. Cincinnati: Richard H. Collins, 1862.

The Case of Dred Scott in the United States Supreme Court: The Full Opinions of Chief Justice Taney and Justice Curtis, and Abstracts of the Opinions of Other Judges; with an Analysis of the Points Ruled, and Some Concluding Observations. New York: Horace Greeley, 1860.

[Collier, R. R.]. *Correspondence and Remarks on Two Occasions in the Senate of Virginia, on the Subject of Martial Law and Arrests and Confinement of Civilians by Military Orders*. Richmond: J. E. Goode, 1863.

Colton, Calvin, ed. *The Speeches of Henry Clay*. 2 vols. New York: A. S. Barnes, 1857.

Communication of the Secretary of War . . . January 27, 1864 [relative to the domestic passport system]. Richmond, Va.: N.p., 1864.

The Confederate Records of the State of Georgia. Atlanta: Charles P. Byrd, 1909. State Secession Debates, 1859–62, Research Publications, microfilm, reel 4.

Cook, Thomas M., and Thomas W. Knox, eds. *Public Record: Including Speeches, Messages, Proclamations, Official Correspondence, and Other Public Utterances of Horatio Seymour: From the Campaign of 1856 to the Present Time*. New York: I. W. England, 1868.

Crandall, Marjorie Lyle. *Confederate Imprints: A Check List Based Principally on the Collection of the Boston Athenaeum*. 2 vols. Boston: Boston Athenaeum, 1955.

Crist, Lynda Lasswell, ed. *The Papers of Jefferson Davis*. Vols. 1–11. Baton Rouge: Louisiana State University Press, 1971–2004.

Curtis, Benjamin R. *Executive Power*. Reprinted in *Union Pamphlets of the Civil War,*
1861–1865, by Frank Freidel. 2 vols. Cambridge: Harvard University Press, 1967.

Dana, Richard Henry, Jr. *Supreme Court of the United States: The Amy Warwick: Brief of*
R. H. Dana, Jr. N.p., [1863?].

Document V, *Report of the Committee of Elections Showing Who Was Elected Members of*
the Convention, 6. State Secession Debates, 1859–62, Research Publications, microfilm,
reel 18.

Dole, Charles F. *Argument for the Plaintiffs in the Case of the Golden Rocket, before the*
Supreme Court of Maine: Taking by Rebels on the High Seas Is Piracy, Not Capture,
Seizure, or Detention by the Law of Nations. Boston: Press of John Wilson and Son,
1862.

Facts and Authorities on the Suspension of the Privilege of the Writ of Habeas Corpus.
N.p., [1863?].

Fisher, Sidney George. *The Trial of the Constitution.* Philadelphia: J. B. Lippincott, 1862.

Fitzhugh, George. "The Conduct of the War." *DeBow's Review,* 32 (January–February
1862): 139–46.

Foner, Philip S., and Yuval Taylor, eds. *Frederick Douglass: Selected Speeches and Writings.*
Chicago: Lawrence Hill Books, 1999.

Freehling, William W., and Craig M. Simpson, eds. *Showdown in Virginia: The 1861*
Convention and the Fate of the Union. Charlottesville: University of Virginia Press,
2010.

Freidel, Frank. *Union Pamphlets of the Civil War, 1861–1865.* 2 vols. Cambridge: Harvard
University Press, 1967.

Goodwin, Philo A. *Biography of Andrew Jackson, President of the United States, Formerly*
Major General of the United States Army. New York: R. Hart Towner, 1835.

[Gross, Charles Heber?]. *A Reply to Horace Binney's Pamphlet on Habeas Corpus.*
Philadelphia: N.p., 1862.

Hamilton, Alexander. *The Federalist . . . Reprinted from the Original with an Historical*
Introduction and Notes by Henry B. Dawson. New York: C. Scribner, 1863.

Hamilton, Alexander, James Madison, and John Jay. *The Federalist Papers.* 1788. Reprint,
Edited by Clinton Rossiter, New York: Penguin, 2003.

Hay, Melba Porter, ed. *The Papers of Henry Clay, Volume 10: Candidate, Compromiser,*
Elder Statesman, January 1, 1844–June 29, 1852. Lexington: University Press of
Kentucky, 1991.

Ingersoll, Charles. "Conscription. Argument before the Judges of the Supreme Court
of Pennsylvania in the Case of Kneedler et al. vs. Lane et al., Dec. 30, 1863." (Page
proofs of a fragment of an unidentified, unpublished printed book, Library Co. of
Philadelphia, 5192.0. Photocopy courtesy of Jonathan W. White.)

Jackson, Tatlow. *Authorities Cited Antagonistic to Horace Binney's Conclusions on the*
Writ of Habeas Corpus. Philadelphia: John Campbell, 1862.

Johannsen, Robert W., ed. *The Letters of Stephen A. Douglas.* Urbana: University of Illinois
Press, 1961.

Jones, John B. *A Rebel War Clerk's Diary at the Confederate Capital.* 2 vols. Philadelphia:
J. B. Lippincott, 1866.

Journal of the Acts and Proceedings of the General Convention of the State of Virginia
Richmond: Wyatt M. Elliott, 1861.

Journal of Both Sessions of the Convention of the State of Arkansas. Little Rock: Johnson
and Yerkes, 1861.

Journal of the Convention of the People of Florida at a Called Session Begun . . . January 14, 1862. N.p., n.d.

Journal of the Convention of the People of North Carolina, Held on the 20th Day of May, A.D. 1861. Raleigh: John W. Syme, 1862.

Journal of the Convention of the People, South Carolina, Held in 1860-'61. Charleston: Evans and Cogswell, 1861. State Secession Debates, 1859–62. Research Publications, microfilm, reel 14.

Journal of the Convention of the People of South Carolina, Held in 1860, 1861 and 1862. Columbia: R. W. Gibbes, 1862. State Secession Debates, 1859–62. Research Publications, microfilm, reel 14.

Journal of the Convention of the People of the State of Alabama . . . Commencing . . . 7th Day of January, 1861. Montgomery: Shorter and Reid, 1861.

Journal of the Convention of the State of Arkansas. Little Rock: Johnson and Yerkes, 1861.

Journal of the State Convention and Ordinances and Resolutions Adopted in January 1861 with an Appendix. Jackson, Miss.: [1861?]. State Secession Debates, 1859–62. Research Publications, microfilm, reel 17.

Kaminski, John P., and Gaspare J. Saladino, eds. *Documentary History of the Ratification of the Constitution.* 23 vols. Madison: University of Wisconsin Press, 1976–2009.

Kennedy, Joseph C. G. *Population of the United States in 1860: Compiled from the Original Returns of the Eighth Census.* Washington, D.C.: U.S. Government Printing Office, 1864.

———. *Preliminary Report on the Eighth Census, 1860.* Washington, D.C.: U.S. Government Printing Office, 1862.

Kirkland, Charles P. *A Letter to the Honorable Benjamin R. Curtis, Late Judge of the Supreme Court of the United States, in Review of His Recently Published Pamphlet on the "Emancipation Proclamation" of the President.* 2nd ed. New York: Anson and D. F. Randolph, 1863.

Lieber, Francis. *Guerrilla Parties Considered with Reference to the Laws and Usages of War.* New York: D. Van Nostrand, 1862.

———. *On Civil Liberty and Self-Government.* 2 vols. Philadelphia: Lippincott, Grambo, 1853.

Lord, William Blair. *Arguments of Counsel in the Court of Appeals of the State of New York, upon the Power of Congress to Make United States Treasury Notes a Legal Tender.* New York: Wm. C. Bryant, 1863.

Lowrey, Grosvenor P. *The Commander-in-Chief; A Defence upon Legal Grounds of the Proclamation of Emancipation; and an Answer to Ex-Judge Curtis' Pamphlet Entitled "Executive Power."* New York: G. P. Putnam, 1862. Reprinted in Frank Freidel, *Union Pamphlets of the Civil War, 1861–1865.* 2 vols. Cambridge: Harvard University Press, 1967.

Marshall, John A. *American Bastile: A History of the Arbitrary Arrests and Imprisonment of American Citizens in the Northern and Border States.* 1869. Reprint, Philadelphia: Thomas W. Hartley, 1885.

Marx, Karl, and Frederick Engels. *The Civil War in the United States.* New York: International Publishers, 1937.

Memoir of the Hon. William Whiting, Ll.D. Boston: Clapp and Son, 1874.

Myers, Robert Manson, ed. *The Children of Pride: A True Story of Georgia and the Civil War.* New Haven, Conn.: Yale University Press, 1972.

"The Next General Election." *North American Review* 205 (October 1864): 557–72.

Nicholas, S. S. *Martial Law: Part of a Pamphlet First Published in 1842 over the Signature of a Kentuckian.* Philadelphia: John Campbell, 1862.

Niven, John, ed. *The Salmon P. Chase Papers, Volume I: Journals, 1829–1872*. Kent, Ohio: Kent State University Press, 1993.

[Norton, Charles Eliot]. "Immorality in Politics." *North American Review* 201 (January 1864): 105–28.

Opinions Delivered by the Judges of the Court of Appeals, on the Constitutionality of the Act of Congress Declaring Treasury Notes a Legal Tender. Albany, N.Y.: Weed, Parsons and Co., 1863.

Opinions of the Judges of the Supreme Court of Pennsylvania, on the Constitutionality of the Act of Congress of March 3, 1863. Philadelphia: Kay and Brother, 1864.

Ordinances Adopted by the Convention of Virginia at the Adjourned Session, in June and July 1861. N.p., n.d.

Ordinances Adopted by the Convention of Virginia at the Adjourned Session, in November and December 1861. N.p., n.d. State Secession Debates, 1859–62. Research Publications, microfilm, reel 18.

Ordinances and Constitution of the State of South Carolina. Charleston: Evans and Cogswell, 1861.

Ordinances and Resolutions Passed by the State Convention of the People of Florida begun . . . January 3, 1861. N.p., n.d.

Ordinances of the State Convention, Which Convened in Little Rock, May 6, 1861. Little Rock, Ark.: Johnson and Yerkes.

An Ordinance Touching Contested Elections, Passed by the Convention, February 21, 1861. State Secession Debates, 1859–62. Research Publications, microfilm, reel 18.

Parker, Joel. "Constitutional Law." *North American Review* 92 (April 1862): 435–63.

———. *Constitutional Law: With Reference to the Present Condition of the United States*. Cambridge, Mass.: Welch, Bigelow, 1862.

———. *Habeas Corpus and Martial Law: A Review of the Opinion of Chief Justice Taney, in the Case of Merryman*. 2nd ed. Philadelphia: J. Campbell, 1862.

———. *Revolution and Reconstruction: Two Lectures Delivered in the Law School of Harvard College, in January 1865, and January 1866*. New York: Hurd and Houghton, 1866.

———. *The Three Powers of Government: The Origin of the United States, and the Status of the Southern States on the Suppression of the Rebellion*. New York: Hurd and Houghton, 1869.

———. *To the People of Massachusetts*. Cambridge, Mass.: N.p., 1862.

Peckham, Wheeler H. *A Review of the Arguments of Counsel in the New York Court of Appeals: On the Constitutionality of the Law Making United States Treasury Notes a Legal Tender*. New York: Banks and Co., 1864.

Peterson, Merrill, ed. *Thomas Jefferson: Writings*. New York: Library of America, 1984.

Pollard, Edward. *Life of Jefferson Davis, with a Secret History of the Confederacy*. 1869. Reprint, New York: Books for Libraries, 1969.

Porter, John K. *Treasury Notes a Legal Tender: Argument of John K. Porter, in the Court of Appeal of the State of New York, in the Case of the Metropolitan Bank and Others, Respondents agt. Henry H. Van Dyck. . . . Appellant. June 27, 1863*. Albany, N.Y.: Weed, Parsons and Co., 1863.

Presidential Power over Personal Liberty: A Review of Horace Binney's Essay on the Writ of Habeas Corpus. Philadelphia: N.p., 1862.

Proceedings of the Missouri State Convention, Held at Jefferson City, July 1861. St. Louis: George Knapp, 1861.

Read, John M. *Opinion of Hon. John M. Read of the Supreme Court of Pennsylvania, in Favor of the Constitutionality of the Act of Congress Making Treasury Notes a Legal*

Tender in Payment of Debts: Delivered at Harrisburg, on Wednesday, May 24, 1865. Philadelphia: C. Sherman, 1865.

————. *Opinions of Hon. John M. Read of the Supreme Court of Pa. in Favor of the Constitutionality of the Act of Congress of March 3, 1863.* Philadelphia: Caxton Press of C. Sherman and Son, 1864.

Report of the Committee of Elections upon the Resolution of Mr. Wyser with Regard to Absent Members. N.p., n.d. State Secession Debates, 1859–62. Research Publications, microfilm, reel 18.

Revised U.S. Army Regulations of 1861. Washington, D.C.: Government Printing Office, 1863.

Richardson, James D., ed. *A Compilation of the Messages and Papers of the Confederacy Including the Diplomatic Correspondence, 1861–1865.* 2 vols. Nashville: U.S. Publishing Co., 1906.

Roberts, Oran Milo. *Speech of Judge O. M. Roberts of the Supreme Court of Texas, at the Capital, on the 1st Dec., 1860, upon the "Impending Crisis."* [Austin: N.p., 1860].

Sears, Stephen W., ed. *The Civil War Papers of George B. McClellan: Selected Correspondence, 1860–1865.* New York: Ticknor and Fields, 1989.

Sickel, H. S. J. *Thanksgiving: Its Source, Philosophy and History with All National Proclamations and Analytical Study Thereof.* Philadelphia: International Printing, 1940.

Silbey, Joel H. *The American Party Battle: Election Campaign Pamphlets, 1828–1876.* 2 vols. Cambridge: Harvard University Press, 1999.

Smith, William Russell. *The History and Debates of the Convention of the People of Alabama, Begun and Held in the City of Montgomery, on the Seventh Day of January 1861; in Which Is Preserved the Speeches of the Secret Sessions, and Many Valuable State Papers.* Montgomery: White, Pfister, and Co., 1861; Tuscaloosa: D. Woodruff; Atlanta: Hanleiter, Rice and Co., 1861. State Secession Debates, 1859–62, Research Publications, microfilm, reel 1.

Stephens, Alexander H. *A Constitutional View of the Late War between the States: Its Causes, Character, and Results.* 2 vols. Philadelphia: National Publishing Co., 1868–70.

Stowell, Daniel W., ed. *The Papers of Abraham Lincoln: Legal Documents and Cases.* 4 vols. Charlottesville: University Press of Virginia, 2008.

Urofsky, Melvin I., and Paul Finkelman, eds. *Documents of American Constitutional and Legal History.* 2 vols. 2nd ed. New York: Oxford University Press, 2002.

Wakelyn, Jon L., ed. *Southern Pamphlets on Secession, November 1860–April 1861.* Chapel Hill: University of North Carolina Press, 1996.

————, ed., *Southern Unionist Pamphlets and the Civil War.* Columbia: University of Missouri Press, 1999.

The War of the Rebellion: A Compilation of the Official Records of the Union and Confederate Armies. 128 vols. Washington, D.C.: U.S. Government Printing Office, 1880–1901.

[Welles, Gideon]. *Diary of Gideon Welles, Secretary of the Navy under Lincoln and Johnson.* 3 vols. Boston: Houghton Mifflin, 1911.

White, Jonathan W., ed. *A Philadelphia Perspective: The Civil War Diary of Sidney George Fisher.* New York: Fordham University Press, 2007.

Whiting, William. *Military Government of Hostile Territory in Time of War.* Boston: John L. Shorey, 1864.

————. *The War Powers of the President and the Legislative Powers of Congress in Relation to Rebellion, Treason and Slavery.* 2nd ed. Boston: John L. Shorey, 1862.

Widmer, Ted, ed. *American Speeches: Political Oratory from the Revolution to the Civil War*. New York: Library of America, 2006.

Wilson, Douglas, and Rodney O. Davis, eds. *Herndon's Lincoln*. Urbana: University of Illinois Press, 2006.

Wilson, Woodrow. *Congressional Government: A Study in American Politics*. Boston: Houghton Mifflin, 1885.

Wiltse, Charles M., ed. *The Papers of Daniel Webster: Speeches and Formal Writings, I, 1800–1833*. Hanover, N.H.: University Press of New England, 1986.

The Writ of Habeas Corpus. N.p., 1862.

The Writ of Habeas Corpus and Mr. Binney. Philadelphia: N.p., 1862.

Younger, Edward, ed. *Inside the Confederate Government: The Diary of Robert Garlick Hill Kean*. 1957. Reprint, Baton Rouge: Louisiana State University Press, 1993.

Secondary Sources

THE UNION

Adams, Michael C. C. *Fighting for Defeat: Union Military Failure in the East, 1861–1865*. Originally published as *Our Masters the Rebels: A Speculation on Union Military Failure in the East, 1861–1865*, 1978. Lincoln: University of Nebraska Press: 1992.

Altschuler, Glenn C., and Stuart M. Blumin. *Rude Republic: Americans and Their Politics in the Nineteenth Century*. Princeton, N.J.: Princeton University Press, 2000.

Amar, Akhil Reed. *America's Constitution: A Biography*. New York: Knopf, 2005.

———. *The Bill of Rights: Creation and Reconstruction*. New Haven, Conn.: Yale University Press, 1998.

Anbinder, Tyler. "Which Poor Man's Fight? Immigrants and the Federal Conscription of 1863." *Civil War History* 52 (December 2006): 344–72.

Anderson, Benedict. *Imagined Communities: Reflections on the Origin and Spread of Nationalism*. 1983. Rev. ed., London: Verso, 1991.

Bailyn, Bernard. *The Ideological Origins of the American Revolution*. Enlarged ed. Cambridge: Harvard University Press, 1992.

Banner, James M., Jr. *To the Hartford Convention: The Federalists and the Origins of Party Politics in Massachusetts, 1789–1815*. New York: Knopf, 1970.

Beard, Charles. *An Economic Interpretation of the Constitution of the United States*. 1913. Reprint, New York: Free Press, 1986.

Belz, Herman. *Abraham Lincoln, Constitutionalism, and Equal Rights in the Civil War Era*. New York: Fordham University Press, 1998.

———. *Reconstructing the Union: Theory and Policy during the Civil War*. Ithaca, N.Y.: Cornell University Press, 1969.

Benedict, Michael Les. *The Blessings of Liberty: A Concise History of the Constitution of the United States*. 2nd ed. Boston: Houghton Mifflin, 2006.

Bensel, Richard Franklin. *The American Ballot Box in the Mid-Nineteenth Century*. Cambridge: Cambridge University Press, 2004.

Benton, Josiah H. *Voting in the Field*. Boston: Privately printed, 1915.

Berwanger, Eugene H. *The Frontier against Slavery: Western Anti-Negro Prejudice and the Slavery Extension Controversy*. Urbana: University of Illinois Press, 1967.

Bestor, Arthur. "The American Civil War as a Constitutional Crisis." *American Historical Review* 69 (January 1964): 327–52.

Beveridge, Albert J. *Abraham Lincoln, 1809–1858*. 2 vols. Boston: Houghton Mifflin, 1928.

Billias, George Athan. *American Constitutionalism Heard Round the World, 1776–1989*. New York: New York University Press, 1989.

Binney, Charles Chauncey. *The Life of Horace Binney with Selections from His Letters*. Philadelphia: J. B. Lippincott, 1903.

Boritt, Gabor S. *Lincoln and the Economics of the American Dream*. 1978. Reprint, Urbana: University of Illinois Press, 1994.

Boucher, Chauncey F. "In Re That Aggressive Slaveocracy." *Mississippi Valley Historical Review* 8 (June–September 1921): 13–80.

Bradley, Erwin Stanley. *The Triumph of Militant Republicanism: A Study of Pennsylvania and Presidential Politics, 1860–1872*. Philadelphia: University of Pennsylvania Press, 1964.

Brock, W. R. *An American Crisis: Congress and Reconstruction, 1865–1867*. New York: St. Martin's, 1963.

Buel, Richard, Jr. *America on the Brink: How the Political Struggle over the War of 1812 Almost Destroyed the Young Republic*. New York: Palgrave, Macmillan, 2005.

Burgess, John W. *The Civil War and the Constitution, 1859–1865*. 2 vols. New York: Charles Scribner's Sons, 1901.

Burlingame, Michael. *Abraham Lincoln: A Life*. 2 vols. Baltimore: Johns Hopkins University Press, 2008.

Burrows, Edwin G., and Mike Wallace. *Gotham: A History of New York City to 1898*. New York: Oxford University Press, 1999.

Carwardine, Richard J. *Lincoln: Profiles in Power*. London: Pearson, 2003.

Chester, Alden. *Courts and Lawyers of New York: A History, 1609–1925*. 4 vols. New York: American Historical Society, 1925.

Cole, Arthur Charles. *The Era of the Civil War, 1848–1870*. 1919. Reprint, Freeport, N.Y.: Books for Libraries Press, 1971.

Degler, Carl N. "Lincoln: Was He America's Bismarck?" *New York Times*, February 12, 1991.

———. *One among Many: The Civil War in Comparative Perspective*. Gettysburg, Pa.: Gettysburg College, 1990.

Dimunation, Mark G., and Elaine D. Engst. *A Legacy of Ideas: Andrew Dickson White and the Founding of the Cornell University Library*. Ithaca, N.Y.: Cornell University Library, 1996.

Donald, David Herbert. *Lincoln*. Simon and Schuster, 1995.

———. *Lincoln Reconsidered: Essays on the Civil War Era*. 2nd ed. New York: Knopf, 1956.

Donald, David Herbert, Jean Harvey Baker, and Michael F. Holt. *The Civil War and Reconstruction*. New York: Norton, 2001.

Doyle, Don Harrison. *Nations Divided: America, Italy, and the Southern Question*. Athens: University of Georgia Press, 2002.

Dusinberre, William. *Civil War Issues in Philadelphia, 1856–1865*. Philadelphia: University of Pennsylvania Press, 1965.

Eicher, David J. *The Civil War in Books: An Analytical Bibliography*. Urbana: University of Illinois Press, 1997.

Farber, Daniel. *Lincoln's Constitution*. Chicago: University of Chicago Press, 2003.

Fehrenbacher, Don E. *The Dred Scott Case: Its Significance in American Law and Politics*. New York: Oxford University Press, 1978.

———. *The Slaveholding Republic: An Account of the United States Government's Relations to Slavery*. New York: Oxford University Press, 2001.

Fellman, Michael. *Inside War: The Guerrilla Conflict in Missouri during the American Civil War*. New York: Oxford University Press, 1989.

Foner, Eric. *Free Soil, Free Labor, Free Men: The Ideology of the Republican Party before the Civil War*. New York: Oxford University Press, 1970.

Fredrickson, George M. *The Black Image in the White Mind: The Debate on African-American Character and Destiny, 1817–1914*. New York: Harper and Row, 1971.

———. "The Coming of the Lord: The Northern Protestant Clergy and the Civil War Crisis." In *Religion in the American Civil War*, edited by Randall M. Miller, Harry S. Stout, and Charles Reagan Wilson, 110–30. New York: Oxford University Press, 1998.

———. *The Inner Civil War: Northern Intellectuals and the Crisis of the Union*. New York: Harper and Row, 1965.

Freidel, Frank. *Francis Lieber: Nineteenth-Century Liberal*. Baton Rouge: Louisiana State University Press, 1947.

Friedman, Lawrence M. *A History of American Law*. New York: Simon and Schuster, 1973.

Gaddis, John Lewis. *Surprise, Security, and the American Experience*. Cambridge: Harvard University Press, 2004.

Gallman, Matthew. *Mastering Wartime: A Social History of Philadelphia during the Civil War*. 1990. Reprint, Philadelphia: University of Pennsylvania Press, 2000.

Garner, Brian A., ed. *Black's Law Dictionary*. 8th ed. St. Paul, Minn.: Thompson/West, 2004.

Geary, James W. *We Need Men: The Union Draft in the Civil War*. DeKalb: Northern Illinois University Press, 1991.

Gellner, Ernest. *Nations and Nationalism*. Ithaca, N.Y.: Cornell University Press, 1983.

Gienapp, William E. *The Origins of the Republican Party, 1852–1856*. New York: Oxford University Press, 1987.

Gillespie, Michael Allen, and Michael Lienesch, eds. *Ratifying the Constitution*. Lawrence: University Press of Kansas, 1989.

Gillette, William. *Jersey Blue: Civil War Politics in New Jersey, 1854–1865*. New Brunswick, N.J.: Rutgers University Press, 1995.

Guelzo, Allen C. *Abraham Lincoln: Redeemer President*. Grand Rapids, Mich.: William B. Eerdmans, 1999.

———. *Lincoln's Emancipation Proclamation: The End of Slavery in America*. New York: Simon and Schuster, 2004.

Harper, Robert S. *Lincoln and the Press*. New York: McGraw-Hill, 1951.

Heidler, David S., and Jeanne T. Heidler. *Encyclopedia of the War of 1812*. Santa Barbara, Calif.: ABC-CLIO, 1997.

Hickey, Donald R. *The War of 1812: A Forgotten Conflict*. Urbana: University of Illinois Press, 1989.

Historical Statistics of the United States, 1789–1945. Washington, D.C.: U.S. Government Printing Office, 1949.

Hobsbawm, Eric J. *Nations and Nationalism since 1780: Programme, Myth, Reality*. Cambridge, U.K.: Cambridge University Press, 1990.

Hobsbawm, Eric J., and Terence Ranger. *The Invention of Tradition*. Cambridge, U.K.: Cambridge University Press, 1983.

Holt, Michael F. "An Elusive Synthesis: Northern Politics during the Civil War." In *Writing the Civil War: The Quest to Understand*, edited by James M. McPherson and William J. Cooper, 112–34. Columbia: University of South Carolina Press, 1998.

———. *The Political Crisis of the 1850s*. New York: Norton, 1978.

Horwitz, Morton J. *The Transformation of American Law, 1780–1860*. New York: Oxford University Press, 1992.

Howe, Daniel Walker. *What Hath God Wrought: The Transformation of America, 1815–1848*. New York: Oxford University Press, 2007.

Hyman, Harold M. "Election of 1864." In *History of American Presidential Elections, 1789–1968*, 4 vols, edited by Arthur M. Schlesinger Jr., 2:1155–1246. New York: Chelsea House, 1971.

———. *A More Perfect Union: The Impact of the Civil War and Reconstruction on the Constitution*. New York: Knopf, 1973.

Jensen, Merrill. *The Articles of Confederation: An Interpretation of the Social-Constitutional History of the American Revolution*. Madison: University of Wisconsin Press, 1940.

Johannsen, Robert W. *Stephen A. Douglas*. 1973. Reprint, Urbana: University of Illinois Press, 1997.

Johnson, Ludwell H., III. "Abraham Lincoln and the Development of Presidential War-Making Powers: Prize Cases (1863) Revisited." *Civil War History* 35 (September 1989): 208–24.

———. "The Confederacy: What Was It? The View from the Federal Courts." *Civil War History* 32 (March 1986): 5–22.

Kammen, Michael. *A Machine That Would Go of Itself: The Constitution in American Culture*. New York: Knopf, 1986.

Keegan, John. *The Mask of Command*. New York: Viking, 1987.

Kelly, Alfred H., Winfred A. Harbison, and Herman Belz. *The American Constitution: Its Origin and Development*. 2 vols. New York: Norton, 1991.

King, Willard L. *Lincoln's Manager: David Davis*. Cambridge: Harvard University Press, 1960.

Klement, Frank L. *Dark Lanterns: Secret Political Societies, Conspiracies, and Treason Trials in the Civil War*. Baton Rouge: Louisiana State University Press, 1984.

———. *The Limits of Dissent: Clement L. Vallandigham and the Civil War*. 1970. Reprint, New York: Fordham University Press, 1998.

Kramer, Larry D. *The People Themselves: Popular Constitutionalism and Judicial Review*. New York: Oxford University Press, 2004.

Kutler, Stanley I. *Judicial Power and Reconstruction Politics*. Chicago: University of Chicago Press, 1968.

Lalor, John J. *Cyclopaedia of Political Science. . .* 3 vols. New York: Charles E. Merrill, 1893.

Lawson, Melinda R. *Patriot Fires: Forging a New American Nationalism in the Civil War North*. Lawrence: University Press of Kansas, 2002.

Leach, Jack Franklin. *Conscription in the United States: Historical Background*. Rutland, Vt.: Charles E. Tuttle, 1952.

Lerner, Ralph. "The Supreme Court as Republican School Master." In *The Supreme Court Review 1967*, edited by Philip B. Curland, 127–55. Chicago: University of Chicago Press, 1967.

Levy, Leonard. *Jefferson and Civil Liberties: The Darker Side*. 1963. Reprint, New York: Quadrangle, 1973.

Maier, Pauline. *Ratification: The People Debate the Constitution, 1787–1788*. New York: Simon and Schuster, 2010.

Marten, James. *The Children's Civil War*. Chapel Hill: University of North Carolina Press, 1998.

McC., R. W. "Enlistment or Mustering of Minors into Military Service." *University of Pennsylvania Law Review and American Law Register* 91 (November 1942): 255–59.

McDonald, Forrest. *The Formation of the American Republic, 1776–1790*. Originally published as *E Pluribus Unum: The Formation of the American Republic, 1776–1790*. Baltimore: Pelican Books, 1967.

McGinty, Brian. *Lincoln and the Court*. Cambridge: Harvard University Press, 2008.

McKitrick, Eric. "Party Politics and the Union and Confederate War Efforts." In *The American Party Systems: Stages of Development*, edited by Walter Dean Burnham and William Nisbet Chambers, 117–51. New York, Oxford University Press, 1967.

McLauchlan, William P. *The Indiana State Constitution: A Reference Guide*. Westport, Conn.: Greenwood Press, 1996.

McPherson, James M. *Battle Cry of Freedom: The Civil War Era*. New York: Oxford University Press, 1988.

———. *For Cause and Comrades: Why Men Fought in the Civil War*. New York: Oxford University Press, 1997.

———. *How Lincoln Won the War with Metaphors*. Fort Wayne, Ind.: Louis A. Warren Lincoln Library and Museum, 1985.

———. "What Did He Really Think about Race?" Review of James Oakes, *The Radical and the Republican: Frederick Douglass, Abraham Lincoln, and the Triumph of Antislavery Politics* in the *New York Review of Books*, 18–19, March 29, 2007.

McPherson, James M., and William J. Cooper, eds. *Writing the Civil War: The Quest to Understand*. Columbia: University of South Carolina Press, 1998.

Miller, Randall M., Harry S. Stout, and Charles Reagan Wilson, eds. *Religion and the American Civil War*. New York: Oxford University Press, 1998.

Miller, William Lee. *President Lincoln: The Duty of a Statesman*. New York: Knopf, 2008.

Mitchell, Stewart. *Horatio Seymour of New York*. Cambridge: Harvard University Press, 1938.

Monaghan, Jay. *Lincoln Bibliography, 1839–1939*. 2 vols. Springfield: Illinois State Historical Library, 1943–45.

Morgan, Edmund S., and Helen M. Morgan. *The Stamp Act Crisis: Prologue to Revolution*. 1953. Reprint, New York: Collier Books, 1962.

Morison, Samuel Eliot. "Dissent in the War of 1812." In *Dissent in Three American Wars*, by Samuel Eliot Morison, Frederick Merck, and Frank Freidel, 1–31. Cambridge: Harvard University Press, 1970.

Mulford, Elisha. *The Nation: The Foundation of Civil Order and Political Life in the United States*. 1887. Reprint, New York: Augustus M. Kelly, 1971.

Murdock, Eugene Converse. *One Million Men: The Civil War Draft in the North*. Madison: State Historical Society of Wisconsin, 1971.

———. *Patriotism Limited, 1862–1865*. Kent, Ohio: Kent State University Press, 1967.

Neely, Mark E., Jr. "Abraham Lincoln's Nationalism Reconsidered." *Lincoln Herald*. 76 (Spring 1974): 12–28.

———. *The Boundaries of American Political Culture in the Civil War Era*. Chapel Hill: University of North Carolina Press, 2005.

———. *The Civil War and the Limits of Destruction*. Cambridge: Harvard University Press, 2007.

———. "The Civil War and the Two-Party System." In *"We Cannot Escape History": Lincoln and the Last Best Hope of Earth*, edited by James M. McPherson, 86–104. Urbana: University of Illinois Press, 1995.

———. "Colonization and the Myth That Lincoln Prepared the People for Emancipation." In *Lincoln's Proclamation: Emancipation Reconsidered*, edited by William A. Blair and Karen Fisher Younger, 45–74. Chapel Hill: University of North Carolina Press, 2009.

———. "The Constitution and Civil Liberties under Lincoln," in *Our Lincoln*, edited by Eric Foner, 37–61. New York: Norton, 2008.

———. *The Fate of Liberty: Abraham Lincoln and Civil Liberties*. New York: Oxford University Press, 1991.

————. "Justice Embattled: The Lincoln Administration and the Constitutional Controversy over Conscription in 1863." In *The Supreme Court and the Civil War*, edited by Jennifer M. Lowe, 47–61. Washington, D.C.: Supreme Court Historical Society, 1996. Special issue of the *Journal of Supreme Court History*.

————. "Politics Purified: Religion and the Growth of Antislavery Idealism in Republican Ideology during the Civil War." In *The Birth of the Grand Old Party: The Republicans' First Generation*, edited by Robert F. Engs and Randall M. Miller. Philadelphia: University of Pennsylvania Press, 2002.

————. "'Seeking a Cause of Difficulty with the Government': Reconsidering Freedom of Speech and Judicial Conflict under Lincoln." In *Lincoln's Legacy: Ethics and Politics*, edited by Phillip Shaw Paludan, 48–66. Urbana: University of Illinois Press, 2008.

————. *The Union Divided: Party Conflict in the Civil War North*. Cambridge: Harvard University Press, 2002.

————. "War and Partisanship: What Lincoln Learned from James K. Polk." *Journal of the Illinois State Historical Society* 74 (Autumn 1981): 199–216.

Neff, Stephen C. *Justice in Blue and Gray: A Legal History of the Civil War*. Cambridge: Harvard University Press, 2010.

Nevins, Allan. *The War for the Union: The Organized War to Victory, 1864–1865*. Vol. 4. New York: Charles Scribner's Sons, 1971.

Nevins, Allan, James I. Robertson Jr., and Bell I. Wiley, eds. *Civil War Books: A Critical Bibliography*. 2 vols. Baton Rouge: Louisiana State University Press, 1967.

Nicolay, John G., and John Hay. *Abraham Lincoln: A History*. 10 vols. New York: Century, 1890.

Niven, John. *Connecticut for the Union*. New Haven, Conn.: Yale University Press, 1965.

Oakes, James. *The Radical and the Republican: Frederick Douglass, Abraham Lincoln, and the Triumph of Antislavery Politics*. New York: Norton, 2007.

Orr, Timothy J. "'A Viler Enemy in Our Rear': Pennsylvania Soldiers Confront the North's Antiwar Movement." In *The View from the Ground: Experiences of Civil War Soldiers*, edited by Aaron Sheehan-Dean, 171–98. Lexington: University Press of Kentucky, 2007.

Paludan, Phillip S. *A Covenant with Death: The Constitution, Law, and Equality in the Civil War Era*. Urbana: University of Illinois Press, 1975.

————. *"A People's Contest": The Union and Civil War, 1861–1865*. New York: Harper and Row, 1988.

Parrish, William E. *A History of Missouri, Vol. 3, 1860 to 1875*. Columbia: University of Missouri Press, 1973.

Perry, Thomas Sergeant. *The Life and Letters of Francis Lieber*. Boston: James R. Osgood, 1882.

Posner, Richard A. *Overcoming Law*. Cambridge: Harvard University Press, 1995.

Potter, David M. *The Impending Crisis, 1848–1861*. New York: Harper and Row, 1976.

Randall, James G. *Constitutional Problems under Lincoln*. 1926. Reprint, Urbana: University of Illinois Press, 1951.

————. *Lincoln the President: Midstream*. New York: Dodd, Mead, 1952.

————. *Lincoln the President: Springfield to Gettysburg*. 2 vols. New York: Dodd, Mead, 1945.

Randall, James G., and Richard N. Current. *Lincoln the President: Last Full Measure*. New York: Dodd, Mead, 1955.

Rawley, James A. "The Nationalism of Abraham Lincoln." *Civil War History* 9 (September 1963): 283–98.

Richards, Leonard. *The Slave Power: The Free North and Southern Domination*. Baton Rouge: Louisiana State University Press, 2000.

Richardson, Heather Cox. *The Greatest Nation of the Earth: Republican Economic Policies during the Civil War*. Cambridge: Harvard University Press, 1997.

Riddle, Donald W. *Congressman Abraham Lincoln*. Urbana: University of Illinois Press, 1957.

Rovere, Richard. *Howe and Hummel: Their True and Scandalous History*. New York: Farrar, Strauss, 1947.

Sandow, Robert. *Deserter Country: Civil War Opposition in the Pennsylvania Appalachians*. New York: Fordham University Press, 2009.

Schlesinger, Arthur M., Jr. *History of American Presidential Elections, 1789–1968*. 4 vols. New York: Chelsea House, 1971.

Schneider, Thomas E. *Lincoln's Defense of Politics: The Public Man and His Opponents in the Crisis over Slavery*. Columbia: University of Missouri Press, 2006.

Sellers, Charles. *The Market Revolution: Jacksonian America, 1815–1846*. New York: Oxford University Press, 1991.

Silbey, Joel H. *The American Political Nation, 1838–1893*. Stanford, Calif.: Stanford University Press, 1991.

———. *A Respectable Minority: The Democratic Party in the Civil War Era, 1860–1868*. New York: Norton, 1977.

Smith, Adam I. P. *No Party Now: Politics in the Civil War North*. New York: Oxford University Press, 2006.

Smith, Dwight L. *The War of 1812: An Annotated Bibliography*. New York: Garland Publishing, 1985.

Snay, Mitchell. *Fenians, Freedmen, and Southern Whites: Race and Nationality in the Era of Reconstruction*. Baton Rouge: Louisiana State University Press, 2007.

Stampp, Kenneth M. *And the War Came: The North and the Secession Crisis, 1860–1861*. Chicago: University of Chicago Press, 1950.

———. "The Concept of a Perpetual Union." In *The Imperiled Union: Essays on the Background of the Civil War*, edited by Kenneth M. Stampp, 3–36. New York: Oxford University Press, 1980.

———. *The United States and National Self-Determination: Two Traditions*. Gettysburg, Pa.: Gettysburg College, 1991.

Stone, Geoffrey R. *Perilous Times: An American Dilemma, 1790 to the Present*. New York: Norton, 2007.

———. *War and Liberty: An American Dilemma, 1790 to the Present*. New York: Norton, 2007.

Swisher, Carl Brent. *The Oliver Wendell Holmes Devise History of the United States Supreme Court, Volume V: The Taney Period, 1836–1864*. New York: Macmillan, 1974.

———. *Roger B. Taney*. New York: Macmillan, 1935.

Taylor, Alan. *The Civil War of 1812: American Citizens, British Subjects, Irish Rebels, and Indian Allies*. New York: Knopf, 2010.

Teachout, Woden. *Capture the Flag: A Political History of American Patriotism*. New York: Basic Books, 2009.

Thornbrough, Emma Lou. *Indiana in the Civil War Era, 1850–1880*. Indianapolis: Indiana Historical Bureau, 1965.

———. "Judge Perkins, the Indiana Supreme Court, and the Civil War." *Indiana Magazine of History* 60 (March 1964): 79–96.

———. *The Negro in Indiana before 1900*. Indianapolis: Indiana Historical Bureau, 1957.

Voegli, V. Jacque. *Free but Not Equal: The Midwest and the Negro during the Civil War*. Chicago: University of Chicago Press, 1967.

Vorenberg, Michael. *Final Freedom: The Civil War, the Abolition of Slavery, and the Thirteenth Amendment*. Cambridge, U.K.: Cambridge University Press, 2001.

Waldstreicher, David. *In the Midst of Perpetual Fetes: The Making of American Nationalism, 1776-1820*. Chapel Hill: University of North Carolina Pres, 1997.

Warshauer, Matthew. *Andrew Jackson and the Politics of Martial Law: Nationalism, Civil Liberties, and Partisanship*. Knoxville: University of Tennessee Press, 2006.

———. *Connecticut in the American Civil War*. Middletown, Conn.: Wesleyan University Press, 2011.

Weber, Jennifer L. *Copperheads: The Rise and Fall of Lincoln's Opponents in the North*. New York: Oxford University Press, 2006.

Wheare, K. C. *Abraham Lincoln and the United States*. New York: Macmillan, 1949.

White, Jonathan W. *Abraham Lincoln and Treason in the Civil War: The Trials of John Merryman*. Baton Rouge: Louisiana State University Press, 2011.

———. "'Sweltering with Treason': The Civil War Trials of William Matthew Merrick." *Prologue* 39 (Summer 2007): 26-36.

White, Ronald C., Jr. *The Eloquent President: A Portrait of Lincoln through His Words*. New York: Random House, 2005.

———. *Lincoln's Greatest Speech: The Second Inaugural*. New York: Simon and Schuster, 2002.

Wilson, Douglas. *Lincoln's Sword: The Presidency and the Power of Words*. New York: Knopf, 2006.

Wilson, Edmund. *Patriotic Gore: Studies in the Literature of the American Civil War*. New York: Oxford University Press, 1966.

Wood, Gordon. *The Creation of the American Republic, 1776-1787*. Chapel Hill: University of North Carolina Press, 1969.

Wubben, Hubert H. *Civil War Iowa and the Copperhead Movement*. Ames: Iowa State University Press, 1980.

Yoo, John. *Crisis and Command: A History of Executive Power from George Washington to George W. Bush*. New York: Kaplan, 2009.

THE CONFEDERACY

Andrews, J. Cutler. *The South Reports the Civil War*. 1970. Reprint, Pittsburgh: University of Pittsburgh Press, 1985.

Baum, Dale. *The Shattering of Texas Unionism: Politics in the Lone Star State during the Civil War Era*. Baton Rouge: Louisiana State University Press, 1998.

Beringer, Richard E., Herman Hattaway, Archer Jones, and William N. Still Jr. *Why the South Lost the Civil War*. Athens: University of Georgia Press, 1986.

Berlin, Ira. *Generations of Captivity: A History of African-American Slaves*. Cambridge: Harvard University Press, 2003.

Blair, William. *Cities of the Dead: Contesting the Memory of the Civil War in the South, 1865-1914*. Chapel Hill: University of North Carolina Press, 2004.

———. *Virginia's Private War: Feeding Body and Soul in the Confederacy, 1861-1865*. New York: Oxford University Press, 1998.

Bonner, Robert E. *Colors and Blood: Flag Passions of the Confederate South*. Princeton, N.J.: Princeton University Press, 2002.

———. *Mastering America: Southern Slaveholders and the Crisis of American Nationhood.* Cambridge: Cambridge University Press, 2009.

———. "Roundheaded Cavaliers? The Context and Limits of a Confederate Racial Project." *Civil War History* 48 (March 2002): 34–59.

———. "Slavery, Confederate Diplomacy, and the Racialist Mission of Henry Hotze." *Civil War History* 51 (September 2005): 288–316.

Buenger, Walter L. *Secession and the Union in Texas.* Austin: University of Texas Press, 1984.

Cauthen, Charles Edward. *South Carolina Goes to War, 1860–1865.* Chapel Hill: University of North Carolina Press, 1950.

Cooper, William J., Jr. *Jefferson Davis: American.* New York: Knopf, 2000.

Crandall, Marjorie Lyle. *Confederate Imprints: A Check List Based Principally on the Collection of the Boston Athenaeum.* Boston: Boston Athenaeum, 1955.

Crofts, Daniel. *Reluctant Confederates: Upper South Unionists in the Secession Crisis.* Chapel Hill: University of North Carolina Press, 1989.

Current, Richard N. *Encyclopedia of the Confederacy.* 4 vols. New York: Simon and Schuster, 1993.

Davis, William C. *"A Government of Our Own": The Making of the Confederacy.* New York: Free Press, 1994.

DeRosa, Marshall L. *The Confederate Constitution of 1861: An Inquiry into American Constitutionalism.* Columbia: University of Missouri Press, 1991.

Dew, Charles B. *Apotheosis of Disunion: Southern Secession Commissioners and the Causes of the Civil War.* Charlottesville: University Press of Virginia, 2000.

Dumond, Dwight Lowell, ed. *Southern Editorials on Secession* New York: Century, 1931.

Eaton, Clement. *A History of the Southern Confederacy.* 1954. Reprint, New York: Free Press, 1965.

Edgar, Walter. *South Carolina: A History.* Columbia: University of South Carolina Press, 1998.

Escott, Paul D. *After Secession: Jefferson Davis and the Failure of Confederate Nationalism.* Baton Rouge: Louisiana State University Press, 1978.

Faust, Drew Gilpin. *The Creation of Confederate Nationalism: Ideology and Identity in the Civil War South.* Baton Rouge: Louisiana State University Press, 1988.

Fehrenbacher, Don E. *Constitutions and Constitutionalism in the Slaveholding South.* Athens: University of Georgia Press, 1989.

Freehling, William W. *Prelude to Civil War: The Nullification Controversy in South Carolina, 1816–1836.* New York: Harper and Row, 1965.

———. *The Road to Disunion: Secessionists at Bay, 1776–1854.* New York: Oxford University Press, 1990.

———. *The Road to Disunion, Volume 2: Secession Triumphant, 1854–1861.* New York: Oxford University Press, 2007.

Freehling, William W., and Craig M. Simpson, eds. *Showdown in Virginia: The 1861 Convention and the Fate of the Union.* Charlottesville: University Press of Virginia, 2010.

Furgurson, Ernest B. *Ashes of Glory: Richmond at War.* New York: Knopf, 1996.

Gallagher, Gary W. *The Confederate War: How Popular Will, Nationalism, and Military Strategy Could Not Stave Off Defeat.* Cambridge: Harvard University Press, 1997.

Genovese, Eugene. *The World the Slaveholders Made: Two Essays in Interpretation.* New York: Pantheon Books, 1969.

Ireland, Robert M. *The County Courts in Antebellum Kentucky.* Lexington: University Press of Kentucky, 1972.

Johnson, Michael. *Toward a Patriarchal Republic: The Secession of Georgia.* Baton Rouge: Louisiana State University Press, 1977.

Lee, Charles Robert. *The Confederate Constitutions.* Chapel Hill: University of North Carolina Press, 1963.

Marks, Bayly Ellen, and Mark Norton Schatz, eds. *Between North and South: A Maryland Journalist Views the Civil War: The Narrative of William Wilkins Glenn, 1861–1869.* Rutherford, N.J.: Fairleigh Dickinson University Press, 1976.

McCardell, John. *The Idea of a Southern Nation: Southern Nationalists and Southern Nationalism, 1830–1860.* New York: Norton, 1979.

McCurry, Stephanie. *Confederate Reckoning: Power and Politics in the Civil War South.* Cambridge: Harvard University Press, 2010.

Memminger, Christopher. *The Mission of South Carolina to Virginia.* Baltimore: James Lucas and Son, [1861].

Moore, Albert Burton. *Conscription and Conflict in the Confederacy.* New York: Macmillan, 1924.

Neely, Mark E., Jr. "Abraham Lincoln vs. Jefferson Davis: Comparing Presidential Leadership in the Civil War." In *Writing the Civil War: The Quest to Understand,* edited by James M. McPherson and William J. Cooper Jr., 96–111. Columbia: University of South Carolina Press, 1998.

———. *Southern Rights: Political Prisoners and the Myth of Confederate Constitutionalism.* Charlottesville: University Press of Virginia, 1999.

Neely, Mark E., Jr., Harold Holzer, and Gabor S. Boritt. *The Confederate Image: Prints of the Lost Cause.* Chapel Hill: University of North Carolina Press, 1987.

Nieman, Donald. "Republicanism, the Confederate Constitution, and the American Constitutional Tradition." In *An Uncertain Tradition: Constitutionalism and the History of the South,* edited by Kermit L. Hall and James W. Ely Jr., 201–24. Athens: University of Georgia Press, 1989.

Owsley, Frank Lawrence. *State Rights in the Confederacy.* 1925. Reprint, Gloucester, Mass.: Peter Smith, 1961.

Parrish, T. Michael, and Robert M. Willingham Jr. *Confederate Imprints: A Bibliography of Southern Publications from Secession to Surrender.* Austin, Tex.: Jenkins Publishing, n.d.

Potter, David M. "The Historian's Use of Nationalism and Vice Versa." In *The South and the Sectional Conflict,* edited by David M. Potter, 34–83. Baton Rouge: Louisiana State University Press, 1968.

———. "Jefferson Davis and the Political Factors in Confederate Defeat." In *Why the North Won the Civil War,* edited by David Donald, 91–114. Baton Rouge: Louisiana State University Press, 1960.

Rable, George. *The Confederate Republic: A Revolution against Politics.* Chapel Hill: University of North Carolina Press, 1994.

Ringold, May Spencer. "Robert Newman Gourdin and the '1860 Association.'" *Georgia Historical Quarterly* 55 (1971): 501–9.

Robbins, John B. "The Confederacy and the Writ of Habeas Corpus." *Georgia Historical Quarterly* 55 (1971): 83–101.

Robinson, William M. *Justice in Grey: A History of the Judicial System of the Confederate States of America.* Cambridge: Harvard University Press, 1941.

Saum, Lewis O. "Schlesinger and the 'State Rights Fetish': A Note." *Civil War History* 24 (December 1978): 357–59.

Silver, David M. *Lincoln's Supreme Court.* Urbana: University of Illinois Press, 1956.

Snay, Mitchell. *Gospel of Disunion: Religion and Separatism in the Antebellum South.* New York: Cambridge University Press, 1993.

Stout, Harry S., and Christopher Grasso. "Civil War, Religion, and Communications: The Case of Richmond." In *Religion and the American Civil War,* edited by Randall M. Miller and Harry S. Stout, 313–59. New York: Oxford University Press, 1998.

Thomas, Emory M. *The Confederacy as a Revolutionary Experience.* Englewood Cliffs, N.J.: Prentice-Hall, 1971.

——. *The Confederate Nation: 1861–1865.* New York: Harper and Row, 1979.

——. *The Confederate State of Richmond: A Biography of the Capital.* 1971. Reprint, Baton Rouge: Louisiana State University Press, 1998.

Thornton, J. Mills, III. *Politics and Power in a Slave Society: Alabama, 1800–1860.* Baton Rouge: Louisiana State University Press, 1978.

Trexler, Harrison A. "The Davis Administration and the Richmond Press, 1861–1865." *Journal of Southern History* 14 (May 1950): 177–95.

Williams, David. *Bitterly Divided: The South's Inner Civil War.* New York: New Press, 2008.

Wish, Harvey. *George Fitzhugh: Propagandist of the Old South.* Baton Rouge: Louisiana State University Press, 1943.

Wooster, Ralph A. *The Secession Conventions of the South.* Princeton, N.J.: Princeton University Press, 1962.

Acknowledgments

Professor Jonathan W. White of Christopher Newport University read much of this book and offered valuable criticism. Moreover, he shared with me the results of his research on points he knew would be of interest to me. All of this was offered in a generous and cheerful way. Sylvia Neely, who is now retiring from the History Department at Penn State, has always helped and never hindered my work and did more than ever this time to help my text and my thoughts. William A. Blair, also a professor in the History Department at Penn State, discussed several of the issues in this book with me in ways that benefited my thinking and writing. This book would not have been possible without the great database called Westlaw Campus. Also helpful was the OCLC database. Incidental references to *The Federalist* and the Constitution in this book come from that beloved teaching tool, Clinton Rossiter's edition of *The Federalist Papers*.

Index